"This is the first study guide to the book of Revelation that I can see using in our women's Bible studies. As I read through this study, I see it as an inviting, effective tool to gain an understanding of this often-daunting book of the Bible. The unique format of this study guide and its questions give us an experience of digging out the text's meaning for ourselves and finding new possibilities for application to our lives and to our hopes for the future in Christ."

—**Kari Stainback**, Director of Women's Ministries, Park Cities Presbyterian Church, Dallas

"Sarah Ivill's studies of Scripture are a reflection of the wonderful influences that have shaped her as a scholar and teacher. There is the disciplined textual skill of exegesis and exposition. This flows seamlessly into real-life application. Yet pervading this blend of the scholar-teacher and spiritual counselor is a recognition of the majesty of God and the awe-inspiring privilege of having in one's hands the panorama of the history of redemption accomplished by the triune God of sovereign grace. I highly commend *Revelation* as the firstfruits of Ivill's careful investigation into Christ's truth and grace."

—**Peter A. Lillback**, President, Westminster Theological Seminary, Philadelphia

"Rich, rich, rich. Sarah's book on Revelation digs deep into the Word of God. She brings the whole of Scripture to bear in her expositions so that you truly see the unity of Revelation with the rest of the Bible. And she shows with clarity and without a doubt that the one writer of all Scripture could only be God the Holy Spirit himself, because of the wonder and grandeur of the Holy Scriptures on full display through her careful explanation of the text. In addition, the book contains an excellent study guide with questions designed to give readers the opportunity to dig into Scripture for themselves, enabling them to read, digest, and apply the truths it contains."

—**Donna Dobbs**, Director of Christian Education, First Presbyterian Church, Jackson, Mississippi

"Revelation can be an intimidating book to read. Its many complexities and pitfalls require careful navigation. But Sarah Ivill proves to be a steady guide, steering the reader through these difficult waters. In this study, she reminds us that the book of Revelation is not just some puzzle to solve or some code to crack. Rather, it is a wonderful and glorious vision of the person and work of Jesus Christ. Thus, she helps us to see that Revelation is a book not just about the future, but also very much about the present."

—**Michael J. Kruger**, Professor of New Testament, Reformed Theological Seminary, Charlotte

"This study is a banquet: it feeds the hungry soul with riches from the Word. Sarah covers every facet of Bible study, from teaching the beginning Bible student how to study to helping the seasoned student plumb the depths of each passage. Sarah is a careful, thoughtful student of the Word who makes the complicated passages and images of

Revelation very understandable and accessible. Throughout this study, she encourages students to dig deeper and reach further as they apply the Scriptures to their hearts."

—**Helen Holbrook**, children's director, Grace Presbyterian Church of the North Shore, Winnetka, Illinois

"The book of Revelation, often a closed book to many, is to be read. Sarah Ivill has given us a carefully crafted pattern that enables us to see Revelation through covenantal eyes. She leads us with clarity, focus, and life-impacting applications. She is a faithful guide, using her gifts to open the rich blessings from God found in Revelation. We appreciate her objective in doing so: to speak to the mind, the heart, and the hands—and to have us open the door and sit at the table with Jesus through this study."

—**Charles Dunahoo**, Coordinator of Christian Education and Publications for the PCA

"I commend this book for bridging the gap between a commentary and a fill-in-the-blank exercise for women. The study of Revelation has become less challenging and more edifying with Ivill's book. It is an annotated Bible study, providing Old Testament background, salient commentary, and personal exhortations and examples from a covenantal perspective. Questions for each Bible chapter enhance and encourage group discussion that is focused on Scripture interpreting Scripture."

—**Diane M. Poythress**, wife, mother, author, founder of Women's Weekend Seminary, Bible study leader, teacher, and speaker

"Sarah Ivill invites women to explore the treasures of the book of Revelation and to mine the spiritual riches of the visions granted to John for the comfort and encouragement of Christ's church. Ivill approaches Revelation from the perspective of Reformed theology and inaugurated (amillennial) eschatology. Among the strengths of *Revelation* are its sensitivity to the Old Testament background of John's visions and to the symbolic genre of the book, the personal illustrations that open and close each lesson, and the insightful study questions that encourage thoughtful engagement with the text."

—**Dennis E. Johnson**, Professor of Practical Theology, Westminster Seminary California

"Sarah Ivill's new Bible study is wonderful and fills a gap that has long been avoided in women's ministry, particularly within Reformed circles. Ivill does a remarkable job of showing the applicability of the prophecies to us women as we are today, without resorting to sensationalism. Ivill reminds us that this oft-neglected book is just as important for women as Proverbs 31, Titus 2, Ephesians, and the other books and passages that get so much 'airtime' today. The Introduction alone taught me more than I had previously known about Revelation, and it set a great foundation for the rest of the book's teaching."

—**Jennifer Smithfield**, Bible Study Leader, Scientific Information and Research Specialist

Revelation

Revelation

LET THE ONE WHO IS
THIRSTY COME

SARAH IVILL

P&R
PUBLISHING
P.O. BOX 817 • PHILLIPSBURG • NEW JERSEY 08865-0817

ISBN: 978-1-59638-423-1 (pbk.)
ISBN: 978-1-59638-573-3 (ePub)
ISBN: 978-1-59638-574-0 (Mobi)

Printed in the United States of America

Library of Congress Cataloging-in-Publication Data

Ivill, Sarah.
  Revelation : let the one who is thirsty come / Sarah Ivill.
    p. cm.
  Includes bibliographical references (p.   ) and indexes.
  ISBN 978-1-59638-423-1 (pbk.)
  1. Bible. N.T. Revelation--Textbooks. 2. Christian women--Religious life.
I. Title.
  BS2825.55.I95 2012
  228'.06--dc23
                        2012025637

"To him who loves us
and has freed us from our sins by his blood
and made us a kingdom, priests to his God and Father,
to him be glory and dominion forever and ever.
Amen."
Revelation 1:5–6

Contents

Foreword ix

Acknowledgments xiii

A Personal Note from Sarah xv

Introduction xix

Lesson 1: Revelation 1 1

Lesson 2: Revelation 2 21

Lesson 3: Revelation 3 39

Lesson 4: Revelation 4–5 57

Lesson 5: Revelation 6 73

Lesson 6: Revelation 7 87

Lesson 7: Revelation 8 101

Lesson 8: Revelation 9 115

Lesson 9: Revelation 10 127

Lesson 10: Revelation 11 139

Lesson 11: Revelation 12 155

Lesson 12: Revelation 13 173

Lesson 13: Revelation 14:1–13 189

Lesson 14: Revelation 14:14–15:4 203

Foreword

THE BIBLE IS A COMPLEX BOOK. In fact, the Bible is a divine library of sixty-six books, all conveying to us the history of redemption. As a series of books, and as one volume, the Bible has a logical structure to it. Genesis 1–11 is the introduction to the entire Bible, setting forth the major themes that will be developed throughout the remaining books of Scripture. Chronologically speaking, Exodus 20 and the Ten Commandments appear to be the first Scripture revealed to Moses and the first to be written. This would immediately be followed by Exodus 21–40 and Leviticus: the Lord's statutes for the proper worship of God, his "regulative principles" for Israel. Moses would then backtrack and explain to his readers why God destroyed the country and army of the world's greatest monarch of the time—Pharaoh. The reason was that God chose a man and his family to be his covenant people, and through Abraham and his descendants—especially Christ—all the families of the earth would be blessed. Genesis 1–11 tells us how mankind came to need the blessings of redemption brought by Eve's son and Abraham's seed: "salvation is from the Jews" (John 4:22).

The Old Testament books of history, prophesy, worship, and wisdom lay out God's covenant plan, progressively unfolding toward the person and work of Jesus Christ. The four Gospels tell of this God incarnate and his once-for-all atonement: "the Lamb of God who takes away the sins of the world" (John 1:29). The Acts of the Apostles and the Epistles written by the apostles tell of the gospel mission and how the "God story" (i.e., "gospel" from the old German *gotts spiel*, "God's play" or "God's story") moved beyond Israel in blessing all the families of the earth—Jew and Gentile. The Epistles make the God of Abraham, the work of Christ, and membership in the people of the Spirit accessible to all men, women, and children around the world and across all barriers of time.

This body of divine revelation has an *epilogue*: the Revelation of John. Genesis 1–11 tells the story of a mankind in need of salvation from the human perspective. Revelation recapitulates the story of redemptive history from a divine perspective. In Revelation 4:1, John sees "a door standing open to heaven." In the Apocalypse, the veil between angels and men and between heaven and earth is removed. The great cosmic conflict (Rev. 12) that lies behind all human struggle, suffering, and sorrow is now removed. John is given the formidable task of unveiling the mysteries of redemptive history for the entire world to see.

In this study, my friend Sarah Ivill, a member of my congregation, will take you deep inside this wonderful book of mysteries revealed. In so doing, she will expose you to new ideas and age-old concepts that may well have been obscured by all our "last days madness." Who is the Antichrist? How long is the millennium? What is the great battle of Armageddon? These types of questions have caused many to shy away from a marvelous book given to the church in times of great persecution. I encourage you to follow Sarah's sensitive and balanced guidance through a book that promises a blessing to those who read it—the only book in the Bible to do so (Rev. 1:3)! Human history is linear: it moves from "in the beginning" to the end of history as we know it. Unlike all other religions, Christianity does not possess an unbroken circle and cycle of fertility as our paradigm for history. God is moving creation and mankind from Eden, paradise lost, to the City of God, paradise regained. The cycle of repetition in the book of Revelation merely recapitulates (restates) the linear flow of history—the story of the Hero of it all: "who is and who was and who is to come" (Rev. 1:8).

Caution is called for. People have often used the Scriptures in a manner that reads into the text their own experiences or the current issues of their time. This is a dangerous thing to do, especially with the book of Revelation. Lesslie Newbigin comments on this: "The Bible is concerned with the public history of the world; this reductionist conversion of it into religious psychology is a product of the contemporary western culture, which accepts another public 'myth' and 'privatizes the gospel.'" Sarah Ivill will guard the reader against such tendencies. Remaining true to the historical context of John's Revelation, and explaining the greater story (metanarrative) of Scripture, this Bible study will move from text to context and then into personal application. Let Revelation speak for itself:

> I warn everyone who hears the words of the prophecy of this book: if anyone adds to them, God will add to him the plagues described in this book, and if anyone takes away from the words of the book of this prophecy, God will take away his share in the tree of life and in the holy city, which are described in this book. (Rev. 22:18–19)

So, come! Come to this book, come to a great story of the kingdom of God, come to those things opened for us by this window in heaven. Most of all, come to the Lamb that was slain, the King of kings and the Lord of lords, and drink of the waters of life! May you be refreshed by these things that are, have been, and are yet to come.

Michael F. Ross
Senior Pastor, Christ Covenant Church
Matthews, North Carolina

Acknowledgments

I wish to thank those in my life who have been a part of this writing process. Charles Dunahoo, Dennis and Cindy Bennett, Jane Patete, and Jim and Linda Bland have all been a great source of encouragement to me as I shared my hope of publication with them.

Thank you to P&R Publishing's Marvin Padgett, who first approached me to write a book and who was more than willing to have me submit a Bible study instead. Thank you to P&R's Bryce Craig, whose personal review of the study encouraged me, and to P&R's John J. Hughes and Rick Matt for their editorial work.

Thank you to the women of Ivy Creek Church (PCA) who first encouraged me to publish Bible studies and who have prayed for me, encouraged me, and believed in the work that the Lord is doing through me.

Thank you to the pastors and women of Christ Covenant Church (PCA) who have been a part of this process and who have encouraged me to keep writing Bible studies for women.

Thank you to the men and women of Dallas Theological Seminary who taught me what it means to be a gracious student of Scripture and who instilled in me the importance of expository teaching and the love of God's Word.

Thank you to Westminster Theological Seminary and to the professors who have served there. The many books that have been written and recommended by the professors, as well as the many online class lectures and chapel messages, have been of tremendous benefit to me. They have taught me what it means to see Christ in all of Scripture and to understand more deeply the history of redemption and the beautiful truths of Reformed theology.

Thank you to my many dear friends (you know who you are!) who prayed for me and encouraged me to make the dream of writing a reality.

Thank you to my mom and dad, who have always supported me in my love of the Word and encouraged me to do that which the Lord has called me to do. I love you both more than words can express.

Thank you to my husband, Charles, who has always given me his love, support, and encouragement in the writing process and in what the Lord has called me to do.

And thank you to my two children, Caleb and Hannah, whose sweet smiles, loving hugs, prayers for "Mom's Bible studies," and patience as I "finish another thought" before tending to one of their many needs are a constant source of encouragement to me as I pray for the next generation of believers to love the Lord and his Word with all their hearts and minds.

Finally, thank you to my heavenly Father, to my Lord and Savior Jesus Christ, and to the Spirit, who helps me in my weakness. To the triune God be the glory for what he has done through me, a broken vessel and a flawed instrument, yet one that is in the grip of his mighty and gracious hand.

A Personal Note from Sarah

WHEN I WAS ASKED to consider writing a Bible study on the book of Revelation, I was very excited. I have always loved Revelation, though I have to admit that, like many I have talked with, the imagery in the book has often been confusing and perplexing. But even with all of the symbolism, I can never help being left breathless with the majestic picture that John paints of our Lord and Savior Jesus Christ coming again to complete God's plan of judgment and salvation. As I studied, some passages made me want to get on my knees and worship alongside the saints and angels in heaven. Some passages made me want to go to battle against the evil of this world. Some exhorted me to be more obedient, holy, and faithful. And all of them pointed me to the ultimate purpose of my life: to be a witness and a worshiper of Jesus Christ to the glory of God. I hope and pray that as you read and study, you will be overwhelmed with the majesty of Jesus Christ and the glorious plan of God's redemption, which in turn will also lead you to a life of witness and worship.

My love for teaching the Word of God was inspired by my own hunger to study it. Longing for the "meat" of God's Word and finding it lacking in so many churches today, I enrolled in Bible Study Fellowship after graduating from high school. It was there that I realized my desire to attend seminary and was influenced and encouraged by a strong, godly woman and mentor in my life to attend Dallas Theological Seminary

(DTS). During this time I was leading women through in-depth Bible studies and caught a glimpse of how much women desired to be fed the depth of God's Word. This encouraged me even further to receive an education that would best prepare me to deliver God's Word to women who hungered for the truth.

Upon graduating with my Master of Theology from DTS, I took a position as assistant director of women's ministry at a large church where I served under a woman who shared my same passion to teach the "meat" of God's Word. Within the year, I had assumed the role of director and delved into teaching the Word of God in an expository and applicable manner. After three years, I resigned in order to stay home with my first child. During those years at home, the Lord used my experience in seminary and ministry to lead me back to my roots and the full embracing of Reformed theology. Raised for the first half of my childhood in the Associate Reformed Presbyterian Church and a conservative Independent Presbyterian Church, I had been grounded in the Reformed faith and Reformed catechisms from an early age. But from middle school on I was not in Reformed churches. The questions in my twenties then became "Who am I?" and "What do I really believe?"

One of the first steps on my journey was contacting a Reformed seminary and asking for a list of books covering everything I would have missed by not attending a Reformed seminary. That began my reading of some of the most renowned Reformed theologians in the world. It was during those days that the question, "Who am I?" was finally answered, and I began teaching women based on my understanding of the historic Reformed and covenantal tradition. In fact, that is how my first Bible study came to be written. I had the incredible privilege of teaching that first study to a wonderful group of women for a morning Bible study at our Presbyterian Church in America (PCA) church. And it was from their encouragement and exhortation that I submitted the study for publication.

I know it is difficult to pick up a Bible study written by another author and either teach it or study it. It is for this reason that I offer you the following suggestions as you prepare to teach or study *Let the One*

Who is Thirsty Come. It is my practice that before I ever begin to study a book of the Bible I read it through several times. I try to read it as if I were reading a letter from a personal friend for the first time. This is reading to get a feel for the "big picture" of the book and how it fits into the rest of the books of Scripture. Then, with my own pen, paper, and Bible, I divide each chapter (or sometimes half a chapter or two halves from two different chapters) into my own divisions.

Next, I try to grasp what the divisions are saying in a nutshell and write that down. From that point, I move to writing application questions appropriate for each division, with at least one, if not several, questions for each division. This gives me "ownership" of the passage. Before going to read what anyone else has to say, I have studied it by myself and allowed the Holy Spirit to speak to my own heart about it. This adds "uniqueness" to your teaching. You don't want simply to regurgitate what someone else has said. You want to make it your own.

Following this, though, it is important to enhance your understanding by studying what others have learned from the book. So, I try to have at least three good, solid Reformed commentaries for the book I am studying, as well as other study tools such as a Bible dictionary and concordance. One of my favorite tools for this particular study was *The Book of Revelation*, by G. K. Beale (see the Bibliography for information on this book as well as on other helpful sources for learning about Revelation). As I studied this and other commentaries chapter by chapter, I would highlight what I felt was important for the women I would be teaching to know in this study. Then I would begin writing the lesson notes, using my own outlines and notes, as well as what I had learned from others.

The final step is writing the questions for Bible study participants to answer. I always have them read and work on the questions for the passage that will be covered in the following week's lesson. This gives them the opportunity to "own" it for themselves before they ever hear or read the lesson.

I want to encourage you as you embark upon the study of the book of Revelation. It will require prayer and diligence, but the reward will be great. Revelation is the culmination of all of Scripture. It reveals the glorious plan of God's judgment and salvation. It shows the body of Christ where we have been, where we are, and where we are headed. It defines who we are as worshipers and witnesses for God. And it gives us a tremendous example of worshiping God to emulate in our own lives. So, let us join our voices together and cry out, "Hallelujah! For the LORD our God the Almighty reigns. Let us rejoice and exult and give him the glory" (Rev. 19:6b–7a)!

Introduction

AT THE BEGINNING of every lesson we will identify the *aim* of the lesson concerning our:

- *Mind*: What do we need to know from this passage in Scripture?
- *Heart*: How does what we learn from this passage affect our internal relationship with the Lord?
- *Hands*: How does what we learn from this passage translate into action for God's kingdom?

In the spring of 1802, Ludwig van Beethoven began losing his hearing. Even the finest doctors in Vienna could not help. It would not be long before he would be completely deaf. His days as a concert pianist would come to an end. But music was Beethoven's passion, so he set out to find a way to save his career.

Finally he thought of a solution: he would become a great composer. But he would need something or someone to inspire him to put his solution into a great symphony. During this time there was a war moving across Europe for the freedom of all people. There was one war hero, Napoleon Bonaparte, who rose above all the rest. A young boy gave Beethoven a magazine with Bonaparte's picture on it. Napoleon was portrayed as valiantly riding forward on a majestic stallion, fearless, and confident of victory. Beethoven pondered his own struggles with deafness and found the confidence to carry on in his own life and career. That was when a heroic tune came to his mind. He immediately began writing a new symphony. It wasn't long before the four movements took form.

The first movement is a battle scene. Napoleon fights the injustice in the world that touches us all. The second section is a description of the sorrows of humanity. The third movement is a dance of celebration. The battle is over. Fear and death have been conquered. Hope appears on the horizon, warm and bright, a joyous homecoming! The fourth movement is about peace and freedom.

Several weeks later, after putting the final touches on his symphony, Beethoven heard that Napoleon had betrayed the people and crowned himself Emperor of France. Angry, Beethoven ripped his symphony to shreds crying, "I did not write my symphony for a tyrant!"

Slowly, Beethoven's anger subsided and he realized that his symphony was never about Napoleon, but about himself and humanity, the hero in each and every person. So, he named it *The Heroic Symphony*, and it was first performed in 1804. No one in the audience knew the story behind the music, but each person was moved by it. In the majesty of each movement, listeners discovered their own dreams and fears. *The Heroic Symphony* touched their hearts.[1]

The book of Revelation could well be entitled *The Heroic Symphony*. But the melody came to John from Jesus Christ. And it was the revelation of Jesus Christ that inspired John to write this great symphony. A war is raging across the world, a war to free God's people and judge those who are not his own. It is clear that one figure towers above all the rest, a war hero named Jesus Christ. He charges forward on his war horse, certain of victory, afraid of nothing. One after another we see the movements of John's symphony take form. The movements all blend into another and interrelate. One cannot be understood nor appreciated without the others. Each movement builds toward a grand climax. And when the symphony is finished being written John does not have to fear that the Great War Hero will betray him. His Word is faithful and true. He did not write the symphony for a tyrant, he wrote it for the Lamb of God by the Spirit of God.

1. This story is adapted from Anna Harwell Celenza's beautiful children's book *The Heroic Symphony*, illustrated by JoAnn E. Kitchel (Watertown, MA: Charlesbridge, 2004).

DATE

Most recent commentators view Revelation as being written about 95 A.D. during the reign of the Roman Emperor Domitian, instead of around the late 60s prior to the destruction of Jerusalem and during Nero's reign. Several indicators in the book itself point to the date in the mid-90s.

First, the book seems to point to persecution that has recently grown bad and is soon going to get even worse, which fits better the circumstances around Domitian's reign than those of Nero's. Even John's exile to Patmos is more likely under Domitian's reign than under Nero's because persecution for not taking part in emperor worship was more strictly enforced under Domitian.

Second, the situations of the churches referred to in Revelation point to a later date. The Ephesian church most likely left its "first love" in the second generation of its existence rather than the first. The church of Laodicea, which is called "wealthy," would more likely have taken to the 90s to recover from the devastating earthquake of the early 60s and to establish the economic security that the book portrays it having at the time of John's writing. The church in Smyrna is thought to have formed in the 60s, so it would fit better with a late date for Revelation also.

Third, John refers to Rome as "Babylon," a title given to it only after Rome destroyed Jerusalem in 70 A.D., just as Babylon had destroyed Jerusalem in the sixth century B.C.

Fourth, many of the early church fathers, including Irenaeus, believe John to have been writing around 95 A.D. This evidence alone would be hard to overcome for someone holding to an early date.

PURPOSE

If God is on the throne, why does evil continue to reign? This question has come to the fore in evangelical Christianity in recent decades, but it has plagued all Christians from the very beginning. The first readers of Revelation struggled with it just as we do and thus, this issue stood as one of John's main purposes for writing the book. He had to help people understand why persecution was on the rise, especially in light of the fact that he had been an eyewitness to the resurrection of Christ, which symbolized Jesus' victory, not his defeat. But the Lord himself had prepared the apostles for such a question when he said, "A servant is not greater than his master. If they persecuted me, they will also persecute you. . . . I have said all these things to you to keep you from falling away. They will put you out of the synagogues. Indeed, the hour is coming when whoever kills you will think he is offering service to God. And they will do these things because they have not known the Father, or me. But I have said these things to you, that when their hour comes you may remember that I told them to you" (John 15:20; 16:1–4).

John himself had dealt with antichrists that had come during the time when he was writing the letter we know as 1 John. He spoke of this when he said, "Children, it is the last hour, and as you have heard that antichrist is coming, so now many antichrists have come" (Rev. 2:18). And John had dealt with false prophets, as he noted elsewhere: "Beloved, do not believe every spirit, but test the spirits to see whether they are from God, for many false prophets have gone out into the world (1 John 4:1).

With Christianity being seen as distinct from Judaism following 70 A.D., new temptations to compromise one's faith arose. Previous to 70 A.D. Christians were still considered part of Judaism, which was accepted by Rome and would have been an umbrella of protection for Christians. But after that date both Jews and Rome persecuted Christians. Since the cost of discipleship was so high, John was writing to Christians who were tempted to compromise, were facing persecution for standing firm in their faith, or were willing to deny and walk away from their faith. So, we see John throughout the book of Revelation exhorting Christians to stand strong as witnesses for Christ in the midst of a world that had no regard for Christ, and in the midst of so-called Christians who were willing to compromise their faith and worship idols under the pressure of persecution.

AUTHOR

As you can tell by the previous paragraphs, I believe that the apostle John wrote the book of Revelation. Though some have pointed to the differences in writing style between the Gospel of John and the Epistles of John as an argument against the apostle being the author, I see the similarities between these writings as a much more persuasive argument. Those who do not believe the apostle John wrote Revelation generally believe either that John the Elder, another disciple of Jesus, or someone using the name John as a pseudonym, which was popular among authors of apocalyptic writings, wrote it.

GENRE

Though the book certainly has elements of apocalyptic and prophetic literature, and is written in an epistolary form, the major thrust of the book is prophetic. In this light, it must be remembered that prophecy is not just about the future. The prophecies of the Old Testament had much to say to the people of their own day, as does Revelation. However, the book is put in the form of an epistle, which strongly points to its practical use for the churches of John's day. Nevertheless, the book deals with the future and climactic second coming of Christ and joins the ranks of the prophetic books in the Old Testament that also pointed to the consummation of the kingdom of God.

The book also has elements of apocalyptic literature, which is important for us to understand as we interpret the highly symbolic language. Like Daniel, Ezekiel, Job 1:6–12, certain parts of Isaiah, and Zechariah in the Old Testament, the book of Revelation is considered to be apocalyptic in its genre. Dan McCartney and Charles Clayton define apocalyptic as "that literary genre which interprets earthly events, especially the struggles of God's people, as manifestations of the heavenly warfare between God and the forces of evil, and depicts the coming victory of God over those forces by means of symbolic images." They also list three distinctives of apocalyptic literature: symbolism, dualism, and messianism. Symbolism must be looked at in the context of the individual book as well as of the entire Bible, and in the context of the culture of the time in which the book was written. Though symbolism may be difficult to interpret, it points to God's victory, which we know is certain. Dualism is the element of apocalyptic literature that describes the battle between God and Satan, although unlike in true dualism, Satan is not the direct opposite of God, but the counterfeit of God. Finally, messianism means that God will win the battle with Satan through a messiah, a savior, whom we know to be Jesus Christ.[2]

INTERPRETATIONS OF REVELATION

When studying the book of Revelation, it doesn't take very long to realize that different people have interpreted the book in different ways over the centuries since it was written. In my opinion, this is one of the biggest barriers that keeps many people from studying the book at all. What a shame! Revelation was a gift to the church. It was not given so that we would argue over its meaning and application; it was given to inspire, to exhort, to inform, and, most of all, to lead us to be witnesses and worshipers of the triune God to whom all glory and honor is due.

Nevertheless, if we are going to be good students of the book, we need to be informed of the major ways in which people have interpreted it. No matter what study you do on Revelation, it becomes immediately evident what view the author of the study holds. That will be true in this study as well. But I would like to remind all of us to hold our views humbly and loosely, for among those of each view are devoted evangelical Christians who love the Lord and seek to do justice to the biblical text. Though we may not agree with one another's views, we must recognize that these are not to divide us but unite us, for we are all in need of encouragement upon this pilgrim road that has many trials and tribulations. We all believe that we are to be witnesses in this world for Christ, that Christ is coming again, and that we are to glorify God.

2. Dan McCartney and Charles Clayton, *Let the Reader Understand: A Guide to Interpreting and Applying the Bible*, 2nd ed. (Phillipsburg, NJ: P&R Publishing, 2002), 240–42.

In the end, this is all that matters. The main views of Revelation that we'll look at are the *preterist view*, the *historicist view*, the *futurist view*, and the *idealist view*.

The *preterist view* takes two forms. The first says that Revelation was written for the seven historical churches of Asia Minor. It is seen as a prophecy of the destruction of Jerusalem in 70 A.D. Preterists believe that the great tribulation and other judgment passages in the book occurred in the first century A.D. with the persecution by Nero, the Jewish war with Rome, and the destruction of the temple. They believe that the Antichrist also came in the first century. The second form of this view sees Revelation as a prophecy of Rome's fall in the fifth century A.D.

The *historicist* view sees the symbols in the book of Revelation—such as the seals, trumpets, and bowls—as being fulfilled by the unfolding of specific, identifiable, and chronological events in history, most of which have already occurred, but some of which are applicable to our own time.

The *futurist* view takes two forms. Both forms take Revelation 4:1–22:5 as referring only to the time immediately before Christ's second coming. The first form is known as dispensational futurism, which interprets Revelation very literally and chronologically. In this view, the order of events would go like this:

1. Ethnic Israel is restored to its land.
2. The church is raptured to heaven.
3. The seven-year tribulation begins.
4. The antichrist reigns.
5. The evil nations assemble to fight for Jerusalem.
6. The second coming of Christ occurs.
7. Christ reigns on earth for a literal one thousand years.
8. Satan rebels for one final time at the end of the millennium by assembling unbelievers to fight against Christ and the saints.
9. Christ begins his eternal reign with the saints in a new heaven and a new earth.

The second form of the futurist view believes that the church is the true Israel and that the church will go through the tribulation, but those who hold this view still see the majority of the book as referring only to the future.

The *idealist* view identifies Revelation as symbolic of the struggle between God and Satan. Some believe that the book is timeless and does not point to any particular historical event. Rather, it can be applied to all times and all situations as a representation of the struggle between good and evil.

I don't know about you, but I can see a grain of truth in all of these approaches, which again reminds us that we must approach with humility the task of interpreting the text, and we must be wise and discerning in deciding which texts are speaking about the past, or the present, or the future. As for the idealist approach, the book certainly does portray the struggle between good and evil. The futurists are correct in affirming that the book does deal with the second coming of Christ and the events leading up to it. The preterists are certainly correct in affirming that the book is written to and for the seven historical churches of Asia Minor. And even the historicists are correct in that the book surely has application for our own day. But we must recognize that to put ourselves in any one of these boxes exclusively does not do the best justice to the biblical text, which, if interpreted carefully in a grammatical-historical way, leads to the conclusion that the book speaks to realities of the past, present, and future.

SYMBOLISM IN REVELATION

Before we begin our study of Revelation, it would be helpful to discuss how to interpret the symbolism found in the book. When I first began my own study, I wanted to physically draw out each vision that John gave and try to figure out the "puzzle" by interpreting each picture I created. I quickly realized that this presented a rather confusing and sometimes contradictory and illogical picture of what John was really saying. I had my logical left brain turned on and my artistic right brain turned off. But when I turned my right brain on, sat back, and "played the music," John's words made much more sense. I urge you to do the same.

The book itself tells us that most of the language is symbolic. In Revelation 1:1 we are told that what we are reading is "The *revelation of Jesus Christ, which God* gave him to *show* to his servants the things *that must soon take place*. He *made it known* by sending his angel to his servant John" (the italics here are mine). The only other time in the Scriptures that the words in italics occur together is in Daniel 2:28–30, 45, which strongly indicates that John is alluding to Daniel's symbolic vision and that symbolism will also be a key part of his writings as well. Furthermore, in the English Standard Version (ESV) translation of Revelation 1:12–16, the word "like" is used seven times, which tells us that these descriptions are not be taken literally, but as portraying truth about Christ in a figurative manner.

Certainly not everything in the book is symbolic, but most of it is figurative; where we have difficulty deciding between literal and non-literal understandings, it would be better to err on the side of the figurative. As we read, we must remember to keep in mind several different aspects of the text. First, we must remember that verse 1:1 tells us to "hear" the words of the book. Second, we must remember that many passages are records of John's real visions happening in real historical time. Third, we must remember that each vision speaks of true historical referents. Fourth, we must remember that each historical referent has a mostly symbolic meaning. Fifth, we must remember that John makes many allusions to the Old Testament throughout the book that inform our interpretation and understanding of his meaning.

The numbers three, four, seven, twelve, and their derivatives are also used in the book symbolically to convey completeness. Thus, though seven historical churches are in view in chapters 2–3, these historical churches are also symbolic for the complete/universal church. Additionally, the seven seals, seven trumpets, and seven bowls convey the fact that God's judgment upon the world will be complete. Other such symbolic numbers include the 144,000 in chapter seven who are sealed; these stand for all of the redeemed saints. In Revelation 13:8, the number 666, which is, in a sense, one less than 777 (the symbolic number of the perfect and complete Trinity), most likely stands for the lack of perfection of the counterfeit trinity (the dragon, the beast, and the false prophet), though, as some commentators point out, both a literal (the emperor Nero, for example) *and* a symbolic notion could be in view here. The 1,000 years mentioned in verse 20:1 is most likely referring to the entire church age between Christ's ascension and his second coming. The dimensions of the city (the people of God) in verse 21:15 and following connotes the completeness of God's people secured since the foundation of the world.

As we discussed with regard to the interpretations of Revelation, and specifically with regard to the dispensational futurist view, not everyone interprets the book in quite as symbolic a manner as I have been describing. Many wonderful, godly, evangelical Christian men and women believe the majority of the book is to be taken literally and that, unless absolutely necessary, the numbers and descriptions are to have a literal fulfillment, which is why in this view the majority of the book gets pushed to the timeframe of the future.

THE USE OF THE OLD TESTAMENT IN REVELATION

The book of Revelation contains more allusions to the Old Testament than any other book in the New Testament. It is imperative to be familiar with the Old Testament background if we are going to understand the book. More than half of the Old Testament allusions are from Psalms, Isaiah, Ezekiel, and Daniel, with Daniel being the most significant influence. In any given verse of Revelation, references to anywhere from one to five or even more different Old Testament passages may be collapsed into one portrayal. Not all Old Testament allusions are used with their original meanings. Like other New Testament authors, John takes the liberty to take Old Testament texts and apply them to his own purposes as the Holy Spirit leads him.

THE STRUCTURE OF REVELATION

As already noted, the book of Revelation is <u>more like a piece of art or music than it is a textbook.</u> As we read through the book, we see many words, phrases, and ideas that are similar to or are repetitions of earlier ones. In keeping with the numbers four and seven as symbolic for completeness, commentators have observed a broad four-fold division of the book as well as a smaller seven- or eight-fold division.[3]

Table I.1 Structure of Revelation

Four-Fold Division	Seven-Fold Division	Eight-Fold Division
Rev. 1:1–20	Rev. 1–3	Rev. 1–3
Rev. 1:20–3:22	Rev. 4–7	Rev. 4–7
Rev. 4:1–22:5	Rev. 8:1–11:14	Rev. 8:1–11:14
Rev. 22:6–21	Rev. 11:15–14:20	Rev. 11:15–14:20
	Rev. 15–16	Rev. 15–16
	Rev. 17:1–21:8	Rev. 17:1–19:10
	Rev. 21:9–22:21	Rev. 19:11–21:8
		Rev. 21:9–22:21

Those who hold to a futurist position will see that the section of the book from verse 4:1 through verse 22:5 speaks of future events that will occur in a chronological and mostly literal manner. Those who hold to a progressive recapitulation (parallelism) position will see the structure more like a cone, where each series of seals, trumpets, bowls, and so on, are parallel but emphasize different dimensions, the seventh of each representing the final judgment. Thus, there are several places where the final judgment and salvation are portrayed before we get to the end of the book (see, for example, Rev. 11:14–18). They also hold that while the seventh seal, seventh trumpet, and seventh bowl each represent the final judgment, the previous six seals, trumpets,

---

3. G. K. Beale, *The Book of Revelation: A Commentary on the Greek Text*, New International Greek Testament Commentary (Grand Rapids: Eerdmans, 1999), 114.

and bowls are not necessarily placed in chronological order. Again, we must "listen to the music" rather than logically diagramming it. Furthermore, there are many connections between the historical letters of chapters 2–3 and the visions of the later chapters, showing further that the section from 4:1 to 22:5 is not to be taken as referring to the future only. Thus, the first three chapters and the last two chapters of the book form a boundary around the five (or six) inner sections of the book that parallel one another.

The structure of the book serves to convey the themes of judgment, persecution, and redemption. The angel's words in Revelation 14:7 sums up the entire message of the book: "Fear God and give him glory, because the hour of his judgment has come, and worship him who made heaven and earth, the sea and the springs of water." And all of us who are seeking the Lord, no matter what position we take on interpreting the book, can join hearts, hands, and voices in fearing God and worshiping him.

OUTLINE: THE BOOK OF REVELATION, THE BOOK OF SEVENS

Prologue (Rev. 1)

    The Seven Churches (2–3)

        Ephesus (2:1–7)

        Smyrna (2:8–11)

        Pergamum (2:12–17)

        Thyatira (2:18–29)

        Sardis (3:1–6)

        Philadelphia (3:7–13)

        Laodicea (3:14–22)

The Throne in Heaven (Rev. 4–5)

    The Seven Seals (6:1–8:5)

        First Seal (6:1–2)—occurs throughout the church age

        Second Seal (6:3–4)—occurs throughout the church age

        Third Seal (6:5–6)—occurs throughout the church age

Fourth Seal (6:7–8)—occurs throughout the church age
Fifth Seal (6:9–11)—approaching final judgment
Sixth Seal (6:12–17)—final judgment
Interlude (7:1–8)—the servants of God are sealed (occurs
    during the church age)
        (7:9–17)—the great multitude worship God at
    the throne (church age)
Seventh Seal (8:1–5)—final judgment

The Seven Trumpets (Rev. 8:6–11:19)
    First Trumpet (8:7)—occurs throughout the church age
    Second Trumpet (8:8–9)—occurs throughout the church age
    Third Trumpet (8:10–11)—occurs throughout the church age
    Fourth Trumpet (8:12)—occurs throughout the church age
    Fifth Trumpet (9:1–12)—occurs throughout the church age
    Sixth Trumpet (9:13–21)—occurs throughout the church age
    Interlude (10)—the mighty angel with the little scroll
    (occurs during the church age)

The Seven Thunders (Rev. 10:3–4)—occurs during the
    church age
    Interlude (11:1–14)—the measuring rod and two
      witnesses (church age)
    Seventh Trumpet (11:15–19)—final judgment

The Seven Signs (Rev. 12:1–15:4)[4]
    First Sign (12)—mostly during church age
    Second Sign (13:1–10)—church age
    Third Sign (13:11–18)—church age
    Fourth Sign (14:1–5)—final reward
    Fifth Sign (14:6–13)—final judgment
    Sixth Sign (14:14–20)—final judgment
    Seventh Sign (15:2–4)—final reward

4. Chapters 1–11 are now retold in chapters 12–22, but with more detail.

The Seven Bowls (Rev. 15:5–16:21)

    First Bowl (16:2)—occurs throughout the church age

    Second Bowl (16:3)—occurs throughout the church age

    Third Bowl (16:4–7)—occurs throughout the church age

    Fourth Bowl (16:8–9)—occurs throughout the church age

    Fifth Bowl (16:10–11)—occurs throughout the church age

    Sixth Bowl (16:12–16)—final judgment

    Seventh Bowl (16:17–21)—final judgment

The Seven Descriptions of Babylon's Judgment (Rev. 17:1–18:24)

    First Description (17:7–18)—final judgment

    Second Description (18:1–3)—final judgment

    Third Description (18:4–8)—final judgment

    Fourth Description (18:9–10)—final judgment

    Fifth Description (18:11–17)—final judgment

    Sixth Description (18:18–19)—final judgment

    Seventh Description (18:20–24)—final judgment

The Seven Last Things (Rev. 19:1–22:5)

    The Consummation of the Marriage (19:1–10)

    The Consummation of the Battle (19:11–21)

    The Consummation of Evil (20:1–10)

    The Consummation of Judgment (20:11–15)

    The Consummation of the New Heaven and New Earth (21:1–8)

    The Consummation of the New Jerusalem (21:9–27)

    The Consummation of the New Eden (22:1–5)

Epilogue (Rev. 22:6–21)[5]

---

5. I am indebted to Dr. Vern Poythress's "Heptads in Revelation" for prompting my writing of this outline. See Vern S. Poythress, *The Book of Revelation: A Guide for Understanding* (Glenside, PA: Westminster Theological Seminary Bookstore, 2002), 3.8a.

THEOLOGY

As we study the theology of Revelation, we should seek to:

- Read it with a covenantal perspective in mind.
- Understand what the book is teaching us about God.
- Understand what the book is teaching us about his Son, Jesus Christ.
- Understand what the book is teaching us about God's covenant with his people.
- Understand how the book helps to further reveal God's covenantal story of redemption and restoration.
- Understand how the Holy Spirit would have us apply what we have learned to our own lives.

A Covenantal Perspective

First, God is fulfilling his covenant promises. We see each covenant represented in the book of Revelation and the fulfillment of all of them portrayed.

Covenant of Works. God made a covenant with Adam to work and keep the garden, to be fruitful and multiply, all leading to life in the garden. Through sin we lost access to the garden of Eden. But Christ paved the way back for us. The book of Revelation shows us the new Eden, the new heaven and the new earth.

God's Covenant with Noah. God promised that as long as this earth remained, a flood would never again cut off all flesh. His sign was a rainbow, which we see in Revelation 4:3 and 10:1. In this book we see that the period of common grace is over. The world will be completely judged and only the redeemed will be saved.

God's Covenant with Abraham. The Lord promised Abraham land, offspring, blessing, blessings on all nations through him, and a curse on those who cursed Abraham. The book of Revelation displays the fulfillment of the Promised Land in the new heaven and the new earth with God dwelling in the midst of his people, the fulfillment of the offspring in Jesus Christ as the One who came to redeem God's people, and the fulfillment of the blessings of the nations as both Jew and Gentile who make up the redeemed people of God in the new heaven and the new earth.

God's Covenant with Moses. The law was added to govern a theocratic nation that would be a kingdom of priests in the land. The book of Revelation displays the true Israel, the church, as a royal priesthood and holy nation in the church age, but also reveals that this will not be consummated until the new heaven and the new earth.

God's Covenant with David. God promised an eternal kingdom and an eternal king on the throne of David, which is fulfilled in Jesus Christ as King of kings and Lord of lords. The redeemed make up the kingdom of God, which is inaugurated in the present age, but will not be consummated until Christ's second coming.

The New Covenant. God promised the indwelling of the Holy Spirit within his people, forgiveness of sins, the law written on believers' hearts and minds, and knowledge of God. The book of Revelation portrays God's people as able to stand firm through persecution because of the indwelling Holy Spirit and able to enter the new heaven and the new earth because of forgiveness of sins by Jesus Christ, the Lamb of God.

God

Second, the book teaches us that God has had a purpose and a plan from all of eternity to judge those who are not his own and to redeem those who are. He, along with Christ, is on the throne, and worthy of all worship, praise, and adoration. He executes his purpose and plan through the Son and the Spirit and is Creator over all.

Jesus, the Son of God

Third, Jesus Christ is on the throne with the Father, as King of kings and Lord of lords. He is worthy to judge because he was obedient to death on the cross and crowned as King upon his ascension. He is worthy of our worship and our praise and is the One who has gained us entrance into the new heaven and the new earth. He has provided an example for us of how to live on this earth and endure persecution for the sake of the kingdom, and how to stand firm as a witness for the kingdom of God.

God's Faithfulness to His Covenant Promises

Fourth, God is faithful to fulfill his covenant promises to his people that can be summed up in Revelation 21:3: "Behold, the dwelling place of God is with man. He will dwell with them, and they will be his people, and God himself will be with them as their God."

The Climax of Redemption

Fifth, the book of Revelation stands as the final and climatic book in the New Testament to reveal God's plan of redemption and restoration. God has redeemed his people and restored them to Eden, the new heaven and the new earth. If Genesis is the kingdom prologue,[6] Revelation is the kingdom epilogue.

Application to Our Lives

Sixth, the Holy Spirit wants us to apply what we learn from this book to our lives in many ways that will be discussed throughout this study. But I think the ones that come to the forefront are (1) to stand firm as witnesses for Jesus Christ in this world through persecution and tribulation, and (2) to fear God and worship him.

CONCLUSION

Unfortunately, it does not seem that Beethoven believed in the Christian God. More of a tragedy than his physical deafness was his spiritual deafness. He could not hear the voice of God. Repeatedly in the book of Revelation it is said, "He who has an ear, let him hear what the Spirit says to the churches." This is the exhortation before us: to open our eyes and listen to the music of the book, to hear the victory and see the battle scenes in our mind. And, ultimately, to hear the truth behind it all and be moved at the end to rise to our feet with loud applause in order to stand firm as witnesses for Jesus Christ, and to give our worship and praise to the One to whom all glory and honor is due.

6. I am indebted to Meredith G. Kline's book *Kingdom Prologue: Genesis Foundations for a Covenantal Worldview* (Eugene, OR: Wipf and Stock, 2006) for this thought.

LESSON 1

Revelation 1

PLEASE USE THE QUESTION paradigm from pages 353–54 as you work through the following. See the introductory comments there that explain each part of the process below in more detail.

- **Pray**.
- **Ponder the Passage**. Read Revelation 1 once a day from different translations for the entire week, looking for its:
  - Point
  - Persons
  - Patterns
  - Persons of the Trinity
  - Puzzling Parts
- **Put It in Perspective**.
  - Place in Scripture
  - Passages from Other Parts of Scripture

1. Based on your observations of the text, what is the basic content of this passage? Try to summarize it in your own words, using a sentence or two.
2. Whose revelation is this (Rev. 1:1)? What is the purpose of the revelation (Rev. 1:1)?

3. What five parties are involved in the chain of communication (Rev. 1:1–3)?

4. What does the word "must" convey in Revelation 1:1?

5. Since John was living in the first century A.D. and it has been more than two thousand years since "what must soon take place" was written, what does this phrase mean (Rev. 1:1)?

6. What is the blessing in Revelation 1:3? Look up "blessed" in a concordance. Where are the other blessings in Revelation? How many are there total? Make a list of them.

7. Look up each of the seven churches in a Bible dictionary and write down what you learn (Rev. 1:4).

8. What type of genre does Revelation 1:4–8 convey that the book of Revelation is?

9. What person of the Godhead is "the seven spirits who are before his throne" (Rev. 1:4)?

10. Explain in your own words the titles used of Jesus Christ in Revelation 1:5.

11. What has Christ made us by his action on the cross (Rev. 1:6)?

12. Compare Revelation 1:4 with 1:8. What similarities exist?

13. When will the tribulation and the kingdom occur, according to Revelation 1:9?

14. Where was John? Why was he there and when (Rev. 1:9–10)?

15. What was John commanded to do (Rev. 1:11)?

16. Look up *trumpet* in a Bible dictionary or concordance. What did a trumpet usually signify in the Old Testament (Rev. 1:11)?

17. What are the "seven golden lampstands" in Revelation 1:12 (compare with Rev. 1:20)?

18. Compare Daniel 3, 7, and 10 with Revelation 1:13–15. What do you find?

19. What was John's response to the vision of Revelation 1:12–15 (Rev. 1:17)? What was Christ's response to John's response (Rev. 1:18)?

20. Compare Revelation 1:4 and 1:8 with 1:19. What similarities exist?

21. Go back and interpret Revelation 1:12 and 1:16 in the light of 1:20.

• **Principles and Points of Application.**

1. It is so easy to read Scripture without hearing it. It's also easy to hear Scripture without doing anything about it. We can observe, but not interpret. Or we can observe and interpret, but not apply. But the Lord is telling us here in the introduction of Revelation that we must observe, interpret, and apply his Word in our lives. Use your lesson's questions to spend time this week in Revelation 1 observing, interpreting, and applying.

2. Make a list, title by title or description by description, of the names of God presented in Revelation 1:4–8. What does each name tell you about Christ? Which one is most meaningful to you? Most comforting for your season of life right now? Hardest for you to grasp? Easiest for you to understand?

3. How are you demonstrating your kingship and priesthood in God's kingdom? In other words, how are you ruling over that which/those whom he's put underneath you (children, those who are under your leadership environment, etc.) and how are you worshiping God and leading others to worship him? How are you interceding for others?

4. How does Revelation 1:9 make you feel connected to your brothers and sisters in Christ in the past? How does this encourage you? Read Hebrews 11 and then read verse 1:9 again. Pray that one day your life too will be an encouragement to others long after you've passed away. Then live each day in light of this.

5. When have you "seen Jesus" in such a way that you have fallen "facedown"? Write about the circumstances and pray about whether to share it with your group this week.

6. As we move through the book of Revelation this year, it will aid our worship to write down the names of God in each chapter

as we study. I have separated the page into names for God the Father, God the Son, and God the Holy Spirit. Of course, some names apply to all three. At the end of each lesson, fill out the names you have seen in that lesson's text. Keep this page nearby and use it often as a reference for worship and adoration of God during your individual and/or group prayer time. Add as many pages of your own as you need to complete the list of names found throughout the book. I have done the first chapter for you below as an example.

- *Father*, you are God (Rev. 1:1), the One who is and who was and who is to come (Rev. 1:4, 8), the Alpha and the Omega (Rev. 1:8), the LORD God (ibid.), the Almighty (ibid.).
- *Jesus*, you are Jesus Christ (Rev. 1:1), the faithful witness (Rev. 1:5), the firstborn of the dead (ibid.), the ruler of kings on earth (ibid.), the one who loves us (ibid.), the one who has freed us from our sins by your blood (ibid.), the one who has made us a kingdom of priests to God the Father (ibid.), the one to whom belong glory and dominion forever (Rev. 1:6), the one who is coming with the clouds (Rev. 1:7), one like a Son of Man (Rev. 1:13), the first and the last (Rev. 1:17), the living one (Rev. 1:18), the one who died and is alive forevermore (ibid.), the one who has the keys of death and hades (ibid.).
- *Holy Spirit*, you are the seven spirits who are before God's throne (Rev. 1:4).

NOTES FOR REVELATION 1

Aim: Ponder the aim of this lesson concerning our:

Mind: What do we need to know from this passage in Scripture?

That John is instructed by Jesus to write to the seven churches in Asia concerning his vision on Patmos of the things that he's seen, that are, and that are about to take place.

Heart: How does what we learn from this passage affect our internal relationship with the Lord?

It prepares us to be kingdom disciples who read, hear, and keep the Word of God given through Revelation.

Hands: How does what we learn from this passage translate into action for God's kingdom?

It enables us to:

1. Make a list of the descriptions of God presented in Revelation 1:4–8 and meditate on them, thanking God for who he is and what he has done.
2. Demonstrate our kingship and priesthood in God's kingdom by leading those under our care in a Christlike way by the Spirit's power, and by interceding for those in our lives who need prayer.
3. Live each day in light of the fact that after we die our life legacy should be an encouragement to others in the faith.
4. Rely on the Holy Spirit to "see Jesus" in such a way in our lives that we fall "facedown" and worship him and lead others to do the same.

INTRODUCTION

The music began as a cue for people to stop talking and take their seats before the worship service. After a time of Scripture reading and singing, the pastor assumed his position at the pulpit to preach the Word of God. As he got under way, I purposefully looked around me to see what people were doing. Some were sleeping. Some were yawning. Others were reading their bulletins. A few were taking serious notes. A couple were tending to antsy children. Several were looking straight ahead at the preacher. I wondered how we looked to the One who was supposed to be the center of our worship. Was he pleased? I couldn't help wondering if he was offended at our conduct. It seemed to be another Sunday morning that we showed up at church because we knew that was where we were supposed to be, but it seemed as if we were not impressed with the One we were worshiping. Perhaps we had grown too familiar with the church building and the preacher. Perhaps we were tired from the week before and trying to figure out how we were going to make it through the next one. Or maybe we were still thinking about this whole God idea and if we really bought into it. But few of us seemed overwhelmed to be in the presence of the Holy and Almighty God.

I knew it wasn't all of the many trials and pains and hardships that kept us from being overwhelmed. One of the ladies in the audience was on the verge of physical death and she looked more radiant and more engaged than anyone. She had battled cancer—a cancer that would take her life in a week—but she was ready to go home to be with her Lord and Savior. No, the difference among the people, biblically speaking, was, first, the presence (or lack of it) of the indwelling Holy Spirit. I knew that not everyone in the seats was saved. The second difference had to do with whether or not we had quenched the Holy Spirit in our lives or were attuned to the Spirit and ready to hear what God had to say to us through him. I knew that few of us had taken the time to prepare our hearts for worship before coming to church. And the third difference was in knowing God through knowing the Word of God so that we were able to worship in spirit and in truth. I knew that many had not opened the Word of God since last Sunday. These three differences—the indwelling of the Spirit, being attuned to the Spirit, and knowing God through his Word—are important for opening our eyes to the spiritual things taking place around us and preparing our hearts to worship God as he deserves on Sunday mornings.

Revelation 1 has much to say about embracing Christ, being attuned to the spiritual things around us, and knowing the Word of God. And the response is not to stay comfortably seated. John's response in this chapter is to fall at Christ's feet as though he, John, were stricken dead.

When is the last time that we saw Jesus and fell at his feet as though we were dead? When is the last time that we were so overwhelmed with who he is and what he has done that we have fallen facedown to worship him? When was the last Sunday that we spent time preparing our heart to meet with the Living God and worship him?

We will study this chapter by dividing our lesson into three main sections:

   I. The Revelation of Jesus Christ (Rev. 1:1–3)
  II. John's Greeting to the Seven Churches in Asia (cf. John 1:4–8)
 III. God Gives John a Vision on Patmos (Rev. 1:9–20)

I. The Revelation of Jesus Christ (Rev. 1:1–3)

Revelation 1:1. The first thing we see is that this is a revelation of Jesus Christ—that is, it is about him and comes to John through him. It has been said that every book in the Bible whispers Christ's name; in Revelation, we have a book that shouts his name. But that shout does not originate with Christ; it originates with God the Father. And God the Father had a purpose in giving his Son this revelation. The message was not only for the churches in Asia Minor during John's day; it was for you and me as well, to show us the things that must soon take place. The word "must" here is an imperative. If we say this word in our own lives—"this must happen"—we reveal that we are being selfish and prideful. But for God to say it reveals that he is Sovereign over all things and that his plan and purpose is certain to come to pass. This should instill great hope in us that our Father's plan and purpose will, indeed, *must*, come to pass. God made this known to believers like you and me by sending an angel to his servant John who recorded what he saw for the church. So, we see that there is a chain of communication involved here that looks like this: God the Father to Jesus Christ to his Angel to John to all believers.

Old Testament Background to Revelation 1:1. Daniel 2:28–30, 45–47 says, "But there is a God in heaven who reveals mysteries,

7

and he has made known to King Nebuchadnezzar what will be in the latter days . . . thoughts of what would be after this, and he who reveals mysteries made known to you what is to be . . . just as you saw that a stone was cut from a mountain by no human hand, and that it broke in pieces the iron, the bronze, the clay, the silver, and the gold. A great God has made known to the king what shall be after this." This background helps us define "soon" in 1:1. What was future for Daniel, who is looking toward Christ's first and second comings, has already been inaugurated in John's day. John has been an eyewitness to the death and resurrection of Jesus Christ and is now living in a time when the kingdom has been inaugurated but not consummated, just as we do today.

Revelation 1:2. John was faithful in his task. He was a faithful servant and obeyed God's command to write down the visions that he saw. How much we would have missed if John had not been obedient to his calling! How important it is for you and for me to be sensitive to the ministry that the Lord has for us as we join together to serve the kingdom of God through the power of the Holy Spirit. What is the "testimony of Jesus Christ"? It is defined by its parallel phrase in the verse, "the word of God." John 1:1 tells us that the Word was God and this Word was Christ and he came to earth to be a witness to God's Word, that we might know the Father since the Son has revealed him to us in our world. He stands as a witness to the truth of God's Word.

Revelation 1:3. We see here the first "blessing" of seven in the book. John uses the number seven to connote completeness. Thus, the seven blessings in Revelation convey that the ones who follow the exhortations connected with the blessings will be completely and fully blessed in glory. The seven blessings in Revelation can be found in the following verses:

- Revelation 1:3: "Blessed is the one who reads aloud the words of this prophecy, and blessed are those who hear and who keep what is written in it, for the time is near."

- Revelation 14:13: "Blessed are the dead who die in the Lord from now on." "Blessed indeed," says the Spirit, "that they may rest from their labors, for their deeds follow them!"
- Revelation 16:15: "Blessed is the one who stays awake, keeping his garments on, that he may not go about naked and be seen exposed!"
- Revelation 19:9: "Blessed are those who are invited to the marriage supper of the Lamb."
- Revelation 20:6: "Blessed and holy is the one who shares in the first resurrection!"
- Revelation 22:7: "Blessed is the one who keeps the words of the prophecy of this book."
- Revelation 22:14: "Blessed are those who wash their robes, so that they may have the right to the tree of life and that they may enter the city by the gates."

All of the blessings have to do with embracing and persevering in faith so that we will receive the promise of eternal life. These blessings are important because they are glimmers of hope for us. The church in John's day that was undergoing persecution and the temptation to compromise with the world especially needed to be reminded of the blessing that was theirs if they remained faithful to Christ. But we need such a reminder just as much today, as we are tempted to compromise our own faith with the world of materialism and false ideology around us.

Let's look at the first blessing: "Blessed is the one who reads aloud the words of this prophecy . . ." We should not skim over that instruction too quickly. So many people find the book of Revelation difficult to study. They make it through the first few chapters and then put it down when the "weird visions" begin. But if we were to sit and read this out loud to our children and grandchildren and add pictures alongside it, ask them if they understood it, they would look up at us with wide eyes and say, "Yes." They would say this because children are so good at seeing the big picture and using their imaginations and not getting stuck on details. For example, when my son, Caleb, was four, we began reading *Dangerous Journey*, which is a children's book based on John Bunyan's *The Pilgrim's Progress*.[1] Each page is illustrated with some of the most disturbing pictures to convey our journey through this life to the next. But Caleb loved the book and even when he was four understood the majority of the message. He wanted it read to him over and over again. So we would do well to pick up Revelation and read it all in one sitting, out loud, and if we have children or grandchildren, to read it to them too. Don't get caught up in the logic of it all; rather, remember that this is more like a piece of great art or a symphony composed by a master musician. It is to be read with emotion and flare, but the truth behind it is not embellished. The truth behind it is *truth* and will certainly take place.

The second part of the first blessing of the book is also found in this verse: "Blessed are those who hear and who keep what is written in it." We are not just supposed to read John's message; we are to hear it. That is a great difference. We can read something and not hear it, in the sense that the content quickly leaves our minds and we move on to the next bit of information in our world. But John tells us that we are to hear it in the sense that it touches our hearts and minds in such a way that we are moved to action to keep the exhortations written in it.

Our motivation for persevering in the faith is because "the time is near." This phrase will confuse us here and throughout the whole book if we think of it only in terms of the second coming of Christ. But Revelation is not only concerned with the second coming. The book is concerned with the period of time between Christ's first and second comings. We see in the book of Revelation what we see elsewhere in Scripture, the tension between the already and the not yet. Christ has already come and won the victory over Satan at the cross, but Satan is still allowed to roam around the world looking for someone to devour (1 Peter 5:8). He is not yet confined to the "lake of fire" for all eter-

---

1. *Dangerous Journey: The Story of Pilgrim's Progress*, selected from John Bunyan's original work by Oliver Hunkin, illustrated by Alan Parry (Grand Rapids: Eerdmans, 1995).

nity. So, too, Christ has already inaugurated his kingdom with his death and resurrection, but it will not be fully consummated until he comes again. So, we can say that Christ will "come quickly" because this refers not just to his visible second coming, but also to the comings of judgment depicted in chapters 2–3, in which Christ removes those in the church who do not serve him faithfully. Of course, we should always recognize that the time of his second coming is near in the sense that it is the next main event in the history of redemption that God has revealed in his Word. And, we should always recognize that because we do not know the day or the hour of Christ's return, it could take place any day of our lives and we need to be found faithful. Only if we are found faithful will we receive the blessing. And we should be faithful not only because of what Christ has already done for us through his death and resurrection, but also because of what he will do for us when he returns to establish his eternal kingdom in its fullest form and allow us entrance into it.

II. John's Greeting to the Seven Churches in Asia (cf. John 1:4–8)

Revelation 1:4–5a. These verses clearly display that the book of Revelation is first and foremost an epistle. The book does use prophetic and apocalyptic genres, but it is primarily a letter to seven historical churches in Asia Minor, although these are most likely representative for all the churches in Asia Minor at the time and for all churches of all times.[2] We must not forget that Revelation not only had an application for the readers of John's day, but has a message for the church of our day as well. Thus, the book is not just about the future, it is about today and yesterday and forever. We must be discerning as we try to understand which parts of Revelation apply to the past, the present, and the future. And we must hold our conclusions humbly and loosely, as we acknowledge that many in the church who love the Lord and seek to know his Word hold to different interpretations of the book.

---

2. G. K. Beale, *The Book of Revelation: A Commentary on the Greek Text*, New International Greek Testament Commentary (Grand Rapids: Eerdmans, 1999), 37–39.

Figure 1.1. The Seven Churches in Asia[3]

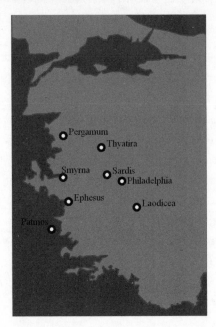

The Asia Minor of John's day was an oppressive place for Christians to live. No longer did they enjoy the protection of being considered an offshoot of Judaism, which was tolerated by Rome. By this time, Jews had become increasingly intolerant of Christians as the beliefs of the two groups separated them from one another. In fact, Jews most likely were the ones accusing Christians before the Roman government of disturbing the peace, not being part of Judaism, and refusing to worship Caesar. The imperial cult of ancient Rome, which acknowledged the emperors as having divine authority, infiltrated every area of life at the time so that Christians who did not participate were left at a severe economic and social disadvantage. Penalties for not worshiping the Roman emperor would involve exile and death.

Ephesus was a significant city because it had been the center of Paul's ministry and because John had lived there and been influential in

3. I am indebted to Robert Mounce, *The Book of Revelation*, New International Commentary on the New Testament, rev. ed. (Grand Rapids: Eerdmans, 1998), 67–115, for specific information on the cities and churches.

the church. Geographically, it was located at the best entry point from the port in that region of Asia Minor. Three trade routes met at the city and a wide, column-lined street led from the port to the center of the city, which contained a stadium, market, and theater. The Temple of Artemis, one of the seven wonders of the ancient world, and several other temples built to emperors were a significant presence in the city.

Smyrna is the only one of these seven ancient cities that remains active and vital today (as Izmir). It too had a great entry point from the Aegean Sea and contained an important road to get exports out of the region. It contained a well-known stadium, library, and the largest public theater in Asia. Like Ephesus, it too had a large population. It too built temples in honor of emperors and gods. It held strong allegiance to Rome and was mainly made up of Jews who persecuted Christians. Polycarp, one of the early church fathers, was the twelfth martyr of Smyrna.

Pergamum was about ten miles east of the Aegean Sea. It was the capital city of Asia Minor and known as the most distinguished city of the region. Its library was the largest and it was the center of worship for the pagan cults of Zeus, Athene, Dionysos, and Asklepios.

Thyatira was the least elaborate and known city of the region, but did have a large number of trade guilds that developed and succeeded there. Since trade guilds were closely linked with allegiance to the imperial cult, it was difficult for Christians to be involved in these guilds without compromising their faith, which hurt them economically.

Sardis was a famous and wealthy city, as it was the first to strike gold and silver coins and discover how to dye wool. The environment was pagan, but there appeared to be no heresy or outside opposition coming into the churches.

Philadelphia was known as the "gateway to the East" for commerce and a "missionary city" for Greek culture to Lydia and Phrygia. It had many temples, cults, and religious festivals.

Laodicea was the wealthiest city in Phrygia. It was famous for the soft, glossy black wool it produced from its sheep. This fame and wealth brought the banking industry to the region. The city was also famous for its medical school and physicians. Two famous medicines invented in Laodicea were an ear ointment and an eye-salve. However, the city had to bring its water in from an outside source through stone pipes, which could be cut off and did not provide the freshest water.

The phrase "grace and peace" is seen frequently in the New Testament letters, as the author knows that it will only be by God's grace that readers will be able to keep and apply the words they are reading that were written under the inspiration of the Holy Spirit, and it is only the peace of God (which he alone can give) that will get them through external pressures. But grace and peace are theirs from "him who is and who was and who is to come." This is an allusion to both Exodus 3:14 ("I AM Who I AM") and Isaiah (multiple verses in which God refers to himself in a similar way) and would have instilled great confidence in the readers that the same God who was with believers in the Old Testament is with them today and is holding all of their tomorrows in his hand as well. This allusion serves the same purpose for us today. The God of the Old and New Testaments is the same God who today is bringing his promises to pass, filling our lives with his grace and peace as we walk through this world that is not our home. Not only are grace and peace and the book of Revelation from God the Father, but also from the Holy Spirit, "the seven spirits who are before his throne" (Rev. 1:4). The "seven" connotes perfection and completion. The Holy Spirit is not only the one who assists John in writing Scripture (2 Peter 1:21), but also the one who applies God's grace and peace to our lives. We see in verse 5a that this grace and peace are also from Jesus Christ, who is given three descriptions here. He is the faithful witness because he has been sent from the Father to testify about the Father. If we know the Son, then we know the Father (John 10:30). He was faithful even unto death on the cross. Thus, despite the persecution that he faced, Jesus stood strong as a faithful witness to God in the midst of it, never wavering or compromising his faith. He is the example that the churches in Asia Minor were to follow and that we are to follow today. He is also the "firstborn of the dead." Christ's resurrection inaugurated the new creation, and thus he is the firstborn of the new creation in whose footsteps all believers will follow. Finally, he is "the ruler of kings on earth." At the cross he defeated all of his enemies and thus rules over them.

Old Testament Background to Threefold Description. Psalm 89:27, 37: "And I will make him the firstborn, the highest of the kings of the earth. Like the moon it shall be established forever, a faithful witness in the skies."

This psalm speaks of David as the anointed king who reigns over his enemies and whose seed will be established on the throne for eternity. Christ is the ultimate fulfillment of the ideal Davidic king who reigns forever on his throne that was established at his resurrection (Rev. 1:5b–6).

Now John breaks into worship, a theme we will see throughout the book. John's worship stems from three things. First, Christ has loved us. The epitome of his love was shown to us on the cross. Second, he has freed us from our sins by his blood on the cross. He died in our place. Third, he has made us a kingdom of priests to his God and Father. Upon his ascension, the kingdom of which we are priests was inaugurated and we are thus participants in his kingdom as priests now although not yet in the fullest sense. It is because of these three actions that Christ is to be worshiped; his will be the glory and the dominion forever.

Old Testament Background to Revelation 1:6. Exodus 19:6: "And you shall be to me a kingdom of priests and a holy nation."

Christ fulfilled what the Passover lamb could never do. He was the final and complete sacrifice. Christ's death not only made him priest and king, but also made all believers priests and kings with him. Believers function in these two offices now by being witnesses to the world around us of Christ's office of king and priest so that others, too, might become a part of the kingdom. We do this by standing firm in our testimony despite any persecution and temptation to compromise our faith. This will be revealed to us throughout the pages of Revelation. The church functions as the new Israel, which no longer has to offer the Passover lamb but proclaims and testifies to the true Lamb of God. And he alone is worthy to receive glory for the salvation that he accomplished for the people of God on the cross.

Revelation 1:7. This one who has loved us and freed us from our sins when he came the first time to accomplish his work on the cross is

15

coming again. But this time it will not be as a baby; this time it will be as the Son of Man coming with the clouds. And he will not be hidden in a stable, but every eye will see him and all the tribes of the earth will wail on account of him. However, his ultimate coming is already inaugurated as all throughout the history of this interadvent age he continues to bless and to judge.

Old Testament Background to Revelation 1:7.

- Daniel 7:13: "And behold with the clouds of heaven there came one like a son of man, and he came to the Ancient of Days and was presented before him."
- Zechariah 12:10: "When they look on me, on him whom they have pierced, they shall mourn for him."

Revelation 1:8. All three titles in Revelation 1:8 convey the same idea. God is over all of history. He was at the beginning and he will be at the end, and consequently he will be over all that is in between. Alpha is the first letter of the Greek alphabet and omega is the last. He is almighty over all things and is directing its end to accomplish his purposes.

Old Testament Background to Revelation 1:8.

- Isaiah 44:6 and 48:12: "I am the first and I am the last."
- Haggai repeatedly uses "Almighty" to refer to God, as do Zechariah and Malachi.

III. God Gives John a Vision on Patmos (Rev. 1:9–20)

Revelation 1:9. John's words here remind us that he is our brother as much as he was the brother of the Christians in the churches of Asia Minor. Also, the tribulation and the kingdom are spoken of as present realities so we know that they have been inaugurated. He is also a partner with his readers in "the patient endurance," as is clear by his location on the island of Patmos. He was there because he had stood firm in his faith and testimony, which means he had probably been banished to the island because of his faith.

Revelation 1:10–11. Evidently John had his heart attuned to worship by the Holy Spirit's working on a certain Sunday when he received this vision. What an appropriate model for us today who have largely forgotten what it's like to be in the Spirit on Sunday morning. Rushing about trying to get ourselves and our children ready in order to fly out the door to make it to church on time, sometimes even having an argument with our spouse on the way, leaves us in a poor condition to hear from the Lord or worship him. But thankfully, John had prepared his heart and was able to hear from the Lord, and because he had done this and heard, he was able to bless the church with one of the most encouraging books of the New Testament. How many blessings we must miss on the Lord's Day by not having our hearts prepared!

The loud voice like a trumpet alludes to the many instances in the Old Testament where trumpets were associated with judgment (Ex. 19:16, 19–20 and Josh. 6), and thus gives us an idea that the book of Revelation will deal with judgment as one of its themes. Just as the Old Testament prophets were commanded to communicate to the people of Israel their visions, which also had judgment as one of their themes, so too John is asked to write down his visions for the seven churches of Asia Minor, and ultimately for the universal church.

Revelation 1:12–16. John turns and sees seven golden lampstands, which represent the church and in the midst of them, one like a son of man.

Old Testament Background to Revelation 1:12. Zechariah 4:2–6: "A lampstand . . . and seven lamps on it."

Note that there was only one lampstand in Zechariah, whereas here there are seven. This is due to the fact that John is now applying the lampstands to the church universal and to all peoples, not just Israel. The long robe and golden sash (Rev. 1:13) around Christ emphasize his priestly role of tending to the churches. He is the one who speaks words of promise, words of affirmation, or words of warning or rebuke to them. The hairs of his head being white not only convey wisdom, but purity as well. His eyes being like a flame of fire describes Christ's judicial role (Rev. 1:14). His feet that were like burnished bronze refined in a furnace (Rev. 1:15) display his moral purity and set the precedent for what his followers should reflect as well.

Old Testament Background to Revelation 1:13–15. See Daniel 3, 7, 10. Note that the attributes of God the Father (Ancient of Days) is

17

here ascribed to Christ ("one like a son of man"), thus solidifying the deity and place of Christ alongside the Father on the throne. The seven stars in Christ's right hand are the angels of the seven churches (Rev. 1:20), conveying that Christ is not only Lord of the earthly church, but the heavenly church as well. The sharp two-edged sword continues to convey his role as judge (Rev. 1:16a).

Old Testament Background to Revelation 1:16a.

- Isaiah 11:4: "And he shall strike the earth with the rod of his mouth."
- Isaiah 49:2: "He made my mouth like a sharp sword."

The idea here is that his face was like the sun shining in full strength, which reveals a victorious warrior.

Old Testament Background to Revelation 1:16b. Judges 5:31: "So may all your enemies perish, O Lord! But your friends be like the sun as he rises in his might."

Revelation 1:17–18. John's response to the vision was to fall face-down, as though dead. Isn't that the response that God's Word should evoke in us? When we are attuned to the Spirit as John was and are ready to hear his Word to us, we are overwhelmed by it. John lay before him as though dead, but you can almost hear Jesus say to John, "I died so that you don't have to. Because I live you will live too. Because I broke the bonds of death, you do not have to fear. Because I am the first and the last, you do not have to worry; I have everything under my control. Because I have the keys of Death and Hades, Satan and his powers cannot destroy you. Thus, do not fear!" I don't know about you but there have been moments in my life when I have been seized by fear. The news of layoffs coming in the company leaves us wondering if we will be next. The doctor leaves a message on the voice mail saying the test results are not good and we need to come in immediately. The pregnancy doesn't seem like it's going well and there is the possibility of miscarriage. The neighbor down the street tells us she's seen our husband with another woman. We have reason to believe that our child has disabilities. We have evidence that our teen is struggling with an addiction. Our adult child has abandoned the faith and is on the road of destruction. But Jesus takes us by the shoulder and lays his right hand on us, displaying his kingship over our lives, and speaks to us, saying, "Do not fear. I have died so that you may live. I am sovereign over your circumstances. I am almighty over the events in your life." And he invites us to live as kings and priests with him.

Old Testament Background to Revelation 1:17–18.

- Isaiah 22:22: "And I will place on his shoulder the key of the house of David. He shall open, and none shall shut; and he shall shut, and none shall open."
- Isaiah 41:4; 44:6; 48:12: "I am the first and the last."

Revelation 1:19–20. Again John is commanded to write. He is to write "the things you have seen, those that are and those that are to take place after this." In light of the threefold description of Christ in Revelation 1:4 and 1:8, it seems likely that this verse is referring equally to the entire book. "What will happen after these things" may very probably be an allusion to Daniel 2, which provides an already and not-yet tension, as we have seen exists in the book. To understand this verse as separating the book into three different chronological sections does not do justice to the literary genre of Revelation, the biblical text, or the already and not-yet tension found in the New Testament. The "mystery" in 1:20a further confirms the use of Daniel 2 in these verses.

Old Testament Background to Revelation 1:19–20. Daniel 2:29, 47: "Of what would be after this" and "a revealer of mysteries."

Now the seven stars and seven lampstands are defined as the angels of the seven churches and the churches themselves. The angels here refer to the earthly church that they represent as well. They are in a sense accountable for the churches and the churches benefit from the angel's activity on their behalf. They have heavenly assistance for the churches' earthly trials. The churches are already seen as taking part in the heavenly realm, and the angels remind them of this. Though they are struggling on earth, they are already in a

19

sense taking part in the heavenly worship of heaven. Thus, it is even more imperative that they stand firm as witnesses.

CONCLUSION -we for our conclusion

John saw Jesus and fell at his feet as though he were dead. He was so overwhelmed with who Christ is and what he has done that John fell facedown to worship him. He was prepared to be in the Spirit on the Lord's Day. He was prepared in his heart to meet with the Living God and worship him. He had allowed exile to soften rather than harden his heart. He had joyfully embraced suffering for the cause of Christ. He was ready to be used by God to build up the churches. And he was able to do all of these things because he knew the one that he worshiped and he recognized the enablement of the Holy Spirit. He knew that Jesus was the Christ who had died and rose again. He knew the grace and peace that only comes from God. He knew that Christ was the faithful witness and he wanted to follow in his Master's footsteps. He knew Christ was the firstborn of the dead and that he too would receive a glorified body. He knew that Christ was the ruler of kings on earth and that they could not harm him even if they put him in exile. He knew that Christ loved him and had freed him from his sins by his blood and he wanted to be willing to give his blood for the cause of Christ as well. He knew that Christ had made him part of a kingdom and made him a priest to his God and Father. And he knew that his whole life was to glorify the Lord. He knew that one day Jesus would come with the clouds and every tongue would confess that Jesus is Lord. John knew Jesus and because he knew him, he was a faithful witness.

May we follow in the footsteps of John and see Jesus in such way that we fall at his feet in worship and stand as faithful witnesses for him in the midst of our world.

How do we stand in the midst of trials & persecution? By knowing the One who gave His life so we might live & recognizing the enablement of the Holy Spirit!

The time to prepare for [20] suffering & persecution is before it comes, not while you're in the midst of it. Example- Vacation planning?

LESSON 2

Revelation 2

PLEASE USE THE QUESTION paradigm from pages 353–54 as you work through the following. See the introductory comments there that explain each part of the process below in more detail.

- **Pray.**
- **Ponder the Passage**. Read Revelation 2 once a day from different translations for the entire week, looking for its:
  - Point
  - Persons
  - Patterns
  - Persons of the Trinity
  - Puzzling Parts
- **Put It in Perspective**.
  - Place in Scripture
  - Passages from Other Parts of Scripture

1. Based on your observations of the text, what is the basic content of this passage? Try to summarize it in your own words, using a sentence or two.
2. As you go through each letter to the seven churches, make a comparative chart that shows the similarities and differences between the churches.

3. Where have you seen the description of Christ in verse 2:1 before in the book? In light of that passage, define the seven stars and seven golden lampstands in 2:1.

4. What does Christ commend about the Ephesian church (Rev. 2:2–3, 6)?

5. What does the Lord have against the Ephesian church (Rev. 2:4)?

6. What does Christ exhort the Ephesians to do (Rev. 2:5a)?

7. What is his warning in Revelation 2:5b if they do not follow his exhortation?

8. Look up the word "hear" in a Bible concordance. Where else have you seen this in the book? In light of this, what do you think it means here (Rev. 2:7a)?

9. Go through the questions above with the church of Smyrna in mind now (Rev. 2:8–11), continuing to fill out your chart. Is there an accusation and warning for the church in Smyrna?

10. Go through the questions above with the church of Pergamum in mind now (Rev. 2:12–17), continuing to fill out your chart.

11. Skim Numbers 22:5–25:3. How does this inform your understanding of the teaching of Balaam in Revelation 2:14?

12. Where have you already seen the Nicolaitans mentioned in the book (Rev. 2:15)?

13. Look up "manna" in a concordance. Where else is manna mentioned in the Bible? Do you see any connection with the manna in Revelation 2:17?

14. Go through questions 5–10 above with the church of Thyatira in mind (Rev. 2:18–29), continuing to fill out your chart.

15. Read 1 Kings 21. How does this inform your understanding of Revelation 2:20–23?

16. Who is behind Jezebel's teaching (Rev. 2:24)? Who is behind all false teaching?

- **Principles and Points of Application.**

1. Who and what do you allow to give counsel in your life? Do you take their words and compare them to the truth or do you

readily accept the advice of newscasters, talk shows, newspaper columnists, friends, family, and/or church members? Begin this week evaluating what you hear with the truth of God's Word. In order to do that, we must know God's Word as revealed to us in Scripture. So, if you do not already have a time set aside to study Scripture daily, begin to implement such a time this week, relying on the strength of the Holy Spirit.

2. In what areas of your life are you enduring patiently and bearing for Christ's name's sake? Meditate on Isaiah 40:27–31, praying and asking the Lord to continue to strengthen you, as those in Ephesus.

3. Think about a time in your life when you were most fervent for the Lord and for his people, a time when studying God's Word and giving of your time and resources to the church came easily. Pray and ask God's forgiveness for any lack of fervency you have now, and ask him to help cultivate that first love again. Then act on it this week by the enablement of the Spirit of God.

4. In what area of your life are you suffering? How does it help you to know that you have to share in Christ's sufferings in order to share in his crown of life? Pray and ask God to help you stand firm under the testing. Then memorize or meditate on Scripture having to do with suffering (look up "suffer" and associated words in a concordance) this week.

5. What sphere in your life (neighborhood, career, school, etc.) is bringing you down to its level instead of you raising the bar and standing as a light among others? Repent and fight against this by putting on the spiritual armor of God described in Ephesians 6:10ff.

6. How are you continuing to develop and increase the effectiveness of your spiritual gifts? If you don't know what your spiritual gifts are, ask one of the leaders in your church to help you determine them. Then use them to benefit the body of Christ beginning this week, remembering to rely on the Spirit's enablement instead of your own.

7. Who or what do you "tolerate" in your life that you shouldn't, and how are you going to change this today beginning with

repentance? (It may be television shows, radio stations, language, music, false teaching, immorality, laziness, overindulgence, etc.)

NOTES FOR REVELATION 2

Aim: Ponder the aim of this lesson concerning our:

Mind: What do we need to know from this passage in Scripture?

> Christ's words through John to the churches in Ephesus, Smyrna, Pergamum, and Thyatira speak to the universal church throughout all of history.

Heart: How does what we learn from this passage affect our internal relationship with the Lord?

> It helps us to be kingdom disciples who hear what the Spirit says to our churches, strengthening our weaknesses, continuing our strengths, and repenting of our sin.

Hands: How does what we learn from this passage translate into action for God's kingdom?

> It teaches us to:

1. Evaluate what we hear from the media, family, and friends with the truth of God's Word.
2. Endure patiently difficult areas in our lives for Christ's name's sake.
3. Confess any lack of fervency for the Lord and his people and ask the Lord to help cultivate a strong witness for him within us.
4. Endure suffering in light of the fact that we have to share in Christ's sufferings in order to share in the crown of life.
5. Put on the spiritual armor of God and stand strong as a witness for Christ in our various spheres of influence.

6. Discern, develop, and use our spiritual gifts for the building up of the body of Christ by relying on the Spirit's enabling power.
7. Discern Satan's propaganda in different spheres of our life and remove it by the power of the Spirit.

INTRODUCTION

I sat around a meeting table for pastoral staff on a weekly basis for two years. Each Monday we were responsible to inform the other church leaders of what was going on in our ministries, and together we were to evaluate what was going on in the church. There was a large emphasis on programs and on the number of people who were being drawn into the church on a weekly basis. Two questions were always asked: "What do the people want?" and "What do the people need?" The thought behind these questions was that if we gave the people what they wanted and needed, more people would attend and the church would grow and be "successful."

But these questions themselves were wrong. The question that needed to be asked was, "What does *Christ* want?" The acknowledgment that needed to be made was that Christ was in the midst of our church. What works does he want us to be doing or not doing? We needed to be Christ-centered and Christ-driven rather than people-centered and people-driven. If we let anyone or anything other than Christ center us and drive us, our ministries will always end up in the wrong place.

Like John in Revelation 1, we need to lead women to a portrait of Christ first and foremost so that they will grasp who he is and fear him alone. Then we need to lead women to the picture of Christ standing in the midst of our ministries, overseeing them and judging them or commending them. The question should always be, "What does Christ want for this ministry?" rather than, "What do the people want or what do I want for this ministry?"

Revelation 2 has much to say about Jesus Christ standing among his people, the church, commending, exhorting, warning, and promising them according to their ways. He is not a God who is far off; he is near us and cares about what we are doing and where we are going.

25

The church is his body; it is not ours. We do not have the liberty to sit around a table and ask the question, "What do the people want or what do we want?" The question should always be, "What does Christ want?"

We can divide this lesson into four sections:

   I. The Words of Christ to the Church in Ephesus (Rev. 2:1–7)
  II. The Words of Christ to the Church in Smyrna (Rev. 2:8–11)
 III. The Words of Christ to the Church in Pergamum (Rev. 2:12–17)
 IV. The Words of Christ to the Church in Thyatira (Rev. 2:18–29)

I. The Words of Christ to the Church in Ephesus (Rev. 2:1–7)

Revelation 2:1. For two chapters we will study the specific letters to the seven historical churches of Asia Minor, which also represent the church universal. The letters begin with the church in Ephesus, perhaps because it was the church that John would have spent the greatest amount of time with and, as the greatest port city, Ephesus begins the clockwise geographical circuit of the order in which John writes to the churches. Notice that the letter is addressed to "the angel of the church." The angel should be identified closely with the church, as the heavenly representative of the earthly reality, and as being responsible to help the church.[1] In this sense the angel would encourage the church to know that it not only has heavenly help, but that it is already a part of the heavenly realm, its members already citizens of heaven and already taking part in the heavenly worship and reign of Christ. The words to the church come from "him who holds the seven stars in his right hand, who walks among the seven golden lampstands." This alludes to Revelation 1:12, 16, and 20. It is Christ who is speaking; he has the seven angels of the seven churches at his command and walks among the seven churches. Immediately, we realize from this verse that God is not a God who is far away, but he is near his people; indeed, he walks among his people, and, as we will see in the following verses, he is intimately acquainted with our

---

1.1 Leon Morris, *The Book of Revelation: An Introduction and Commentary*, Tyndale New Testament Commentaries (Leicester: InterVarsity; Grand Rapids: Eerdmans, 1987), 61.

ways. He cares about what his people are doing with their time, talents, and testimony for his name.

Revelation 2:2–3. Christ has a word of praise for the Ephesian church. They are not doing everything wrong. He has observed some good among them and he begins with the positive. We would do well to learn from Christ's example as we deal with our own churches. When we are in leadership roles and have to evaluate a ministry, we would do well to always begin with the positive. The Ephesian church is doing good works. The people are toiling and enduring patiently and are not bearing with evil. They have tested the false apostles and have not grown weary in doing so. They are solid on doctrine and theology, unlike many "false prophets" in our churches today, men and women who are zealous for false teaching. Such false prophets say a lot that sounds right and gather a following through their charisma and personalities. What they say contains just enough truth to hook a woman and then lead her astray. Our Christian television stations sometimes feature such "prophets," our local bookstores have them, and, unfortunately, our local churches often have them as well. We must be zealous for women's hearts and minds in our women's ministries and other ministries. We must be zealous for our own hearts and minds. We must hold one another accountable as to who and what we are allowing to influence us.

I remember one morning when I was getting ready to teach the morning Bible study at the church where I served as director of women's ministry. The ladies were in their small groups talking and discussing the week's questions. I overheard one of the small group leaders promoting a popular speaker and author and praising this lady's teaching. My heart started pounding. I knew this woman was a false teacher. What was I to do? I knew that I must deal with it. So, after my teaching time, I asked to speak with the small group leader in private, and I gently and lovingly explained to her that this lady she held in such high esteem and had gotten "hooked" on was a false teacher. The leader was shocked and very apologetic. She wanted nothing to do with that kind of teaching. More often than not, the ladies in our ministries are ignorant rather than "wolves in sheep's clothing." But don't be fooled, there are "wolves" in our midst as well and we must discern those too.

Revelation 2:4. Though the church in Ephesus is commended, not all is well. In their fervency for the truth and sound doctrine, the church has lost the love of and warmth for God's people. The church members have become heady, not hearty. They have become theology police but have lost mercy. They have put doctrine over love. And God says this is not good. He has this "against them." He is not pleased. We must pay attention to this. We too in Reformed theological circles are in danger of putting more emphasis on our doctrine than we are on love. It is not that doctrine is not important, but it cannot be separated from our hearts or from the hearts of others. We must have doctrine plus love. There must not be a dichotomy between them.

Revelation 2:5. Christ now exhorts the Ephesians and warns them. They are to remember the time when they did have love and return to it. They are to repent for falling from the love they had at first. So, at one point they were doing well at loving one another and at loving Christ. But over time their heads got in the way of their hearts. And if they don't repent and change, the Lord is going to close the doors of the church. One of the saddest things to me is when I am driving around a town and see a church building that has been abandoned. I always wonder what happened. Did the church move because it had grown or did the church not survive, and if not, why not? The Lord will not allow his church to exist as an unfaithful witness. At some point, he will close the doors of such a church. He will not allow a body that is supposed to reflect him to give a false witness of who he is to a watching world.

Revelation 2:6. Christ now cushions his exhortation and warning between another word of praise. How gracious he is in his dealings with us! He commends the Ephesians for hating the works of the Nicolaitans, which he also hates. The Nicolaitans were most likely a sect of false teachers who were trying to infiltrate the churches. Specifically, they taught that it was permissible to participate with the pagan world in order to not compromise their social and economic standing among pagan trade guilds, and still identify themselves with the church.[2] The Ephesian church, sound in its doctrine, was able to identify such false teaching and repudiated it.

We have Nicolaitans in our churches today, men and women who teach that it is fine to have one foot in the world and one foot in the church in order to stay socially acceptable to both. They blend the best of Oprah with the best of the Omega. They blend Doctor Phil with Doctor Jesus. They blend Dear Abby with Dear Alpha. These are "compromisers," not "overcomers." Their witness is weak because it is not strong in anything. It is a blending of beliefs that becomes their own personal ideology in order to meet their own desires and wants. And Christ hates it.

Now dwell on that picture for a moment. Too often I think we have this preschool picture of Jesus in our minds, seeing him as a tender man who holds us and strokes our hair and loves everything about us. In his eyes we can do no wrong. It's as if he is saying, "It's okay, honey, you can have the world and have me too." But Revelation paints a very different picture of Jesus. The compassion is far from gone, but with it is conviction of truth. And what is not truth, he does not merely have distaste for; he *hates* it. We would do well to evaluate the teachings in our own homes and churches that the Lord may hate.

Revelation 2:7. The exhortation here alludes to Revelation 1:3, the first of the book's seven blessings: "Blessed is the one who reads aloud the words of this prophecy and blessed are those who hear, and who keep what is written in it, for the time is near." Implicit, then, in the exhortation is not just that the people will hear, but that they keep what is written in the book. For the time when God's judgment will come and remove their lampstand is near if they do not repent and begin loving one another and Christ again in the same way that they did at first. This exhortation is found at the conclusion of all seven letters, as well as being sprinkled throughout the concluding chapter of the book (Rev. 22:7–8, 10, 16, 18). It is a firm indication that the letters are not meant only for the individual churches they

2. Robert H. Mounce, *The Book of Revelation*, New International Commentary on the New Testament, rev. ed. (Grand Rapids: Eerdmans, 1998), 71.

address, but for all seven churches in Asia Minor and for the church universal as well.

Then there is a promise. To the one who conquers, Christ will give access to eat of the tree of life, which is in the paradise of God. We see this again in Revelation 22:2, 19, where God says he will take away one's share in the tree of life and in the holy city if one takes away from the words of Revelation. Thus, the promise in 2:7 is to give eternal life to those who stand strong in their witness and worship during their pilgrimage as part of the earthly church.

II. The Words of Christ to the Church in Smyrna (Rev. 2:8–11)

Revelation 2:8. Again, the letter is addressed to the angel of the church (see notes on Rev. 2:1), but this time it is the church in Smyrna that is in view, and Christ is identified as "the first and the last, who died and came to life." This is another allusion to chapter 1, but this time it is Revelation 1:17–18 that is in view. Each description of Christ correlates with the exhortation and/or warning and/or promise to the different churches. Thus, a different title of Christ is emphasized according to the church that is being addressed. Here, the focus is on God's sovereignty. As the first and the last, he is also over everything that comes in between. The focus is also on God's victory over Satan as Jesus conquered death through his crucifixion, resurrection, and ascension.

Revelation 2:9. Again, Christ knows the situation of the church. He is not distant from the people, but walks in the midst of them and is intimately acquainted with their ways. He knows their tribulation; indeed, he relates to their tribulation because he has already walked the road of suffering. He also knows their poverty, but he takes a different view of it than they do. They think that they are poor, and they are in the world's eyes, but in Christ's eyes they are rich, because he has nothing to warn them about concerning their conduct; they are faithful to him and he will be faithful to them. And Christ knows the ones who are false Jews, those devoted to the sect of Judaism who are intolerant of Christians who have accepted the Messiah that they themselves considered to be false; indeed, these are those who constitute a synagogue of Satan.

How blinded the Jews were that rejected Christ. They go on thinking they are right in abiding by the law and waiting for the real Messiah, while all the time they have fallen prey to the lie of Satan himself and joined the ranks of his army.

Revelation 2:10. Christ tells the Smyrnaeans to not fear what they are about to suffer, an allusion to the same verse in chapter 1 that was referred to in Revelation 2:9 concerning his title. Chapter 1:17 says, "Fear not, I am the first and the last." Christ is able to say this only because he has gone before them as an example of one who overcomes. They are about to suffer what he has already suffered. Some of them are about to be thrown into prison by the devil to be tested and will have tribulation for ten days. But Christ has a promise for them. If they overcome, they will receive the crown of life upon their physical death. Christ too was thrown into prison by the devil on the cross and had tribulation for three days, but he was faithful unto death and received the crown of life upon his resurrection and ascension. He is the "pioneer of our faith" (Heb. 6:20).

Revelation 2:11. Again, we have an exhortation to hear (see the note on Rev. 2:7) and a promise: "The one who conquers will not be hurt by the second death." This refers to the death of unbelievers in eternal separation from God in hell. All Christians, unless living at the time when Christ returns, will undergo the first physical death, but then they will be alive forevermore with Christ. But nonbelievers not only go through the first physical death, they also go through the second, spiritual, death of an eternity in hell.

III. The Words of Christ to the Church in Pergamum (Rev. 2:12–17)

Revelation 2:12. Again, the letter is addressed to the angel of the church (see notes on Rev. 2:1), but here it is the church in Pergamum that is addressed. Christ's title here is "him who has the sharp two-edged sword," another allusion to chapter 1, but this time to verse 1:16. Again, this title coincides with the message being given to this specific church. Christ's two-edged sword connotes his judgment that he will use against this church if it does not repent (Rev. 2:15).

Revelation 2:13. Five of the seven letters to the churches begin with the words, "I know your works . . ." but here and in the previous letter to Smyrna, there is no reference to "works." Here Christ says that he knows where "you dwell." They dwell "where Satan's throne is." Now if you remember from Lesson 1, Pergamum was the center of worship for the pagan cults of Zeus, Athene, Dionysos, and Asklepios. So the Christians in the Pergamum church were not exactly dwelling in the most conducive of environments for the Christian faith. It would have been extremely difficult to be a witness for Christ, yet they were standing firm. They had already witnessed one martyr among them, Antipas, who stood firm for his faith, but instead of denying Christ, they chose to follow in Antipas's footsteps and stand strong in their faith as well.

Revelation 2:14–15. But the church in Pergamum is not doing everything right. There were some in their midst who held to the teachings of Balaam. This is an allusion to Numbers 22:5–25:3 and 31:8, 16, where Balaam leads Israel into idolatry and immorality. In that passage Balaam too is threatened with the "sword of the LORD" and, when he did not obey the Lord's warning, he was killed by it. The same situation is repeating itself in John's day where some in the church of Pergamum are leading people to compromise with the pagan culture around them. The church also contains some who hold to the teaching of the Nicolaitans, the same group we saw addressed in the letter to Ephesus; but there the church hated the Nicolaitans, whereas here some are embracing their teaching. Some have one foot in the world and one foot in the church. And the pressure to do so is great because if they don't they would be ostracized from the trade guilds that existed in ancient Rome at the time and would face tremendous economic and social loss.

We find ourselves in the same situation today. The church is conforming to the culture around us. We modify the gospel in order to fit the needs of the people. If Christ's blood offends, we'll take it out of the gospel message. If recitation of creeds, Scripture, and public confession of sin seems too remote and removed from relevance, we'll remove it from the liturgy. If hymns seem to belong to another age, we'll throw them out, and sadly, much good theology will go with them. If Bible studies are too difficult, too long, too boring, or too academic, we'll offer book studies instead in order to keep things lighter and easier for our women to attend and understand. I am not saying that there is anything wrong with book studies per se, but they should always be a supplement to rather than a replacement of Bible studies.

Some have gone to the opposite extreme in an effort to resist conformity to culture and have disposed of culture altogether. They pull out of all secular spheres and make their church their world, spending every day of the week serving there and having little or no interaction with nonbelievers at all. If women would rather be at coffee shops, book clubs, country clubs, and gyms, we'll just bring all of those venues into the church so that they can accomplish everything in the same place without ever interacting with the "secular" culture. Those who are called to be firemen, policemen, lawyers, public school teachers, and so on, are almost seen as having a lesser calling than those in "full-time ministry."

Others have made political agendas their main concern. I was reminded of this when I was at a birthday party a couple of years ago that was made up mostly of evangelical Christians. At one point, it seemed to turn into a time for political party-bashing rather than a birthday celebration. Shouldn't we spend more time praying for our political leaders and the political situation rather than criticizing the people themselves? But many churches continue to get more and more involved with political and social agendas, forgetting the purpose of the church in the world.

Revelation 2:16. Christ now exhorts the Pergamites to repent. And if they do not, he will come to them with the same sword with which he killed unrepentant Balaam and he will wage war against them. This is holy war. God will not stand by and let his witness be profaned. He is holy and he expects his people to be holy as well.

Revelation 2:17–18. Again, we have an exhortation to hear (see the note on Rev. 2:7) and a promise: "To the one who conquers I will give some of the hidden manna." This may go back to the Balaam story. There in the wilderness the Israelites are hungry, but instead of being content with the heavenly manna provided by their heavenly Father, they want the meat sacrificed to idols. It is interesting to note that the next day's manna was always hidden from their sight. It was only the manna they would get for that day that was revealed. So too the Christians of John's day and Christians today have to rely in faith on God's promises that if we persevere we will overcome the tribulations in this world and spend eternity with Christ. Though we cannot see the "manna" of the heavenly banquet table now, we know that God has promised it to us and will remain faithful to his promises.

Is God's promise enough for me?

"And I will give him a white stone with a new name written on the stone that no one knows except the one who receives it." There may be several meanings behind the white stone. First, it served as an indication of innocence, as opposed to a black stone that signified guilt. Thus, if one has a white stone, one may enter the heavenly banquet and partake in the manna. Second, manna itself looks like white stones, so again those with white stones can partake of the manna at the heavenly banquet.[3] Christ also had a name that no one knows but himself (Rev. 19:12). Christ's name, his character, will be revealed at the end. To some his name will be life, and to others it will be death. These are not individual names that we will have, but the name of Christ that will be on our foreheads and the name/character that will be fully realized as ours when we dwell with him in the new city (Rev. 22:3–4).

IV. The Words of Christ to the Church in Thyatira (Rev. 2:18–29)

Revelation 2:18. Again, the letter is addressed to the angel of the church (see notes on Rev. 2:1), but here it is the church in Thyatira that is addressed. Christ's title here is "Son of God, who has eyes like a flame of fire, and whose feet are like burnished bronze," an allusion to Revelation 1:14b–15a. This description conveys his judgment and, like the other letters, coincides with the warning, exhortation, and promise to this specific church.

3. G. K. Beale, *The Book of Revelation: A Commentary on the Greek Text*, New International Greek Testament Commentary (Grand Rapids: Eerdmans, 1999), 252–53.

Revelation 2:19. Like the first letter to Ephesus and all the remaining letters, this letter begins with "I know your works." God is not far from us; he is in the midst of our churches and knows the works that we are and are not doing. The church in Thyatira was full of love, faith, service, and patient endurance. The people had grown in their works. This was commendable, but a holy God cannot overlook any sin, and so he turns to an accusation and a warning.

Revelation 2:20–21. All is not well in the church. Though "love covers a multitude of sins" (1 Peter 4:8), it was not enough to cover the seriousness of immorality and idolatry. There was a lead woman who called herself a prophetess, but was far from that in the eyes of the Lord. She was actively teaching and seducing God's servants to practice immorality and idolatry. If we compare this woman and her children (Rev. 2:23) with the "elect lady and her children" in 2 John 1, it is likely that there is a group of people teaching seductively, not just one woman. Jezebel alludes to the Old Testament Jezebel who led King Ahab and Israel to idolatry involving the worship of Baal (1 Kings 21:25). It was prophesied of her that "the dogs shall eat Jezebel within the walls of Jezreel. Anyone belonging to Ahab who dies in the city the dogs shall eat, and anyone of his who dies in the open country the birds of the heavens shall eat" (1 Kings 21:23–24). The Lord gave the group time to repent, but they continued in their seductive teaching.

We have "Jezebels" in the midst of our churches today, women who have crept into the churches, into the Christian bookstores, onto Christian radio and television stations, who are leading women astray. They speak a lot of truth, just enough to hook women and make them think that they are standing firm on the Word of God in their teaching. They are deceptive and secretive and very appealing to the emotions and the needs of women. They are "Christian" counselors who counsel women according to their own wants and desires; they are small group leaders who tell women it's fine to have one foot in the world and one foot in the church. They are authors who promote the "prosperity gospel." They are retreat leaders who say God will heal you if you only have enough faith. We must be careful of these "Jezebels." We must be so grounded in the objective truth of the Word of God that we recognize the subjective teaching of false teachers who play to the needs and emotions of women in an unbiblical manner.

Some of these prosperity teachers have made their way even into conservative evangelicalism. As noted above, I had to pull one of my small group leaders aside one morning after hearing her quote one of these teachers to her group. Innocently, she thought this teacher was a trustworthy source of the truth and she latched onto her subjective message. This particular teacher herself has said, "I finally realized that the gospel is not about rules; it's about loving God and each other. So what have you done this week to help out someone you know?" While this sounds appealing to many women, we must evaluate her comments in light of Scripture. First of all, Matthew 22:36–40 makes it very clear that there is no dichotomy between love and the law. Love is the foundation of the law. Second, this woman adds her own law in her question, "What have you done this week to help someone you know?" Ironically, her message is one of law, of works-righteousness, not of grace.

Scripture makes it very clear that winning the battle of the mind is not about our strategy; it is about being in Christ's armor. We cannot manage our emotions, only the Holy Spirit can. The way of the cross is most often not enjoyable, though it is true that the glory that follows will far exceed what we can hope or imagine. Overcoming life's challenges is not about relentless determination; it is about accepting the determination of Christ to accomplish his Father's will on the cross. Peace is not to be pursued; it has already been given in Christ. Where in the Bible are we given permission to lighten up? All of the authors of Scripture make it clear that we are in a cosmic battle; suffering is involved and it can be intense. Over and over again we are called to discipline and perseverance. Many false prophets teach works-righteousness behind the health, wealth, and prosperity gospel. This is totally out of line with Scripture. Christ's work alone has saved us once and for all; we are not promised health, wealth, and prosperity in this life, but we are promised the abundant wealth of Christ himself in the new heaven and new earth to come.

Revelation 2:22–23. The Lord now warns the church concerning his actions toward this group of false prophets and teachers. If they do not repent, he will cause great suffering and will not protect them spiritually from the great tribulation, part of which was already occurring in John's day (see Rev. 7:14), and would cause death among them. His judgment proves to all the churches of John's day, and to the church universal, that Jesus is Judge of all and repays according to works done. Only those who are hidden with Christ in God will be covered by the work of Christ.

Old Testament Background to Revelation 2:23. Jeremiah 17:10: "I the Lord search the heart and test the mind, to give every man according to his ways, according to the fruit of his deeds."

Revelation 2:24–25. The Lord now singles out the faithful in the church and encourages those who do not hold to Jezebel's teaching that he lays no other burden on them. Notice that Satan himself informs the false teaching. We would do well in our churches to recognize that there are people of darkness, promoting Satan's agenda, who walk among us, and we have to be wise and discerning to recognize false teaching by knowing true teaching. If we do not know the truth, we will not recognize the lies. But there was a faithful group who knew the truth and the Lord exhorts them to hold fast their love, faith, service, and patient endurance until he comes.

Revelation 2:26–28. Then the Lord gives the Thyatirans a promise. If they conquer and keep his works until the end of their journey on earth, they will have authority over the nations to rule them in judgment. This alludes to Psalm 2:8–9, which speaks of Christ himself being given the authority by his Father to break the nations with a rod of iron and dash them in pieces like a potter's vessel. Now this is applied to Christ's followers as well. We will reign with him. "I will give him the morning star" expands on this promise of believers reigning with Christ and sharing in his messianic rule.

Old Testament Background to Revelation 2:28. Numbers 24:17: "A star shall come out of Jacob, and a scepter shall rise out of Israel; it shall crush the forehead of Moab and break down all the sons of Sheth."

Revelation 2:29. Again, we have an exhortation to hear what the Spirit says to the churches (see the note on Rev. 2:7), but this time it follows the promise rather than precedes it, as in the previous three letters. This is an exhortation to heed Christ's call to repentance so that they will receive his promise. The same holds true for the church of Christ today.

CONCLUSION

The church at which I served went through some difficult times. The Lord disbanded the leaders who were asking the wrong questions. The mentality of running the church like a business, where the next marketing and advertising ploy is used to boost consumers' interests, doesn't work. That's because the church is not a business operation; it is an *organism*. It is the body of Christ, and it is to serve its Head at every turn. The question must always be, "Where is the Head turning us?" We should ask, "Where does our Head say we should go?" "What would please our Head?" When we leave our Head, we cease to exist as the church, for we are no longer his body. And he will remove our lampstand from its place.

LESSON 3

Revelation 3

PLEASE USE THE QUESTION paradigm from pages 353–54 as you work through the following. See the introductory comments there that explain each part of the process below in more detail.

- **Pray**.
- **Ponder the Passage**. Read Revelation 3 once a day from different translations for the entire week, looking for its:
  - Point
  - Persons
  - Patterns
  - Persons of the Trinity
  - Puzzling Parts
- **Put It in Perspective**.
  - Place in Scripture
  - Passages from Other Parts of Scripture

1. Based on your observations of the text, what is the basic content of this passage? Try to summarize it in your own words, using a sentence or two.
2. Finish filling out your chart today on the seven letters to the churches, beginning with the church in Sardis.

3. Note the verse in chapter 1 to which each of the titles of Christ refers in Revelation 3:1, 7, and 14.

4. To what passage in Matthew does Revelation 3:3 refer?

5. How do we know that the statment, "I will never blot his name out of the book of life," in Revelation 3:5 does not mean that we can lose our salvation? What other passages of Scripture help us understand this?

6. To what passage in Isaiah does Revelation 3:7 allude (use a concordance for "key"/"David")?

7. What three names are mentioned in Revelation 3:12? What do these names convey is the believer's?

8. What does it mean that Christ is the "beginning of God's creation" in Revelation 3:14?

9. What do you think "neither cold nor hot" means in Revelation 3:15?

10. Contrast Christ's view of the Laodicean church with the church's view in Revelation 3:17.

11. How does Christ's counsel in Revelation 3:18 apply to the "poor, blind, and naked" mentioned in Revelation 3:17?

12. What do you learn about discipline in Revelation 3:19? Look up Hebrews 12:3–11. What does this passage add to illuminate Revelation 3:19?

13. Who is being addressed in Revelation 3:20, believers or unbelievers?

• **Principles and Points of Application.**

1. Think for a moment about your reputation among family and friends. How do others perceive you? Does their external evaluation match up with the internal reality of who you really are? Confess any hypocrisy and ask God to help you be in public what you are in private and vice versa by the power of his Spirit.

2. What "work" or "spiritual gift" do you know that you have, but that you've let dwindle down to almost nothing by not using it or nurturing it? Ask God to forgive your negligence and begin

today to revitalize that work or spiritual gift for the glory of God through the power of his Spirit.

3. How are you preparing yourself for Christ's second coming through the enablement of God the Spirit? Is your name written in the book of life? When was the last time that you confessed the name of Christ before men?

4. In what area of your life right now do you feel like you're barely making it? Or in what area are you trying to hold on and do the right thing according to God's Word, but are finding Satan's tactics so strong that you feel like you're about to lose the battle? Meditate on Revelation 3:8–12. Ask God to strengthen you with his power so that you remain faithful to his Word and his name and will receive your crown.

5. What "name" are you focused on most, yours or God's? Are you spending time making a name for yourself or are you spending time glorifying God's name? Notice whose name you will assume in Revelation 3:12. How are you submitting and bringing glory to it now? If you're married, reflect on how you felt when you assumed your husband's name. How did this make you feel? What relationship did it signify? What roles and obligations did it represent? How is Revelation 3:12 a greater picture of this in the context of the church being the bride of Christ?

6. Too often the churches and individual believers in America today are lukewarm in their faith. They don't "spit on the name of Christ," but neither do they depend on and glorify him as they should. We spend our days working hard, building our own security and provision, and thinking we're getting along just fine. We think we're wealthy in America because of our materialism, but in reality we are in spiritual poverty. Reflect today on the reality of your spiritual life. In what areas are you sinful? Ask God to save you with his amazing grace. In what areas are you poor? Ask God to give you his riches in Christ (Eph. 1:3–14). In what areas are you blind? Ask God to help you see. In what areas are you naked? Ask God to clothe you with the righteousness of Christ.

7. In what area of your life do you feel God's discipline? Meditate on Revelation 3:19. How does this encourage you?

8. Who/what do you have placed on the throne of your heart? For whom/what do you live? Confess any idols in your heart to God and ask him to help you keep Christ on the throne.

NOTES FOR REVELATION 3

Aim: Ponder the aim of this lesson concerning our:

Mind: What do we need to know from this passage in Scripture?

That Christ's words through John to the churches in Sardis, Philadelphia, and Laodicea are also his Word to our churches today.

Heart: How does what we learn from this passage affect our internal relationship with the Lord?

It enables us to be kingdom disciples who hear what the Spirit says to our churches, strengthening the weaknesses, continuing the strengths, and repenting of the sin through the power of the Holy Spirit.

Hands: How does what we learn from this passage translate into action for God's kingdom?

It enables us to:

1. Confess any hypocrisy in our lives and ask God to help us be in public what we are in private and vice versa.

2. Ask God's forgiveness for any spiritual gifts that we've neglected and begin to revitalize that spiritual gift for God's glory by relying on the Spirit's power.

3. Accept Christ by faith and confess his name before others through the Spirit's help.

4. Ask God to strengthen us with his power so that we remain faithful to his Word and name and receive our crown.
5. Acknowledge that God's name alone should be our focus, not our own name, and that we should live our lives in light of glorifying his name, not ours.
6. Reflect on the reality of our spiritual life and ask God to change sinful, poor, blind, and/or naked areas by his Spirit's work in our lives.
7. Be encouraged by God's discipline in our lives and heed its message by relying on the Spirit's power.
8. Confess any idols in our hearts to God and ask him to help us keep Christ on the throne.

INTRODUCTION

Katie looked nervously around the large room. She'd never been around so many women before for a morning Bible study. There must have been more than a hundred in the room. Several groups of busily chatting women had formed. It seemed that everyone in the room had the latest style haircut, the newest and trendiest clothing, and nails perfectly done. Katie knew that most of these women lived in nice homes and never worried about money. The small group she was a part of seemed so empty to her. Most of the talk seemed to hover at the surface, and the women seemed to be blinded to their true dependence on Christ. After all, they were well supported, well fed, and had the house of their dreams.

Katie, on the other hand, had just returned to the States from a Muslim country in Asia. She felt like her five years there had been mostly a failure. She had poured her heart into language study the first two years and then tried to minister to the women of the area while she was playing the role of wife and mother to her own family. She had made some friends with the Muslim women, but she had seen little fruit. Her husband had put his life on the line many times as a witness for Christ in a dark country. He'd had things thrown at him, been spit on, and had taken verbal abuse for his Christian faith. After five years and little fruit, they were denied their visas to stay in the country and had to come home. Katie knew that the Lord was not angry with them, but she struggled with the seemingly fruitless years that they had had in a place that so desperately needed the light.

She had struggled even more since she'd been home with the churches in her city that seemed to have little interest in or enthusiasm for evangelism. Katie couldn't understand how Christians who lived in a free country and could share their faith at any time did not take the opportunity to do so. It seemed that these people cared little about those around them and the fact that their destructive lifestyles were leading them down a path of perdition. Individual Christians seemed to keep to their individual churches, not wanting to come across as "pushing" their faith upon anyone else.

Katie isn't alone in her struggle. The author of Revelation has much to say about the church that is so inwardly focused that it is not doing any outward good, about the materially wealthy but spiritually poor church, and about the small church that has remained faithful but seen little spiritual fruit in its midst.

We can divide this lesson into three sections:

   I. The Words of Christ to the Church in Sardis (Rev. 3:1–6)
  II. The Words of Christ to the Church in Philadelphia (Rev. 3:7–13)
 III. The Words of Christ to the Church in Laodicea (Rev. 3:14–22)

I. The Words of Christ to the Church in Sardis (Rev. 3:1–6)

Revelation 3:1. As in the previous chapter, the letter is addressed to the angel of the church (see notes on Rev. 2:1), but this time it is the church in Sardis that is in view, and Christ is identified as "him who has the seven spirits of God and the seven stars." This is another allusion to chapter 1, but this time it is Revelation 1:4b and 1:16 that are in view. Each description of Christ correlates with the exhortation and/or warning and/or promise to the different churches, thus, a different title of Christ is emphasized according to the church that is being addressed. Here, the focus is on the close association that Christ has with his Spirit and angels that are at work among his heavenly and earthly body, the church.

44

As with the Ephesian church and the following churches, Christ knows the works of the church in Sardis. He acknowledges its reputation of being alive among those on earth, but he informs the people of their reputation in heaven, where they are seen as dead.

Revelation 3:2–3. Christ now moves from his accusation to an exhortation and a warning. First, he tells the Sardinians to wake up. They are "sleeping" through their condition, oblivious to their true state. They are to wake up so that they can strengthen what remains before it dies. We know from the following clause that what is about to die are their incomplete works. Evidently they had started a lot of good works but had not completed them. God's Word says that "he who began a good work in you will bring it to completion at the day of Jesus Christ" (Phil. 1:6). The Lord's reputation was on the line here and they were sleeping through it. How often we do this in our own churches as well! The Lord lays a ministry on our hearts and we set out with great fervor and zeal to accomplish it. But as time goes on and momentum dies down, or struggles occur or resources slow down, we are discouraged and leave God's work undone. We must be faithful not only to begin God's work that he lays on our hearts, but to finish it as well by relying on the Holy Spirit's power.

Second, they are to remember what they received and heard. They are to have before them the initial call of God to the work at hand. If we do not do this then we lose the purpose of the ministry and it is easy for us to throw in the towel when the going gets tough. If we cannot see the big picture, we will get lost and discouraged in the details.

Third, they are to keep what they received and heard and repent. They are to repent of their sleeping and keep their initial word of commitment to the good works for God's kingdom. If they do not keep it, the Lord will come like a thief against them. This is an allusion to Matthew 24:42–44, which speaks of the final coming of Christ. We will see this language later in the book in Revelation 16:15, in the context of the sixth bowl. Here it is also appropriate to associate it with Christ coming in judgment to close the doors of the church at a point in time before the culmination of history. The Lord will not have inactive soldiers. He requires active duty at all times, and he has provided the power that we need by sending his Spirit to the church.

Since the description of Christ here is similar to that in Revelation 2:1, the same problem is probably in view here as in the Ephesian church. The Sardinian church is not a witnessing church. The people have the Holy Spirit's power with them and the heavenly angels' aid to assist them, but they are not awake with regard to evangelism in their world. It is easy today to get so inwardly focused in our churches that we do no outward good. We are to be a light for the world around us, but if others never see us, how will they ever know our witness? We are to be unashamedly different and accessible. We are not to withdraw into ourselves and make our own comfortable communities of faith; we are to explode into the world with the gospel of light and love.

Revelation 3:4. Unlike the letter to the Ephesian church, here Christ reserves his praise for the end of the letter. There are still some in Sardis who "have not soiled their garments" and are worthy to walk with Christ in white. This is an indication that many in the church had "stained their garments" by taking part in the idolatry of the pagan culture in order to not be persecuted by economic or social hardship.[1] As has been noted earlier in this study, if one did not take part in the idolatrous feasts of one's trade guild, one was ostracized. Thus many tried to have one foot in the world and one foot in the church. But this destroys the purpose of the church to be a witness to the watching world. If we are not willing to stand strong for our faith, it will never be attractive to others. People are attracted to that which we are willing to live and die for, not to that which we hold with such low regard that we have only half our hearts invested in it. Christ demands all of our worship and all of our witness and gives us the means to fulfill this by his Spirit.

Revelation 3:5. Now Christ gives a promise, as in the other six letters. For the one who overcomes the temptation to have one foot in the world (in order to save his earthly life) and one foot in the church (in order to save his soul), and who confesses Christ's name before men,

---

1. G. K. Beale, *The Book of Revelation: A Commentary on the Greek Text*, New International Greek Testament Commentary (Grand Rapids: Eerdmans, 1999), 276.

Christ will clothe him in his own white garments and confess his name before his Father and before his angels (Matt. 10:32). "And I will never blot his name out of the book of life" should not be taken to mean that one can lose salvation, but should be seen as a guarantee of salvation, which here is portrayed in a negative way. This meaning is secured by the fact that the other five times John speaks of the "book of life" in Revelation (Rev. 13:8; 17:8; 20:12; 20:15; 21:27) all connote the security of one's salvation by the work of Christ.[2]

Revelation 3:6. Again, we have an exhortation to hear what the Spirit says to the churches (see the note on Rev. 2:7), and like the letter to the church in Thyatira it follows the promise rather than precedes it, as in the first three letters.

II. The Words of Christ to the Church in Philadelphia (Rev. 3:7–13)

Revelation 3:7. Again, the letter is addressed to the angel of the church (see notes on Rev. 2:1), but this time it is the church in Philadelphia that is in view. Christ is identified as "the holy One, the true One, who has the key of David, who opens and no one will shut, who shuts and no one opens." This is another allusion to chapter 1, but this time it is Revelation 1:5 and 1:18 that are in view. Here, the focus is on Christ's faithful witness and his power over death and Hades. He alone is both the Judge and the Savior because he is the final and ideal Davidic king.

Old Testament Background to Revelation 3:7. Isaiah 22:22: "the one having the key of David, who opens and no one shuts, and who shuts and no one opens."

Revelation 3:8. Just as with the churches of Ephesus, Thyatira, and Sardis, Christ here knows the works of the church in Philadelphia. He walks among the people and is intimately acquainted with their situation and their ways. The open door that Christ has set before them is the door into the kingdom of God. He has made a covenant with them and has insured their salvation with his own work. No one can shut the door on his or her salvation; they are secure in Christ. Though they have

2. Ibid., 279.

had "little power" in regard to being effective witnesses for change in the world around them, they have been faithful witnesses and Christ is pleased with that. We are never responsible to save; we are only responsible to bear witness to the Savior. Christ alone does the saving while we do the witnessing. We must be faithful to do our part, and trust the Lord with his. This takes a tremendous amount of pressure off of us. We don't need to stand wringing our hands and choking our family members into a confession of faith; we must allow the Spirit of God to do his part as we do ours. We speak, he saves. The most important witness we have is not a tract, but the witness of our very lives. As we keep God's Word ourselves and confess his name consistently and faithfully, others are drawn to him through the work of the Holy Spirit.

Revelation 3:9. Ironically, the ethnic Jews who are deceived and blinded to the truth by Satan will be made to bow before the Gentiles and acknowledge that Christ did not come just for the Jews, but for the Gentiles as well. The true Israel is the church of God, which is made up of Jews and Gentiles who confess Christ as their Lord and Savior.

Old Testament Background to Revelation 3:9.

- Psalm 86:9: "All the nations you have made shall come and worship before you, O LORD, and shall glorify your name."
- Isaiah 45:14: "The wealth of Egypt and the merchandise of Cush, and the Sabeans, men of stature, shall come over to you and be yours; they shall follow you; they shall come over in chains and bow down to you. They will plead with you, saying: Surely God is in you, and there is no other, no god besides him."
- Isaiah 49:23: "Kings shall be your foster fathers, and their queens your nursing mothers. With their faces to the ground they shall bow down to you, and lick the dust of your feet. Then you will know that I am the LORD; those who wait for me will not be put to shame."
- Isaiah 60:14: "The sons of those who afflicted you shall come bending low to you, and all who despised you shall bow down at your feet; they shall call you the City of the LORD, the Zion of the Holy One of Israel."

This acknowledgment is different from the universal one Paul speaks of in Philippians 2:10–11 where every tongue will confess (speaking of unbelievers as well as believers) that Jesus Christ is Lord at the second coming; this one will involve ethnic Jews confessing the name of Christ because of the witness of the church in Philadelphia.[3] Thus, though the church only sees that it has "little power" in evangelism at the present time, the Lord has not only set before the people an open door to the kingdom of God, but sets that door also before many unconverted in their midst whom he himself will usher into the kingdom through their witness.

Revelation 3:10. Now Christ gives the Philadelphians a promise. Since they have patiently endured according to his Word, he will keep them from the "hour of trial that is coming on the whole world, to try those who dwell on earth." It is not clear whether this speaks of the final heightened period of tribulation against the church immediately prior to the second coming or to the final judgment of the world before the second coming or to an immediate trial about to come upon the Asia Minor of John's day.[4]

Revelation 3:11. Christ now tells the Philadelphians that he is coming soon to encourage them through the trials and persecution that they are facing. Then he exhorts them to "hold fast what you have, so that no one may seize your crown." It is not their perseverance that saves them and gains them the crown, but Christ's preservation of them, although the two ideas work hand in hand and display to a watching world that as Christ's saints persevere, Christ preserves them in the midst of trial and tribulation.

Revelation 3:12. Now Christ makes a promise, as in the other six letters. "The one who conquers, I will make him a pillar in the temple of my God." For those in a city that suffered from earthquakes, this promise of a firm pillar in a firm temple would have been especially reassuring and comforting. For the one who remains as a strong witness in the world will become a strong pillar in the heavenly temple, which

3. Ibid., 288.
4. Ibid., 290.

is synonymous with the presence of God. Thus, those who present a faithful witness to Christ on earth will be presented with God's own presence in heaven. "Never shall he go out of it" alludes back to the door that no one is able to shut in Revelation 3:8. The "name of my God," the "name of the city of my God," and "my own new name" all speak of God's presence with his people. Thus in Revelation 2:17 the name on the stone is God's very presence, which no one can know unless they receive it themselves. This promise has already been inaugurated during the church age, as we know God's presence through the indwelling of the Holy Spirit. We wait for its consummation at his second coming.

Old Testament Background to Revelation 3:12.

- Isaiah 56:5: "I will give in my house and within my walls a monument and a name better than sons and daughters; I will give them an everlasting name that shall not be cut off."
- Isaiah 62:2: "The nations shall see your righteousness, and all the kings your glory, and you shall be called by a new name that the mouth of the LORD will give."
- Isaiah 65:15: "You shall leave your name to my chosen for a curse, and the LORD God will put you to death, but his servants he will call by another name."
- Ezekiel 48:35: "And the name of the city from that time on shall be, 'The LORD is There.'"

Revelation 3:13. Again, we have an exhortation to hear what the Spirit says to the churches (see the note on Rev. 2:7), and like the previous two letters it follows the promise rather than precedes it, as in the first three letters.

III. The Words of Christ to the Church in Laodicea (Rev. 3:14–22)

Revelation 3:14. Again, the letter is addressed to the angel of the church (see notes on Rev. 2:1), but this time it is the church in Laodicea that is in view. Christ is identified as "the Amen, the faithful and true witness, the beginning of God's creation." This is another allusion to chapter 1, but this time it is Revelation 1:5a that is in view. Here, the focus is on Christ's faithful witness to his Father during his ministry on earth, as well as his continuing witness in heaven. "The beginning of God's creation" does not mean that Christ was created, for he is eternal and always has been God along with the Father and the Spirit. Rather, he is the one who began God's creation. The Father created the world through the Son by the power of the Holy Spirit.

Old Testament Background to Revelation 3:14. Isaiah 43:10–12: " 'You are my witnesses,' declares the Lord, 'and my servant whom I have chosen, that you may know and believe me and understand that I am he. Before me no god was formed, nor shall there be any after me. I, I am the Lord, and besides me there is no savior. I declared and saved and proclaimed, when there was no strange god among you; and you are my witnesses,' declares the Lord, 'and I am God.' "

Revelation 3:15–16. Just as with the churches of Ephesus, Thyatira, Sardis, and Philadelphia, Christ knows the works of the church in Laodicea. But he is not pleased. In fact, he gives no word of praise to this church. He goes straight to the accusation and warning. Because these people are lukewarm in their witness, meaning that such witness either doesn't exist or is being compromised with the world, the Lord will spit them out of his mouth. If the church does not want to stand strong as a witness for him, neither will he stand as a witness for it. He will spit them out of his mouth at the final judgment.

To understand the metaphor in these verses, we must understand Laodicea's water supply. Evidently Laodicea was only able to get warm water, which was not good. But, the hot waters of the surrounding region of Hierapolis were medically good for a person, and the cold waters of the surrounding nation of Colossae were refreshing and pure for a person. Thus, the unbelievers in Laodicea were neither receiving the hot water that would have doctored their souls nor the cold water that would have refreshed them. Instead, they were receiving lukewarm water at best, and that was doing them nothing but harm, since it left their souls in a lost state.[5] It is easy for us to grow warm and complacent to those around

5. Ibid., 303–4.

us. We so easily forget the state of the souls of our family and neighbors. While they might look refreshed and nourished on the outside, they are sick on the inside and in need of medicinal or refreshing water.

Revelation 3:17. The people of the Laodicean church were deceived. Their wealth had blinded them to the condition of their own spiritual lives. They had bought into the lie that security lay in worldly wealth. But Christ exposed the truth and told them how poor and pitiable they really were. He calls them five names: wretched, pitiable, poor, blind, and naked. Christ does not define wealth the same way the world does.

Revelation 3:18. He defines wealth by separation from sin. His counsel to buy from him gold refined by fire and white garments refers to purification of one's life. In the context of John's day, this would have included separating from the idolatry of the trade guilds. Though association with the trade guilds brought the people earthly wealth, it would bring them spiritual poverty. They are also commanded to buy salve to anoint their eyes so that they can discern truth from lies. This verse is not implying that we have to "buy" our purification from Christ; his grace is a free gift. Instead, it serves as a contrast for the Laodiceans who are buying resources from the world around them to solve their needs rather than going to Christ himself. Each of the three things Christ tells them to buy relates back to three of the five states of the church mentioned in the previous verse. To understand these references, it is helpful to know the situation of Laodicea in John's day. First, Laodicea had several banking institutions that were well known. Second, the city was well known for its textiles, including woolen tunics. Third, the city was renowned for its medical school that had produced a popular eye salve. Thus, Christ is exposing their reliance on these three things in their midst rather than their reliance on him.[6]

Revelation 3:19. Since Christ gave no word of praise to this church, he gives them the consolation of his love, which is reflected in his discipline and reproof, of which the goal is repentance. Our heavenly Father always disciplines out of a loving relationship with us and it is always for the purpose of bringing us to repentance and to a renewed fervor for

6. Ibid., 305–6.

him. Those of us who are mothers of young children would do well to heed this example of discipline in our own homes. Our children need to know our love before they know our discipline. And our discipline must always lead to the cross, the repentance demanded there, but also the grace received there.

Revelation 3:20. Now Christ gives an invitation to those who are already his children. He invites them to a renewed and restored relationship with him. Of course, for those in the church who were not truly believers, this also functioned as an invitation for them to place their trust in Christ for the first time. But the primary focus is on those who know Christ but are not in fellowship with him as they should be. Some see this as a possible allusion to the Lord's Supper, where believers repent and renew their relationship with Christ, remembering what he has done for them, what he will do for them, and sharing in his fellowship at the table.[7] Again, those of us that are mothers should remember that after we discipline our children, we need to extend the invitation to a renewed and restored relationship with us.

Revelation 3:21. Now we have a promise. For those who conquer the temptation to be rich in the world's eyes and instead become rich in heaven's eyes, it will be granted to sit on Christ's throne. Christ has already gone before us and set the example. He is now seated at the right hand of God the Father. And in part, we are seated with him, but our reign with Christ will not be fully consummated until Christ's second coming.

Revelation 3:22. Again, we have an exhortation to hear what the Spirit says to the churches (see the note on Rev. 2:7), and as in the previous three letters it follows the promise rather than precedes it the way it does in the first three letters. Thus, the first three letters place this exhortation/blessing before the promise, whereas the last four letters place it after the promise.

The study of the seven churches should both humble us and encourage us, for they are representative of all of our churches. First, out of all seven of them, only two do not receive an accusation and a warning.

7. Ibid., 309.

Table 3.1 Comparison of the Seven Churches

Church	Title of Christ	Praise	Accusation/Warning	Exhortation	Blessing/Promise
Ephesus	Holder of seven stars in right hand	Toil, patient endurance	Abandoned first love	Repent	To eat of tree of life
	Walks among seven lampstands	Can't bear with evil	Will remove lampstand	Do first works	
		Exposed false apostles			
		Hate works of Nicolaitans			
Smyrna	First and Last	Spiritually rich in light of persecution	[None]	Do not fear suffering	Crown of life
	Who died and came to life			Be faithful to death	Not hurt by second death
Pergamum	Has sharp two-edged sword	Hold fast Christ's name	Embraced Balaam's teaching	Repent	Receive hidden manna
		Did not deny faith in light of persecution	Allow Nicolaitans' teaching		White stone with new name written on it
			Will war against you with a sword		
Thyatira	Son of God	Love, service, patient endurance	Allow Jezebel's teaching	Hold fast good works	Authority over nations

	Eyes like flame of fire	Latter works exceed first	Judgment		Morning star
	Feet like burnished bronze				
Sardis	Has seven spirits of God	A few who walk with Christ in white	Incomplete works	Remember what you received and heard	Clothed in white
	Has seven stars		Will come like a thief	Keep what you received and heard	Name in book of life
				Repent	Name confessed before Father
Philadelphia	Holy One	Kept Christ's Word	[None]	Hold fast	Pillar in temple
	True One	Have not denied Christ's name			Will have written on him name of God/city
	Has key of David	Patient endurance			
Laodicea	Amen	[None]	Lukewarm	Buy gold from Christ	Communion with Christ
	Faithful		Wretched, pitiable, poor, blind, naked	Buy white garments	
	True witness beginning with God's creation		Will spit you out	Be zealous and repent	

55

Thus, we should remember that churches are not perfect, and that we should always be examining our corporate life and repenting in areas that are in need of change. Second, all of the letters are addressed to an angel, which means that all true churches have the heavenly aid of the Holy Spirit and the angels. We are indeed connected to the heavenly realm even now. Third, Christ walks among us through the Holy Spirit and he demonstrates his power, sovereignty, judgment, holiness, and witness. We are to worship him and exalt him in our churches. Fourth, only one church is left without a word of praise. Thus, we should be reminded that while we need to examine ourselves, we should also encourage one another and praise one another as we see good works being done. Fifth, every church is given an exhortation. While we are here on earth there is always work to be done to stand as a witness in the world and to worship our King, the latter of which will continue into eternity. Sixth, all churches are given a blessing and/or a promise. This is our hope as we work together as the body of Christ here on earth as witnesses and worshipers. If we are faithful, we will receive the heavenly prize.

CONCLUSION

Thankfully, Katie didn't give up on the American church. Instead, she brought her background and spiritual gifts to the women of her church and helped them see and understand the need they had to be dependent upon Christ instead of their own resources. She also was able to get a group of women together to minister to the Muslims in an apartment complex in the downtown area of their city. And though they struggled for many years to see the fruit, they knew that they were being faithful to take the message of the gospel, and that the Lord, not them, was responsible for the conversion of the souls.

LESSON 4

Revelation 4–5

PLEASE USE THE QUESTION paradigm from pages 353–54 as you work through the following. See the introductory comments there that explain each part of the process below in more detail.

- **Pray.**
- **Ponder the Passage.** Read Revelation 4–5 once a day from different translations for the entire week, looking for its:
  - Point
  - Persons
  - Patterns
  - Persons of the Trinity
  - Puzzling Parts
- **Put It in Perspective.**
  - Place in Scripture
  - Passages from Other Parts of Scripture

1. Try and skim Daniel 7 and Ezekiel 1–2 this week after you read Revelation 4–5. What similarities do you see between the passages?
2. Based on your observations of Revelation 4–5, what is the basic content of this passage? Try to summarize it in your own words, using a sentence or two.

3. Where is the vision taking place in Revelation 4:1? How does this relate to believers on earth?

4. Look up the word "trumpet" in a Bible concordance or dictionary. What are they used for throughout Scripture? How does that relate to Revelation 4:1 and its surrounding context?

5. How does the "throne" in Revelation 4:2 relate to the letter to the church in Laodicea (Rev. 3:21)?

6. Where is the first time that we see a "rainbow" in Scripture? What does it signify? Is there any connection with John's use here in Revelation 4:3? What do the jewels convey?

7. Who do you think the twenty-four elders represent in Revelation 4:4? Why?

8. Look up Exodus 19:16. How does this relate to what is going on in Revelation 4:5? What is the context in Exodus? What is the context in Revelation?

9. How does Revelation 4:5 define the "seven torches of fire" and how have we already defined the "seven spirits of God" earlier in the book?

10. Look up the word "sea" in a concordance or Bible dictionary. How is it used in Scripture? What do you think it means in Revelation 4:6?

11. What do you think the living creatures represent in Revelation 4:7?

12. Do the living creatures only reflect creation or do they reflect the Creator as well (note the description of the "eyes all around and within")?

13. What attributes do the living creatures ascribe to God in Revelation 4:8?

14. Who else joins in the worship of God in Revelation 4:10? What attributes do they ascribe to God? What does their casting their crowns before the throne signify?

15. What do you learn about the scroll and the seven seals in Revelation 5:1–5? Why would John weep that no one was found to open it? What do you think it contains? Who alone is found to open it?

16. Is the position of the Lamb significant in Revelation 5:6? Why? To what do you think "as though it had been slain" refers? With what you know now about "seven" in the book, what do you think the "seven horns" and "seven eyes" represent?

17. What happens when Christ takes the scroll from the Father (Rev. 5:8)? What does the mention of "prayers of the saints" convey? Are the saints involved in the unfolding of God's plan of judgment and salvation?

18. Look up "new song" in a Bible concordance. What do you learn? How is it used here in Revelation 5:9?

19. Why does the song tell us that Christ is worthy to open the scroll's seals (Rev. 5:9)?

20. How did Christ "ransom people for God" (Rev. 5:9)?

21. Why is the "from" important in "from every tribe and language and people and nation" (Rev. 5:9) to argue against universal salvation?

22. In Revelation 5:10, what does the tense of "you have made them a kingdom and priests to our God" and "they shall reign on the earth" convey? When do you think this was inaugurated (see Rev. 5:9)?

23. Who else joined in the worship with the living creatures and the elders (Rev. 5:11)? What attributes were they ascribing to Christ?

24. To what time does Revelation 5:13 point if "every" creature is acknowledging Christ (see Phil. 2:9–11)?

- **Principles and Points of Application.**

1. The Holy Spirit is probably the least known and least understood person of the Godhead. This is most likely because he exists to give glory to the Father and the Son, but there is much more to his role than that. Do a word study on the Holy Spirit/Spirit using a Bible dictionary or concordance. What information do you find? If you are a believer, you have the Holy Spirit, the

Spirit that was in Christ when he walked this earth. How does this encourage you?

2. Meditate on Revelation 4:8, 11, using these words to give glory, honor, and thanks today to God the Father.

3. Spend time "weeping" over your sin and thinking about our unworthiness to be able to open the scroll. What if there were no Savior? Think about where we would be. Who in your life do you need to point toward the Savior by relying on the Spirit's power to open up their heart?

4. Reflect on the words in 5:5, 9–10, 13. Use these words to give thanks, worship, glory, and honor to God the Son today.

NOTES FOR REVELATION 4-5

Aim: Ponder the aim of this lesson concerning our:

Mind: What do we need to know from this passage in Scripture?

God the Father and God the Son are to be worshiped; the Father for his sovereignty and holiness, the Son for his kingship and priesthood.

Heart: How does what we learn from this passage affect our internal relationship with the Lord?

It teaches us to be kingdom disciples who join the throngs of heaven in worship of the sovereignty and holiness of God the Father and of the kingship and priesthood of God the Son.

Hands: How does what we learn from this passage translate into action for God's Kingdom?

It enables us to:

1. Learn more about the Holy Spirit's character in order to be encouraged in our ministry for God's kingdom.

2. Assist others in giving glory, honor, and thanks to God the Father by using the paradigm of Revelation 4:8, 11.

3. Point others to our unworthiness and inability to walk through the gates of heaven, and to the worthiness and ability of Christ to open that way for us.

4. Incorporate the worship of Revelation 5:5, 9–10, 13, into our private and corporate worship.

INTRODUCTION

If you were to ask me what or whom I worship, I would tell you that I worship the Lord and Savior Jesus Christ. But a closer look inside my heart would reveal that I worship more than Christ alone. I also worship myself and other things, desires, and dreams. It started when I was a newborn. The nurses hung a sign near me that said, "Feed on Demand." The screams of a 10.5-pound baby when she wants to eat can be very loud. Throughout my childhood there were many signs that I wanted what I wanted when I wanted it, which translated into self-worship. But I began to worship other things too. I began to worship perfectionism. I began to worship the scale on which I weighed myself. I began to worship exercise. I began to worship excellence. As I got older I began to worship the thought of a career, marriage, motherhood, and ministry. It's not that I did not then or do not now worship Christ; it's that I worship Christ plus other wants and desires. I have made Christ share a throne. And he doesn't like that, nor does he deserve that. God has made it clear in his Word that his love is a jealous love, and when we share his glory with another, we are disciplined for it. Yet he has been so gracious in my life to expose and root these objects of worship out of my heart one by one, sometimes two by two, and, more recently, three by three.

Severely restricted in what I can and cannot eat because of medical issues, my diet has often been placed on the throne of my heart. Homeschooling my children when in fact I would really like a "break" from them, I have often placed their education on the throne of my heart.

Moving into a new home in a new city that would later prove to be a long commute to our church family, I placed the location of my home on the throne of my heart. Removing these things from the throne has proven to be agonizing as I wait for God's love and light to break through to me in each circumstance. But waiting is not wringing our hands in anguish, inviting misery on those around us and on ourselves. It is worshiping God while we wait, accepting his plan and timing, inviting him to be Lord over our circumstances and trusting that his way is best. Trust is not total understanding; it is totally resolving to put ourselves under a sovereign and trustworthy God.

Revelation 4–5 has much to say about God alone being deserving of our worship. The persons of the triune God share a throne with one another, but not with any other. The Holy Spirit points us to worship the Son and the Son points us to the Father. Thus, the triune God is worthy of our praise.

We can divide this lesson into two sections:

I. God the Father Is Worshiped for His Sovereignty and Holiness (Rev. 4:1–11)
II. God the Son Is Worshiped for His Kingship and Priesthood (Rev. 5:1–14)

Chapters 4–5 are closely linked with both the chapters that precede them and the chapters that follow them. They are not a "break" in the book. These chapters do not begin the "future only" section of the book. They are integrally related to the book as a whole. In fact, chapter 4 develops from Revelation 3:21, in which Christ is pictured as seated on his Father's throne with his Father. It is important that we remember when Christ assumed this position; Christ was exalted to the right hand of God the Father upon his death, resurrection, and ascension. This was a past historical event that continues to be effective for the present and the future. Thus, these chapters give us a glimpse into heaven during the present church age and as such serve as a model of worship for us here on earth.

I. God the Father Is Worshiped for His Sovereignty and Holiness (Rev. 4:1–11)

Revelation 4:1. John now sees another vision. We need to remember that the events in the book's visions do not necessarily take place in chronological order. We are dealing with a symphony, so to speak, not a textbook. The open door in heaven is inviting John to see what is going on in heaven during the time of the church on earth. Just as Moses was called to go up to the mountain and take God's law back to the people, so too John is called to "come up here" so that he can take the purposes of God's plan back to the people in order to encourage them to stand strong as witnesses and worshipers. The voice "like a trumpet" conveys the judgment and salvation themes that run throughout the book. These two themes are signified in other places in Scripture that also involve the trumpet.

The first time that we see the trumpet mentioned in Scripture is with Israel at Mount Sinai. Here it is accompanied by "thunders and lightnings and a thick cloud on the mountain" (Ex. 19:16). Thus, the trumpet is used in a context of God speaking his law with his people, and the people respond in fear because of the holiness of God. We see the trumpet again in Leviticus in the context of the Feast of Trumpets. Here the trumpet blasts call the people to prepare for the most sacred and restful month of the year (Lev. 23:24). The trumpet was also to be sounded on the Day of Atonement (Lev. 25:9). Numbers illuminates the meaning behind the trumpets even more. The trumpets were to be used for summoning the congregation and for breaking camp. The trumpets were to serve as a perpetual statute throughout Israel's generations. They would be used to remind the Lord of the people's need for salvation from their enemies as well as to remind them that the Lord is their God (Num. 10:1–10). Of course, the trumpets were also significant in the defeat of Jericho (Josh. 6:16, 20), and many of the prophets speak of the trumpet in a context of both warning and salvation. The last trumpet is reserved for the second coming of Christ (1 Cor. 15:52) when Christ will come to judge unbelievers and save believers.

Old Testament Background to Revelation 4:1.

- Ezekiel 1:1: "The heavens were opened and I saw visions of God."
- Daniel 2:28: "But there is a God in heaven who reveals mysteries."
- Daniel 7:1a: "Daniel saw a dream and visions . . . then he wrote down the dream and told the sum of the matter."
- Daniel 7:6a: "After this I looked, and behold, another . . ."

Revelation 4:2. John's visions occurred while he was "in the Spirit," which connected him with the Old Testament prophets (especially Daniel and Ezekiel as seen in the many allusions to their prophecies in chapters 4–5) and solidified his office. He saw a throne standing in heaven with one seated on it. The mention of the "throne" here continues a significant theme in the book that we first saw in Revelation 1:4. But it is not just the throne that is important, but also the one seated on the throne, for this vision will display who is the true King behind all kings.

Old Testament Background to Revelation 4:2.

- Ezekiel 1:26: "And above the expanse over their heads there was the likeness of a throne . . . seated above the likeness of a throne was a likeness with a human appearance."
- Daniel 7:9: "As I looked, thrones were placed, and the Ancient of Days took his seat."

Revelation 4:3. The jewels connote God's glory, majesty, and sovereignty, as they will again later in chapter 21. The brightness of the jewels further enhances the light of God. And the rainbow reminds us of God's covenant with Noah, in which the Lord promised never to "strike down every living creature" while the earth remains (Gen. 8:21–22). It is also an allusion to Ezekiel 1:28, which again is a reference to God's covenant with Noah. These instances remind us that God's mercy in allowing his common grace to be a part of every man's life, which was illustrated in the Noahic covenant, has tempered his judgment upon man for thousands of years; they also convey to us that this same mercy will be part of all the visions of judgment that remain in the book of Revelation. Indeed, in the midst of God's judgment, his mercy is always seen. This vision with the rainbow, which was the first sign of a new creation after the flood, and the precious stones, which were part of Eden and will be part of the new heaven and earth, informs us that the "new creation" was inaugurated at Christ's death, resurrection, and ascension and will be consummated at the final coming of Christ.

Old Testament Background to Revelation 4:3.

- Ezekiel 1:26, 28: "And above the expanse over their heads there was the likeness of a throne, in appearance like sapphire; . . . Like the appearance of the bow that is in the cloud on the day of rain, so was the appearance of the brightness all around."
- Ezekiel 10:1: "Then I looked, and behold, on the expanse that was over the heads of the cherubim there appeared above them something like a sapphire, in appearance like a throne."
- Ezekiel 28:13: "Every precious stone was your covering, sardius, topaz, and diamond."

Revelation 4:4. The number of the thrones and elders should not be taken literally, but figuratively and as representative of the entirety of God's people. The twenty-four elders represent the twelve tribes of Israel and the twelve apostles, which serve to represent the entirety of God's people. The elders here are most likely Old and New Testament saints who have already died and received their white garments and crowns and who serve to encourage those of us who are still persevering through this journey on earth. Yet the vision also presents the reward of all believers, even those yet to die, represented by the elders, so that we are encouraged not only by others' crowns, but also by our own crowns that wait to be put on by us when we reach heaven.[1]

Revelation 4:5–6a. We have already seen that Exodus 19:16 stands behind this passage, but even more appropriately here is Ezekiel 1:13, Ezekiel's first vision of the glory of the Lord. The seven torches of fire are defined for us as the seven spirits of God (an allusion to Zech. 4:2–3, 10), which we have already seen in Revelation 1:4 and are defined as

---

1. G. K. Beale, *The Book of Revelation: A Commentary on the Greek Text*, New International Greek Testament Commentary (Grand Rapids: Eerdmans, 1999), 322.

the Holy Spirit. The sea of glass is also an allusion to Ezekiel's first vision of the glory of God in Ezekiel 1:22. From that passage, we can conclude that the sea here forms the floor for God's throne, and if the sea is representative of evil, which is often the case in the Old Testament, then God's throne would be seen as keeping a lid on the evil, as being sovereign over the evil. Thus, later in the book when John says that there is no sea in heaven (Rev. 21:1), most likely what he means is that there is no evil in heaven.[2]

Revelation 4:6b–8. As the elders are representative of the entirety of God's people, so the four living creatures are most likely representative of all God's animal life through the history of creation. The fact that the four heads of the four species listed are given conveys this idea of representation for all animal life. For indeed, if even the rocks cry out in worship, how much more the animals, and how much more God's people. Not only do the four living creatures represent the creation, though; they also represent the Creator, as seen in their "eyes all around" which conveys God's ability to see all things at the same time (omniscience). But as creatures, they have a continuous role; they are to cry out in witness and worship to God's holiness and sovereignty. Thus, they serve not only as a picture of what consummate life in the new heaven and new earth will be like one day, they also, along with the elders, serve as an example of how all creatures, including mankind, are to worship God now.

Old Testament Background to Revelation 4:6b–8.
- Isaiah 6:1–4: "Above him stood the seraphim. Each had six wings."
- Ezekiel 1:5–21: "And from the midst of it came the likeness of four living creatures."
- Ezekiel 10:12–15, 20–22: "And every one had four faces."
- Hosea, Amos, Nahum, Zechariah, Malachi: "The LORD God Almighty."

Revelation 4:9–11. It is not just the animal life, but also all of God's people that are to fall down and worship the holy and sovereign God.

2. Ibid., 327–28.

His creation is to worship the Creator. He alone is sovereign over creation and worthy of the glory, honor, and praise for such a mighty work that is sustained by him alone. This picture of heavenly worship is not meant to refer only to the future in our minds. We know that even now believers are citizens of heaven and, by the Holy Spirit and the aid of angels, are connected to the heavenly realm of worship (Heb. 12:22–24).

May we remember this in our church services! I wonder how many bored and sleepy church members we would have if we held before them the picture of worship in the heavenly throne room, of which even now we are a part. And if our most incredible worship experiences here on earth are only a glimpse of what they one day will be, how much hope and joy is instilled in us as we wait for that day. Furthermore, our worship of Christ here on earth is one of the most dynamic tools of witness that we have. For as our neighbors note that we leave our comfortable homes every Sunday morning for worship, they will wonder at this God whom we serve. As they observe our praise before meals, as they observe our praise after and during sporting events, as they observe our lives that are lived to bring honor and glory to God, their heads will turn and perhaps their hearts will be softened by the Spirit so that they too might join in worship and witness.

Old Testament Background to 4:9–11.

- Isaiah 6:1: "The LORD sitting upon a throne, high and lifted up."
- Daniel 4:34 and 12:7: "Him who lives forever." This is a contrast with the earthly kings who are only temporal, and thus serves as great encouragement to those in John's day who suffered under human emperors who made themselves out to be gods; such "gods" will not last.
- Daniel 4:37: "Now I . . . praise and extol and honor the King of heaven, for all his works are right and his ways are just."
- Daniel 4:35: "And he does according to his will among the host of heaven and among the inhabitants of the earth."

The people of God can be sure that God does all things according to his will; nothing can thwart his perfect plan.

II. God the Son Is Worshiped For His Kingship and Priesthood (Rev. 5:1–14)

Chapter 5 is inextricably linked to chapter 4, but the background of Ezekiel 1–2 passes with 5:1b, while the background of Daniel 7 remains. The focus also shifts from God the Father to God the Son. The fact that God is sovereign over all things and will carry out his plan was emphasized in chapter 4; now the way that he does that, through the death, resurrection, and ascension of his Son, is emphasized in chapter 5.

Revelation 5:1. The fact that the scroll is held in God the Father's right hand signifies that it is his sovereign plan for the history of his creation. That there is writing on both the front and the back of the scroll signifies the comprehensiveness and completeness of his plan. And, the fact that the scroll is completely sealed (figuratively displayed by "seven" seals) conveys the mystery of it, that God's plan will not be unfolded until his perfect time. But it also conveys the need for someone who is worthy to open it.

Old Testament Background to Revelation 5:1.

- Ezekiel 2:9b–10: "And when I looked, behold, a hand was stretched out to me, and behold, a scroll of a book was in it."
- Daniel 12 and Isaiah 29:11: "And the vision of all this has become to you like the words of a book that is sealed."

Revelation 5:2–4. Even the "strong" angel was evidently not able to open the scroll and break its seals. No matter our strength or the strength of the heavenly beings, it pales in comparison to what is needed to unfold the sovereign decree of God and open the way for judgment and salvation before us. Without someone greater than the angelic beings and ourselves we are hopeless to satisfy God's demand for holiness, righteousness, and justice before him.

What did the scroll contain? Most likely it contains God's plan that was inaugurated with Christ's redemptive work on the cross, which brought both judgment for unbelievers and salvation for believers. The idea of authority as well as inheritance stands behind the scroll as well.[3]

3. Ibid., 340.

Old Testament Background to Revelation 5:2–4.
- Isaiah 29:11 and Daniel 7: "Books."
- Daniel 7:10: "The books were opened."
- Daniel 12:4: "Seal up the book until the time of the end."

For Daniel the "time of the end" looked toward Christ's redemptive work on the cross that inaugurated the time of the end. So, for John, the time of the end had already been inaugurated.

Revelation 5:5. Praise God that there is one who is greater and who is able to open the scroll. He is not just God and he is not just man. He is the God-man who has perfectly satisfied God's justice and has been perfectly obedient unto death on the cross so that he has been exalted to the right hand of God and stands as both Judge and Savior. He is both the Lion and the Lamb. He is both the Root of David and the culmination of the Davidic line. He allowed himself to be conquered so that he could conquer the powers of evil in this world. He alone has opened up the way for judgment and salvation. It is Christ whom we are to place as King on the throne of our hearts. Because of his work, we need not work anymore. Because of his grace, we have the gift of eternal life. Because of his mercy, we are no longer trapped in the misery of our sin. Because of his sacrifice, we are no longer shamed. Because of his judgment on the cross, we are no longer judged. And so our whole lives are to point to him in witness and in worship.

Old Testament Background to Revelation 5:5.
- Genesis 49:9: "Judah is a lion's cub."
- Isaiah 11:1: "There shall come forth a shoot from the stump of Jesse, and a branch from his roots shall bear fruit."
- Daniel 7:10: "And the books were opened."
- Daniel 12:4–9: Books sealed until the end of time.

Revelation 5:6. Between God the Father on the throne and all of God's creatures, and among the church, stands our Mediator. For without him being "between" God and us we would not be able to approach God. And he stands among his Body, the church, as the Elder

Brother, as Lord and Savior, as the Mediator, to usher us into God's presence. "As though it had been slain," points to Christ's work on the cross, where Satan "bruised his heel" (Gen. 3:15). The emphasis on the "Lamb" conveys to God's people in the midst of persecution that though it does not appear that they are conquerors on earth, they are conquerors in heaven. Just as Christ was victorious and won the battle through death, so too would his followers. The seven horns connote the perfection of his power and the seven eyes his complete omniscience, but John also defines them as the Spirit of God who carries out God's purpose and plan on earth.

Old Testament Background to Revelation 5:6.
- Isaiah 53:7: "He was led as a sheep to the slaughter." This refers to the Old Testament Passover lamb.
- Zechariah 3:9: "Seven eyes."
- Zechariah 4:2, 10: "Seven lamps" and "seven eyes."

Revelation 5:7. Just as Christ knew that he must take the form of a servant and come to earth as a baby, just as he knew he must take the "cup" and drink God's wrath in order to save God's people, so too he knows that he is to take the scroll from God the Father.

Old Testament Background to Revelation 5:7. Daniel 7:13: "There came one like a son of man, and he came to the Ancient of Days and was presented before him."

Revelation 5:8. Christ is worshiped for taking the scroll, not only because it conveys the unfolding of judgment and salvation that was inaugurated by his death, resurrection, and ascension, but also because it conveys that he, as the one who accomplished the work on the cross given him by the Father to do, is both Lord of lords and King of kings. The harp, like the trumpet, is associated with both judgment and salvation in the Old Testament, as well as with praise of the Lord for his faithfulness. Here it is seen alongside the prayers of the saints, which evidently play a prominent role in bringing God's plans and purposes to pass. These prayers will be seen in chapters 6 and 8 to be specific to God's judgment upon the ungodly. How much more we would pray if we would understand that our prayers are linked to the plans and purposes of God!

Revelation 5:9–10. Just as the saints were promised a "new name" (Rev. 2:17), so too the saints sing a "new song." It is associated in the Old Testament with praise for his creation, righteousness, salvation, and justice (Pss. 33:3–6; 96:1; 98:1; 149:1), with victory over destruction (Ps. 40:3), and with victory in war (Ps. 144:9). So here, it is associated with the song of Christ's redemption, which began at the new creation, inaugurated with his death, resurrection, and ascension, but that will not be consummated until his second coming.

Christ is worthy to take the scroll because of his obedience to death on the cross, which was a ransom for the people of God, made up of both Jews and Gentiles, who have become even now a kingdom and priests to God on earth, but will be fully consummated as a kingdom and priests to God at the second coming of Christ. It is important that we remember our present state as a kingdom and priests to our God. We are no longer part of the kingdom of this world; our allegiance is not to the kings on earth, but to the King in heaven. And we are priests here to serve as witnesses to a watching world of our God in heaven. This will affect everything that we do and the way in which we do it. All of our lives, every aspect, down to the changing of diapers, the washing of clothes and dishes, the caring for our elderly parents, will be done from an eternal kingdom perspective.

Old Testament Background to Revelation 5:9–10.
- Exodus 19:6: "Kingdom of priests."
- Isaiah 53:7: "He was led as a sheep to the slaughter."
- Daniel 7:10:"And the books were opened."
- Daniel 7:22b–27a: "The saints possessed the kingdom."
- Daniel 12:9: "Words are sealed until the time of the end." Old Testament Passover lamb.

Revelation 5:11–12. Now the angels join in the worship. The numbers are figurative for many angels that worship Christ for his work of redemption, but they are also another allusion to Daniel 7:10. The angels ascribe to him seven attributes, again conveying his complete worthiness of worship. He receives worship for his power, wealth, wisdom, might, honor, glory, and blessing.

Old Testament Background to 5:12.
- 1 Chronicles 29:11–12: "Power, wealth, might, glory."
- Daniel 2:20: "Wisdom."
- Daniel 7:10: "Myriads of myriads and thousands of thousands."

Revelation 5:13–14. Now the creatures and the elders fall down in worship. The creatures ascribe to the Lamb four attributes, again conveying his complete worthiness of worship. He is worthy of blessing, honor, glory, and might forever. But it is not only Christ who is worshiped. Both the Father and the Son are worshiped together, emphasizing Christ's deity, since his humanity in regard to the work of redemption has been heavily emphasized already. And it is not only the heavenly creatures and believers that worship, but all creatures everywhere, which points to the consummation where "every knee [will] bow, in heaven and on earth and under the earth, and every tongue confess that Jesus Christ is Lord, to the glory of God the Father" (Phil. 2:10–11).

Old Testament Background to Revelation 5:13–14. Daniel 7:13–27 presents the same order of events as Revelation 5:9–14.

CONCLUSION

I still struggle with keeping Christ alone on the throne of my heart. Every day I am tempted to put some other desire or dream on the throne with him. He is so gracious to reveal this to me and to give me the grace that I need to enthrone him alone once again on my heart's throne. He alone is worthy of glory, honor, power, wealth, wisdom, might, and blessing forever. May we stand strong as witnesses for him as we worship him.

LESSON 5

Revelation 6

PLEASE USE THE QUESTION paradigm from pages 353–54 as you work through the following. See the introductory comments there that explain each part of the process below in more detail.

- **Pray**.
- **Ponder the Passage**. Read Revelation 6 once a day from different translations for the entire week, looking for its:
  - Point
  - Persons
  - Patterns
  - Persons of the Trinity
  - Puzzling Parts
- **Put It in Perspective**.
  - Place in Scripture
  - Passages from Other Parts of Scripture

1. Based on your observations of the text, what is the basic content of Revelation 6? Try to summarize it in your own words, using a sentence or two.
2. Compare Revelation 4:5 with 6:1. Whose voice stands behind the voice of the living creature that says, "Come!"?

3. Compare Revelation 9:7; 11:7; and 13:7 with 6:2. Who do you think the first rider represents?

4. Who gave the first rider his crown? Why is this significant? What does it reveal about God's sovereignty?

5. Compare Revelation 6:3 with 6:9. What group of people do you think the second horseman primarily targets?

6. Compare Leviticus 26:26 and Ezekiel 4:10, 16 with Revelation 6:5. In light of these Old Testament passages, what do you think the "pair of scales" conveys? In the same light, what does "black" symbolize?

7. How does the fourth seal reflect the first three seals? Were all the inhabitants of the earth killed or only some? Does this convey the time of final judgment then or a time previous to final judgment?

8. Where are the saints (Rev. 6:9)? Do you see any significance?

9. What do they cry out (Rev. 6:10)? How does God answer them? What do you think the white robe symbolizes?

10. Are the cosmic events in Revelation 6:12–14 partial or complete? What does this convey about the time frame of the sixth seal? Is it the final judgment that is in view?

11. List the different groups mentioned in Revelation 6:15. Who do they represent? What are they doing and why? Compare this with Genesis 3:10. What does this tell us about sin?

12. Compare Exodus 10:28 with Revelation 6:16. Why has sinful man never been able to stand before the face of God?

13. Who can stand on the day of judgment? Why?

- **Principles and Points of Application.**
1. How are you preparing your heart today through the power of the Holy Spirit for the second coming of Christ?

2. In what are you hiding yourself and taking refuge? Revelation 6:15 says that many were hiding themselves in caves and rocks because they have never hidden themselves in the Lord God. Have you hidden yourself in the Lord Jesus Christ? If not, speak with someone about that this week.

3. Are you standing before the throne of God on a daily basis, in Christ, who has made a way for you to boldly approach the throne of grace with confidence (Heb. 4:16)?

4. Read Revelation 6:9–11. Take time today to pray for the persecuted church, as well as all believers who must daily choose to be witnesses and worshipers of Jesus Christ. Pray for those in Colombia, Turkey, Cuba, Belarus, China, India, Bangladesh, North Korea, and any others that you may have on your heart.

NOTES FOR REVELATION 6

Aim: Ponder the aim of this lesson concerning our:

Mind: What do we need to know from this passage in Scripture?

The Lamb of God will open the first six seals, which begins judgment and salvation on earth.

Heart: How does what we learn from this passage affect our internal relationship with the Lord?

It encourages us to be kingdom disciples who stand strong as witnesses and worshipers by relying on the strength of the Holy Spirit during persecution and tribulation.

Hands: How does what we learn from this passage translate into action for God's kingdom?

It enables us to:

1. Witness to others by our worship through the power of the Holy Spirit during persecution and tribulation.
2. Approach the throne of grace with confidence, interceding for the persecuted church.
3. Lead others to hide themselves in the Lord Jesus Christ while acknowledging that the Holy Spirit must open up their hearts to the gospel.

INTRODUCTION

In the fall of 2010 musicians who promoted awareness for the persecuted church through Voice of the Martyrs came to our church. I was very convicted that morning that I was not as aware of or involved with praying for the persecuted church as I should have been. I knew that there were many countries that persecuted Christians, and I knew friends serving as missionaries in some of them, whom I prayed for regularly, but I did not know to what extent persecution existed and how many countries restricted the gospel by persecution. That Sunday morning changed all that for me. The Holy Spirit used those musicians to touch a chord deep in my heart that moved me to action. Through the website for Voice of the Martyrs I have been able to pray effectively for my brothers and sisters in Christ who are being persecuted around the world, and I am able to pray for the nations that restrict the gospel.

This has been a very emotional experience for me. The stories of persecuted believers is heavy on my heart and I am burdened for my brothers and sisters around the world daily. My heart hurts for them and for those around them who are enduring so much pain. And yet, God's Word defines suffering as a gift, a purpose, a decree, and a joy. In fact, Scripture does not inform me to pray that the persecution will stop, but rather informs me that the persecution has been sent by God to advance his kingdom purposes. Just as Christ's death was followed by the resurrection, so too the saints' deaths are followed by resurrection to eternal life. As they stand strong as witnesses and worshipers in Colombia, Belarus, Northwest Africa, Turkey, China, India, Bangladesh, North Korea, and many other countries, the kingdom of God advances in the world. And as we join them in standing strong in our spheres of influence as witnesses and worshipers, we too participate in the advancement of the kingdom of God through the work of the Holy Spirit.

Revelation 6 has much to say about God using the evil that others do to accomplish the advancement of his kingdom, about persecution of the saints, and about the final judgment and vindication of such persecution. This chapter holds before us the hope that suffering is purposeful, and provides us the opportunity to take part in God's kingdom work.

We can divide this lesson into three sections:

I. The Lamb of God Opens the First through Fourth Seals (Rev. 6:1–8)
II. The Lamb of God Opens the Fifth Seal (Rev. 6:9–11)
III. The Lamb of God Opens the Sixth Seal (Rev. 6:12–17)

I. The Lamb of God Opens the First through Fourth Seals (Rev. 6:1–8)

Though there is a logical progression in the first four seals, they should most likely be viewed as parallel with each other also. This seems likely because (1) the first three seals are summarized in the fourth one, (2) the Old Testament and Jesus' own eschatological discourse speak of the events occurring in parallel fashion, and (3) the glorified saints spoken of in the section on the fifth seal appear to have endured through the first four seals.[1] The latter makes it clear that the events associated with the first four seals are not reserved for the end of history alone, but were inaugurated by Christ's death, resurrection, and ascension and are occurring throughout the church age. In light of the previous two chapters, believers are assured that God is still on the throne during such troubling events as the seven churches were enduring (see the seven letters in chapters 2–3). Indeed, he has decreed that such events would be suffering/salvation for his saints and judgment for those that are not his own.

Old Testament/New Testament Background to the First through Fourth Seals.

- Leviticus 26:18–28: "I will continue striking you sevenfold for your sins."
- Ezekiel 14:12–13: "And I stretch out my hand against it and break its supply of bread and send famine upon it."

1. G. K. Beale, *The Book of Revelation: A Commentary on the Greek Text*, New International Greek Testament Commentary (Grand Rapids: Eerdmans, 1999), 370–71.

- Zechariah 6:5–8: "Chariot with black horses . . . white ones go . . . dappled ones . . . strong ones."
- Matthew 24:6–8:29: "And you will hear of wars and rumor of wars . . . all of these are but the beginning of the birth pains."

Revelation 6:1. Now John is relieved of his weeping as he watches the Lamb, the only one who is worthy to open the seals, open the first of the seven. The command to "Come!" is sent from the throne, the location of the thunder (see Rev. 4:5). This is significant, for it confirms that God is the one behind these events. History is in his hands and his purposes and plan come to pass certainly.

Revelation 6:2. At first glance it appears that the first horseman is Christ, for white could connote his purity, his crown could be the one given to him upon his ascension, and he certainly conquered the forces of evil by his death. Yet, from the description of the other horsemen in Revelation 6:3–7, a comparison with other background passages (Zech. 1:8–15; 6:1–8), and a comparison within other texts in the book of Revelation (Rev. 9:7; 11:7; 12–13; 13:7), it appears that this is not Christ at all, but rather an evil power masquerading as a heavenly one.[2] The purpose is to deceive believers spiritually and persecute them physically. Notice the phrase "was given to him." God's sovereignty involves his making use of the evil done by others to bring about his plan and purposes of judgment and salvation in the world. Though this may be disturbing, it is less disturbing than the image of him purposelessly permitting evil to run rampant in this world. Instead, he has made even that which is contrary to his character serve his plan. Ironically, the warfare that Satan wages with the saints of God in order to wreck their faith ends up strengthening it instead, and condemns Satan's own satanic kingdom and all unbelievers who are his children.

Revelation 6:3–4. Again, the command to "Come!" is sent from the throne, the location of the thunder (see Rev. 4:5). As we have already seen, this is significant; it confirms that God is the one behind these judgments. History is in his hands and his purposes and plan sovereignly come to

2. Ibid., 375–79.

pass. The purpose of this second horseman is to inflict persecution on God's people and possibly to cause international disunity and warfare among unbelievers.[3] Thus, the "bright red" stands for bloodshed. The word "permitted" should be defined in light of God's authorizing and sending forth these horsemen from heaven. Though evil never originates with God, it is decreed by God to be used for his purposes.

Revelation 6:5–6. Again, the command to "Come!" is sent from the throne. This time the horse is black, which connotes famine, as is obvious from the scales in the rider's hands. Scales in those days were used to ration out food when it was scarce. Yet Christ himself ("a voice in the midst of the four living creatures") limits the famine. A "quart of wheat" would be enough food for a person for a day, and a "denarius," the amount of money one would earn in one day, would be just enough to cover the fee. So, though one's daily income would go solely to food and nothing else, one would still be fed. Thus, the people would not be able to "harm the wine and oil" because they would not be able to buy it. As in the first two seals, the Christians are affected the most severely. This was portrayed in the letters to the churches where Christians were under economic hardship because they were not willing to compromise with the pagan trade guilds. Yet, the plague affects unbelievers as well. Though Christians suffer depletion of food sources during the church age, they can look hopefully and expectantly to the day when the tree of life, with its twelve kinds of fruit, yielding its fruit each month and "the river of the water of life" will be theirs (Rev. 22:1–2).

Revelation 6:7–8. Again, the command to "Come!" is sent from the throne. This time the horse is pale, symbolizing death, as is clear from the rider's name. Death and Hades were given authority by God to kill believers and unbelievers alike, but for different purposes. For God's people, persecution purifies; for unbelievers, death destroys. The ways in which these satanic forces inflict death (sword, famine, pestilence, wild beasts) are representative for all the ways that death occurs. Yet, the plague is limited. It is only allowed for a fourth of the earth. Thus again, we see God's mercy even in judgment. Believers who die no longer

3. Ibid., 379.

suffer here on earth. And three-fourths of unbelievers are still allowed life. "Death and Hades," which were conquered upon Jesus' death, resurrection, and ascension, are now used as tools toward the development of his kingdom. Just as Christ's death appeared as defeat, so Christians' deaths appear as defeat, but in reality the death of Christ and the deaths of Christians serve as the defeat of evil.

II. The Lamb of God Opens the Fifth Seal (Rev. 6:9–11)

Now we see the reaction of Christians to the persecution of Christians under the first four seals. And, we see God's response to how long this persecution will be allowed. Contrary to our tendency to wring our hands over such persecution and our desire to end it immediately, the Lord is carrying out his sovereign plan and actually using the deaths of his people to advance his kingdom, just as he used the death of his Son to advance it. The only way to life is through death.

I have seen this over and over again in my own life as well. I wring my hands over suffering, physical pain, emotional distress, unmet expectations, unfulfilled longings, and tragedies. I want it ended immediately. But the Lord is carrying out his sovereign plan for my life through those very events, advancing Christlike character in my heart and bringing me more into conformity with who he wants me to be. While I am wringing my hands, he is wringing my heart, because he wants it to be submitted to him alone.

Revelation 6:9–10. Contrary to the first four commands by the living creatures to "Come!" here we have a response to those comings by the saints in heaven. Like Christ, they too had been killed for their witness and worship. Their position is significant. They are under the altar, which connotes God's protection of them. But they are associated with the altar because they poured out their blood on earth for the sake of witness and worship of Jesus Christ. This is most likely an allusion to the golden altar of incense (Ex. 30:1–10), which was in the holy of holies, and was used on the Day of Atonement.[4] In this light, the fact that they are "under" the altar also brings to

4. Ibid., 391–92.

80

mind that while Christ is the complete and perfect sacrifice that was on top of the altar, his followers now follow in his footsteps and are fellow sufferers with him under the altar, yet hidden in Christ and saved by his blood alone.

Their response is in the form of a question. But first, they recognize the sovereignty, holiness, and truthfulness of God. This is significant and should inform our own prayers to God. As creatures of the Creator, we place ourselves under his sovereignty, holiness, and truthfulness. We never demand our own way. We delight in his sovereignty, holiness, and truth, presenting our requests in humility and submission. Their question was not, "What are you doing?" but rather "When will you do it?" The saints already knew that their blood would be avenged on unbelievers, but they did not know when. And apparently they were anxious for the vindication to occur, not only because God would finally demonstrate his justice in punishing sin, but also because the world would finally know that Christians were innocent and their persecutors were guilty.

Anyone who has endured chronic pain is sooner or later plagued with the questions, "Why?" and "How long?" Anyone who has endured ridicule for his or her faith is sooner or later plagued with the same questions. Anyone who has endured years of being denied requests of marriage or children or employment or healing asks the same things. We wonder for what purpose God has to put his people through such pain. And even when we know the purpose, it is greatly difficult for us to bear up under the pressure of physical, mental, and emotional pain.

The cross that I have been asked to endure in my own life is very different from yours. It has been carved to conform to my own heart that needs to be molded to that of my Savior's. My own sin and obsessions and tendencies that need to be dealt with are in that cross. Where my will crosses with the Lord's will, crucifixion happens. And it is that crucifixion that leads to true life. The process is painful to say the least, agonizing at points, tolerable at others. The cries of suffering are the loudest when the nail is felt the deepest, but so is the rejoicing loudest when the suffering is finished. Without the pain of the cross, we cannot gain the victory of heaven, and so, we too kneel before our Father in sacrificial obedience, knowing he is molding us and shaping us to the likeness of his Son.

But as we kneel before our Father, we also kneel before a watching world. And as we do so we are empowered by the Spirit of God to be bold witnesses and worshipers of God. The world watches our response to the news of intense anguish in our lives. It watches our interactions with our husbands and our children. It watches our comings and our goings. It hears the words that we speak and sees the lives that we lead. And the world may snicker and ridicule and persecute, but it sees God through seeing our lives. To some we will be a fragrant aroma of life, but to others we will be an aroma of death (2 Cor. 2:16).

It is greatly perplexing to ponder the paradox of the Christian faith that Christ and Christians must suffer at the hands of unbelievers in order to gain the crown of glory. Man would have done it differently. We would have put Christ's second coming in place of his first. But God chose another way. He chose the way of love and grace and mercy. He chose the only way he could choose, in order to satisfy his justice and yet display his grace. And so, he sent his own Son, the Servant, to suffer for the servants of God. And just as Christ suffered, so too we suffer in his footsteps; but just as Christ was glorified for his suffering, so too we will be glorified for ours.

Old Testament Background to Revelation 6:10.
- Psalm 79:2: "They have given the flesh of your faithful to the beasts of the earth."
- Psalm 79:10: "Let the avenging of the outpoured blood of your servants be known among the nations before our eyes."
- Zechariah 1:12: "How long?"

Revelation 6:11. Though it is not yet time for God to make it known to the world that his saints are innocent, he declares it to all of heaven by giving them white robes and rest. Here we especially see that our timing is not the Lord's timing and that he indeed uses the deaths of his children to further his plan. Rather than putting an end to persecution, he increases the persecution purposefully in order to bring judgment to unbelievers and salvation to believers. Though martyrdom is included in "who were to be killed as they themselves had been," this is not just limited to martyrs; this includes all believers who have died as witnesses and worshipers.

III. The Lamb of God Opens the Sixth Seal (Rev. 6:12–17)

The saints' question/pleading in the section on the previous seal is now answered with the opening of the sixth seal. This seal depicts the time when the number of the fellow servants and brothers of the saints already in heaven is complete (when persecution is complete), which will be the final judgment at the end of history.

Revelation 6:12–14. The metaphorical language of these verses connotes the universal and final judgment of unbelievers on the earth at the time of Christ's second coming. This is clear from the totality of the destruction of the sun, moon, stars, and the removal of the sky, every mountain and island. The imagery is that of God's creation being brought down, for man exchanged it for the Creator and worshiped his creation instead. Thus, just as God destroyed idols all throughout the Old Testament, so too here he brings down all that had been idolized on earth (the sun, the moon, the stars, etc.). God will never give his glory to any other. In the end, the Creator will renew his own creation in order to bring glory to himself.

Old Testament/New Testament Background to Revelation 6:12–14.
- Isaiah 13:10–13: "For the stars of the heavens and their constellations will not give their light; the sun will be dark at its rising, and the moon will not shed its light. I will punish the world for its evil and the wicked for their iniquity."
- Isaiah 24:1–6, 19–23: "The LORD will empty the earth and make it desolate . . . for they have transgressed the laws, violated the statutes, broken the everlasting covenant."

- Isaiah 34:4: "All the host of heaven shall rot away, and the skies roll up like a scroll. All their host shall fall, as leaves fall from the vine, like leaves falling from the fig tree."
- Ezekiel 32:6–8: "I will cover the heavens and make their stars dark; I will cover the sun with a cloud, and the moon shall not give its light."
- Joel 2:10, 30–31; 3:15–16 "The sun and the moon are darkened."
- Habakkuk 3:6–11: "The sun and the moon stood still in their place."
- Matthew 24:29: "The sun will be darkened and the moon will not give its light, and the stars will fall from heaven, and the powers of the heavens will be shaken."
- Mark 13:25: "And the stars will be falling from heaven."
- Acts 2:20: "The sun shall be turned to darkness and the moon to blood, before the day of the Lord comes, the great and magnificent day."

Revelation 6:15–17. From the most exalted to the least exalted among unbelievers, all hid from the judgment of the Creator behind his creation. But he uses his creation for his own purposes and glory and so creation became a witness against the unbelievers, as the creation wanted no part in hiding the unbelievers' guilt. Instead those who rebel against God would be exposed before all creation for what they really were, persecutors of the true people of God, and thus, persecutors of God's kingdom. Now that kingdom would turn on them in judgment and wrath, knocking their stance out from underneath them in order to bring them low in worship of the one to whom their worship was always due (see Phil. 2:9–11).

From the time that sin entered the world in the garden of Eden, man hid his face from the face of God. In Exodus 10:28 we learn that men will die if they see the face of God because he is holy and we are not. Sinful creatures cannot stand in the presence of the sinless God. That is why we need a Redeemer, one who will clothe us with his own bloodstained clothes of atonement, so that we might stand face to face before the Father and one day see him as he really is. Thankfully, God in his graciousness sent us his face in the face of his Son so that those who walked the earth in his day and were blessed to look into it would record for us what they learned from him. Even now, we have been sent his Spirit to shine the face of Christ into our hearts so that we might reflect it in our own lives.

Are we living in light of this coming day? What are we hiding behind now in order to keep from facing our Lord and Savior Jesus Christ? What do we need to bring out of the darkness to be exposed in his glorious light of refinement rather than judgment? There will come a day when man will be taken off guard. He will realize what you and I have already realized. One cannot hide from "the face of him who is seated on the throne." What do we need to bring willingly before his face today, confessing our sin and idolatry, and asking him to hide us under the shelter of his almighty wings while there is still time?

Old Testament Background to Revelation 6:15–17.

- Genesis 3:9–10: "I was afraid because I was naked and I hid myself."
- Jeremiah 4:29: "Every city takes to flight; they enter thickets, they climb among rocks; all the cities are forsaken and no man dwells in them."
- Hosea 10:8: "They shall say to the mountains, Cover us, and to the hills, Fall on us."
- Joel 2:10–11: "For the day of the LORD is great and very awesome; who can endure it?"

CONCLUSION

The persecuted church still weighs heavy on my heart. Living in the States where I am free to worship and witness, it is very difficult for me to wrap my mind around what my brothers and sisters in other countries face on a daily basis. Sometimes it is hard to believe that we even live in the same world. And yet we do, and while I have been sovereignly placed in America, they have been sovereignly placed in their respective countries. I have involved my family in praying for the persecuted church on a daily basis. It is very moving to watch my children voluntarily get prostrate on the floor to lift up those suffering in persecuted countries. Their prayers are mature and heartfelt, simple yet profound. Our family wants to be a part of their witness and worship as we seek to stand strong as witnesses and worshipers in our own lives to the glory of God the Father and Jesus Christ, his Son. I hope and pray that you will do so as well.

LESSON 6

Revelation 7

PLEASE USE THE QUESTION paradigm from pages 353–54 as you work through the following. See the introductory comments there that explain each part of the process below in more detail.

- **Pray**.
- **Ponder the Passage**. Read Revelation 7 once a day from different translations for the entire week, looking for its:
  - Point
  - Persons
  - Patterns
  - Persons of the Trinity
  - Puzzling Parts
- **Put It in Perspective**.
  - Place in Scripture
  - Passages from Other Parts of Scripture

1. Based on your observations of the text, what is the basic content of this passage? Try to summarize it in your own words, using a sentence or two.
2. Compare Isaiah 11:12 and Ezekiel 7:2 with Revelation 7:1. What does the phrase "the four corners of the earth" represent?

3. Compare Zechariah 6:5 with Revelation 7:1. To what do you think "the four winds of the earth" refer (see Rev. 6:1–8)?

4. From where does the angel come in Revelation 7:2? Is this usual? What do you think could be the significance?

5. Look up the word "seal" in a concordance or Bible dictionary. Where else is it used in the New Testament? To what does it refer? To what do you think it refers in Revelation 7:2?

6. Are the angels or the result of the angels' action going to harm the earth in Revelation 7:3?

7. Do you think the 144,000 in Revelation 7:4 is a literal number of ethnic Jews that will be saved, or a symbolic number representing the entire people of God? Why?

8. What tribe is listed first in Revelation 7:5? Is this significant (see Gen. 49:8–12)?

9. Do you think that the "great multitude that no one could number" is the same as the 144,000 sealed (Rev. 7:9)? Why? (Different commentators disagree on this. I am just asking what you think from your own reading and study of the book so far.)

10. To what covenant does Revelation 7:9 allude (see Gen. 13:16; 15:5; 22:17; 26:4)?

11. Look up Leviticus 23:40, 43. What do the palm branches signify for John in 7:9–10?

12. To whom is salvation attributed in Revelation 7:10? What role in salvation does each person of the Godhead play?

13. For what do the angels praise God (Rev. 7:11–12)? List each element of worship separately and try to write a brief synopsis of each one.

14. When did "the great tribulation" (Rev. 7:14) begin (see John 19)? Does it intensify at the end of history (see Matt. 24:21–31)?

15. To what does "washed their robes" (Rev. 7:14) refer (see 1 Peter 4:13)? To what does "made them white" refer (see Dan. 11:35)?

16. Why are those coming out of the great tribulation worthy to be before the throne of God in Revelation 7:15 (see 7:14)? What are they doing? What is God doing for them?

17. Why will they not hunger, thirst, or be scorched by heat anymore (see Rev. 7:17)?

- **Principles and Points of Application.**
1. Have you been sealed with the "seal of the living God"? In other words, have you made Jesus Christ Lord and Savior of your life? What fruit in your life do you see as evidence of this? If you've never given your life to Christ, do so today by acknowledging that you are a sinner in need of his grace and by accepting him through faith to be Lord and Savior of your life.
2. Use Revelation 7:10, 12 to worship God today in Spirit and in truth.
3. Meditate on Revelation 7:15–17. How does the truth that Christ is your Shepherd and that the world to come will be free from pain encourage your heart now in your present suffering?

NOTES FOR REVELATION 7

Aim: Ponder the aim of this lesson concerning our:

Mind: What do we need to know from this passage in Scripture?

That God's people are sealed in Christ by the Spirit and are to worship and serve before his throne.

Heart: How does what we learn from this passage affect our internal relationship with the Lord?

It prepares us to be kingdom disciples who joyously worship and serve God.

Hands: How does what we learn from this passage translate into action for God's kingdom?

It enables us to:

1. Lead others to a relationship with Jesus Christ so that they are sealed by the Holy Spirit.
2. Rely on God's power through the Holy Spirit to live the Spirit-filled life in every area of our lives.
3. Worship and lead others to worship God in Spirit and in truth by using the hymns throughout the book of Revelation.
4. Encourage others in present suffering that Christ is their Shepherd and that the world to come will have no pain.

INTRODUCTION

As each year passes, I cannot help but reflect on the joys and the sorrows that have occurred not just in my own life, but in the lives of my family and friends as well. With regard to sorrows, just in the past year we have seen the loss of a loved one, divorce, miscarriage, infertility, a prolonged adoption process, a rebellious adult child, a disobedient and rebellious child still at home, loss of work, a sinful relationship, the heartache of a husband who won't go to church, a move, financial stress, foreclosure of a home, physical pain, depression, an angry husband, an abundance of stress in the home, loneliness, and the inability to cope with grief. Life is difficult to say the least. The greatest moments soon give way to the reality that life is not perfect and the realization that the journey is fraught with pain and hardship.

We cope with these sorrows in many ways instead of turning immediately to the Word of God in order to seek his perspective and his way to deal with them. Too often we turn to food, trying to eat away our pain; or we turn away from food, trying to starve out the pain. Sometimes, we become glued to the television, trying to drown ourselves with someone else's life that looks better than ours; or we turn to getting advice from the talk show hosts. Sometimes, we turn to our books, wanting to escape into a world of fantasy where marriages are much more romantic and money is never a problem. Sometimes, we turn to exercise and become obsessed with our scales and the number of trips we make to the gym each week. Other times, we go shopping and feed the hunger of our distress with a cute new outfit; we try and dress ourselves up on the outside while we're dying on the inside. We may go to the salon to try and make our head, that is spinning out of control, look sleek and controlled; or we get a manicure to make our hands and feet, that are grabbing and running in all the wrong directions trying to cope, look put together and groomed. But none of these work to fill the hole in our hearts and help us endure the suffering in a godly way.

Revelation 7 gives us a different perspective and a different coping mechanism as we walk through suffering and trials during this life. First, it tells us that we are sealed with the Holy Spirit so that no amount of suffering in our lives can separate us from God or defeat our ultimate victory in Christ. We will certainly overcome any trial that we are put through. Indeed, God himself is orchestrating the very suffering that we are trying to escape from in our lives. Second, there is an end. One day the suffering will be over and we will be standing among the redeemed in heaven worshiping our God in glorified bodies. And, the longings in our hearts that were so prevalent here on earth will be fulfilled in heaven by the presence of God himself in all of his fullness.

We can divide this lesson into two sections:

I. God's People Are Sealed (Rev. 7:1–8)
II. God's People Worship and Serve before God's Throne (Rev. 7:9–17)

I. God's People Are Sealed (Rev. 7:1–8)

Before moving on to the opening of the seventh seal, we have a parenthetical section, in which John explains and/or expands on chapter 6. These first eight verses explain how God's people make it through the first four seals when there is deception, martyrdom, famine, and physical death. They make it through because God has spiritually sealed them and no one is able to take from them their eternal life in Christ. Thus, this sealing occurs prior to the time of the opening of the first four seals in Revelation 6:1–8, during the church age.[1]

Revelation 7:1. We need to remember in light of what was said above that "after this" does not speak of how the events will occur in chronological,

---

1. G. K. Beale, *The Book of Revelation: A Commentary on the Greek Text*, New International Greek Testament Commentary (Grand Rapids: Eerdmans, 1999), 405.

historical time, but rather that this was the order of John's visions. The four angels are standing at the four corners of the earth, which represents that they are over the entirety of the earth, holding back the four winds of the earth (see also Jer. 49:36; Dan. 8:8; Matt. 24:31). In light of the fact that (1) this section immediately precedes Revelation 6:1–8, and (2) that Zechariah 6:1–8, which was alluded to in Revelation 6:1–8, identifies the horsemen as the "four winds of heaven," it is likely that the "four winds of the earth" here should be identified with the four horsemen of the first four seals. The purpose of the angels holding them back is so that the evil they will bring on the earth will not yet occur. As we will see in Revelation 7:3, this delay occurs in order to seal the people of God so that they will be protected during the opening of the first four seals.[2]

Revelation 7:2–3. It is interesting that the angel that has the seal of the living God ascends from the rising of the sun, rather than descends from heaven. It is almost as if to say that God is not only over the powers above, but he is also over the evil powers below and he will seal his people from those earthly powers below that will try and destroy them. The "seal of the living God" is not a guarantee of physical protection of believers through their time on earth, but rather a guarantee of spiritual protection. Even death will only be a gateway into their eternal presence with the Lord. This seal then identifies the true people of God, and in light of other New Testament passages, is best identified as the Holy Spirit (Eph. 1:13; 4:30).

The angel commands the other angel that is holding back the first four seals to continue holding them back. The command, "Do not harm," does not imply that the angel is the one doing the harming, but rather that once the angel stops holding the four horsemen back, the harm will follow. Thus, even the four horsemen that bring evil upon the world are under the sovereign timing, plan, and purposes of God. Verse 3 informs us why the four horsemen are being held back: God must protect his people spiritually with the Holy Spirit first.

This should provide great encouragement for us as believers. Living in the world where Satan is still prince, we are given the assurance that

2. Ibid., 406–7.

God's Holy Spirit has sealed us in Christ so that nothing can separate us from the love of God and the presence of God. We are united with him in life and in death, and any trial that occurs in our lives on earth will only conform us more to the image of Christ and bring us closer to the day of Christ Jesus. We can be assured that even when we feel like Satan, the world, or the flesh is winning, we have the power of the Holy Spirit in our lives to help us overcome them. And indeed, we will overcome, for we are sealed with the Spirit of God.

Old Testament Background to Revelation 7:3.

- Exodus 12:7, 13, 22–28: "And when I see the blood, I will pass over you."
- Ezekiel 9:4: "And put a mark on the foreheads of the men who sigh and groan over all the abominations that are committed in it."

Revelation 7:4. John now tells us who is sealed and how many. In light of the context and the use of numbers elsewhere in the book, 144,000 must be taken as symbolic for the entire people of God (though those who see the book from a futurist viewpoint and are literalists believe that these are literally 144,000 ethnic Jews, as will be explained below). This is illuminated by the fact that in chapter 21 we see that the twelve tribes of Israel alongside the twelve apostles make up part of the symbolic structure of the heavenly city. If we multiply 12,000 by 12 we get 144,000, which would stand as representing the entire church of God.[3] The phrase "from every tribe" further identifies that there were many in Israel who were not saved; they were not part of the true Israel, the church of God.

Revelation 7:5–8. It is significant that Judah is listed first here. Judah does occur first in other lists of the Old Testament tribes, but it is rare. Here in the last book of the Bible it portrays the fulfillment of the prophecy in the first book of the Bible (Gen. 49:8–12) that all his "father's sons shall bow down before [him]." And, that "the scepter will not depart from Judah." Ezekiel 37:15–19 develops the prophecy in Genesis by saying that "all the tribes of Israel" will become a part of "the

3. Ibid., 417.

tribe of Judah." Ezekiel goes on in 37:24–25 to speak of the fulfillment of these prophecies as resulting in an ideal Davidic king on the throne forever. As seen in Revelation 5:5, Christ, the one who is worthy to open the seals, is identified as "the Lion of the tribe of Judah, the Root of David." Thus, Judah is first because from its tribe has come Christ, the only one worthy to open the door of salvation for the redeemed out of every tribe.

Those who interpret the book literally and see the events from chapter 4 onward as referring to the future only, believe that 144,000 speaks of a literal number from the literal tribes of Israel. That the twelve tribes no longer existed in John's day should speak against this. Though it is true that God knows each Jew's identity even when they themselves do not, the likelihood of that being the interpretation here does not make logical sense in light of the context. Thus, this number is meant to be representative for the entire people of God who are redeemed by the blood of the Lamb, sealed by the Holy Spirit of God, and soldiers in the army of God to wage war against the spiritual powers of darkness in the world.

This passage serves as a tremendous encouragement to us. We do not stand alone in this world. With Christ as our Head of the army, we join the troops from every tribe and every age that have been sealed with the Holy Spirit of God and make up the true Israel. We march out to battle the destructive forces of this world, knowing for whom we stand in allegiance, knowing we have the fellowship and encouragement of the redeemed, knowing that we have the spiritual armor needed to win the battle, and knowing that the ultimate victory has already been won.

I still remember standing in chapel at the Christian school I attended in second grade, marching and singing, "I'm in the Lord's army, yes, sir! I'm in the Lord's army, yes sir!" That instilled such a sense of warfare in my young mind, although I could not understand the full force of it yet. I knew that this world was a battlefield and that I was to say "Yes, Sir!" to my King at every turn of the battle. Today as a mom singing this song with my own children, I hope and pray that their small hearts and minds are grasping the same. Our allegiance in this war is to Jesus Christ, the Lamb of God, the Lion of Judah, and the Warrior of all warriors.

II. God's People Worship and Serve before God's Throne (Rev. 7:9–17)

This section illuminates Revelation 6:9–11 where the saints who have already suffered and died for their faith are in heaven. It also answers the question posed in Revelation 6:17: "Who can stand" on the great day of wrath? All of those who are sealed by the Spirit of God and persevere to the very end will be left standing after the final judgment before the throne of God worshiping and serving him. Thus, this section gives us both a picture of what is occurring now, as we see by the saints who are already in heaven, and what will occur at the end of time when all the saints of all times will join together to worship and serve God before his throne for eternity.

Revelation 7:9–10. Again, "after this" conveys the order of John's visions, not necessarily the order of history. This verse further confirms our conclusion above that the 144,000 is not a literal number of ethnic Jews, but rather a symbolic number for the entire people of God, which are here referred to as "a great multitude that no one could number from every nation, from all tribes and peoples and languages." Yet, we know that God has numbered every one of his children (the perspective of the "144,000" displays this) and knows those who are his. Whereas Revelation 7:1–8 informed us of the sealing of God to protect them during their time on earth, Revelation 7:9–17 informs us of what takes place in heaven after the redeemed are free from this world. In part, this scene is already taking place as the saints who have gone before us worship the Lord in heaven, but this scene will not be fully consummated until after the final judgment when the new heaven and new earth will be the realm of all of God's people.

We see here the fulfillment of the promise to Abraham that was given in Genesis 13:16, "I will make your offspring as the dust of the earth, so that if one can count the dust of the earth, your offspring also can be counted." We know from both Old and New Testament passages that this offspring did not just consist of national Israel, but is made up of both Jews and Gentiles, all those who by faith are part of the people of God. Thus, here in the book of Revelation we see a culmination of God's covenantal story of redemption and restoration that was prophesied in the Abrahamic covenant.

The people of God are standing before the throne, *just as* their Lord and Savior was standing before the throne (Rev. 5:6) *and because* their Lord and Savior is standing before the throne. It answers the question in Revelation 6:17, "Who can stand" on the great day of wrath. Those who have been sealed by the Holy Spirit of God and are in Christ can stand. Because Christ stands before the Father in front of us, we are able to stand behind him, hidden in him, clothed by his white robes of righteousness and holding the palm branches that signify his victory and thus, our victory, over the war with Satan, the world, and the flesh. The palm branches allude to the Festival of Tabernacles (Lev. 23:40, 43), which was an annual thanksgiving in Israel for their crops, a time to remember God's deliverance of them at the Red Sea, and a time to remember God's protection and provision as they "tabernacled" in tents during their wilderness journey from Egypt to the Promised Land.

The redeemed ascribe salvation to whom it is due, both God the Father and God the Son. God the Father sent his Son into the world to redeem his people, and God the Son, in perfect obedience, accomplished the work of redemption. We might add here that the Holy Spirit applies the work of redemption to us by sealing us as the redeemed people of God.

Revelation 7:11–12. Now the angels fall down and worship the Father and the Son. "Amen" both introduces and concludes their praise, signifying the certainty of God's work and his worthiness of praise. They speak of eight elements of worship. Blessing comes to us from God and we are to bless God. Glory is to be given to him alone for the plan of judgment and salvation. God's plans and purposes are wise. Our lives are to be a continual act of thanksgiving before God, to whom all honor is due. And, it is because of his power and might that redemption has been made possible for the redeemed.

Revelation 7:13–14. It seems that the elder's function is to emphasize the answer to John, to get his attention, so to speak, for the elder clearly knew and answered his own question. The "great multitude" in Revelation 7:9 is here identified as "the ones coming out of the great tribulation." In other words, the ones coming out of the time of the tribulation inaugurated by the opening of the first four seals, as well as those who will come out at the final time of judgment during the last final stage of the tribulation. The great tribulation has already begun in part with Jesus' own death, but will escalate at the end of history, before the final judgment.

The fact that they have "washed their robes" and not merely been "clothed" with them points to the fact they have partaken in Christ's sufferings, a characteristic of all believers. Because they have proved and worked out their salvation by the witness of their suffering, they are worthy to be clothed in white robes of purity and worship the one who redeemed them.

Old Testament Background to Revelation 7:13–14.
- Daniel 11:35: "So that they may be refined, purified, and made white, until the time of the end, for it still awaits the appointed time."
- Daniel 12:1: "And there shall be a time of trouble . . . but at that time your people shall be delivered, everyone whose name shall be found written in the book."

Revelation 7:15. Therefore, because they have washed their robes and are now clothed in them, they alone are able to stand before the throne of God and serve him continually in his temple, which is his presence, as seen in the final clause. They have come out of the tribulation and are now rewarded with the complete shelter of God's presence, in contrast to their partial protection (spiritual but not physical) while they persevered through persecution on earth.

Old Testament Background to Revelation 7:15.
- Exodus 19:10, 14: "Consecrate them and let them wash their garments."
- Ezekiel 37:26–28: "I will make a covenant of peace with them. It shall be an everlasting covenant with them. And I will set them

in their land and multiply them and will set my sanctuary in their midst forevermore. My dwelling place shall be with them, and I will be their God and they shall be my people. Then the nations will know that I am the LORD who sanctifies Israel, when my sanctuary is in their midst forevermore."

Revelation 7:16–17. Though they hungered on earth through the economic disadvantage of not partaking in trade guilds and through famine, they will not hunger anymore in the presence of God. They can freely eat from the tree of life (Rev. 22:2). Though the church in Laodicea was thirsty for either cold or hot water, not the lukewarm that the springs of Laodicea produced, they would not be thirsty in the presence of God. They could freely drink from the river of the water of life (Rev. 22:1). Though the sun struck them and scorched them, there would be no sun in heaven to scorch them, for the glory of God gives the light (Rev. 21:23). The Lamb himself will be their Shepherd, the only Shepherd that has become a Lamb himself in order to identify with his flock. And he will guide them to springs of living water, eternal life, rather than lukewarm water. He will wipe away from their eyes every tear that had been shed on earth, for there is no need of crying in heaven, unless one is crying out in worship to God. It is clear from these verses that this is speaking of the time when the kingdom of God has been consummated and thus, this is a picture of all of God's redeemed people clothed in the righteousness of Christ, worshiping and serving God in the new heaven and new earth.

What an incredible picture of hope for us who are hungry and thirsty for more than this world can give, who are scorched by the "heat" of life, depleted from tears cried over the loss of loved ones, miscarriages, broken marriages, rebellious children, financial disaster, physical pain, and emotional distress. It will not be like this forever! Even now, we can partake in part of the food and drink of heaven, of the light of Christ, and of the healing stroke of God's hand over our tears.

Old Testament Background to Revelation 7:16–17.

- Psalm 23:1–2: "The LORD is my shepherd; I shall not want. He makes me lie down in green pastures. He leads me beside still waters."
- Isaiah 49:10: "They shall not hunger or thirst, neither scorching wind nor sun shall strike them."

CONCLUSION

Though the end of the year always comes, the end of the trials does not. They will be with us throughout this journey on earth. But they are purposeful. They are orchestrated by the Lord himself and under his control. We are sealed by the Holy Spirit in the midst of them and have his power to make it through them. And we can even now take part in the heavenly worship of standing around the throne worshiping God for our salvation. For one day we know that our hunger will be fed, our thirst will be quenched, our sun-scorched hearts will be healed, our Shepherd will have led us into the new heaven and new earth of eternal life, and all of our tears of sorrow will be gone. May we witness to others about this glorious Lamb and Shepherd, and may we worship him and lead others to worship him on earth as it already is in heaven.

Revelation 8

PLEASE USE THE QUESTION paradigm from pages 353–54 as you work through the following. See the introductory comments there that explain each part of the process below in more detail.

- **Pray.**
- **Ponder the Passage.** Read Revelation 8 once a day from different translations for the entire week, looking for its:
  - Point
  - Persons
  - Patterns
  - Persons of the Trinity
  - Puzzling Parts
- **Put It in Perspective.**
  - Place in Scripture
  - Passages from Other Parts of Scripture

1. Based on your observations of the text, what is the basic content of this passage? Try to summarize it in your own words, using a sentence or two.
2. Look up the word "silence/silent" in a concordance. With what is silence usually associated in Scripture? What do you think it conveys concerning the seventh seal in Revelation 8:1?

3. Look up "trumpet/trumpets" in a concordance. With what are trumpets usually associated in Scripture? What do you think they convey in Revelation 8:2?

4. Look up Exodus 27:1–8 and 30:1–10. What two altars were located in the Old Testament sanctuary? For what were they used? How does that illuminate Revelation 8:3–4? To whom does the phrase "all the saints" refer? Where are they located?

5. How does Revelation 8:5 answer Revelation 6:10?

6. Skim Exodus 9 and read Exodus 10:1–7. What similarities do you see between them and Revelation 7–8?

7. Read Exodus 19:16–25. What did the peals of thunder, etc., and the trumpet mean in that context? What do you think they mean here?

8. On which previous verse in this chapter does Revelation 8:6 continue?

9. Look up Exodus 9:24. Compare this with Revelation 8:7. How much of the creation is affected? How does this display God's judgment, yet also his mercy?

10. Look up Exodus 7:20–21. To which plague does Revelation 8:8–9 allude? Read Jeremiah 51:25 and 42. To what do you think "something like a great mountain" refers?

11. Read Exodus 7:15–24. Is this plague still alluded to in Revelation 8:10–11? Read Isaiah 14:12–15. How does this help identify the star?

12. Look up "wormwood" in a dictionary and in a concordance. What do you learn that helps shed light on its meaning in Revelation 8:11? How much of the creation is affected?

13. Look up "darkened" in a concordance. What does it usually convey in Scripture? What does it convey here? Is it limited in its effect? Why? Read Exodus 10:21–23. To what Exodus plague does this allude?

14. Look up the word "eagle" in a concordance. What meaning/meanings is it usually associated with? What does it convey here for unbelievers (and indirectly for believers)? How many times

is "woe" used in Revelation 8:13? Is this related to the "other trumpets that the three angels are about to blow"?

- **Principles and Points of Application.**
1. Our prayers (Rev. 8:3) are said to be part of God's judgment upon the earth. When Jesus taught his disciples to pray, "Thy kingdom come, thy will be done on earth as it is in heaven" (Matt. 6:9), he was telling us to pray for judgment and righteousness upon the earth. And, he uses our prayers to be a part of that. We are a royal priesthood, a holy nation (1 Peter 2:9). Spend time in prayer today for God's justice and righteousness to be displayed in our world.
2. It is hard to look past the judgment in Revelation 8:6–12 and see the grace, but it is clearly there. God is only destroying in thirds rather than in wholes. He is still giving people time to repent. That same grace is evident in our lives today. He has given us another day to bow ourselves before him and accept him as Lord and Savior of our lives. How does your life represent a walk with God? Are you using your life to worship and serve the Creator? With whom in your life do you need to share the message of the gospel this week?

NOTES FOR REVELATION 8

Aim: Ponder the aim of this lesson concerning our:

Mind: What do we need to know from this passage in Scripture?

That the seventh seal, which reflects the last judgment, brings the seals to an end, and John sees the first four trumpets blown.

Heart: How does what we learn from this passage affect our internal relationship with the Lord?

It prepares us to be kingdom disciples who help carry out God's justice and righteousness on earth.

Hands: How does what we learn from this passage translate into action for God's kingdom?

It enables us to:

1. Rely on the Holy Spirit to enable us to display God's justice and righteousness in daily choices that we are called to make.
2. Demonstrate God's grace to those around us through the power of the Spirit.
3. Lead others to worship and serve the Creator.
4. Share the gospel message with someone in our lives who has never heard it or who has heard it but never responded in faith, praying that the Holy Spirit will open up their hearts.

INTRODUCTION

My favorite time of the day is early in the morning before the sun has risen, before my children and husband are awake, and when the house lies silent, shrouded in the pre-dawn darkness. It's the one time of the day when I feel like I can hear my own heart and hear what the Lord wants to say to me. Once the day gets going, this opportunity doesn't leave me, but it is more difficult for me in the midst of a busy schedule. Unless of course, I escape the chattering of my children, the fixing of meals, the laundry, homeschooling, and the list of other things on my job description as a wife and mother.

Such an escape presented itself beautifully the other day. We had a lovely snow and I was able to leave my husband at home with my children and go out to walk the wooded trails in our neighborhood. It was quiet from the start, but the real silence didn't begin until I got back onto the trail away from the streets and houses. Once I was on the trail the most beautiful landscape unfolded before me: snow laden trees, bubbling brooks, squirrels digging for their nuts, birds chasing each other with glee, and the soft sound of snow falling gently on my face and nose. I was so awe-struck at God's creation that I heard myself gasp out loud. Smiles continually broke upon my face as I laughed at God's creatures enjoying the snow. In the silence, I heard God speaking through his creation. All around me worshiped him and so did I.

But sadly, many people do not like silence. They blare their radios in their cars, their televisions remain on continually in their homes, they are constantly chatting on the telephone, or they have some other noisemaker going all the time. Silence seems to make people uncomfortable. It's almost as if they want to hide behind the noise, as if the silence is going to expose them for who and what they really are. Noise seems to help them keep from facing themselves and from facing God.

But God is in the silence. He speaks to us in the silence, but he also acts in the silence. And it is his acting in judgment in silence that is portrayed in Revelation 8. Far from being an empty silence, the silence that takes place with the opening of the seventh seal that precedes the seven trumpets is full of significance. All the earth is silent before God as creation witnesses the wonder of his war with evil, his judgment of it, and his victory over it.

We can divide this lesson into two sections:

I. The Seventh and Final Seal (Rev. 8:1–5)
II. The First Four Trumpets (Rev. 8:6–13)

I. The Seventh and Final Seal (Rev. 8:1–5)

After a parenthetical section in chapter 7, we return to conclude the opening of the seals. Like the sixth seal, the seventh continues to convey the final judgment. Unlike the first five seals, in which the final judgment is seen as inaugurated, the sixth and seventh seals focus on the consummation of the final judgment.

Revelation 8:1. The only information John himself gives us concerning the seventh seal is that when it was opened there was silence in heaven for half an hour. The Old Testament places silence along with judgment in several passages (Pss. 115:17; 31:17; Isa. 47:5; 1 Sam. 2:9–10). Habakkuk 2:20 says, "The LORD is in his holy temple; let all the earth keep silence before him." And, Zechariah 2:13, in a context of judgment on unbelievers, says, "Be silent, all flesh, before the LORD, for he has roused himself from his holy dwelling." Thus, the seventh seal is most likely a continuation of the depiction of final judgment in the sixth seal, and as the consummation of it, produces silence as the final and awesome wrath of God is witnessed. It is not a fearful silence, but a silence of worship at the almighty judgment of God who has finally vindicated his saints. It is significant that the silence is in heaven, for the judgment comes from God's throne; he alone is worthy to judge. Perhaps John does not give us any more information here about the final judgment because he will do so later in the book. For now it is enough to know that the awesome and vengeful wrath of the Lord on unbelievers comes from God himself on the throne and the response is a silent witness of wonder as he executes his plan.

Revelation 8:2. This verse is a transition from the seven seals to the seven trumpets. John sees seven angels (possibly the same ones that are the seven guardian angels of the seven churches?) standing before God, receiving the seven trumpets from him. Again, "given to them" displays God's sovereignty over history. He alone knows his purposes and plans and the timing of them. He is over all; even the powers of darkness simply serve his bidding.

Revelation 8:3–4. The transition from the seals to the trumpets continues. Another angel came and stood at the altar. We have already seen this altar in Revelation 6:9. It was the place at which the saints who had already died asked God how long it would be until their blood would be vindicated. The incense altar and the altar of burnt offering were two different altars in the earthly temple, but here the two ideas are combined at one altar. The golden censer would hold the incense that would be offered with the prayers of the saints. Incense is always involved with sacrifice in both the Old and New Testaments. Here it was the saints' very lives that were sacrificed and for which they want vindication. We have already discussed earlier, in regard to Revelation 6:9–11, that these prayers are part of God's plan to execute his judgment. The smoke of the incense, with the saints' prayers that have already been portrayed in Revelation 6:9–11, is seen here as mediated by the angel and rising to God, who has already heard the prayers and looked favorably upon them. This vision serves to advance the transition between the seals and the trumpets, showing that the trumpets too are intricately related to the saints' request for vindication in Revelation 6:10.

Revelation 8:5. Now God finally answers the saints' request. And he uses their prayers in part to accomplish his final judgment. It was the censer, associated with the saints' prayers and holding the incense (which represented the saints' sacrifice of their very lives), that was thrown down on the earth in judgment.

The fact that the saints' prayers were bound up with God's plan should greatly encourage us and exhort us to pray. Too often prayer has been seen as optional in the believer's life. But if it is true that our prayers are not passive, but active in the plan of God, we need to be on our knees a lot more than we are. Though the context here is specifically in regard to the prayers of the saints as active in the culmination of God's final judgment on unbelievers, it would not be wrong to apply this idea to prayer for God's purpose and plan in all areas of our lives. God uses our prayers to effect change in the lives of others and change in our own circumstances. We must do the work of prayer though. And it is work. It is purposefully and prayerfully relating all our entreaties before a righteous Savior, while worshiping him and submitting our plans to his. It is aligning our requests with the Word of God, so that we may help bring the kingdom of God to earth.

When the censer was thrown down there were peals of thunder, rumblings, flashes of lightning, and an earthquake. Again, this is an allusion to God's appearance at Mount Sinai in Exodus 19:16–18. This is not the first time we have seen this allusion and it will not be the last. Each one of them is linked with the others by their portrayal of final judgment, but each one escalates the allusion, signifying the increasing severity of the seals, trumpets, and bowls.

- Revelation 4:5: "Flashes of lighting, and rumblings, and peals of thunder."
- Revelation 8:5: "Peals of thunder, rumblings, flashes of lightning, and an earthquake."

- Revelation 11:19: "Flashes of lightning, rumblings, peals of thunder, an earthquake, and heavy hail."
- Revelation 16:18–21: "Flashes of lightning, rumblings, peals of thunder and a great earthquake such as there had never been . . . and great hailstones, about one hundred pounds each."

Old Testament Background to Revelation 8:3–5. Ezekiel 10:1–7: "Fill your hands with burning coals from between the cherubim, and scatter them over the city."

II. The First Four Trumpets (Rev. 8:6–13)

The seven trumpets should not be seen as following the seven seals chronologically, as is evident from the fact that the sixth and seventh seals have already described the final judgment. Hopefully, the following chart will prove helpful:

Table 7.1 The Seven Seals and Trumpets

TEMPORALLY PARALLEL (PRECEDE FINAL JUDGMENT/CHURCH AGE)	TEMPORALLY PARALLEL (FINAL JUDGMENT)
The First–Fifth Seals	The Sixth–Seventh Seals
Focus: Tribulation of believers	Focus: Answer to saints' plea (Rev. 6:10)
The First–Sixth Trumpets	The Seventh Trumpet
Focus: Judgment of unbelievers	Focus: Answer to saints' plea (Rev. 6:10)

Revelation 8:6. This verse picks up on Revelation 8:2, continuing the vision of the seven angels that had been given the trumpets. Trumpets in the Old Testament are associated with judgment and salvation, calling God's people together, and the enthronement of a king. In the New Testament, they are associated with the second coming of Christ. The trumpets in Revelation announce judgment upon unbelievers and salvation upon believers because Christ has been enthroned as King. In the Old Testament story of Joshua and the Israelites fighting at the

battle of Jericho, we see several parallels with Revelation, both connoting a holy war of God. At Jericho, God commanded seven priests to bear seven trumpets and on the seventh day to blow the trumpets as the people marched around Jericho. They were to make a longer blow immediately preceding the fall of the walls of Jericho in order to inform the people of the time to shout with a great shout. Just as there had been silence in heaven during the seventh seal preceding the vision of the trumpets, so too there was silence from the people during the first six days that Joshua and the Israelites marched around Jericho. Yet, the trumpets blew continually to announce impending judgment for Jericho and victory for the Israelites (see Josh. 6). In Exodus 19:6, 13–19, the trumpet also brought Israel together to pledge allegiance to God as king after his deliverance of them from Egypt by way of the plagues. Thus, here in Revelation, the trumpets also act as an announcement of God's judgment and yet salvation of the final Exodus of believers to the new heaven and the new earth.

Revelation 8:7. The first trumpet is the fulfillment of what the Egyptian plague of hail and fire in Exodus 9:22–25 was a type.[1] This plague was "thrown upon the earth." Again, God is sovereign over what is happening in history and is, indeed, issuing the judgments from heaven himself. Yet his judgment in the trumpets is still tempered by his grace. He is still willing that some would come to repentance. For though the trumpets function primarily as judgments against unbelievers, they also function as a warning to unbelievers that will repent, to do so before the time is too late. Only a third of creation is touched, rather than the whole. Yet, unlike the plagues in Egypt that were limited to one country, these plagues are universal. It is most likely that the phrase "burned up" is symbolic for famine, possibly the famine of the third horseman in Revelation 6:5–6. That this is likely is seen from Ezekiel 5:2, 12 and Zechariah 13:8–9. Ezekiel 5:12 interprets the judgment of fire in 5:2 as "plague and famine." Revelation 18:8 also links famine with being "burned up by fire."

1. G. K. Beale, *The Book of Revelation: A Commentary on the Greek Text*, New International Greek Testament Commentary (Grand Rapids: Eerdmans, 1999), 473.

Old Testament Background to Revelation 8:7.

- Exodus 9:22–25: "And the LORD rained hail upon the land of Egypt."
- Ezekiel 5:2, 12: "A third part shall be . . . consumed with famine in your midst."

Revelation 8:8–9. The second trumpet announces judgment on "Babylon," which will be further developed in chapters 11–18. That this is true is drawn from the allusion here to Jeremiah 51:25–27 (see below). These verses also allude to the Egyptian plague in Exodus 7:20 where the Nile is turned to blood. The partial death of sea creatures and the partial destruction of sea commerce again connote famine and points forward to Revelation 18:11–19, where Babylon and all sea commerce are completely destroyed.

Old Testament Background to Revelation 8:8–9.

- Exodus 7:20: "And all the water in the Nile turned into blood."
- Jeremiah 51:24–27: "I will repay Babylon. . . . Behold, I am against you, O destroying mountain."

Revelation 8:10–11. The third trumpet continues the famine judgment and continues to have the Egyptian plague of the Nile turned to blood (Ex. 7:15–25) in the background. The "great star that fell from heaven" seems to allude to Isaiah 14:12–15. If this is the case, the star would be Babylon's representative angel, just as each of the seven churches had representative angels, and would be suffering judgment along with them, just as the angels of the seven churches were addressed as being included in the praise, rebuke, and promises of their respective churches. Also, Jeremiah 9:15 and 23:15 are alluded to here, which point to the star representing an evil angelic representative for an evil kingdom (Babylon) that God is judging. "Wormwood" was an herb that had a very bitter taste and led to poisoning if ingested over a lengthy period of time.[2] So too Babylon has "poisoned" those on earth who have taken part in her idolatry, which has brought God's judgment upon them.

2. Ibid., 479.

Like the other trumpets, this served as a judgment upon unbelievers, a warning for those who would actually turn and repent, and, negatively portrayed, it offers a picture of redemption for God's people as evil is destroyed in the world.

Old Testament Background to Revelation 8:10–11.

- Exodus 7:15–25: "And all the water turned into blood."
- Isaiah 14:12–15: "How you are fallen from heaven, O Day Star, son of Dawn!"
- Jeremiah 9:15: "I will feed this people with bitter food and give them poisonous water to drink."
- Jeremiah 23:15: "I will feed them with bitter food and give them poisoned water to drink."

We would be wise to remember that there is "wormwood" all around us, trying to deceive us into idol worship. Materialism, fantasy, education, beauty, career, fame, and anything else that we idolize in our hearts competes for our worship. We must worship Christ alone and give him our whole heart by immersing ourselves in the pure water of the Word of God rather than the bitter water of wormwood.

Revelation 8:12. The fourth trumpet does not continue the famine judgment. Rather, it alludes to the Egyptian plague of darkness in Exodus 10:21. Like the darkness in Egypt that served as a judgment against idolatry, especially the worship of the sun god, so too the darkness here serves as a judgment against idolatry. The darkness represents all divinely orchestrated events that prove that God is on the throne and that the gods of the idolatrous people are not. These events include those of the first three trumpets. Throughout the Old Testament we see that God interrupts the order of creation in order to signify his judgment upon a people that has interrupted their covenant obligations to him. Even unbelievers are bound to his covenant and are to live by his law, and when they do not, judgment ensues (see especially Genesis 6).

Old Testament Background to Revelation 8:12.

- Jeremiah 31:35–36: "Thus says the LORD who gives the sun for light by day and the fixed order of the moon and the stars for light by night . . . 'If this fixed order departs from before me, then shall the offspring of Israel cease from being a nation before me forever.' "

- Jeremiah 33:20–21; 25–26: "If you can break my covenant with the day and my covenant with the night, so that day and night will not come at their appointed time, then also my covenant with David my servant may be broken so that he shall not have a son to reign on his throne, and my covenant with the Levitical priests my ministers."

As noted in the chart at the beginning of this second division, the judgment of the four trumpets is occurring at different points in time and in various places throughout the church age. The judgment comes both because of the unbelievers' idolatry and because of their persecution of the saints. Thus they are judged not only because they have refused to worship God, but also because they have refused to respect his worshipers.

In the beginning God created the heavens and the earth. Then he created man and gave man laws for his good both to establish and to give order to his life. But man changed God's law and brought judgment upon himself. Thus, God has to undo what he has done. We see this in the first four trumpets. He undoes his creation of light, air, vegetation, sun, moon, stars, sea creatures, and humans (though in a different order in Revelation 8) so that he can usher in a new heaven and a new earth where sin (even the possibility of sin) is no more and God is glorified and worshiped forever.

Revelation 8:13. Now John sees an eagle flying directly overhead. Eagles in the Old Testament are symbolic for destruction (Job 9:26; Jer. 4:13; Hos. 8:1) as well as in the New Testament (Luke 17:37). Yet, the eagle is also used in regard to the Lord himself who protects his people (Ex. 19:4) and sustains them (Isa. 40:31). Here it functions in both ways. While it announces judgment upon unbelievers, it also is associated with God's protection of his people during such tribulation.

I don't know about you, but I have always taken great refuge in knowing that I can take shelter underneath the shadow of my Father's wings. So often, I am like a little bird, full of fear, fragile, shaky, and scared to spread my wings. But he carries me on his own wings and shelters me there. He tends to my needs and loves me despite my unloveliness. There is no judgment there, for his Son justifies me and I soar in light of his salvation.

Three woes are announced in this verse (which are the fifth through seventh trumpets). The fifth through sixth trumpets continue to be judgments occurring during the church age, while the seventh focuses on the final judgment.

We should note that the tribulation that exposes so blatantly the hearts of the wicked also exposes the hearts of the righteous. By God's grace, Job used his sufferings to glorify God and recognized that God was using his trials to forge his character in him. So too the sufferings that we endure are an opportunity for us to expose our hearts of witness and worship to a watching world and to recognize that God is developing Christlike character within us.

CONCLUSION

I love silence because I feel safest in silence. It drowns out all the other voices so that I can hear God's Word speak to my heart. He is my Redeemer, and I know that I am safe under the shelter of his almighty wings. But I know that many of my family and loved ones are not, and it is for them that I pray and seek to offer witness with a life of worship to the Creator of all things.

LESSON 8

Revelation 9

PLEASE USE THE QUESTION paradigm from pages 353–54 as you work through the following. See the introductory comments there that explain each part of the process below in more detail.

- **Pray**.
- **Ponder the Passage**. Read Revelation 9 once a day from different translations for the entire week, looking for its:
  - Point
  - Persons
  - Patterns
  - Persons of the Trinity
  - Puzzling Parts
- **Put It in Perspective**.
  - Place in Scripture
  - Passages from Other Parts of Scripture

1. Based on your observations of the text, what is the basic content of this passage? Try to summarize it in your own words, using a sentence or two.
2. Compare Revelation 9:1 with 8:10 and 9:11. Who is "a star fallen from heaven to earth"? What was he given? Who gave it to him? Why is this significant?

3. What environment does the imagery in Revelation 9:2 convey? Where is the smoke coming from? What does this tell us about the smoke?

4. Look up "scorpion" in a dictionary or other resource. What do you learn, especially about their tails?

5. What were the "locusts" told not to harm and what were they told to harm (Rev. 9:4)? Were they limited in their ability to harm (Rev. 9:5)?

6. What do you think Revelation 9:6 means?

7. What does the imagery in Revelation 9:7–10 convey about the "locusts"?

8. Who is king over them (Rev. 9:11)? How does this help interpret Revelation 9:1? Look up Abaddon and Apollyon in a Bible resource. What do these names mean? Who do you think this king is?

9. Compare Revelation 7:1 with 9:14. Are the "four bound angels" the same as "the four winds of the earth"?

10. What does Revelation 9:15 tell us about God's sovereignty?

11. Compare Revelation 9:16 with 5:11. In light of this, are the numbers here to be taken literally or figuratively?

12. What does the imagery in Revelation 9:17 convey about "the horses and horsemen"?

13. What are the "three plagues" in Revelation 9:18 as defined in the verse itself? Are these plagues limited? What does this tell us with regard to whether this is part of the final judgment or not?

14. If the "horses" portray demonic spirits, and their power is in their mouths, do you think it has any connection with the false teachings of the Nicolaitans (Rev. 2:15) and Jezebel (Rev. 2:20)?

15. Compare Exodus 7:23; 8:15, 19, 32; 9:7, 12, 35; 10:20; 11:10; 14:8 with Revelation 9:20–21. Who hardens the heart, God or man? Why? What does this tell us about God?

16. What sin is/sins are spoken of in Revelation 9:20? In 9:21?

- **Principles and Points of Application.**
1. Read Revelation 9:6. This is the opposite of what we find in our culture today. Most people don't seek death; instead, we see anti-aging techniques, cosmetic surgery, and other attempts to preserve youth on the rise. There is a fear of death in our culture. What is your view of death? What emotions does it conjure up within you? Pray and ask God to help you release the fear of death to him, the one who has conquered death for you.
2. Read 9:20–21. Ask the Lord to reveal to your heart today what "works of your hands" or idolatry you need to repent of (to answer this, ask yourself what you are putting your sense of self-worth or security in). With what words/actions are you "killing people"? In what horoscopes/modern-day spirituality are you putting hope? What sexual temptations are you facing or filling your mind with through the media? What time, things, esteem, are you "stealing" from others? Repent of these and then walk in the freedom of forgiveness of sin today.

NOTES FOR REVELATION 9

Aim: Ponder the aim of this lesson concerning our:

Mind: What do we need to know from this passage in Scripture?

That the fifth and sixth trumpets of John's vision continue to bring God's justice and righteousness on earth.

Heart: How does what we learn from this passage affect our internal relationship with the Lord?

It prepares us to be kingdom disciples who help carry out God's justice and righteousness on earth.

Hands: How does what we learn from this passage translate into action for God's kingdom?

It enables us to:

1. Gain a biblical view of death so that we will not fear it, but look forward to being present with the Lord, and to help others who fear death gain this perspective as well.
2. Repent of "the works of our hands" that are not pleasing to the Lord, of idolatry, of murdering people with our words, of putting hope in luck or chance, of sexual immorality, or of stealing people's time or resources, and then to walk in the freedom of forgiveness of sin while leading others to do the same.

INTRODUCTION

Tears stung the back of my eyes as the worship music played on the car CD player. It took an hour to drive to the home of some family members whose household appeared to be running smoothly but was shrouded in the darkness of deception. Finally, I couldn't hold the tears back any longer. They came pouring down my cheeks as I was reminded that some in my family did not join me in the witness and worship of Jesus Christ. Deceived, they had embraced a different way of life and were trying to find happiness in it. I was devastated, heartbroken, wanting them to see the truth. I desperately want all of my family in heaven with me. It is excruciatingly difficult to bear the fact that they may not be. My heart was not filled with judgment, but with pity. I cried out, "How long?"—not for vindication, but for God's mercy to fall upon them and open up their eyes so that they could see.

Around that time I had a conversation with another family member who was hardened toward the gospel. Rather than leaving grieved from that conversation, though, I left angry. I was angry because my arguments seemed to make so little sense to them, and yet I thought that I had spoken so plainly, but was so misunderstood. I was forgetting that I was simply a messenger and had to allow the Author of the message to open up the other person's heart. I was forgetting that the gospel comes across as foolishness to those who don't believe. As the days passed, my heart turned from anger to sadness, sadness that some of my loved ones are so hardened toward the gospel.

It is difficult for me to accept the possibility that not all of my family will be in heaven. Yet the Bible makes it clear that not all are saved. I am not writing the story, God is, and he has written hardened hearts into his plan. Indeed, he uses them to glorify himself. Revelation 9 addresses people who have a hard time understanding and accepting hardened hearts.

We can divide this lesson into two sections:

I. The Fifth Trumpet (Rev. 9:1–12)
II. The Sixth Trumpet (Rev. 9:13–21)

I. The Fifth Trumpet (Rev. 9:1–12)

John continues to describe the vision of the angels blowing their trumpets. Again, the fifth through sixth trumpets are not the final judgment, but precede it in the time of the church age.

Table 8.1 The Seven Seals and Trumpets

TEMPORALLY PARALLEL (PRECEDE FINAL JUDGMENT/CHURCH AGE)	TEMPORALLY PARALLEL (FINAL JUDGMENT)
The First–Fifth Seals	The Sixth–Seventh Seals
Focus: Tribulation of believers	Focus: Answer to saints' plea (Rev. 6:10)
The First–Sixth Trumpets	The Seventh Trumpet
Focus: Judgment of unbelievers	Focus: Answer to saints' plea (Rev. 6:10)

Revelation 9:1. In light of our interpretation of Revelation 8:10 ("a great star fell from heaven" being a sinful angel that represented sinful humanity and was judged alongside them), this "star fallen from heaven to earth" is the same. This angel did not hold the key to the shaft of

119

the bottomless pit, which is the realm of Satan and his demons. Rather, Christ gave it to him. Thus, the one who won the keys of Death and Hades (Rev. 1:18) by his death on the cross, now purposefully gives them to this evil angel, who is none other than Satan himself.[1] Though Satan and his demons still have power on this earth, their power is limited, controlled by the Sovereign God and used for his greater plan.

It is a great encouragement for us to realize that God gives Satan his power in this world; it is under God's control. We do not have to be paralyzed by fear of the darkness because we have the light and the light has already overcome the darkness (John 8:12). When Satan and his powers seem prevalent around you, hold fast to the one who has the keys to his realm. If God has the power to unleash evil, he also has the power to leash it and lock it up, and indeed, one day he will do just that—for all of eternity.

Revelation 9:2. Now the smoke from the bottomless pit (the realm of satanic power), which symbolizes judgment, comes to earth. No longer is the judgment confined to the demonic realm, but now it is unleashed on unbelievers. The darkness caused by smoke anticipates that the form of judgment will be deception among the people, instigated by the demons.[2] The imagery is drawn from Exodus 10:15, the Egyptian plague of locusts, and from Joel 2:10, 31, and 3:15 where locusts are also used to signify judgment.

Old Testament Background to Revelation 9:2.
- Exodus 10:15: "[The locusts] covered the whole land so that the land was darkened."
- Joel 2:10, 31; 3:15: "Sun and moon are darkened, and the stars withdraw their shining."

Revelation 9:3. "Then from the smoke came locusts on the earth" is based on Exodus 10:12, which involves the Lord's instructions to Moses to begin the locust plague. Again, as in Revelation 9:1 when the angel

---

1. Dennis E. Johnson, *The Triumph of the Lamb: A Commentary on Revelation* (Phillipsburg, NJ: P&R Publishing, 2001), 148.

2. G. K. Beale, *The Book of Revelation: A Commentary on the Greek Text*, New International Greek Testament Commentary (Grand Rapids: Eerdmans, 1999), 494.

was "given the key to the shaft," so here God gives the locusts, which were literal in Egypt but here represent demons, power. They are not free to deceive as they please; they are agents in the hand of a sovereign God who allows temporary deception for his eternal sovereign purposes. The power of the locusts was like that of the scorpions of earth, which gave out a poison when it struck its prey. They would hide during the day and seek their prey in the darkness of the night. So too, the demonic forces poison (deceive) their prey (unbelievers) in the dark (unexpected times and places).

Our world has taken the demonic and caricatured it as the witches, ghosts, wizards, devils, and such that we see portrayed in the media and literature. These are a great example of the demonic masquerading as that which is silly, fictional, and not to be taken seriously. But all the while they are deceiving hearts and minds. We must be very guarded toward deception and run the influences in our lives through a biblical grid so that we do not believe the lies of Satan. How many of us have been deceived that good looks gratify, that grand homes glorify, that a husband and children define us, that a career marks us, and that acclaim awards us, only to find out that it all ends, and we are left deceived by that which promised so much. The only one who can lead us to the truth is Truth himself. Jesus is the Way, the Truth, and the Life (John 14:6), and no one escapes darkness or deceit apart from him.

Revelation 9:4. Evidently God did not want any more of the "grass," "green plants" or "trees" harmed, as the first trumpet had already harmed a third of them. Here, unlike the locust plague in Exodus (Rev. 10:15), the focus is on man, but not all men, only those who are not sealed by God with the Holy Spirit. Some are sealed but do not yet know it. The Lord will use the deception to actually lead them to the truth. But the majority will remain hardened in their sin and will be reminded that they are hopelessly lost and separated from God as they are shrouded by darkness.

Too often evangelicals have been known to be judgmental of men and women living in sin. We should be quick to remember that they live under fear and hopelessness as they are separated from God. Let this prick our hearts and bring us to our knees to pray for those in our families, neighborhoods, and even our churches, who need the light of Christ. Let your heart be tender toward them, as they are living in darkness.

Revelation 9:5. Again, as in the sections on the earlier trumpets, we see God's mercy even in his judgment as he limits the deception, here portrayed in time (five months). The locusts were allowed to torment, but not to kill (just as a scorpion's sting cannot kill). This would be mostly spiritual and mental torment of the soul, something we don't see,[3] and another reason to be prayerful and merciful toward unbelievers in our own lives.

Revelation 9:6. We are reminded of the sixth seal here where unbelievers cry out for the mountains and rocks to fall on them to hide them from the face of God and his wrath. So here people will seek death, but part of their torment is that they will not be able to die. Their fear of death will keep them from inducing death upon themselves. Like the Egyptians who were hardened by the plagues, so here unbelievers are not brought to repentance by the plague, but are further hardened toward God. They continue serving their own gods despite their anguish. In contrast, we as believers do not have to fear death. Sealed by the Holy Spirit, we know where we are headed. Death has lost its sting and victory in our lives. For us, it is a gateway to glory where we gain our glorious inheritance in Christ Jesus.

Revelation 9:7–9. John now continues his allusion to Joel 2, with Exodus 10 in the background, along with an allusion to Jeremiah 51:14, 27. All of these serve to strengthen the portrayal of primarily spiritual and mental anguish coming upon the unbelievers for their idolatry. The heightened portrayal of the demons, characterized by locusts and horses, serves to strengthen the idea of a battle between God and Satan.

Old Testament Background to Revelation 9:7–9.

- Exodus 10:12ff: "The locusts, so that they may come upon the land."
- Jeremiah 51:14, 27: "As many as locusts," "bring up horses like locusts."
- Joel 2:4ff: "[The locusts'] appearance is like that of horses."

3. Vern S. Poythress, *The Returning King: A Guide to the Book of Revelation* (Phillipsburg, NJ: P&R Publishing, 2000), 123–24.

Revelation 9:10. The metaphor of scorpions is now added to portray that the locusts do indeed have power to hurt people, but again, that power is limited. Just as a scorpion's sting does not lead to its victim's death, neither do the demons inflict death on unbelievers. Ironically, though, the unbelievers would rather have death than the misery of prolonged spiritual and mental anguish.

Old Testament Background to Revelation 9:10. Jeremiah 8:16–18: "Horses . . . come and devour . . . sending among you serpents . . . they shall bite you."

Revelation 9:11. The king of these demons is the "star fallen from heaven to earth" who was given the key to the shaft of the bottomless pit (Rev. 9:1); he is an evil angel that represents unbelievers and is judged alongside them. The Hebrew Abaddon means "Destruction" and the Greek Apollyon means "Destroyer." Thus, this angel is either Satan or an evil representation of Satan.[4] Either way, the names define his plan; he seeks to kill and destroy. Contrary to our Lord and Savior Jesus Christ, who seeks to save his children, Satan seeks to destroy his. He has no ability to hold out hope that a future with him will be glorious; rather, he stands condemned and wants to take others to his condemnation with him.

Revelation 9:12. A succinct statement is here given to transition us from the fifth trumpet to the sixth and, later, the seventh one. Again, this does not convey the chronological time of the plagues, but the order in which John sees the visions. Thus, John is not saying that the events associated with the fifth trumpet have already occurred in history, but just that he has seen the vision in order to write it down for the edification of the church.

II. The Sixth Trumpet (Rev. 9:13–21)

Revelation 9:13–14. Verse 13 continues the development in Revelation 8:3–5 of the saints' prayer in Revelation 6:10–11. Thus, the voice from "the four horns of the golden altar before God" may be Christ's voice (see Rev. 6:6), or it may be an angel's voice (see Rev. 16:7). The

4. Beale, *The Book of Revelation*, 503.

sixth trumpet then is part of God's answer to the saints' plea for vindication, although it is not the consummate fulfillment of their request, which will come at the final judgment.

The sixth angel is told to "release the four angels who are bound at the great river Euphrates." Like the four angels standing at the four corners of the earth, holding back the four winds of the earth (Rev. 7:1), which were the four horsemen of the first four seals (Rev. 6:1–8), so here the same evil angels are portrayed as bound by God's timing at the Euphrates, and are to now be released. In the Old Testament, much prophecy spoke of a great army that would come from the north, beyond the Euphrates River, in order to judge Israel and surrounding pagan nations (Isa. 7:20). Here the four angels would come to inflict unbelievers.

Old Testament Background to Revelation 9:13–14. Jeremiah 46:4, 22–23: "Harness the horses . . . a serpent . . . more numerous than locusts."

Revelation 9:15–16. The details of this verse convey God's sovereignty. Not one moment of time is out of his control. He knows the very hour of the day of the month of the year that he has planned for this plague. And he limits the plague to a third of mankind. The numbers of evil forces are not to be taken literally, but imply a number too great to count (see Rev. 5:11 for the same intended meaning).

Revelation 9:17. Now John describes the horses and horsemen in his vision. The metaphors convey how dreadful, destructive, and fierce they are. "Fire" and "sulfur" are repeated twice for emphasis of their destruction. Though this language is used in Revelation 14:10; 19:20; 20:10; and 21:8 with regard to the final judgment, here it still precedes the final judgment, as is evident from Revelation 9:15 and 18, which limits its effect on mankind.

Revelation 9:18. The three plagues are defined in the verse as "fire," "smoke," and "sulfur." They literally kill a third of mankind. Again, the plagues are limited in power by the sovereign hand of God. It is not yet time for the final judgment. In his mercy, God still leaves time for repentance.

Old Testament Background to Revelation 9:18.

- Genesis 19:24, 28: "The LORD rained on Sodom and Gomorrah sulfur and fire."
- Deuteronomy 29:22–23: "An overthrow like that of Sodom and Gomorrah."

Revelation 9:19. The demons portrayed as "horses" are evidently the means that the evil angels use to kill a third of mankind. Like the fifth trumpet, the sixth could also deceive spiritually and mentally, but as we have seen, it also intensifies by involving literal death. The power of their mouths probably relates to the false teachers that were prevalent in some of the churches in John's day through the church age. The point of this verse is to emphasize the power that the "horses" have to kill by the comparison of them with serpents. The horses are thus identified with Satan, the ancient serpent, and the one to deceive mankind in the beginning.[5] Thus, Satan continues to destroy and deceive man, leading to both physical and spiritual death.

Revelation 9:20–21. Again, the plague did not result in repentance among the rest of mankind who witnessed it. Like the Egyptians after each plague in Exodus, so too we see that here the unbelievers are further hardened in their hearts against God. They continue their idolatry, which can do nothing for them, and find no room for repentance in their lives. Yet, as has been noted before, there will be some who come to salvation during this time, as was the case in Egypt as well, thus displaying God's mercy in the midst of judgment.

CONCLUSION

The hearts of some of my family members have not changed for years. I am still hopeful and prayerful that God will "grant them repentance leading to a knowledge of the truth, and they may come to their senses and escape from the snare of the devil, after being

5. Ibid., 514.

captured by him to do his will" (2 Tim. 2:26). But I have also surrendered their salvation to the Lord. I do not understand his plan,
but I trust it and I know that it will be for his glory. I also know
that my role is to be a witness for Christ, one who worships him
with my whole life. I hope and pray that the relationship with my
unbelieving family members is such that I am the first person they
call if they want to know more about Jesus.

LESSON 9

Revelation 10

Please use the question paradigm from pages 353–54 as you work through the following. See the introductory comments there that explain each part of the process below in more detail.

- **Pray.**
- **Ponder the Passage.** Read Revelation 10 once a day from different translations for the entire week, looking for its:
  - Point
  - Persons
  - Patterns
  - Persons of the Trinity
  - Puzzling Parts
- **Put It in Perspective.**
  - Place in Scripture
  - Passages from Other Parts of Scripture

1. Based on your observations of the text, what is the basic content of this passage? Try to summarize it in your own words, using a sentence or two.
2. Compare Revelation 1:12–16 and 4:2–3 with Revelation 10:1. Who do you think this angel is? Why?

3. Compare Revelation 5:1–5 with 10:1–3. What was the scroll identified as in chapter 5 (go back to that lesson if you don't remember)? What do you think the scroll might be identified with here?

4. Look up "thunder" in a concordance. How is it used in Scripture? What do you think it conveys here? How does this relate to the seven seals and seven trumpets? What are some reasons you think it does not need to be written?

5. How does Revelation 10:5–7 reflect a scene in a courtroom? Who stands as witness to whom? What does he witness that the Father has done?

6. Of what will there be "no more delay" (Rev. 10:7)?

7. Look up "mystery" in a concordance. How is it used in Scripture? What do you think the meaning is here?

8. What similarities do you see between Christ in Revelation 5:5, 7, and John in 10:8–9?

9. What three verses speak of Christ standing on the sea and on the land in this chapter? What is John emphasizing by this repetition (Rev. 10:8)?

10. In light of John's commission to prophesy "against many peoples and nations and languages and kings," why would the scroll be bitter after he ingests it (Rev. 10:11)?

11. In light of the contents of the little scroll being from Christ, why would it be as sweet as honey in John's mouth (Rev. 10:11)? See Psalm 119:103.

- **Principles and Points of Application.**

1. Read Revelation 10:5–7. Are you being a witness of what God has done for you by raising your hand in worship to heaven in order to proclaim his faithfulness to his covenant? Spend time today doing so. Pray about someone who needs to hear about Christ and with whom you can share your testimony this week. Remember that it is the Spirit's work to save, not yours.

2. The cost of discipleship comes with bittersweet instruction. As pilgrims on this earth, there is nothing in our lives that is

completely sweet, but there is also nothing in our lives that is completely bitter. The cross of Christ stands as our supreme example; each of us as disciples of Jesus must pick up our own cross. What bittersweet events, relationships, or sufferings is God asking you to "eat" right now? How are you responding? Take and eat it this week, thanking God for the sweet and the bitter and asking him to help you receive his grace and power, which he makes available to you to carry you through the bitter.

NOTES FOR REVELATION 10

Aim: Ponder the aim of this lesson concerning our:

Mind: What do we need to know from this passage in Scripture?

Just as John was asked to share in Christ's kingship and in his sufferings as a prophet, so too believers today are asked to share in Christ's kingship and in his sufferings.

Heart: How does what we learn from this passage affect our internal relationship with the Lord?

It prepares us to be kingdom disciples who share in Christ's kingship and in his sufferings.

Hands: How does what we learn from this passage translate into action for God's kingdom?

It enables us to:

1. Place Christ on the throne of our hearts as King of kings and Lord of lords and to lead others to do the same, recognizing the Spirit's enabling to do so.
2. Taste the sweetness of God's Word by studying and meditating on it each day, relying on the Spirit to teach us.

3. Accept suffering in our lives as a gift that allows us to more closely identify with the suffering of Christ and to lead others to view suffering in this light as well.

4. Grow content with grace and suffering coexisting in our lives by the power of the Holy Spirit.

5. Share God's word of judgment and salvation with others, relying on the Spirit's power and praying that he will open up their hearts to accept Christ by faith.

INTRODUCTION

I have always been a romantic at heart. Though I was never one to dream about my wedding day and have it all planned out to the very color of the roses and the design of the cake, I did always dream of being married. But the dream of marriage and the reality of marriage are two different things. I am not sure I could have been any better prepared for marriage, though. My husband and I were twenty-nine and twenty-four respectively when we married, so no one thought that we were too young. We went through months of premarital counseling, so no one thought that we were not prepared. We had somewhat similar backgrounds and were both believers, so no one thought of us as being unequally yoked or mismatched.

So, in the first several years of marriage, I experienced the truth that sinners, not glorified saints, make wedding vows. When my husband was in a bad mood, I didn't like it. It seemed unfair that he should ruin my good mood that day (of course, I shouldn't have let him!). When I left for work and my husband was still in bed because he had quit his job (which I had been in favor of him doing!), and was looking for a new one, I didn't like it because I didn't think he was living up to his responsibility to provide for us. When my husband got sick on a rare occasion, I didn't like it (as if he could help it!), because he was grouchy and not a help to me around the house. On the flip side, when my husband was in a good mood, I loved it because his mood lifted my own. When my husband was not sick (which is most of the time), he was a tremendous help around the house. When he left for work each day and I stayed at home with the children, I felt tremendously blessed to have him as my provider. When my husband's job promotion took us out of state, I loved the thought of a new adventure. I have learned through marriage the difficult lesson that I am to love my husband not just when it is to my advantage, but also when it is to my disadvantage. Identifying with and loving my husband has been difficult at times, but it has been sweet and rewarding as well.

Since the church is compared to the bride of Christ, we know that God has given us marriage as an analogy of Christ's love for the church. We will not only share in Christ's glory; we will also share in his cross. As his bride, we too will be despised and rejected by men. We too will feel at times like a lamb being led to the slaughter. We too will be ridiculed and disbelieved. We too will face pain and suffering. But we will also overcome. We too will gain a crown of kingship. We too will partake in the benefits of being daughters of the King. So while the suffering is difficult, the salvation is sweet, and it preserves us until we reach the presence of our heavenly Bridegroom.

Revelation 10 speaks to this relationship between suffering and salvation and of our identification with Jesus Christ as his bride. Like premarital counseling, it tells us that things will be sweet and bitter if we unite with him as our Lord and Savior. But just as I learned the truth of premarital counseling only after I was married, so too we learn the sweetness and bitterness of God's Word only after we ingest it and identify with it.

We can divide this lesson into two sections:

I. The Mighty Angel Announces No More Delay of Judgment (Rev. 10:1–7)

II. The Mighty Angel Instructs John to Eat the Little Scroll (Rev. 10:8–11)

I. The Mighty Angel Announces No More Delay of Judgment (Rev. 10:1–7)

Just as there was a parenthetical section between the opening of the sixth and seventh seals, so too there is a parenthetical section between

131

the blowing of the sixth and seventh trumpets. Each of them contains two different visions. The sections are not to be taken chronologically, but rather as temporally parallel with the first five seals and first six trumpets during the church age. The previous parenthetical section (Rev. 7:1–17) revealed that believers are sealed during the time of the first five seals and first six trumpets. Here, the section reveals how the unbelievers persecute the believers and how this lays the basis for their judgment. Thus, as has already been noted in previous lessons, the trumpets continue to answer the saints' plea for vindication of their persecutors.

Revelation 10:1. John sees "another mighty angel." Some commentators believe that this angel is meant to reflect God's majesty. Others believe that this is the Angel of the LORD (as in the Old Testament) and thus is to be identified as Jesus Christ himself. They defend this belief by the glorious description given here, which differs from how other angels have thus far been described in the book, and with the background of Daniel 7:13 and Ezekiel 1:26–28. First, the angel is "wrapped in a cloud," which in the Old Testament only refers to God. Second, Revelation 1:7 speaks of one "coming with the clouds," which is identified in Revelation 1:13 as one "like a Son of Man." In Ezekiel 1:26–28 the glory of the Lord is described in part by likening its radiance to a rainbow. In Revelation 4:3 (the only other place "rainbow" occurs in the New Testament), we see that the rainbow is around the throne of God, another indication that this "mighty angel" is God himself. As noted in the lesson on chapter 4, we saw that the rainbow also alluded to God's covenant with Noah. Third, the phrase "his face was like the sun" recalls Revelation 1:16, and "his legs like pillars of fire" recalls Revelation 1:15. In chapter 1, though, Christ's feet are described as "bronze refined as in a furnace." John changes the wording here because his purpose, as we will see, is to encourage God's people that he is with them during their time of tribulation at the hands of the ungodly on earth. Thus, the imagery of the pillar that led the Israelites during the wilderness journey to the Promised Land is used to reinforce this encouragement and promise. As the pillar went before the Israelites to protect and to guide, so too Christ goes before his people to protect them and guide them during the church's wilderness journey to the Promised Land.[1]

Old Testament Background to Revelation 10:1.

- Ezekiel 1:26–28: "Like the appearance of the bow that is in the cloud."
- Daniel 7:13: "With the clouds of heaven came one like a son of man."

Revelation 10:2. Christ has a little scroll open in his hand. The last scroll that we saw was in Revelation 5:1, which was in the right hand of God the Father. The only one found worthy to take that scroll and open it was Christ, who was able to do so because of his death, resurrection, and exaltation, which signified that he had now been crowned as King of kings and Lord of lords and had the authority to reign over all of God's creation. Christ setting his right foot on the sea and the left foot on the land, as well as having the rainbow over his head (Rev. 10:1), further conveys this in Revelation 10:2. The scroll in chapter 5, as we discussed earlier, signified God's plan of judgment and salvation that was inaugurated at Christ's cross and will be consummated at Christ's coming.

In light of the context of this passage, which is to encourage believers in the midst of their persecution by showing them the relationship they have with their persecutors during the church age, this little scroll is almost identical to Christ's, but on a lesser scale. For believers too are to gain their crowns by way of their crosses and thus unleash judgment upon unbelievers and salvation upon themselves. The scroll in chapter 5 was also identified as a covenantal promise of Christ's inheritance, just as here it is a covenantal promise of all that believers will inherit in Christ if they persevere through persecution.[2]

---

1. Beale believes this angel is to be identified with Christ himself, while Morris, Johnson, Poythress, and Mounce believe this is merely a mighty angel who reflects God's majesty. See G. K. Beale, *The Book of Revelation: A Commentary on the Greek Text*, New International Greek Testament Commentary (Grand Rapids: Eerdmans, 1999), 522–24 for the view outlined above.

2. Ibid., 527–28, 545.

Revelation 10:3–4. With his right foot on the sea and his left foot on the land, connoting his divine rulership granted him by his Father, Christ now calls out with a loud voice like a lion roaring. This further connects this passage with Revelation 5, where Christ was named the Lion of the tribe of Judah (Rev. 5:5) who could open the scroll. The Old Testament also likens God's voice to the roar of a lion (Isa. 31:4; Amos 3:8; Hos 11:10). When he called out, the seven thunders sounded. It is usual for thunder to be connected with the voice of God, as we have seen in the Sinai allusions throughout the book and in the summaries of final judgment (Rev. 4:5; 8:5; 11:19; 16:18–21). "Thunder" usually conveys God's judgment in the Old Testament (Ex 9:23–34). Christ's voice, associated with the seven thunders, is most likely declaring another series of judgments parallel with those of the seals, trumpets, and bowls (see the four "sevenfold" plagues in Lev. 26:18, 21, 24, 28), but for whatever reason is not to be written down.[3] Perhaps this is because enough has been written down in the sections dealing with the seals and trumpets concerning the judgments against unbelievers during the church age. Writing about another set of judgments would delay the purpose of this parenthetical section, which is to show the relationship between the unbelievers and believers during the church age. The unbelievers are judged because they persecute God's people.

Old Testament Background to Revelation 10:2. Psalm 29:1–9: "The God of glory thunders."

Revelation 10:5–7. Now John sees Christ raise his right hand to heaven and swear by God the Father that there would be no more delay, but the seventh trumpet would usher in the final judgment, fulfilling God's sovereign plan, just as he had revealed through the prophets in his Word. Thus, Christ stands boldly on earth before his Father in heaven, pointing up to him with his right hand, in order to be a witness of his Father's faithfulness to complete his covenant.[4] This includes not just his covenant with man, but the covenant that the Father, Son, and Holy Spirit had among themselves before the creation of the world concern-

3. Ibid., 536.
4. Ibid., 537.

ing judgment and salvation. His stance on earth before the Father also conveys that the Father has transferred his right of sovereignty, rule, and judgment to his Son.

This imagery should conjure up awe in our hearts, provide encouragement for us, and give us an example to follow. How often can it be said of us that we boldly raise our hands in worship to God the Father and God the Son, testifying of their faithfulness to us in keeping their covenant promises? In the midst of a dark world, we are to shine boldly as lights of witness and worship, pointing others to the Lamb of God who now stands as Warrior and King over the created earth. Though his stance is invisible now, one day it will be visible for all to see "so that at the name of Jesus every knee [will] bow, in heaven and on earth and under the earth, and every tongue confess that Jesus Christ is Lord, to the glory of God the Father" (Phil. 2:9–11).

The fact that there will be "no delay" conveys God's sovereignty over events in history. He waits on nothing or no one. When his time to bring his sovereign decree to pass arrives, he ushers it in without delay. That this is recorded here in chapter 10 of the book is another validation that Revelation is not recording events in chronological order, but rather in the order that John receives the visions.

The "mystery of God" points back to Revelation 6:11, which defines this mystery as God's purpose of the saints' persecution being the grounds for the unbelievers' judgment at the final judgment. That this was inaugurated at Christ's first coming is clear from Romans 16:25–26, where we are told that "the mystery . . . has now been disclosed and through the prophetic writings has been made known to all nations . . . to bring about the obedience of faith." Included in this mystery is the irony that God defeated Satan by the death of his own Son, and would likewise defeat unbelievers with the death of his saints.

Old Testament Background to Revelation 10:5–7.

- Deuteronomy 32:34–35: "Sealed up in my treasuries? Vengeance is mine and recompense."
- Deuteronomy 32:40: "For I lift up my hand to heaven and swear, 'As I live forever.'"

- Daniel 12:7: "He raised his right hand and his left hand toward heaven and swore."
- Amos 3:7: "Without revealing his secret to his servants the prophets."

That the way to glory is through the cross has always perplexed Christians. The irony that the King of kings would arrive as a baby wrapped in swaddling cloths and lying in a manger is mysterious to us. What kind of God is this who does things so contrary to the way of man? He is Alpha, beyond our understanding, Creator, Deliverer, eternal, forgiving, gracious, holy, intentional, judge, King, Lord, mighty and majestic, has a name which is above all other names, omnipotent, worthy of praise, the one who leads us beside quiet waters, Redeemer, Savior, Truth; he unravels his plan in his timing; he is victorious, Warrior, exalted over all, yields to no one, and reigns from Mount Zion.

II. The Mighty Angel Instructs John to Eat the Little Scroll (Rev. 10:8–11)

Revelation 10:8. Just as the Lamb of God was worthy to go and take the scroll from the Father's hand (Rev. 5:7–8), so too one who is worthy (as a witness of Christ) is beckoned to take the little scroll from Christ's hand. For the third time John reminds us of Christ's sovereignty by stating that he is "standing on the sea and on the land." Thus John, as representative of all believers, shares in Christ's rule, and will also share in his sufferings, as all believers do as well.

Revelation 10:9–10. So John willingly obeys and takes the scroll, but when he does so he is given a very important message for the entire church. The contents of the scroll were to be eaten, and this would make his stomach bitter but his mouth sweet. Again, John willingly obeys, and what Christ said proves true. This clearly affirms John as a prophet, as seen in the allusion to Ezekiel's own commission (Ezek. 2:8–3:3). This has already been seen in Revelation 1:10 and 4:1–2. Ezekiel's message, like John's, is primarily one of judgment, but also of salvation. The sweet taste of the scroll in John's mouth conveys that God's spoken Word is sweet to those who obey it and it is a life-giving power to those who proclaim it. But John is also to ingest God's Word of judgment, which means he is to identify closely with it and proclaim it. The hardened hearts that he would face would be bitter for him. The persecution that he would face would also be bitter for him. But the grace of God would remain sweet through the bitterness. Thus, the sweetness in his mouth and the bitterness in his stomach would coexist, both pushing him toward the witness and worship of God.

Old Testament Background to Revelation 10:9–10.

- Ezekiel 2:8–3:3: "Open your mouth and eat what I give you . . . a scroll . . . sweet as honey."
- Psalm 119:103: "How sweet are your words to my taste, sweeter than honey to my mouth!"

As we are in God's Word and ingest it and make it a part of our lives and our hearts, we too can proclaim with the psalmist and with John that his words are like honey to our mouths. His Word will carry us through the journey of this world that is filled with so much sorrow in our own lives. Not just the sorrow of suffering that comes through physical pain, unemployment, miscarriage, infertility, broken marriages, rebellious children, the death of loved ones, and so on, but also the pain of people rejecting Christ and thus, rejecting us. This is the suffering of seeing hardened hearts toward the one we so magnify and love.

Revelation 10:11. Now that John has been reaffirmed as a prophet, he is again commissioned to his task. The sense here is that John must prophesy "against" unbelievers throughout the world as well as against believers who are tempted to compromise their witness and worship within the church. This prophecy does not just contain future judgment, but judgments all throughout the church age. What would John say to us in our church today? Are we standing firm as witnesses and worshipers of Christ, or are we compromising our witness and worship of him? Is our church flavored with more of the world or more with the Lord, Jesus Christ, King of kings, the one who is worthy of our allegiance and praise?

CONCLUSION

I am still a romantic at heart, though the reality of marriage has adjusted this a bit. I still wonder at God's plan of using the sufferings in marriage to make the bond of marriage stronger. It is difficult enough to endure my own sufferings, much less those of my spouse. Yet it is this identification with the sweet and suffering aspects of my husband's life that strengthens the bond between us. So too it is as we identify with the sufferings of our Lord and Savior Jesus Christ that we are also able to partake in his glory. And we too can stand and point our right hand up at him as a witness that he has been faithful to fulfill the covenant that he has made with us, "that he gave himself up for us, that he might sanctify us, having cleansed us by the washing of water with the word, so that he might present us to himself in splendor, without spot or wrinkle or any such thing, that we might be holy and without blemish" (Eph. 5:25–27).

Revelation 11

PLEASE USE THE QUESTION paradigm from pages 353–54 as you work through the following. See the introductory comments there that explain each part of the process below in more detail.

- **Pray**.
- **Ponder the Passage**. Read Revelation 11 once a day from different translations for the entire week, looking for its:
  - Point
  - Persons
  - Patterns
  - Persons of the Trinity
  - Puzzling Parts
- **Put It in Perspective**.
  - Place in Scripture
  - Passages from Other Parts of Scripture

1. Based on your observations of the text, what is the basic content of this passage? Try to summarize it in your own words, using a sentence or two.
2. Read Micah 2:5. What does the "measuring line" mean in this passage? What do you think it means in Revelation 11:1?

3. Look up 2 Corinthians 6:16; Revelation 16:7; 6:9–10; Matthew 21:39; and 1 Peter 2:5. In light of these verses, to whom do you think "temple of God," "altar," "those who worship there," "the court outside the temple," and "the holy city" refers (Rev. 11:1–2)?

4. Now compare Revelation 7:3 with 11:1–2. Do you think the meaning behind "sealing" and "measuring" is the same?

5. Look up Deuteronomy 19:15. What do you think the significance of "two witnesses" is in Revelation 11:3? Why would they be clothed in sackcloth (think about the message they proclaim and why it was bitter for John in 10:10)?

6. Who do you think the "two witnesses" are? Compare Revelation 11:7 with 13:7. Whose lives and ministries serve as a pattern for them (look up Mark 9:4)?

7. How does Revelation 11:4 define the two witnesses? Where else in the book have we seen "lampstands" and to what did it refer (see Rev. 1:19)?

8. Compare what comes from Christ's mouth in Revelation 1:16 with 11:5? What does "fire pours from their mouth and consumes their foes" mean in light of this? (See also John's message of prophecy in Revelation 10:11.)

9. Look up 2 Kings 11 and Exodus 7:17–25. To whom does Revelation 11:6 allude?

10. Compare Revelation 13:5–8 with 11:7.

11. How many days was Christ in the tomb? Compare this with Revelation 11:9. Was Christ placed in a tomb? Who had to place him there? What was the reaction of unbelievers to Christ's death? Compare this with Revelation 11:10. What happened to Christ after three days? Compare this with Revelation 11:11. What happened after Jesus' resurrection and what was its purpose? Compare this to Revelation 11:12.

12. Is the judgment in Revelation 11:13 complete or limited? How do you know?

13. What does the seventh trumpet establish (Rev. 11:15)? Who does the seventh trumpet judge (Rev. 11:18)?

14. Compare Revelation 11:19 with 21:22. What does "God's temple" symbolize? Look up "Ark of the Covenant" in a concordance or Bible dictionary. What do you learn? What do you think it conveys here?

15. Compare Revelation 11:19 with 4:5; 8:5; and 16:18. To what time do all of these references refer?

- **Principles and Points of Application.**

1. Meditate on Revelation 11:9–10. Compare this to what you think it was like during the three days that Jesus was dead. How did people respond? How do people respond in our day? Now meditate on Revelation 11:11–13. Compare this to the resurrection of Christ. How does this encourage you as you journey through the wilderness, where it seems as if Satan is winning the battle at times?

2. There is coming a day when God will reward his servants, those who fear his name (Rev. 11:18). How are you serving him in your life today through the power of the Holy Spirit? What evidence is there that you fear his name? Give thanks to him today, using Revelation 11:17. Also, ask the Lord to show you areas in which you need to serve him and areas in which you need to fear his name, not man's name. Then begin doing this today by the Spirit's power.

NOTES FOR REVELATION 11

Aim: Ponder the aim of this lesson concerning our:

Mind: What do we need to know from this passage in Scripture?

John is given a message of judgment for persecutors of God's people and a message of hope for the persecuted, that God will be with them while they witness and worship in the midst of persecution.

Heart: How does what we learn from this passage affect our internal relationship with the Lord?

> It prepares us to be kingdom disciples who are encouraged by God's presence to witness and worship despite persecution and suffering.

Hands: How does what we learn from this passage translate into action for God's kingdom?

> It enables us to:

1. Encourage others with the message of resurrection that follows the cross of Christ, which is also the pattern for believers' lives.
2. Serve the kingdom of God by being effective witnesses and worshipers of the King Jesus Christ.

INTRODUCTION

When my children were young, they made up a game called "Jericho! Jericho!" Caleb, who was five at the time, invented it, but my daughter, Hannah, who had just turned three, always begged him to play it with her. "Let's play Jericho! Jericho!" she would yell while jumping up and down. So off to her room they would go, where they walked around her bed, banging toy kitchen pots and shouting in loud voices. When it would come time for Jericho to fall, they would throw everything off of her bed, including all the pillows, sheets, blankets, books, and toys, making a loud crash on the laminate floors. Since I was usually downstairs when they were playing this, I would get the full sound effect of the crash, and I couldn't help but laugh at the thrill they got out of acting out such a victory.

We all love and thrive on victory, don't we? Just watch the mother at the sports game whose child has scored the winning point. Or the mother at the hospital who has just heard that her child's cancer is in remission. Or the mother who witnesses her rebellious child repent of sin. Or the mother who leads her child to Christ. Or what about when the walls of sin come crashing down in our own lives? What happens when the pride that we've held onto for so long crumbles? When the beauty that we've idolized gets put in its proper place? When the career we've prized is willingly given up so we can stay at home with our children? When the pull toward materialism gets replaced with the pull to true spirituality? When the family member stops ridiculing us or the ridicule stops bothering us? When we've overcome a specific habitual sin?

A lot of the time, though, we are circling our "Jericho" for six days over and never feel like the seventh day is going to come. We never feel like we're going to overcome the world, our own flesh, or Satan. But Revelation 11 tells us differently. John tells us that one day the city of man will be captured. As God's people march around the city in faith, as witnesses and worshipers of God, as soldiers in his army, as a kingdom of priests carrying the Ark of the Covenant (symbolizing God's judgment and mercy), and silently enduring until the time comes to shout, the time *will* come for the walls to crumble and for the city of man to become the city of our God.

We can divide this lesson into two sections:

I. Witnesses Are Rewarded While Their Persecutors Are Judged (Rev. 11:1–14)
II. The Seventh Trumpet Announces the Kingdom of God (Rev. 11:15–19)

I. Witnesses Are Rewarded While Their Persecutors Are Judged (Rev. 11:1–14)

The parenthetical section between the events associated with the sixth and seventh trumpets continues, but the emphasis changes. Whereas in chapter 10 we saw that John was again commissioned to be a prophet who spoke a word of judgment for unbelievers and, thus, salvation for believers, here we see that the emphasis is on the content of John's message.

143

Revelation 11:1–2. In Revelation 3:12, Christ figuratively promises four things to the one who conquers: he will make him a pillar in the temple so that he will never have to go out of the temple of God (both pillar and temple are applied to the believer, thus counting as two of the five promises); he will write on him the name of God the Father; he will write on him the name of the city of God (Jerusalem); and he will write on him Christ's own new name. Here again we see God figuratively promising five things to the persevering believers in light of persecution. They are called a temple, an altar, those who worship at the altar, the court outside the temple, and the holy city.[1] All five are names for the church that suffers during the church age, yet even now takes part in heavenly worship. Each name emphasizes a different aspect of the church's situation, which is related to God's promises. Believers are called a temple because God's presence is with them on earth. They are called an altar because they have been called to sacrifice their very lives for the kingdom of God. They are called "those who worship at the altar" because their way of life is one of sacrifice. They are "the court outside the temple" because for a time God has allowed them to be physically (not spiritually) unprotected during their time of persecution on earth. And they are the holy city because they are a people set apart for God's glory and a people among whom the holy God dwells.

John is figuratively given a staff like a measuring rod to measure the people of God in order to ensure them that God has sealed them for the time of tribulation on earth ("forty-two months"). This tribulation began with the first coming of Christ and will culminate at his second coming, with a final escalation of suffering. Thus, the measuring found here in the parenthetical section between the sixth and seventh trumpets serves the same purpose as the sealing found in the parenthetical section between the sixth and seventh seals. The "forty-two months" serves to recall Elijah's prophetic message of judgment (Luke 4:25), the length of Christ's ministry on earth, and the number of encampments of Israel during the wilderness journey (Num. 33:5–49). It is the same

---

1. G. K. Beale, *The Book of Revelation: A Commentary on the Greek Text*, New International Greek Testament Commentary (Grand Rapids: Eerdmans, 1999), 571.

length of time as the three and a half years and 1,260 days that we see in other places of the book, the background for which can be found in the book of Daniel.

We should note that those who take Revelation to be literal and future-oriented only interpret these verses as referring to a literal future temple with an altar where sacrifices are made, not for atonement, but to remember Christ's atonement, as is conveyed in Ezekiel 40–48. But Ezekiel's prophecy must be interpreted in light of Hebrews 10:1–12, which makes it clear that there is no longer any need for sacrifice (atoning or memorial). Furthermore, the book of Revelation itself says that there is no need of a temple in heaven, for God himself is the temple (Rev. 21:22). Thus, it is best to interpret Revelation 11:1–2 figuratively.

That Christ's forty-two months of suffering ministry is a pattern for believers is clearly seen in these verses. He too was "the temple of God" (God with us as "Immanuel"), "the altar" as the final and complete sacrifice, the "one who worshiped at the altar" as his whole life was one of sacrifice, "the court outside the temple" because God forsook him for a time in order for him to accomplish redemption, and "the holy city" because he was the perfect God-man.

Old Testament/New Testament Background to Revelation 11:1–2.
- Exodus 19:6: "You shall be to me a kingdom of priests and a holy nation."
- Ezekiel 40–48: Vision of the new temple.
- Daniel 7:25; 9:29; 12:7, 11–12: "They shall be given into his hands for a time, times, and half a time."
- Hebrews 10:1–12: "Sanctified through the body of Jesus Christ once for all."
- 1 Peter 2:5: "To be a holy priesthood, to offer spiritual sacrifices."

Revelation 11:3. The same one who gives the people of God over to the nations to be trampled physically but not spiritually is the same one who gives them authority to be his witnesses during the church age. Thus, the "two witnesses," while alluding to both Moses and Elijah, are symbolic for the entire people of God during the church age who are to

145

function as God's witnesses, just as Moses and Elijah did in their own day. The time period of 1,260 days is synonymous with the forty-two months in Revelation 11:2, which we defined as the entire church age. The church is clothed in sackcloth, just as Elijah and John the Baptist, because it too proclaims the same message to repent for the kingdom of God is near. The sackcloth represents mourning, and here it represents mourning over judgment, just as in chapter 10 the scroll was bitter in John's stomach because of the message of judgment. It is never easy for the people of God to minister in the midst of hard hearts that are bound for eternal judgment by God.

With the new covenant came the fulfillment of the promise that the church would be given the Holy Spirit's gift of prophecy (Joel 2:28–32; Acts 1:8). We are to use this gift of prophecy to be witnesses and worshipers of God in the midst of persecution and suffering in this world. "For we are the aroma of Christ to God among those who are being saved and among those who are perishing, to one a fragrance from death to death, to the other a fragrance from life to life. Who is sufficient for these things . . . men of sincerity, as commissioned by God, and speaking in Christ in the sight of God" (2 Cor. 2:15–17). Does this characterize our womanhood? Are we sincere in our faith? Do we know our commission? Are we speaking as Christ's ambassadors in the sight of God? We are to lay our lives at the altar and be the aroma of Christ, not just among believers, but among unbelievers as well. Indeed, God will even use our fragrant aroma of sacrifice to condemn our persecutors.

Revelation 11:4. The two witnesses are now further defined. They are the two olive trees and two lampstands that stand before the Lord of the earth in his temple. This is an allusion to Zechariah 4:14 where the olive trees are on each side of the lampstand providing oil for the lamp to keep it burning. Just as the Holy Spirit of God empowered Joshua and Zerubbabel, as priest and king, so here the Holy Spirit of God empowers the entire people of God to be a royal priesthood and a holy kingdom as they act as witnesses for him. The "two witnesses, two olive trees, and two lampstands" are significant, for the law required at least two witnesses in making judgment with regard to an offense of the law (Deut. 17:6). That the lampstands in Revelation 2–3 represent the church as a whole lends further support that here too the lampstands represent the entire people of God.

Old Testament Background to Revelation 11:4.

- Zechariah 1:16–17; 2:1–5: "The measuring line shall be stretched out over Jerusalem."
- Zechariah 3:1–2; 4:7: "Who are you, O great mountain? Before Zerubbabel you shall become a plain."
- Zechariah 4:14: "The two anointed ones who stand by the LORD of the whole earth."

Revelation 11:5. The church, as protected by God's presence, cannot be harmed spiritually. Instead, the church brings down judgment upon unbelievers by its message ("fire pours from their mouths and consumes their foes"). The persecutors will be harmed in the same way that they kill the believers, which recalls the "eye for an eye" aspect of the law (Lev. 24:19–20).

Revelation 11:6. The people of God have the same power of God behind them that the great prophets of old, Elijah and Moses, had when they shut up the sky with their prayer (Elijah) and brought on the Egyptian plagues (Moses). Their power is used in judgment against their persecutors. It is not just Elijah and Moses that are in view, but all true prophets of God who have proclaimed his judgment and salvation through the ages. Though the church of God does not perform the same miracles as Elijah and Moses, we are empowered by the same Spirit of God to stand boldly in this world as witnesses and worshipers of God. And as we do so, the trumpet plagues fall upon the persecutors of God's people.

Old Testament Background to Revelation 11:6.

- Exodus 7:17–25: The first plague, water turned to blood.
- 1 Kings 11: Solomon turns from the Lord.

Revelation 11:7–8. "And when they have finished their testimony" refers to the very end of history immediately prior to the second coming of Christ, when the people of God appear to be defeated, as Christ appeared to be defeated at the cross. It is an incredible phrase of hope that God preserves his people until his plan for them is finished. He allows us to be "trampled" no less, but no more, than what is decreed by his sovereign plan. "The beast that rises from the bottomless pit" is the counterfeit of Christ who has been active throughout the church age, but here makes one last and final war on the saints at the end of history. The people of God will appear to be dead/defeated ("dead bodies will lie in the street"), just as Christ appeared to be dead on the cross. The "great city" is ironically the ungodly world that thinks it is great in its own eyes, but is bound for destruction. It is like Sodom because it is doomed for judgment by destruction, and it is like Egypt because it has been a people who have persecuted the people of God. The word "symbolically" clearly states that the great city is not to be identified as a geographical location, but speaks of the entirety of unbelievers. An allusion to Jerusalem comes last, "where their Lord was crucified." "Their" is not speaking of believers, but unbelievers, as he is their Lord too despite their not acknowledging him as such. And shamefully, it was their only Lord and hope of salvation that they killed. They nailed their own bodies to the cross when they nailed their Lord's there. They put to death their only hope of salvation. How often people do the same today!

Old Testament Background to Revelation 11:7–8.
- Deuteronomy 29:22–26: "An overthrow like that of Sodom and Gomorrah."
- Joel 3:19: "Egypt shall become a desolation and Edom a desolate wilderness."
- Amos 4:10–11: "As when God overthrew Sodom and Gomorrah."

Revelation 11:9–10. The unbelievers are relieved that finally the church, which has spoken judgment against them, is out of their lives. They can go on with their worldly pleasures, doing as they please without being reminded of their doom. In fact, it appears that there is no doom at all. It appears that the witnesses and worshipers had been wrong and the unbelievers pity them for believing in such a lie. Just as Jesus appeared to be defeated for three days, so too his church appears to be defeated for three (and a half) days. In contrast to the three (and a half) years of Christ's ministry and the figurative three (and a half) years of the saints' ministry, the Antichrist's seeming victory is short and irrelevant. Just as the ungodly did not bury Jesus, but rather a disciple of Jesus (Joseph of Arimathea) asked permission from Pilate to bury him (John 19:38–42), so too the ungodly did not bury the believers who lay dead on the street.

Old Testament Background to Revelation 11:9–10. Psalm 79:3: "And there was no one to bury them."

Revelation 11:11. Just as God raised Jesus from the dead, so too he will raise his people from the dead. The unbelievers who were so relieved that they had been right and those that tormented them mentally had been wrong, fearfully discover that the God of those they had persecuted was real after all, and thus, they were in the end the true persecuted. We must remember the figurative language in these verses, so that rather than literal bodies lying dead on the street and a literal resurrection, this could refer to the very small and seemingly defeated church being vindicated by God's judgment on unbelievers. But, it could be a literal description as well (see notes on next verse).

Old Testament Background to Revelation 11:11.

- Exodus 15:16: "Till your people O LORD pass by, till the people pass by whom you have purchased."
- Psalm 105:38: "Egypt was glad when they departed for dread of them had fallen upon it."
- Ezekiel 37:5: "I will cause breath to enter you and you shall live."
- Ezekiel 37:10–13: "And the breath came into them and they lived."
- Jonah 1:10, 16: "Then the men feared the LORD exceedingly."

Revelation 11:12. This verse most likely refers symbolically to God's divine approval before their enemies for the believers' witness and worship. This was indeed one of the purposes of Christ's ascension. Thus, this entire passage continues to answer the cry of the saints in Revelation 6:9–10 concerning how long it will be before they are vindicated.

149

In comparison with Revelation 1:10–11 and 4:1–2, the voice here is Christ's. The one who was also questioned and persecuted for his witness and worship now validates his followers who have been questioned and persecuted for theirs.[2]

Revelation 11:13. In comparison with Revelation 6:12 and 16:18, this great earthquake speaks of final judgment at the end of history. It is not the end of the final judgment, though, but rather the beginning, as is made clear from the limit of "a tenth of the city fell" and "seven thousand people were killed." In light of other Old and New Testament passages listed below, it is most likely that "the rest" who were "terrified and gave glory to the God of heaven" acknowledged God, but did not have faith in God.

Old Testament/New Testament Background to Revelation 11:13.
- Daniel 4:34: "I, Nebuchadnezzar . . . I blessed the Most High and praised and honored him."
- Jonah 1:9–10: "The God of heaven . . . then the men were exceedingly afraid."
- Micah 7:8–17: "They shall turn in dread to the LORD our God."
- Matthew 28:1–4: "And for fear of him the guards trembled and became like dead men."

Revelation 11:14. This verse takes us back to where we left off before the parenthetical section of Revelation 10:1–11:13 began, that is, verse 9:21. The second woe was identified with the sixth trumpet. Now we move to the third woe, which is a result of the seventh trumpet. Again, John's visions are not in chronological order, as is clear from the events that happen in different visions. If they were chronological, they would be horribly illogical and inconsistent with the rest of Scripture.

II. The Seventh Trumpet Announces the Kingdom of God (Rev. 11:15–19)

Revelation 11:15. As with the seventh seal, and as we will see with the seventh bowl, the seventh trumpet speaks of the end of history, the

2. Ibid., 599.

final judgment, and the establishment of the kingdom of God on earth. God now resumes the rule over the world that he had allowed Satan to have for a limited time. God the Father and God the Son are both rulers in the kingdom, though here the Father is placed first because the Son is always in submission to the Father (1 Cor. 15:24–28).

Old Testament Background to Revelation 11:15. Daniel 7: Daniel's vision of the four beasts, the reign of the Ancient of Days, and the Son of Man given dominion.

Revelation 11:16–17. The twenty-four elders, whom we defined as heavenly representatives of the church in chapter 4, now fall on their faces and worship God. This is the appropriate posture of worship. Whether we are literally facedown or whether we are facedown in the posture of our hearts, we are to humble ourselves before the Almighty God who has accomplished his kingdom purposes. The elders gave thanks to him. This is something that we do not do often enough. Too often we are grumbling and complaining, or we are requesting help for something or someone. But we need to give thanks to the Lord continually for who he is and for all that he has done for us. Here he is the Lord God Almighty who is and who was. The "who is to come" of Revelation 1:4, 8; 4:8 is not included here because this is the time of the consummated kingdom. Thus, "who is to come" has been replaced by "you have taken your great power." He has come and he now reigns for eternity by his great power. It was his power that overcame the darkness and his power that enables him to reign over all. This aspect of God's sovereignty is also often overlooked in our prayer life. So often we offer our pleas before God and then go about trying to fix the problem on our own, or make the situation happen that we wanted, or overcome sin by our own strength. But God is sovereign over the details of our lives and is the only one who has the power to accomplish his purposes for our lives.

Revelation 11:18. This is the culmination of God's answer to the saints' plea for vindication in Revelation 6:9–10. Its time immediately precedes the consummation of God's kingdom described in the previous three verses, for God's kingdom in verse 15 is to reign *forever*. First, God judges the nations for their rage against him and his people. Second, all dead unbelievers are judged for destroying the earth, God's people. The punishment clearly fits the crime. In between the description of the unbelievers' judgment is the description of the believers' reward, which conveys that part of their reward is the satisfaction that their blood has been vindicated. The five descriptions of believers all speak of the same group, the entire people of God.

Old Testament Background to Revelation 11:18. Jeremiah 51:25: "I am against you, O destroying mountain, which destroys the whole earth."

Revelation 11:19. The final judgment is reached, as God's temple in heaven is opened. The Ark of the Covenant conveys both judgment and mercy. In the account of the fall of Jericho, the ark came behind the trumpet blowers who blew for six days, and then on the seventh day the trumpet blasts caused the wall to come down. Thus, the ark was involved with the judgment of Jericho. But it also conveys mercy. The blood of the sacrifices was sprinkled on the mercy seat of the ark in order to cover the nation's sins on the Day of Atonement. Thus, it was a symbol of God's presence, as it is here. So, the temple and the ark are both figurative for the presence of God who has now ushered in the final judgment.[3]

This is the third time that we have seen "flashes of lightning, and rumblings and peals of thunder" in the book of Revelation. But as noted in the lesson on chapter 8, each successive repetition grows a little more intense in its description of the final judgment.

- Revelation 4:5: "Flashes of lighting, and rumblings, and peals of thunder."
- Revelation 8:5: "Peals of thunder, rumblings, flashes of lightning, and an earthquake."
- Revelation 11:19: "Flashes of lightning, rumblings, peals of thunder, an earthquake, and heavy hail."
- Revelation 16:18–21: "Flashes of lightning, rumblings, peals of thunder and a great earthquake such as there had never been . . . and great hailstones, about one hundred pounds each."

3. Ibid., 619.

152

Old Testament Background to Revelation 11:19. Exodus 15:13–18: "You will bring them in and plant them on your own mountain . . . the LORD will reign forever and ever."

CONCLUSION

I am still marching around my "Jerichos." It is a glorious time when God helps me to overcome one of them. But there are so many more! Thankfully, I know that one day all of my sin, all of my suffering, and all of the ridicule I face will come crashing down at the final trumpet blast when Jesus Christ appears in judgment and mercy, and the kingdom of this world becomes the "kingdom of our Lord and of his Christ."

Revelation 12

PLEASE USE THE QUESTION paradigm from pages 353–54 as you work through the following. See the introductory comments there that explain each part of the process below in more detail.

- **Pray**.
- **Ponder the Passage**. Read Revelation 12 once a day from different translations for the entire week, looking for its:
  - Point
  - Persons
  - Patterns
  - Persons of the Trinity
  - Puzzling Parts
- **Put It in Perspective**.
  - Place in Scripture
  - Passages from Other Parts of Scripture

1. Based on your observations of the text, what is the basic content of this passage? Try to summarize it in your own words, using a sentence or two.
2. John moves from seeing the seventh trumpet to seeing what in heaven (Rev. 12:1)? Why is this significant?

3. Read Genesis 37:9–10. Whom do you think the "woman" is in Revelation 12:1?

4. In light of Genesis 3:15; 17:19; and 2 Samuel 7:12, to whom is the woman giving birth?

5. With what you have learned about the symbolism of seven and ten in this study, what would "seven heads" and "ten horns" on the dragon convey (Rev. 12:3)?

6. Read Revelation 1:16, 20. What do you think the stars represent in those verses? What do you think the stars represent in Revelation 12:4 and what is Satan doing to them? Who is he waiting to devour?

7. To what events of Christ's life does Revelation 12:5 refer?

8. What did you learn in Revelation 11:3 about the 1,260 days and the protection of the church during this time? Compare this to Revelation 12:6.

9. Read Zechariah 3:1–5. What do you think "there was no longer any place for him in heaven" means? What was Satan doing in Zechariah? What event has now happened in John's day that would keep him from doing that?

10. When else were Satan and his angels thrown down to earth (Rev. 12:9)? Look up Isaiah 14:12.

11. Of what does the hymn in Revelation 12:10–12 consist? What event caused Satan to be thrown down? How have the saints conquered Satan? Why are the heavens to rejoice, but the earth to take warning? Who on earth is warned? Why?

12. Whom does Satan pursue now that he's on earth (Rev. 12:13)?

13. Look up Exodus 19:4; Deuteronomy 1:31–33; 32:10–12; and Isaiah 40:31. To whom does the "great eagle" refer (Rev. 12:14)?

14. Read Genesis 3:1ff. What did Satan use to deceive Eve in these verses? Do you see any connection with his "mouth" here? To what do you think this refers in the context of Revelation, especially the letters to the churches?

15. How do Exodus 15:12 and Numbers 16:31–35 shed light on Revelation 12:16?

16. To whom do you think the "woman" refers in Revelation 12:17? What about "her offspring"?

- **Principles and Points of Application.**
1. In what area of your life do you feel like Satan is about to devour you, or a loved one, a dream, a career, a ministry, a reputation, etc.? Take it to the Lord and let it be caught up to him and to his throne. It is safe in the arms of the Sovereign Ruler over all. Then flee to his presence, to his Word, and to the fellowship of believers for nourishment. Be comforted and encouraged by him and his people today and stand firm in the faith by the power of the Holy Spirit.

2. Read Revelation 12:10–11 carefully. Though Satan has been thrown down from heaven, he is actively at work in our world among believers trying to persecute, deceive, and tempt us. Look carefully at how God's Word tells us to overcome Satan's accusations in our lives. When he comes to us and wants to accuse us of those things or remind us of wrongs done in the past, he can't because they are conquered by Christ's blood. Our righteousness is in Christ. We are forgiven in him. Now look at Revelation 12:12. We can rejoice because we are in Christ and thus, in heaven. So, put the accuser of your specific situation behind you today and rejoice.

3. We are foolish if we forget that our time here on earth is war. We are in active combat. We dare not retreat. We dare not think that we can relax for one moment. Peter says that Satan roams around like a roaring lion ready to devour. Revelation 12:17 tells us that the dragon is furious with us. How do you perceive this war? Or do you? How do you envision the Christian life? Did anyone prepare you for the warfare? Read Ephesians 6:10–20 today and pray through the spiritual armor of God, asking him to equip you to do battle against Satan and his angels in a specific "battle" you are facing right now.

NOTES FOR REVELATION 12

Aim: Ponder the aim of this lesson concerning our:

Mind: What do we need to know from this passage in Scripture?

> That although Christ defeated Satan on the cross of Calvary, he still actively persecutes the church and is prince of this world until the consummation of God's kingdom.

Heart: How does what we learn from this passage affect our internal relationship with the Lord?

> It prepares us to be kingdom disciples who flee to God's presence during times of Satan's persecution, temptation, and deception.

Hands: How does what we learn from this passage translate into action for God's kingdom?

> It enables us to:

1. Take the area(s) of our life that we feel is being devoured by Satan to God and find shelter in his presence and comfort in his Word.
2. Overcome Satan's accusations in our life by the power of the Holy Spirit, recognizing that our righteousness is in Christ.
3. Recognize and help others recognize spiritual warfare in this life and to put on the full armor of God, as described in Ephesians 6:10–20, in order to stand firm in the faith.

INTRODUCTION

The year 2008 was incredibly difficult for me. I was afflicted with a range of physical trials, some of them quite severe. The trials began in January with gastrointestinal complications during which I almost lost my life. Chronic pain that had begun years before continued to plague me. Sinus infections, unexplained foot pains, and a bad running injury came in the spring, and the diagnosis of hypothyroidism finished off the year. All of this started prior to my being asked to teach a women's Bible study, and I knew when I was asked that, despite the pain, I was to teach. I felt like Satan was trying to keep me out of ministry, and I was not going to succumb to his ploy. Instead, I did the only thing I knew to do. I bowed myself down before my Father, literally weeping some days, and asked him to carry me through. I knew that I had no strength, not physically, emotionally, or mentally. I needed him to get me through the waters that were overwhelming me. And I knew from his Word that he would do it. I knew that my Father was involved in every aspect of my suffering, using even Satan's tactics for my good and to accomplish his own divine plan in my life. That did not stop the intense amount of pain and suffering that I had to endure. It did not keep me from crying for mercy. It did not keep me from wanting out, but it did keep me pressed close underneath the shelter of his wings, where I was nestled as he carried me through the wilderness, nourishing my soul and comforting me in my pain.

Revelation 12 has much to say about Satan intensely pursuing us to persecute us, to tempt us, and to deceive us. He uses all kinds of things in our lives in order to do so. And if we're not careful, we will fall prey to his snares. So John gives us a look behind the scenes at what is happening in the kingdom of this world.

We can divide this lesson into three sections:

I. The Sign of the Woman and the Sign of the Dragon (Rev. 12:1–6)
II. The War between the Good and Bad Angels in Heaven (Rev. 12:7–12)
III. The Dragon Is Thrown Down to Earth and Persecutes the Woman (Rev. 12:13–17)

In between the seven trumpets and the seven bowls, we come to a section that describes seven signs, signaled by the phrases, "and a great sign appeared" (Rev. 12:1, 3), "and I saw" (Rev. 13:1), "then I saw" (Rev. 13:11), "then I looked" (Rev. 14:1), "then I saw" (Rev. 14:6), "then I looked and behold" (Rev. 14:14), and "and I saw" (Rev. 15:2). Like the sections on the seven seals and the seven trumpets, which featured an interlude between the sixth and seventh seals/trumpets, so too here there is an interlude between the sixth and seventh signs (Rev. 15:1). Chapters 12–22 almost seem to begin the book of Revelation over again, covering the same time frame as chapters 1–11 and the same topics, but addressing them and explaining them at a deeper level. Here we see more prevalently that Satan himself is behind the evil described in chapters 1–11. By showing us the spiritual reality behind the physical events, John encourages his readers to persevere because Christ has already defeated Satan at the cross. Though Satan may torment believers for a time, he is limited in his power and in the length of time he has for his evil work. Thus, Christ's people can stand firm knowing that the battle is already won; it is only a matter of time before they are vindicated. Satan, the beast, the false prophet, and Babylon (in that order) are pictured as rising and then falling in chapters 12–22.

I. The Sign of the Woman and the Sign of the Dragon (Rev. 12:1–6)

Revelation 12:1. The time in heaven is right before Christ's birth, a time in which God's people existed just as they will after Christ's birth, thus emphasizing the unity of the people of God between the Old and New Testaments. In the Old Testament, Jacob, his wife, and Joseph's brothers (the eleven tribes of Israel) who bow down to Joseph (the twelfth tribe) in his dream are depicted as "the sun, the moon, and eleven stars" (Gen 37:9). Thus, the description here in Revelation conveys the chosen people of God. The twelve stars, symbolizing the twelve tribes of Israel, also call to mind the imagery of twelve stars seen in the sky, conveying Israel's heavenly calling as the people of God who were to shine as a light among the nations. It is not just ethnic Israel that is in view here, since the church is also seen as the seven stars in Revelation 1:16, 20. This is a further validation that Israel and the church are one body. The crown that the woman (the people of God) wears symbolizes her share in Christ's rule and the reward that they receive for overcoming persecution, temptation to compromise their faith, and deception by Satan. Here, before the battle and persecution is conveyed in the following verses, John gives us a picture of the church. She is illuminated, protected, and purified by Christ; this picture instills confidence and courage in the earthly community. Despite the earthly appearance of the persecuted church, the heavenly appearance is the true reality.[1]

Old Testament Background to Revelation 12:1.

- Genesis 37:9: "The sun, the moon, and eleven stars were bowing down to me."
- Isaiah 60:19–20: "But the LORD will be your everlasting light and glory."

Revelation 12:2. The Old Testament church ("she") was awaiting painfully the promised deliverer/king/messiah who had been prophesied all through the Old Testament. She was waiting painfully because the people of Israel had come through judgment and exile and their only hope was the promised deliverer, who had not arrived. In fact, between the Old and New Testament periods there were 400 long years of silence from God.

Old Testament Background to Revelation 12:2.

- Genesis 3:15–16: "I will put enmity between you and the woman, and between your offspring and her offspring; he shall bruise your head, and you shall bruise his heel. . . . I will surely multiply your pain in childbearing."
- Isaiah 7:10, 14: "A sign . . . the virgin shall conceive and bear a son."
- Isaiah 26:17–18: "Like a pregnant woman . . . we were because of you, O LORD."
- Isaiah 51:2–3, 9–11: "And makes her wilderness like Eden . . . joy and gladness will be found in her."

1. G. K. Beale, *The Book of Revelation: A Commentary on the Greek Text*, New International Greek Testament Commentary (Grand Rapids: Eerdmans, 1999), 625–27.

- Isaiah 52:2: "Loose the bonds from your neck, O captive daughter of Zion."
- Jeremiah 4:31: "A cry as of a woman in labor . . . the cry of the daughter of Zion gasping for breath."

Revelation 12:3. The "great red dragon," an allusion to Ezekiel 29:3, represents Satan himself on one level, while also representing all of the evil kingdoms throughout the ages through which he has worked to oppress believers. As has been seen earlier in the book, the numbers seven and ten convey completeness, as with the Lamb of God, but here it is completeness of evil power and the complete effect it has on the world. The seven diadems are representative of the blasphemous claim Satan makes to have the authority that only Christ has.[2]

Old Testament Background to Revelation 12:3.

- Ezekiel 29:3: "I am against you, Pharaoh king of Egypt."
- Daniel 7:7, 24: "A fourth beast . . . out of this kingdom ten kings shall arise."

Revelation 12:4. The time frame here is prior to Christ's birth where the true Israel suffers an attack from Satan physically, though not spiritually. In light of "stars" in the previous verse representing true Israel, and in light of the context of Daniel 8, which stands behind this chapter, representing the people of God as being delivered, it is best to see the stars here as representing the true people of God. However, it is also a possible interpretation to see the third of the stars of heaven that were swept down to earth as a group of deceived Israelites that fell away from the true Israel, never having truly been a part of it.[3]

To complete his persecution of God's people, Satan wants to destroy Christ before his birth, which he cannot do (so he later attempts to do so by tempting Christ in the wilderness, and through his arrest and crucifixion). Again, God's people are depicted as "about to give

2. Ibid., 633–35.
3. Ibid., 637.

birth," which connotes pain and is thus another reference to their persecuted state.[4]

Old Testament Background to Revelation 12:4.

- Daniel 8:10: "And some of the stars it threw down to the ground and trampled on them."
- Daniel 8:22–25: "His power shall be great, but not by his own power, and he shall cause fearful destruction."

Revelation 12:5. Here we have a summary of Christ's birth, the fulfillment of Old Testament prophecy concerning his rule of the nations, his resurrection, ascension, and reward of kingship.

Old Testament Background to Revelation 12:5. Psalm 2:7–9: "And I will make the nations your heritage and the ends of the earth your possession. You shall break them with a rod of iron and dash them in pieces like a potter's vessel."

Just as Christ's entire life was protected spiritually by the hand of God and in time he was caught up to heaven, so too the church's entire life is protected spiritually by God's hand and in time she will be caught up to heaven too (1 Thess. 4:17).

Revelation 12:6. The woman, here representing God's people after Christ's resurrection and thus, God's people throughout the entire church age, escapes to God's place of protection and provision.[5] Just as the "sealing" in chapter 7 and the "measuring" in chapter 11 stand for God's spiritual protection, so here "a place prepared by God" conveys his spiritual protection of his people. Yet, just as Israel faced temptation in the wilderness, so too the church is faced with the temptation to compromise and must contend with deception in the wilderness. As we have already noted, the 1,260 days (elsewhere in the book seen as 42 months and three and a half years) represents the protection of God's people throughout the entire church age. It recalls Israel's own wandering for 42 years through the wilderness, spiritually protected and provided for by God. Like the temple in Revelation 11:1, here the "place prepared

4. Ibid., 637.
5. Ibid., 642.

by God" represents God's dwelling with his people, which keeps them from spiritual harm but not physical harm.

Old Testament Background to Revelation 12:6.

- Exodus 16:32: "The bread with which I fed you in the wilderness."
- Deuteronomy 1:31: "In the wilderness where the LORD your God carried you."
- Deuteronomy 8:14–16: "Who led you through the terrifying wilderness with its fiery serpents and scorpions."
- Isaiah 32:15: "Until the Spirit is poured upon us and the wilderness becomes a fruitful field."
- Daniel 7; 9; 12: "Three and a half years."

As we journey through this world, God has given us a place of protection and provision that is invisible to the naked eye, but is felt by every true believer who is sealed with the Holy Spirit. We feel his presence with us through the everyday trials that we face because the Spirit indwells us. And we are strengthened and encouraged that though we may feel small, our God is big and he has already defeated the enemy before us.

II. The War between the Good and Bad Angels in Heaven (Rev. 12:7–12)

We now step behind the curtain of Revelation 12:1–6, which portrays events happening on earth, in order to see the heavenly perspective of those same events, as described in 12:7–12.

Revelation 12:7–8. Here we see that the symbolic war in heaven between the good and bad angels is won by the good angels. Michael represents Israel, and thus represents the true Israel, Christ, in heaven while Christ fights on earth. Thus, this scene in heaven relates to the scene of the cross and resurrection on earth. It was not Michael who won the victory, but Christ. It was because of Christ's redemption that the victory in heaven was won. Yet, ironically, this victory begins a struggle that lasts through the church age (the last days), ending only with the second coming of Christ. Even so, God's judgment that is inaugurated with the death, resurrection, and ascension of Christ is universally absolute, as the following verses will make clear.

Old Testament Background to Revelation 12:7–8.

- Daniel 2:35: "The stone that struck the image became a great mountain and filled the whole earth."
- Daniel 7:21: "This horn made war with the saints and prevailed over them."
- Daniel 10:20: "But now I will return to fight against the prince of Persia."

Revelation 12:9. Now the great dragon is further identified as that "ancient serpent, the devil, Satan, and the deceiver of the whole world." This recalls his work in the garden with Adam and Eve, but compares his smaller-scale work there with the vastly larger scale in which he now attempts to deceive and destroy all of mankind. But with Christ's death and resurrection, the allowance formerly given by God to Satan to accuse and deceive (see the Job and Zechariah passages noted below) is even more restricted. This is because Christ's blood has paid the penalty for the people's sins.[6]

Old Testament Background to Revelation 12:9.

- Genesis 3:1, 14: "Now the serpent . . . said to the woman . . . because you have done this cursed are you."
- Job 1:6–11; 2:1–6: "And Satan also came among them . . . to present himself to the LORD."
- Zechariah 3:1–2: "And Satan standing at his right hand to accuse him."

Revelation 12:10. This is the beginning of a hymn that lasts through verse 12. It clearly portrays that what Michael does in heaven is symbolic of what Christ does on earth. The loud voice in heaven represents the saints of God who have already died and are awaiting the full number of their brothers to be brought in before vindication can occur (Rev. 6:9–11). That Satan has now been thrown down out of heaven means

---

6. Ibid., 656.

that the kingdom of God has now been inaugurated and the saints in heaven are celebrating its inauguration.

Just as Satan was expelled from heaven at the first creation, so here he is thrown out of heaven at the beginning of the new creation and, indeed, he will be thrown into the lake of fire at the consummation of the new creation. We need not fear his victory, for he is already defeated by Christ's work on the cross. Though he still physically torments us, we are spiritually safe in the presence of our Father. There is nothing that can separate us from the love of Christ (Rom. 8:35–39). There is nothing that will keep us from entering the Promised Land. Though the journey is long and the way difficult, our completion of it is sure, and because it is certain we travel in hope and faith as witnesses and worshipers of God in this world.

Old Testament/New Testament Background to Revelation 12:10.
- Psalm 2: "And I will make the nations your [Christ's] heritage."
- Daniel 2: "A fourth kingdom that will crush and break all these."
- John 12:31–33: "Now will the ruler of this world be cast out . . . when I am lifted up from the earth."

Revelation 12:11. This is not only the key verse in this section, but in the entire chapter as a whole. As paradoxical as it seems to our experience, suffering Christians are victorious Christians. This is because the suffering Christ was the victorious Christ. We are identified with him and his victory on the cross, and his resurrection is the firstfruits for our own victory and resurrection. Not only his death, but also our witness as ones who have faith in the gospel as we live out our lives on earth, is the foundation of our conquering. Not only was Satan cast out of heaven because his accusation against the saints was proved false by Christ's blood, which paid the penalty for it, but also because he falsely accused and persecuted Christ, the perfect Son of God. The "ones who loved not their lives even unto death" are not just those who were martyred, but all Christians everywhere who stand firm in their faith for a lifetime. Their suffering helps to advance the kingdom of God until its consummation. So, they conquered not just by the one whom they worshiped, but also by their witness of worshiping him alone in the face of persecution, temptation, and deception.

Revelation 12:12. Therefore, because Christ's work of redemption has expelled Satan from heaven a second time at the inauguration of the new creation, the ones who will inherit the new creation are to rejoice. But the saints on earth are warned of even more rampant evil because Satan is angrier than ever that he's been even more restricted in his power and time to wreak havoc before he is thrown into the lake of fire. This serves then to inform Christians of the intensity of the battle on earth. Because Satan has been cast from heaven where he accused believers before the throne of God, now he puts all his efforts toward destroying and deceiving believers on earth. While believers know the time is short before Christ returns and are fervently doing good works, so too Satan knows the time is short before he's destroyed and is fervently doing evil works. However much he tries, though, God's people are protected from spiritual harm because the Holy Spirit of God seals them.

We would be wise to take heed of the fact that Satan is, more than at any other time in history, fervently doing evil works as the time of his destruction draws near. We would be foolish to close our eyes to the forces of evil behind the media, government, unbelievers, and other channels of our world through which Satan works to persecute, tempt, and deceive us. We must stand firm in our faith, turning away from such forces and defeating them with the Word of God, while recognizing that Satan is defeated and the Spirit of God protects us spiritually. The war is fierce, but the victory is certain because Christ has already defeated Satan on the cross.

III. The Dragon Is Thrown Down to Earth and Persecutes the Woman (Rev. 12:13–17)

Revelation 12:13. Because Satan is so angry over being thrown out of heaven, he now pursues God's people in order to persecute them. He pursues the church because she is identified with Christ ("the male child"). Satan's anger toward Christ, who is now in heaven, is transferred to Christians on earth.

167

Revelation 12:14. This verse expands on 12:6 by stating the reason why the church flees to the wilderness. She flees from the serpent. And the way she flees is stated by an allusion to Exodus 19:4; Deuteronomy 1:31–33; and Deuteronomy 32:10–12. She was "given the two wings of the great eagle." We know from the allusions that it is God himself who brings his church safely into the wilderness to nourish her there. This nourishment is an allusion to Isaiah 40:31 where again the "wings like eagles" imagery is used, along with a promise that God's people will "walk and not grow faint." It is also an allusion to the manna that God provided for Israel in the wilderness, which has already been mentioned in the book in the letter to the church of Pergamum (Rev. 2:17). The "time, times, and half a time," as has been discussed several times in the book, is the same as the 1,260 days, forty-two months, and three and a half years, which are all symbolic for the entire church age.

We have not been left alone in the fires of this world to fend for ourselves. When the phone call comes from the doctor that we have cancer, our Father is with us. When the officer comes to the door to inform us that our husband has been in a tragic car accident, our Father holds us. When our best friend tells us she has seen our husband with another woman, God is there. When our teenaged son turns to drinking and drugs, our Father is beside us. When our heart breaks over infertility our Father sees us. When our sobs break over miscarriage our Father hears us. When we are deceived into believing the same old lie again, our Father knows. And he picks us up and carries us into his presence. He nourishes us on his Word of truth and comforts us with his presence and plants our feet upon solid ground. He does not remove us from the battle, but he calms and protects us in the midst of it. We will not go through it alone, and when we cannot walk anymore, he carries us through.

Old Testament Background to Revelation 12:14.

- Exodus 19:4: "How I bore you on eagle's wings and brought you to myself."
- Deuteronomy 1:31–33: "In the wilderness, where you have seen the LORD your God carry you, as a man carries his son, all the way that you went until you came to this place."

- Deuteronomy 32:10–12: "Found him in the wilderness . . . like an eagle . . . the LORD alone guided him."
- Isaiah 40:31: "They shall mount up with wings like eagles; they shall run and not be weary."

Revelation 12:15. The imagery in this verse (see the Old Testament verses below) alludes to Satan trying to destroy God's people through the use of false teaching and deception. Just as Satan deceived Eve with words, so he tries to deceive "the woman" (the church) with words. Thus, deceivers creep into our churches to ask, "Did God really say . . . ?" We see this deception all over our churches today. Did God really say that you had to marry a man instead of a woman? Did God really say that you needed to dress modestly? Did God really say that you had to love him with all of your heart? Did God really say that material-ism could get in the way of your love of him? Did God really say that you couldn't have whatever you wanted to have whenever you wanted it? Did God really say that you needed to put the Word of God at the center of your life? And on and on it goes. And so our churches are fall-ing prey to lies and the truth is being compromised all around us. We must stand on the Word of God and take notice. We must have sound doctrine with sound love and sound works in our ministries. We must seek to teach women the pure, unadulterated Word of God. We must seek to replace lies with truth.

Old Testament Background to Revelation 12:15.
- Exodus 14:21: "And the LORD drove the sea back with a strong east wind."
- Isaiah 42:15: "I will turn the rivers into islands, and dry up the pools."
- Daniel 9:26: "Will be cut off with a flood."

Revelation 12:16. The imagery here alludes to the crossing of the Red Sea when the Egyptians were drowned in the waters after the Israelites had crossed safely (Ex. 15:12). It also alludes to the time that the "earth opened its mouth and swallowed" the families of Korah,

Dathan, and Abiram because of their rebellion against Moses and thus, God (Num. 16:12–14). In other words, God will ensure the protection of his church; not even the gates of hell will prevail against it (Matt. 16:18). God will use whatever means he wills to establish and preserve his church in the midst of Satan's deception, temptation, and persecution.

Old Testament Background to Revelation 12:16.
- Exodus 15:12: "You stretched out your right hand; the earth swallowed them."
- Numbers 16:32: "And the earth opened its mouth and swallowed them up with their households and all the people who belonged to Korah and all their goods."

Revelation 12:17. This verse is difficult to interpret, so we must look at the context closely. In Revelation 12:1–2 the woman is pictured in heaven, whereas in 12:6, 13–16 she is pictured on earth. Thus, both the heavenly church and the earthly church are in view in this verse. Because the heavenly church (the woman here) is unable to be harmed and stands as the hope for the earthly church that will one day join with believers in heaven, Satan turns from her (he's been cast out of heaven) to the earthly church (the rest of Christ's offspring) in order to persecute, tempt, and deceive those who are witnesses ("hold to testimony of Jesus") and worshipers (by "keeping the commandments of God" they worship God with their actions) of God.[7]

Old Testament Background to Revelation 12:17. Genesis 3:15: "I will put enmity between you and the woman, and between your offspring and her offspring; he shall bruise your head and you shall bruise his heel."

The ESV has the phrase "And he stood on the sand of the sea" as part of Revelation 12:17, but it is better placed with 13:1 since Satan takes his stand upon the sea to show that he rules over evil, and in order to oversee and rule the beast (that is introduced in 13:1), which he will use to try and conquer the saints.

7. Ibid., 676–79.

CONCLUSION

Satan still has not left me alone and I know he won't until the end of history when the kingdom of God has become the kingdom of this world. But God's Word helps me to identify his persecutions, temptations, and deceptions better and God himself provides provision and protection for me through the devil's onslaughts. So when Satan pursues me, I flee to the presence of my heavenly Father. And it is there, underneath the shelter of his wings, that he carries me through the trial, nurturing me every moment and sustaining me every day so that by his grace I continue to witness to and worship him. I pray that the same will be true of you.

Revelation 13

PLEASE USE THE QUESTION paradigm from pages 353–54 as you work through the following. See the introductory comments there that explain each part of the process below in more detail.

- **Pray**.
- **Ponder the Passage**. Read Revelation 13 once a day from different translations for the entire week, looking for its:
  - Point
  - Persons
  - Patterns
  - Persons of the Trinity
  - Puzzling Parts
- **Put It in Perspective**.
  - Place in Scripture
  - Passages from Other Parts of Scripture

1. Based on your observations of the text, what is the basic content of this passage? Try to summarize it in your own words, using a sentence or two.
2. Who is standing over this beast (Rev. 12:17)? What does this imply?

3. Compare the description of the beast in Revelation 13:1 with the description of the dragon in 12:3 and the Lamb in 5:6. What do you find? What does this imply?

4. Read Daniel 7:3–8 and compare it with Revelation 13:2. How many empires are represented in Daniel? How many in Revelation? What does this imply? Who gave the beast his power?

5. Was the beast's mortal wound really healed (Rev. 13:3)? Why or why not? Why did the whole earth marvel?

6. What is the reasoning behind worshiping the dragon and the beast (Rev. 13:4)? Look up Exodus 15:11 and compare it with the question in Revelation 13:4. What do you notice?

7. Compare Revelation 13:5 with 12:15. What did we learn about the mouth in the previous lesson? How does the beast imitate the dragon here?

8. Who does the beast blaspheme? How does the information we learn about "his dwelling" here inform our understanding of "the temple of God" in Revelation 11:1?

9. How is this present age, in which Satan and his followers persecute the church, characterized (Rev. 13:7)? From the context of the book, what does "conquer" mean in Revelation 13:7?

10. How does Revelation 13:8 illuminate your understanding of salvation? Who pursues whom?

11. Look up Jeremiah 15:2; 43:11; and Ezekiel 14:12–23. Who goes into captivity and why? Are believers included in this? How does that illuminate the meaning of Revelation 13:10, especially when combined with the last phrase, "here is a call for the endurance and faith of the saints"?

12. From where does the second beast arise (Rev. 13:11)? Compare this with the first beast.

13. What person of the triune God does Revelation 13:12–17 remind you of in a counterfeit form?

14. Think through Revelation 13:18 and try to "calculate the number of the beast" from what you have learned in the book of Revelation so far. Don't take too much time here or get too

frustrated. This is a difficult and debated verse; just ponder it as best you can. It will be discussed in the lesson notes.

- **Principles and Points of Application.**

1. Man will always worship someone or something. If we're not worshiping the truth, we're worshiping the counterfeit of truth. Analyze your own life. Who or what makes you marvel and want to follow them? If it's anyone or anything other than Christ, repent of this and pledge your allegiance to the true God today.

2. Too often Christians are unprepared for the fact that Satan makes war on us. Though it seems as if he wins sometimes, if we are God's children we are safe and our names are written in the Lamb's book of life. How do you rely on the power of the Holy Spirit each day for war between the kingdom of Satan and the kingdom of God? Read Ephesians 6:10–20 and pray through each piece of armor today.

3. As we engage in warfare, we need endurance and faith. Spend some time looking up "endurance" and "faith" in a concordance. Write down other passages of Scripture that use these words and that are of particular benefit to you in your present situations. Review them throughout this week and hide God's Word in your heart.

4. Think about a time in the past month when you have been deceived, maybe by the world, Satan, or your own flesh. Ask God to grant you wisdom and understanding to recognize deception in your life. He will do this as you study his Word and hide its truth in your heart. Make it a priority to do this each day by relying on the help of the Spirit.

NOTES FOR REVELATION 13

Aim: Ponder the aim of this lesson concerning our:

Mind: What do we need to know from this passage in Scripture?

Just as there is one true triune God—the Father, the Son, and the Holy Spirit—there is also one false triune god—the dragon, the beast, and the false prophet.

Heart: How does what we learn from this passage affect our internal relationship with the Lord?

It prepares us to be kingdom disciples who are wise and understanding, recognizing the deception of the false triune god in our lives.

Hands: How does what we learn from this passage translate into action for God's kingdom?

It enables us to:

1. Analyze our lives and ministries to see if there is anything or anyone other than Christ that makes us want to marvel at them and follow them.
2. Repent of any allegiance to false gods in our lives and renew our pledge of allegiance to God alone.
3. Daily prepare for war between the kingdom of God and the kingdom of Satan by praying through and applying the full armor of God, as described in Ephesians 6:10–20.
4. Meditate on and memorize Scripture passages about endurance and perseverance in the Christian life in order to be encouraged and to encourage others in situations in which we are tempted or deceived.
5. Be prepared to recognize deception by being immersed in the truth of God's Word so that we might guard against false teaching in the ministries in which we are involved.

INTRODUCTION

It saddens me to see how many women in our churches today are having affairs with the ideologies of our culture. Opportunities for spiritual conversations are turned into discussions of the latest television shows, talk show host advice, dieting plan, or fashion. Even worse, what a "Christian" counselor told someone is taken as absolute truth that gets circulated around and adopted as the right response for everyone. One person's opinion becomes everyone's rule and the speaker with the most charisma wins the teaching position for the year. As long as you look good, talk right, and say something that sounds like the truth, you're in and become a woman of influence. After all, we wouldn't want to offend anyone by asking how they spend their time, what television channels and Internet sites they frequent, what the last book was that they read, how their marriage is, how they spend their money, or what their private life is like. We are more concerned with having enough leaders and enough minds and hands to share the work of the ministry than to have women of the Word in leadership positions and to be grooming a body of women that will mature into faithful leaders.

If women only knew the voice behind the voices of this world, I believe they would be quicker to change the channel, click off of the site, drop the newspaper, and get out of some of the circles that influence them so heavily. But too often we are naïve to who is promoting such false ideology and we are actually impressed with it. So much so that we buy into that which is diametrically opposed to God's Word.

This is what John addresses in Revelation 13. He exposes the other two beings of the counterfeit trinity and in doing so warns us of falling prey to spiritual deception both inside and outside of the church.

We can divide this lesson into two sections:

I. John's Vision of the Beast Rising out of the Sea (Rev. 13:1–10)
II. John's Vision of the Beast Rising out of the Earth (Rev. 13:11–18)

I. John's Vision of the Beast Rising out of the Sea (Rev. 13:1–10)

Whereas chapter 12 defined Satan's pursuit of believers in order to persecute, tempt, and deceive, now he is described as doing that through his two primary agents, the beast rising out of the sea and the beast rising out of the earth.

Revelation 13:1. This begins the second of seven signs that we see in this section of the book (Rev. 12:1–15:4), which follows the trumpet judgments and precedes the bowl judgments. As noted in the previous lesson, the ESV has "And he stood on the sand of the sea" as part of Revelation 12:17, but it is better placed with Revelation 13:1 since Satan takes his stand upon the sea to show that he rules over evil, and in order to oversee and rule the beast (that is introduced in 13:1), which he will use to try and conquer the saints. The beast with ten horns rising out of the sea is an allusion to Daniel 7:2–3, 7, 20, 24. The seven heads then are a combination of the heads of the four beasts of Daniel 7, which displays its immense power and influence. The ten diadems on the ten horns also allude to the fourth beast in Daniel while the "blasphemous names" allude to the "blaspheming one" of Daniel 7:8ff. As we have seen, the numbers ten and seven convey completeness, which here means that this beast is completely evil, completely universal, and transcends time. The passage closely identifies him with the dragon of Revelation 12:3, who has seven heads, ten horns, and seven diadems on his heads. This beast also stands in stark contrast to Christ, who is said to have "seven horns" in Revelation 5:6 and is said to have "many diadems" on his crown (Rev. 19:12, 16). As the fourth beast in Daniel is identified as Rome in Jewish writings, so too this beast in John's day would have been identified as Rome. But it is not limited to Rome. Satan continues to work through the "Romes" throughout our day as well.

Old Testament Background to Revelation 13:1.
- Job 40:15–41: The descriptions of "Behemoth" and "Leviathan."
- Daniel 7:2, 3, 7, 20, 24: "Four great beasts came up out of the sea . . . ten horns . . . shall be different."

Revelation 13:2. This is another allusion to Daniel 7 (verses 3–8), but here the descriptions of Daniel's four beasts are applied to this one beast. This conveys not only its fierce character, but also the fact that it transcends time and is universal. Throughout the ages this beast has manifested itself in different ways through different world powers. The same evil that existed in the Rome of John's day still exists in our "Romes" today, but is manifested differently. John would have been able to look back to the empires of Assyria, Egypt, Babylon, Persia, Greece, and Sodom and see the same evil character of the beast manifested in different ways before it manifested itself in Rome. So too, Satan, as ruler of this world, continues to give power to earthly kingdoms to act for his own purposes of persecution, temptation, and deception.

One look at the persecuted church around the world today will display how many "Romes" Satan is working through to persecute the people of God. Oppressed under the ideology of Islam, many believers are losing their lives, rights, jobs, and family members for the faith. Satan is actively working through the Islamic governments of these countries as well as the active militant groups in order to try and defeat God's people. But the Holy Spirit spiritually protects God's people and many of them are standing firm, even unto death, in the face of such persecution and the temptation to turn away from Christianity. We need to pray faithfully for our brothers and sisters in Christ who are undergoing such severe persecution, that they will persevere as witnesses and worshipers of Christ.

Old Testament/New Testament Background to Revelation 13:2.

- Daniel 7:3–8: "The first was like a lion . . . second like a bear . . . another like a leopard . . . the fourth was different."
- Daniel 7:12: "As for the rest of the beasts their dominion was taken away, but their lives were prolonged for a season and a time."
- 1 John 2:18: "Antichrist is coming, so now many antichrists have come."
- 2 John 7: "Such a one is the deceiver and the antichrist."

Revelation 13:3. That "one of its heads seemed to have a mortal wound" is better translated "one of its heads was slain" in order to convey that he is slain.[1] This sharpens the stark contrast with the "Lamb

---

1. G. K. Beale, *The Book of Revelation: A Commentary on the Greek Text*, New International Greek Testament Commentary (Grand Rapids: Eerdmans, 1999), 689.

standing as though it had been slain" (Rev. 5:6). The word for "wound" here is the same Greek word as "plague" and is translated as such in every other instance in the book. Thus, this surely refers to the defeat of Satan at the cross of Christ. Though the wound killed him, it appears that it has healed, not only because the whole earth marvels at his ability to overcome the slaying at the cross of Christ and follows him, but also because of the continued oppression, deceit, and temptation that he's allowed to work on earth. This appearance of having overcome is one of the beast's great deceptive ploys to keep unbelievers in his ranks and to try and persecute, deceive, and tempt the people of God to give allegiance to him. That "the whole earth marveled as they followed the beast" refers to the entire period of the church age, though we know from 2 Thessalonians 2 and from 1 John 2:18 and 2 John 7 that there will be a final appearance of the Antichrist, which will be a culmination of all of the manifestations throughout history of the "mystery of lawlessness that is already at work."

Revelation 13:4. Just as God the Father transferred his authority to the Son and the Son is to be worshiped and praised alongside the Father, so too Satan has transferred his authority to the beast and the beast is worshiped and praised alongside Satan. "Who is like the beast and who can fight against it" is similar to "Who is like you, O LORD, among the gods?" in Exodus 15:11. This is another validation that Satan is trying to imitate the triune God through his use of the beast rising out of the sea and the beast rising out of the earth (Rev. 13:11–18).

Of course, the answer to the question is that Christ is like the beast and can fight against it, and, indeed, he already has and he has won. Believers must remember, as Satan masquerades as the victor, that he is not the victor and has no power or authority over us. Christ has won and his Spirit seals us. No tactic of the beast can separate us from the grip of God on our lives.

Revelation 13:5. Satan has not yet come up with a new scheme since the garden of Eden. He is still using the mouth as his agent to utter haughty and blasphemous words against the almighty God in order to try and tempt and deceive God's people. "It was allowed to exercise authority" not by Satan, but by God. And it is limited in that to forty-two months, which we have already defined elsewhere as the entire church age. That the beast has to be allowed authority and that it is limited in time by God should encourage us toward bolder witness and worship of the almighty God who is over even the most oppressive powers of this world. Again, for John, Rome would have been in view during his day, but it is not limited to Rome. The beast works through the words of evil empires throughout the entire church age.

Old Testament Background to Revelation 13:5. Daniel 7:6, 8: "And dominion was given to it . . . came up among them another horn, a little one."

Revelation 13:6. The beast did not waste his authority, but blasphemed the name of God's people. This verse further confirms that God's temple in 11:1 represents God's people, both on earth and in heaven, since it defines it for us here. That "those who dwell in heaven" is stated is significant; though the church may look like it is being destroyed on earth, it is linked to the heavenly church that cannot be seen or destroyed. The word for "dwell" here, used twice, is used twice again in only one other verse, Rev. 21:3, where at the new creation "the dwelling place of God is with man and he will dwell with them, and they will be his people, and God himself will be with them as their God." So even here we see the theme of the covenants of God (that he will be our God and we will be his people) in the background, giving assurance that God's promises are sure; no matter how much he and his people are blasphemed against, God's kingdom is victorious.

Old Testament Background to Revelation 13:6. Daniel 7:25: "Shall be given into his hand for a time, times, and half a time."

Revelation 13:7. Not only was the beast allowed to exercise authority, but it was also allowed to make war on the saints and to conquer them. This describes the persecution that Christians face all through the church age, which can end in physical death (thus, the word "conquer"), but will never lead to spiritual death. Thus, though it appears that the beast has conquered the saints by their deaths, just as it appeared that

Christ had been conquered by his death on the cross, we know that just as Christ was raised again to the heavens, so too believers will be raised for eternal life in heaven. The beast was also given universal authority over unbelievers, and he would use these unbelievers, who had not been chosen as God's people from the foundation of the world, in order to accomplish his purposes of persecution, temptation, and deceit toward the church.

Too often we forget that we are targets of Satan. We pity the people who are blinded by the spiritual darkness of the world, but we forget that the prince of that darkness would still like to blind us, persecute us, and tempt us. He is unleashing his anger upon the church of God, but how often are we really prepared for the attack? Do we have the truth planted firmly in our minds so that we dismiss the lies we are told, lies that a career woman is more acceptable than a stay-at-home mom, that it is fine to respond to the man down the street who pays us more attention than our husband, that we have to be thin in order to be loved, and that we have to be fashionable to be acceptable? Do we have righteousness over our hearts so that we are careful not to trust the ideologies of the television shows, of the talk shows, of the newspaper columns? Do we believe that the gospel applies to our present, everyday life, or have we relegated its power only to those who are lost while forgetting its power for the saved? Do we stand firm in our faith, trusting in God's Word and believing in his promises, or do we trust in the empty promises of man? Do we revel in our salvation, or are we still trying to save ourselves from that mistake we made at work, that blunder we made in that relationship, that sin we committed before a holy God? Do we take advantage of the Spirit's power in our lives, or do we use any other resource we can find before realizing that it is powerless and only then turn to God? Do we pray without ceasing, or are we too busy with our schedules to squeeze that in, thus relegating it to the realm of the unimportant and inconsequential in our lives? Are we alert to the evil around us, or do we go around naively thinking that spiritual warfare isn't real?

Old Testament Background to Revelation 13:7–8.
- Daniel 7:10: "A stream of fire issued and came out from before him."
- Daniel 7:14: "His dominion is an everlasting kingdom."

Revelation 13:9. In case we have forgotten that we are targets of Satan, the Word of God here reminds us with an exhortation that we have seen before in Revelation 1:3 and at the conclusion to all the letters to the seven churches: "If anyone has an ear, let him hear." This further validates the conclusion that this section of Revelation is not just speaking about the future, but is directly linked with the historical seven churches, which are representative for all churches throughout the church age.

Revelation 13:10. This is a call for the endurance and faith of the saints. It is an allusion to Jeremiah 15:2 and 43:11, which was a prophecy concerning Israel's captivity for its sin and unbelief. Along with the unbelievers, the believers went into captivity. Even the faithful remnant had to suffer exile. So too, during the church age, the church is a remnant in the captivity of suffering in this world where Satan has been given authority to persecute, tempt, and deceive. Indeed, not only is the believer told that he will be taken "captive," but also that he may have to endure the sword on behalf of his witness and worship of the truth.

It may be more difficult for Americans to grasp the idea of "captivity" and "the sword" than it is for our brothers and sisters suffering in restricted nations. In Eritrea, a country in northeast Africa, which is devastated by war and drought, hundreds of people flee to Ethiopia or Sudan each week as they try to escape the oppression of a Marxist government. This government is purposeful in its plan to destroy evangelicalism in the country. We know that there are at least 2,000 Eritreans who are imprisoned for their faith. Some are put in underground cells without proper nutrition and medical attention; others are left to die. Some are placed in metal shipping containers that are either extremely hot or extremely cold.[2] These brothers and sisters know the meaning

---

2. This information is taken from the Voice of the Martyrs website, in the section on Eritrea under "Restricted Nations," accessed March 31, 2012, at http://www.persecution.com /public/ restrictednations.aspx?country_ID=MTc%3dwww.persecution.com.

of this verse in Revelation firsthand. They live it every day. And they are choosing to endure and have faith that their reward is in heaven and that the Lord will take vengeance upon their persecutors. Pray for them. Pray for those of us here in the States who face a different kind of "captivity" and "sword" (deception and temptation) that are just as detrimental to our witness and worship of God.

Old Testament Background to Revelation 13:10.

- Jeremiah 15:2: "Those who are for pestilence to pestilence, and those who are for the sword."
- Jeremiah 43:11: "Giving over to the pestilence those who are doomed to the pestilence, to captivity those who are doomed to captivity, and to the sword those who are doomed to the sword."
- Ezekiel 14:12–23: "But some survivors will be left in it, sons and daughters who will be brought out."

II. John's Vision of the Beast Rising out of the Earth (Rev. 13:11–18)

Revelation 13:11. Now we come to the third of seven signs in this section of the book (Rev. 12:1–15:4), signaled by the phrase "then I saw." Contrary to the beast that rose out of the sea in the last section, this one rises from the earth. Like the Lamb (Christ) in Revelation 5:6, this beast also has horns like a lamb, but only two instead of seven. This reflects the two witnesses in chapter 11, but also is an allusion to Daniel 8:3, "a ram that had two horns," which depicts an evil ruler. This beast, like the second one, has been given authority by Satan to speak persecution, deceit, and temptation. It will later be identified as "the false prophet" in Revelation 16:13, which makes it clear that the beast takes on a religious role. He could also be identified with the Rome of John's day and the "Romes" of our own day, but it also represents false prophets in the church itself.

Old Testament Background to Revelation 13:11. Daniel 8:3–4: "A ram . . . two horns . . . he did as he pleased and became great."

Revelation 13:12. Here we see clearly that the second beast is the counterfeit to the Holy Spirit. Just as the Holy Spirit enables believers to worship Christ, so this second beast draws the unbelievers to worship the first beast, the counterfeit to Christ. Because he is so closely linked with the second beast, which symbolizes the state, the second beast too now becomes clearly linked with the state.[3]

Revelation 13:13–14. The great sign alluded to in verse 13 occurred when Elijah challenged the prophets of Baal to call upon the name of their God to answer by fire upon the bull sacrifices on the altar. It was only the true God who answered by fire, consuming the burnt offering and the wood, the stones, the dust, and the water that had been laid around the altar. And Elijah slaughtered the prophets of Baal (1 Kings 18:20–40). By these signs the beast deceives those on earth, leading them to idolatry. That this beast stands in contrast to a true prophet is demonstrated by his following in the footsteps of the first beast in his ministry and in his authority, by his persuasion being linked to the one who was wounded and yet lived, and by the miraculous signs that he performs.[4]

When leaders in the church take their message from the world instead of from the Word, they corrupt the Christian church. We must be on guard against culturally influenced messages in our churches. Christ is changeless and timeless. God's Word is to be applied to our lives at all times and is to be the standard of absolute truth. When our sisters in Christ take their ideologies from secular sources, we must confront them lovingly with the truth. And if they are unwilling to stop promoting their false views, we must ask them, again lovingly, to step down from their leadership positions. Whether we are talking about women's ministry, the welcoming ministry, the children's ministry, the sports ministry, or any other ministry, teaching that is more influenced by the world than by the Word is not to be tolerated in Christ's church.

Revelation 13:15. We see further that this beast is a counterfeit to the Holy Spirit as he "gave breath" to the idol that represented the beast. Though this could include magic, it is more than that; it is anything that makes people believe that the idol symbolizes God.

3. Beale, *The Book of Revelation*, 708.
4. Ibid., 709.

LESSON 12

It is anything or anyone that people put in the place of truth. The reference at the end of the verse to have those slain who would not worship the beast alludes to Nebuchadnezzar's decree that any who would not worship his image should be killed (Daniel 3). In John's day there were increased demands on citizens to worship the emperor. If Christians refused, they were in danger of being killed. It is not just death that is in view here, but suffering for the faith in any measure, which is applicable to all Christians of all times.[5]

Revelation 13:16–17. The mark on the right hand or forehead most likely symbolizes the state's "mark of approval" on citizens who were devoted to the emperor. If one was not, they were ostracized both socially and economically (at the very least).[6] Just as Christians are identified with an invisible seal and the name of Christ, so too unbelievers are identified with an invisible mark and the name of the beast. The placement of the mark on the forehead symbolizes the fact that one's character is lined up with that of the beast, while the placement of the mark on the hand symbolizes the fact that one's conduct is in line with that of the beast. In John's day, the second beast, while related to the first beast (which represented Rome), was more specifically associated with the councils in certain provinces made up of representatives who met to discuss political affairs.[7]

Revelation 13:18. Just as Christians wear the name of Christ, so nonbelievers wear the name of the counterfeit Christ, which is the first beast discussed in Revelation 13:1–10. It should not surprise us that much debate centers on the meaning of the number "666" in this verse. After all, John himself says, "it calls for wisdom" to understand. But the book of Revelation was written for all believers to understand. This is simply another way of saying, "He who has an ear, let him hear what the Spirit of God says to the churches." And what we are to hear is that we need to be wise and discerning in spiritual matters to protect ourselves from the deceit of evil.

5. Ibid., 711–13.
6. Leon Morris, *The Book of Revelation: An Introduction and Commentary*, Tyndale New Testament Commentaries, rev. ed. (Leicester: InterVarsity; Grand Rapids: Eerdmans, 1987), 167.
7. Beale, *The Book of Revelation*, 717.

Because God gives us wisdom to understand his Word, we seek to "calculate the number of the beast." Given the symbolic use of numbers in Revelation, "666" is most likely symbolic as well. Since "seven" is used to symbolize completeness and perfection, it would be logical to assume that "six" falls short of completeness and perfection.[8] And given the fact that we are talking here about the counterfeit trinity, it would make sense to use "six" three times to connote that the counterfeit trinity has missed the mark of completion and perfection that the true Trinity represents. Yet it is not only the counterfeit trinity that is in view, but also all of its followers, who fall short of God's perfect and complete plan for mankind, including especially false teachers in the church.[9]

Old Testament Background to Revelation 13:18.

- Daniel 11:33: "The wise among the people shall make many understand."
- Daniel 12:10: "But those who are wise shall understand."

CONCLUSION

We will always worship someone or something. If we are not worshiping the truth, we are worshiping the counterfeit of truth. God's purposes for our lives are not found through the ideologies of this world. They are found in God's Word. Anything short of God's complete and perfect purposes is not to be adopted as truth. We must be wise and discerning as to who and what we listen to, read, and interact with. We are called to be witnesses and worshipers of the truth and the truth is found in one place and one place alone: the Word of God.

8. Vern S. Poythress, *The Returning King: A Guide to the Book of Revelation* (Phillipsburg, NJ: P&R Publishing, 2000), 147.

9. Beale, *The Book of Revelation*, 722.

LESSON 13

Revelation 14:1–13

PLEASE USE THE QUESTION paradigm from pages 353–54 as you work through the following. See the introductory comments there that explain each part of the process below in more detail.

- **Pray**.
- **Ponder the Passage**. Read Revelation 14:1–13 once a day from different translations for the entire week, looking for its:
  - Point
  - Persons
  - Patterns
  - Persons of the Trinity
  - Puzzling Parts
- **Put It in Perspective**.
  - Place in Scripture
  - Passages from Other Parts of Scripture

1. Based on your observations of the text, what is the basic content of this passage? Try to summarize it in your own words, using a sentence or two.
2. Look up "Mount Zion" in a concordance (Rev. 14:1). To what does it usually refer in Scripture?

189

3. In what chapter in Revelation have we already seen the "144,000"? To what did the number refer there? To what do you think it refers in Revelation 14:1? How do you know (what does the verse say that they had on their foreheads and what happened in chapter 7)?

4. Look up the phrase "new song" in a concordance (Rev. 14:3). What does it usually celebrate? Why do you think only the redeemed could sing it?

5. What three attributes do we see that characterize the redeemed in Revelation 14:4–5? Look up "virgin" in Scripture. Does it ever refer to the church? Where? Look up Ephesians 5:25–27. What metaphor is used to describe Christ's relationship with the church? How does this help you interpret Revelation 14:4? Look up "firstfruits" in a concordance. With what are they associated? How does that apply here?

6. To what time period does Revelation 14:6–7 refer in light of the phrase, "because the hour of his judgment has come"? Do you think this is a call for salvation, or has the time for salvation passed and this is an announcement of judgment (look at the context of the entire passage)?

7. Look up "Babylon" in a concordance. Does "Babylon" always refer to the geographical city of Babylon in Scripture or is it symbolic in places? If so, what does it symbolize? What do you think it means in Revelation 14:8? What is the reason for her judgment?

8. Contrast the "wine" of Babylon in Revelation 14:8 with the "wine of God's wrath" in 14:9. What differences do you find?

9. How does Revelation 14:11 affirm that hell is a place of eternal torment?

10. How is Isaiah 14:12 a key to the purpose of the entire passage?

11. Look up the word "blessed" in a concordance. Where are the seven blessings found in the book of Revelation? What is pronounced in the blessing of Revelation 14:13? Which dead are blessed? Why is this significant in light of the previous verses?

- **Principles and Points of Application.**

1. Sing or write a song of your own today to the Lamb of God, Jesus Christ, for redeeming you from your sin and eternal death. Look up "redeemed/redeemer/redemption" in a concordance and write down some of the verses that most speak to your heart and present circumstances. Ask the Lord to help you commit them to memory this week.

2. Fear God and give him glory for the day of his judgment is coming. Who or what has that place of fear or glory in your life at present? Come back to worshiping Christ alone today.

3. How does our world today resemble the sexual immorality, idolatry, and materialism of Babylon? What parameters do you have in your personal life and family to guard against the "Babylons" of our day by relying on the Holy Spirit's power to escape them?

4. Meditate on Revelation 14:10a. This is what Christ did for you. He drank the wine of God's wrath, poured full strength into the cup of his anger. Thank Christ today for the work of redemption on the cross and worship him for who he is, for what he has accomplished, and for what both he and the Holy Spirit have applied to you.

5. What "deeds" will follow you to heaven? The Scriptures say that we will be rewarded for the work done for God's glory here on earth. What work does God want you to be involved with now? Pray for God to reveal this to you and then take action to get involved.

NOTES FOR REVELATION 14:1–13

Aim: Ponder the aim of this lesson concerning our:

Mind: What do we need to know from this passage in Scripture?

That God is glorified by the believers' final reward and the unbelievers' final judgment.

Heart: How does what we learn from this passage affect our internal relationship with the Lord?

> It prepares us to be kingdom disciples who fear and glorify God in the face of final judgment and reward, turning away from immorality and idolatry.

Hands: How does what we learn from this passage translate into action for God's kingdom?

> It enables us to:

1. Write a poem, song, or letter to the Lamb of God, thanking him for redeeming us from sin and eternal death.
2. Commit to memory, by relying on the Spirit, Bible verses concerning redemption.
3. Give God alone the fear and the glory that he is due.
4. Place boundaries in our personal and family lives, relying on the Spirit's strength, to keep us from falling into sexual immorality.
5. Pray about what "good works" God wants to accomplish through us and take action this week to get involved while relying on the Spirit's power.

INTRODUCTION

I recently completed an intense house-hunting frenzy. This was the second one within six months, but this time it was not to buy, it was to alleviate my own stress over feeling like my husband and I had made a "mistake" with the first one. The first house-hunting trip lasted a total of two weekends, one of which, we later found out from my husband's employer, involved looking in the wrong section of the city in which he'd be working. The second weekend, both of our small children were with us and both were sick, whiny, and not content to be in car seats driving around looking at homes. To say the least, it was not a positive experience and was very draining emotionally. We probably should have rented until we knew the city better, but hindsight is always clearer than what you see when you are going through some experience, so we ended up buying a home. The purpose of the second house-hunting trip, then, was not to find a new home, but to find contentment with the one that I had. I knew that I was kicking and screaming against the Lord. He was the one who had orchestrated the events of this move. He was the one who had provided this home for us, and I was grumbling and complaining against him.

I knew when I went looking that I was in trouble. Materialism latched onto me and I saw bigger and better homes that I would like to have; indeed, felt I even "deserved" to have. I saw areas of the city that I liked much better than ours, but we couldn't afford these. While my discontentment could have continued to grow, the Lord did a very gracious thing in my heart. I had set out to prove that we were wrong in the choice of our home, but what ended up happening was that the Lord proved himself right in the choice of our home. As I looked, he revealed to me that he had chosen a nice neighborhood and a nice home for us to live in, and over time he would reveal to me different reasons why it right for us to be located where we were. So, a deep trust overcame my lack of understanding and I finally settled down into contentment.

If it had not been for the grace of God, though, materialism would have had its way in my heart and I would have exchanged the God of glory for the god of gold and gotten into a heap of trouble. This indeed is what Satan wanted me to do. Hiding behind the god of materialism is the god of the kingdom of darkness, who tempts and deceives and lures us in ways that ensnare our hearts. This god (and all that he represents) is judged in this chapter of Revelation, which thus opens up our eyes to the truth behind the lies.

We can divide this lesson into two sections:

  I. The Song of the Redeemed before the Throne (Rev. 14:1–5)
 II. The Call by Three Angels for the Endurance of the Saints (Rev. 14:6–12)

The final four signs (Rev. 14:1ff; 14:6ff; 14:14ff; 15:2–4) concern the *final* judgment of unbelievers and the *final* reward of believers.

I. The Song of the Redeemed before the Throne (Rev. 14:1–5)

Revelation 14:1. In contrast to the dragon that "stood on the sand of the sea" (Rev. 12:17), we now see the Lamb standing on the mountain of Zion. And just as it was implied that those who had his name and his mark stood with the dragon, so here those who have Christ's name and God the Father's name written on their foreheads are with the Lamb. "Mount Zion" is used nineteen times in the Old Testament; almost half of the occurrences refer to a remnant being saved on behalf of God's name and/or sovereignty. So here it refers to the final city where God dwells with his people, providing for and protecting them. The name of God the Father and God the Son that is "written on our foreheads" is a figurative way of saying that God is with us, protecting us and preserving us until the very end of the age. This recalls the seal placed on the 144,000 in Revelation 7:1–8. In contrast to the imperfect and incomplete number of the unregenerate, "666," who have failed to fulfill God's purposes for mankind, stand the perfect and complete number of the regenerate, "144,000."

We are citizens now of this Mount Zion (Heb. 12:22–24). Although it has only been inaugurated, God is with us now, protecting us and preserving us. Are we living as a citizen of Mount Zion, or are we living as citizens of this world? Are we seeking to fulfill God's purposes for mankind, or are we listening to the purposes of this world? As citizens of Zion, we stand secure in our worship because we know that we have a reason to worship. The Light has overcome the darkness. As those made to fulfill God's purposes, we stand strong and bold as witnesses to the Light that has overcome the darkness of this world and of our own sinful hearts.

Revelation 14:2–3. What John has just seen with his eyes, he now hears with his ears. And what he hears confirms that Mount Zion is a place where the people of God dwell with him in protection, praising him for the victory that he has won over Satan and sin. The two other

times where we see the harpists and heavenly hosts singing a new song
are in Revelation 5:8–9 and 15:2–3, and these too are singing for victory
over Satan and sin. In Isaiah 35:10 (see below) the prophet prophesied
that this would occur. We saw earlier in this study that God's people,
to praise him for victory over their enemies, sang the "new song" in the
Old Testament. Now the final new song is sung as the final victory is
completed. Only those who know the "new name" of God can sing the
"new song" that concerns God's victory. Both the redeemed in heaven
(represented by cherubim and elders in Rev. 5:8–10) and the redeemed
on earth sing this song.

Are we singing this "new song" as we go about our days in which
God's mercies are new every morning? Do we have joy in our hearts
when we get up in the morning, knowing that we have a new song to
sing, or do we get out of bed to face the same old relentless schedule
of the day before? Every day is an opportunity for us to give God the
glory and worship that he deserves for his victory over Satan and sin.
To know that he has overcome sin and that the Holy Spirit has been
given to us to overcome it in our own lives is great reason indeed for
us to sing a new song! We have been made new creatures in Christ—so
let us sing!

Old Testament Background to Revelation 14:2–3.

- Psalm 96:1–2: "Oh sing to the LORD a new song . . . tell of his
  salvation."
- Isaiah 35:10: "And the ransomed of the LORD shall return and
  come to Zion with singing."
- Isaiah 42:10: "Sing to the LORD a new song."

Revelation 14:4–5. "It is these" refers back to the "144,000," which
represents the entire redeemed people of God. Thus, this must inform
our understanding of the following words. First, the redeemed are said
to be virgins, those who have not defiled themselves with women. In
the Old Testament, the word "virgin" is often applied to Israel, as is
the imagery of betrothal with God, which she is so often portrayed as
breaking. Here then the reference is to the redeemed people of God

195

who have remained faithful to their heavenly Bridegroom, not defiling themselves with the idolatry of the world.

Second, "they follow the Lamb wherever he goes," which conveys absolute allegiance and surrender to his plan and purposes. Indeed, they are presented as "firstfruits" to God and the Lamb, which alludes to the sacrificial system in which the firstfruits were to be given to God to signify that one was giving him the very best that he or she had. Here the saints were willing to sacrifice their very selves for the sake of the kingdom of God. These "firstfruits" (the redeemed) stand in contrast to those who will be judged, since this passage speaks of the final judgment. God harvests the firstfruits (his chosen people) and sets them aside from the rest of mankind that is defiled by idolatry and immorality.

Third, "in their mouth no lie was found." This stands in contrast to the Jews of John's day "who say that they are Jews and are not, but are a synagogue of Satan" (Rev. 2:9) and "those of the synagogue of Satan who say that they are Jews and are not, but lie" (Rev. 3:9). The final clause, "for they are blameless," does not mean that they are sinless, but that God stands as witness of his witnesses that they have no reason to be condemned by their persecutors; indeed, in the final judgment their persecutors are condemned by him.[1] For the allusions in these verses to Isaiah and Zechariah see below.

Do these three qualities characterize our own lives? Are we committed to our Lord and Savior Jesus Christ as our Bridegroom, or are we having affairs with the gods of our culture, the god of materialism, the god of beauty, the god of pride, the god of selfishness, the god of independence? Are we absolutely surrendered to God's plan for our lives, or do we follow him only when it is convenient for us? Are we unashamedly witnesses and worshipers of Christ, or do we stand up for him only when it is socially acceptable, politically correct, and economically advantageous?

Old Testament Background to Revelation 14:4–5.
- Isaiah 37:22: "The virgin daughter of Zion."

---

1. G. K. Beale, *The Book of Revelation: A Commentary on the Greek Text*, New International Greek Testament Commentary (Grand Rapids: Eerdmans, 1999), 739–46.

- Isaiah 53:9: "He had done no violence and there was no deceit in his mouth."
- Jeremiah 2:2–3: "Your love as a bride . . . the firstfruits of his harvest."
- Hosea 1:2: "For the land commits great whoredom by forsaking the LORD."
- Zephaniah 3:13: "And speak no lies, nor shall there be found in their mouth a deceitful tongue."

II. The Call by Three Angels for the Endurance of the Saints (Rev. 14:6–12)

This is the fifth of seven signs that began at Revelation 12:1 and end with 15:2–4.

Revelation 14:6–7. The first angel that John sees is flying overhead with the gospel, announcing judgment to the unbelievers on earth immediately preceding the final judgment (elsewhere in the book the unbelievers are also described as "those who dwell on earth, to every nation and tribe and language and people"). The message of the angel is good news to the believers because the hour has come for God's kingdom to be established on earth and for them to be vindicated. But the message is bad news to unbelievers, who are doomed to eternal separation from God. The fear and glory and worship that are called for here are the same that were required in Revelation 11:13, and the same that are required in Philippians 2:9–11. When Christ returns every knee will bow and every tongue confess that Jesus Christ is Lord to the glory of God the Father. Thus, this is not a call to salvation, for that time is past; this is now a forced acknowledgment of God's sovereignty that the unbelievers denied all throughout their lifetimes. If we understand it differently, and take it to be one last invitation to turn to saving faith before the final judgment, then from the following verses, we must conclude that the invitation is rejected. Thus, the result is the same either way it is understood.

These verses should compel us toward evangelism while the day is still called "today." The Lord is still holding out his invitation to mankind to follow him. He has chosen to reveal his Son through the witness of believers (John 1:6–8). The Great Commission (Matt. 28:16–20) is not an option; it is a command. We must be prepared "in season and out of season" to "do the work of an evangelist" and "fulfill [our] ministry" (2 Tim 4:2, 5). The best witness is our worship of God in every aspect of our lives. Our neighbors will pay little attention to our words if they observe the work of our hands to be diametrically opposed to what we say. When Christians live out their lives based on the Word of God, the Spirit uses them to draw others to the King of kings and Lord of lords.

Old Testament/New Testament Background to Revelation 14:6–7.

- Daniel 4:34: "[Nebuchadnezzar] blessed the Most High and praised and honored him who lives forever."
- Matthew 24:14: "And the gospel of the kingdom will be proclaimed throughout the whole world as a testimony to all nations and then the end will come."
- Philippians 2:9–11: "At the name of Jesus, every knee will bow . . . and every tongue confess that Jesus Christ is Lord to the glory of God the Father."

Revelation 14:8. The second angel announces the fall of "Babylon the Great" and the reason why she fell. She deceived the nations into idolatry and immorality. This is not speaking of a particular geographical city, but symbolizes the entire evil world system, driven by Satan, to promote idolatry and immorality. As will be seen in chapter 18, "the wine of the passion of her sexual immorality" is also a metaphor for her promise of economic welfare for all of her followers, which she could not uphold in the end. She deceived herself as much as she deceived others, as her destruction in the end testifies. The god of materialism continues to be prevalent among many economically wealthy countries today. Certainly believers in America are in danger of falling prey to "Babylon's" lies that wealth provides security and independence. If we are not careful, we will find ourselves pursuing wealth at all costs, only to find in the end that we are enslaved to its demands. People everywhere in our society are crumbling underneath the pressure and devastation of foreclosure, bankruptcy, and the like because they bought into the American dream that says that wealth delivers happiness and that we should do whatever we can to acquire it, no matter what the cost. But God's Word speaks of a different wine than that of Babylon; it is the wine of wrath. Materialism leads to idolatry, which leads to destruction.

Old Testament Background to Revelation 14:8.
- Isaiah 21:9: "Fallen, fallen is Babylon; and all the carved images of her gods he has shattered to the ground."
- Jeremiah 51:7–8: "Babylon was a golden cup in the LORD's hand, making all the earth drunken; the nations drank of her wine; therefore, the nations went mad."
- Daniel 4:30: "And the king answered and said, 'Is not this great Babylon, which I have built by my power as a royal residence and for the glory of my majesty?' "

Revelation 14:9–11. Now John sees a third angel, which also announces judgment. The unbelievers are not done drinking with Babylon. Her wine is only temporary. They will move on to drink the wine of God's wrath, which is eternal. There will be no dilution of judgment; they will suffer eternal consequences for their disbelief, being eternally separated from God. Their torment will be before the very one they refused to acknowledge, the Lamb of God, whom they pierced. Thus, all unbelievers of every age are finally judged for their allegiance to the kingdom of darkness and enter into eternal torment.

Old Testament Background to Revelation 14:9–11. Isaiah 34:9–10: "And the streams of Edom shall be turned into pitch . . . its smoke shall go up forever."

This is hard for so many to grasp in our society today. We want instant pleasure and instant results. We don't count the consequences beforehand. We dive headlong into sin because it feels good now, and we never stop to think that we have launched ourselves onto a road of destruction. Sin and its pleasures are only temporary but the results are eternal. If we would stop and contemplate whether we want to drink the wine of success, materialism, and worldly beauty, which all lead to drinking the wine of God's wrath, the choice would seem easy. But we rarely stop to contemplate in this way. That is why John continues to call us to be wise and discerning.

Revelation 14:12. The purpose of the angels' announcement was not merely for judgment, but also to call the saints to endure through persecution, to resist the temptation to compromise, and to recognize the deception of Satan, so that they will receive an eternal reward. This recalls the call in Revelation 13:18: "This calls for wisdom: let the one who has understanding calculate the number of the beast." We saw that this meant being wise to calculate the deceptive nature of Satan and his power so that one is not caught off guard and led astray. The same meaning is in view here. Where are we turning for wisdom and understanding? There is only one basis for truth, and it is the Word of God. We must wake with it, parent with it, educate with it, rest with it, eat with it, and sleep with it; indeed, we must live out our very lives with it. It is the only Word that will grant us wisdom to walk away from the snares of Satan.

Note here also that endurance consists in keeping the commandments of God and having faith in Jesus. Too often the second is emphasized and the first overlooked. John tells us that to love God, which is to know God, is to keep his commandments (1 John 5:3). Thus, we must stress in our churches today that God is just as concerned with our conduct as he is with our confession. The former proves that the latter is genuine.

Revelation 14:13. This is the second of seven blessings that John records in his book (Rev. 1:3; 16:15; 19:9; 20:6; 22:7; 22:14 are the others). It is not simply the dead who are blessed, but the "dead who die in the Lord." For they will be eternal dwellers with God, and their good deeds done here on earth will follow them to heaven, giving evidence that they have a place there, so that they can enter into Sabbath rest for eternity.

So many believers fear death or fear the death of their loved ones. But John calls death for believers a blessing. It is a blessing because we will finally rest in the presence of our Lord and Savior Jesus Christ for all of eternity. All of the "good works" that we do here on earth validate our faith as genuine and grant us the privilege of resting after the hard work on earth is done. It is not that work will be over, but that the work done in the face of sin, persecution, deception, and temptation will be behind us forever.

CONCLUSION

I am so thankful for the Lord's gracious discipline in my life as he brought me to the point of surrender and submission concerning our home. I will never understand all of the reasons why we moved where we did, but I trust that my heavenly Father moved us there for his own purposes and plans. I am even more thankful that he saved me from the snare of materialism that I did not even think was so close to the surface of my heart. For the snare of materialism is a distraction to our witness and our worship, of both of which the Lord is more than worthy.

LESSON 14

Revelation 14:14–15:4

PLEASE USE THE QUESTION paradigm from pages 353–54 as you work through the following. See the introductory comments there that explain each part of the process below in more detail.

- **Pray**.
- **Ponder the Passage**. Read Revelation 14:14–15:4 once a day from different translations for the entire week, looking for its:
  - Point
  - Persons
  - Patterns
  - Persons of the Trinity
  - Puzzling Parts
- **Put It in Perspective**.
  - Place in Scripture
  - Passages from Other Parts of Scripture

1. Based on your observations of the text, what is the basic content of Revelation 14:14–15:4? Try to summarize it in your own words, using a sentence or two.
2. Read Daniel 7:13, Matthew 24:30, and Revelation 1:12–18. Who is "one like a son of man" in Revelation 14:14? What does the

"golden crown" on his head represent? Look up Jeremiah 50:16 and Joel 3:13. What is the context in these verses? How do you think "sickle" should be interpreted in Revelation 14:14? Is it used for judgment or redemption?

3. How does the phrase "for the hour to reap has come" reflect Revelation 14:7? What was the context in that passage? What do you think the context is here?

4. Who tells whom to reap in Revelation 14:15? What does this imply (read Mark 13:32)? From where does the angel's voice come? Read Revelation 6:1–5; 9:13; 16:7, 17 for the other places in the book where a command comes from the temple. What is always the context? What is the context here?

5. How did Christ respond (Rev. 14:16)? How does this reflect Christ's obedience and submission to his Father?

6. What similarities do you see in Revelation 14:17–20 with 14:14–16? What differences? Read Joel 3:13. What imagery is used there? How does this compare to these two different passages of Revelation?

7. Read Revelation 6:6–11 with 8:3–5 and 14:18. What do you see?

8. To whom/what does the city refer in Revelation 14:20 (read 20:8–9; 21:8, 27; 22:15)?

9. Read Revelation 19:17–18. How does this help define Revelation 14:20?

10. What is introduced in the interlude of Revelation 15:1?

11. What color would a "sea of glass mingled with fire" be? Where else have we seen a sea this color in the Bible? What was the context? How would that relate to the second exodus of God's people from this world?

12. Look up Exodus 15 and Deuteronomy 32. What is the context of these passages? How does it relate to the saints' praise in Revelation 15:3–4?

13. What characteristics of God are being praised in Revelation 15:3–4? What conduct of God is being praised? Why will "all nations" come and worship God? In the context of "worship"

as opposed to acknowledgment, is "all nations" a reference to all people everywhere or a reference to the fact that there will be believers called out from all the nations?

• **Principles and Points of Application.**

1. How is the Holy Spirit using you to sow a rich harvest for the kingdom of God? Who in your life needs to hear the gospel? How will you share it with them this week, relying on the power of the Holy Spirit? Are you part of the ripe harvest? What fruit in your life displays this?

2. Spend time today praying for specific people in your life who have heard the gospel, but are hardened toward its message. Use 2 Timothy 2:25–26 to pray that God will "grant them repentance leading to a knowledge of the truth, [that] they may come to their senses and escape from the snare of the devil, after being captured by him to do his will."

3. Meditate on Deuteronomy 32:1–43 and Exodus 15:1–18. Now write your own song of praise to the Lord for what he has done in your past, what he is doing your present, and what he will do for you in your future.

NOTES FOR REVELATION 14:14-5:4

Aim: Ponder the aim of this lesson concerning our:

Mind: What do we need to know from this passage in Scripture?

That God is glorified with the believers' final reward and the unbelievers' final judgment.

Heart: How does what we learn from this passage affect our internal relationship with the Lord?

It prepares us to be kingdom disciples who fear and glorify God in the face of final judgment and reward.

Hands: How does what we learn from this passage translate into action for God's kingdom?

It enables us to:

1. Recognize that the Spirit uses us to sow a rich harvest for the kingdom of God as we faithfully witness and worship.
2. Pray for those in our lives who have heard the gospel, but are hardened toward it.
3. Write our own song, patterned after the "Song of Moses," that relates to God's deliverance in our past and present, and to what he has promised to do in our future.
4. Share with others how to approach the throne of grace boldly and with confidence through faith in Jesus Christ, rather than hiding from his judgment.

INTRODUCTION

I spotted her out of the corner of my eye. It was dusk on a cold winter night. I had run down to get the mail and hadn't expected to see anyone out for a walk, but her downcast figure painfully walked the streets. Though her burden was not visible, I could still see it in the way her shoulders were hunched over and her head was down. As she got closer, I could see it in her eyes. She was tired. Tired of life. She had asked me a few weeks earlier to pray for her, but this was the first time I had seen her face to face. We were meant to intersect paths that night; God had orchestrated our meeting. As we talked, I could see the hole in her heart. She was beaten and bruised, not physically, but emotionally and mentally. Her expectations had been dashed and she couldn't climb out of the darkness. Most of her pain concerned a rebellious son and the state of his soul.

As I pondered our conversation later the next day, my thoughts turned to those whom I love dearly who are in serious rebellion against God. My expectations too have been burst, and my burden for my loved ones is great. I pray that God will "grant them repentance leading to a knowledge of the truth, [that] they may come to their senses and escape from the snare of the devil, after being captured by him to do his will" (2 Tim. 2:25–26).

So many days I long for Jesus to come back. I am tired of the kingdom of this world. I long for righteousness to reign and justice to have its final say. But then I remember that if this happened my loved ones would be judged and eternally separated from God, so I long instead for another day of God's longsuffering patience, hoping that he will have mercy on them and bring them to repentance.

It is these two themes that John is concerned about in this passage of Revelation: judgment and redemption. Both lead to worship of the King of the nations, the almighty God.

We can divide this lesson into two sections:

I. The Gathering of Believers and the Judgment of Unbelievers (Rev. 14:14–20)
II. The Introduction of the Bowls and the Believers' Worship of Almighty God (Rev. 15:1–4)

The last two signs, along with the previous two (Rev. 14:1ff; 14:6ff; 14:14ff; 15:2–4), concern the *final* judgment of unbelievers and the *final* reward of believers.

I. The Gathering of Believers and the Judgment of Unbelievers (Rev. 14:14–20)

Revelation 14:14. This begins the sixth of seven signs in this section (Rev. 12:1–15:4), which, from a literary perspective, follows the trumpets and precedes the bowls, but chronologically is temporally parallel with them. It is Christ whom John sees seated on the white cloud with a golden crown on his head, signifying his kingship and his right to judge, and with a sharp sickle in his hand, signifying that he will judge.

Old Testament/New Testament Background to Revelation 14:14.
- Daniel 7:13: "With the clouds of heaven there came one like a son of man."

- Matthew 24:30–31: "All the tribes of the earth will mourn and they will see the Son of Man coming on the clouds of heaven with power and great glory. And he will send out his angels and they will gather the elect."

Revelation 14:15–16. "And another angel came out of the temple" means that the angel has come from being in the presence of God. Commands from God's presence in the book always refer to God's judgment (Rev. 6:1–5; 9:13; 16:7, 17). The angel comes to tell Christ (who is also in God's presence) that the hour to reap has come, for not even the angels in heaven nor Christ knew when the time of judgment would be, but only God the Father (Mark 13:32; Acts 1:7). The nine other times that "hour" occurs in the book, it always refers to judgment (Rev. 3:3, 10; 9:15; 11:13; 14:7; 17:12–13; 18:10, 17, 19), as it does here.

The metaphor that is used here is one of the harvest. This is appropriate, for in God's covenant with Noah he made a promise that "while the earth remains, seedtime and harvest, cold and heat, summer and winter, day and night, shall not cease" (Gen. 8:22). Implicit in Genesis 8:22 is that there will be a time when the earth does not remain. And that is the time that has come in these verses. God has proven faithful to his covenant, but now as the one over the harvest of the crops and over the harvest of souls, he commands his Son, whom he gave the right of Judge, to reap. So Christ, in perfect obedience to his Father and in his Father's time, just as he was perfectly obedient on the cross, puts in his sickle and reaps the earth.

From the context, it seems that these verses portray the judgment of the unrighteous, rather than the gathering of the elect.[1] However, some interpreters see these verses as describing God's gathering of his people, with the following verses showing the gathering of unbelievers

---

1. For this view see G. K. Beale, *The Book of Revelation: A Commentary on the Greek Text*, New International Greek Testament Commentary (Grand Rapids: Eerdmans, 1999), 770; Vern S. Poythress, *The Returning King: A Guide to the Book of Revelation* (Phillipsburg, NJ: P&R Publishing, 2000), 152; and Robert H. Mounce, *The Book of Revelation*, New International Commentary on the New Testament, rev. ed. (Grand Rapids: Eerdmans, 1998), 278.

for judgment.[2] However one interprets this text, it is clear from other Old and New Testament passages that there will also be a gathering of the righteous at the end of the church age (Isa. 27:12; Hos. 6:11; Matt. 9:27–38; Luke 10:2; John 4:35–38).

Old Testament/New Testament Background to Revelation 14:15–16.

- Jeremiah 51:33: "The daughter of Babylon is like a threshing floor at the time when it is trodden; yet a little while and the time of her harvest will come."
- Joel 3:13: "Put in the sickle for the harvest is ripe. Go in, tread, for the winepress is full. The vats overflow, for their evil is great."
- Zechariah 5:1–3: "A flying scroll . . . this is the curse that goes out over the face of the whole land."
- Mark 13:32: "But concerning that day or hour, no one knows, not even the angels in heaven, nor the Son, but only the Father."
- Acts 1:7: "It is not for you to know times or seasons that the Father has fixed by his own authority."

There is coming a day to end all days. Are we ready for it? Is our relationship with Christ one of saving faith? What about our loved ones? Are we praying fervently for their salvation? Are we using every opportunity to share the gospel with them in word and in action, relying on the Holy Spirit to open up their hearts? God makes it very clear that his longsuffering will come to an end. Let us make haste to order our relationship with him and with others so that we might be found faithful when Jesus Christ returns.

Revelation 14:17–19. That these verses describe the same events with such similar imagery seems to further confirm that the first harvest was also one of judgment and that both accounts are depicting the same judgment. This would be in line with the Old Testament background of Joel 4:13, which also uses the imagery of harvest and a winepress together, both conveying judgment. That these two accounts are the same and are repeated serves to emphasize the final and climactic judgment.

2. For this view see Dennis E. Johnson, *The Triumph of the Lamb: A Commentary on Revelation* (Phillipsburg, NJ: P&R Publishing, 2001), 209–12.

Now another angel comes from God's presence, and has a sharp sickle in his hand. And another angel gives a command from the altar, which is where the saints cried out, "How long?" concerning their vindication in Revelation 6:9–10 (another indication that this is a context of judgment). It is also where, in Revelation 8:3–5, the angel throws fire down to earth (still another confirmation of judgment). This angel commanded the angel with the sickle to "gather the clusters from the vine of the earth." In the Old Testament this metaphor is always used for judgment. So this angel too obeys the heavenly decree and gathers the grape harvest, throwing it into the great winepress of the wrath of God. This angel is the seventh heavenly being (six angels and Christ) seen in the fifth and sixth signs of judgment combined (Rev. 14:6–20), again conveying the completeness of God's judgment. Whatever one's conclusion with regard to Revelation 14:15–16, these verses clearly denote that this gathering (Rev. 14:17–19) is of the unbelievers only, and for the purpose of judgment.

Old Testament Background to Revelation 14:17–19.

- Isaiah 63:2: "Why is your apparel red, and your garments like his who treads in the winepress?"
- Joel 3:13: "Put in the sickle for the harvest is ripe. Go in, tread, for the winepress is full. The vats overflow, for their evil is great."

Revelation 14:20. God's wrath is certain and eternal for those who do not turn to him in saving faith. This is portrayed here in graphic imagery. The winepress for unbelievers stands "outside the city," which is made up of God's people (Rev. 11:2; 20:8–9; 21:8). Thus, God's people are protected from this winepress by being in his presence. He preserves their blood from flowing because the blood of his Son, Jesus Christ, flowed for them instead. But this is not so for the unbelievers. In graphic war imagery, John depicts the defeat of God's enemies. And the defeat is universal and complete, as the number "1,600" being a multiple of the squares of four and ten (numbers that symbolize completeness in the book) makes clear. The time has come for God to answer his people's cry for vindication. And so for those who made the blood of his children flow, God's judgment now makes their blood flow as well.

Throughout Scripture God repeatedly reminds us that vengeance is his business and he will repay. Believers are not to take vengeance or sit in judgment upon their enemies. The role of judge is reserved for God alone. We are to be faithful witnesses and worshipers of God, willingly laying down our lives, even to be "trampled" on, knowing that one day our persecutors will be trampled in the winepress of the wrath of God. When we read accounts of the apostles or the early church fathers being martyred for their faith, we wonder how they stood so calm and remained so firm in the face of violent death. This is the truth onto which they held: They knew that their persecutors were enabling their (the believers') entrance to heaven, while closing that entrance to their own unbelieving souls. They knew that they didn't have to rise up in violence against the violent, because God's justice would one day be shown to all who persecute his people. God does not turn a blind eye to bloodshed. Rather, he waits until the final number of unbelievers is ready to be trodden in the winepress of his wrath, and then carries out his divine and supremely just vengeance.

This should give great hope to our brothers and sisters throughout the world who are living in the face of persecution every day. They are losing to the sword loved ones who stood firm for their faith. They are watching their churches burn. They are enduring fines and imprisonment. They are enduring the confiscation of their medical and food supplies. Yet they are remaining faithful to their Lord and Savior Jesus Christ, knowing that he went through persecution before them and was glorified on the other side. So we too join hands with them and stand firm as witnesses and worshipers of Christ.

Old Testament Background to Revelation 14:20.

- Isaiah 63:2–3: "Why is your apparel red, and your garments like his who treads in the winepress? I have trodden the winepress alone, and from the peoples no one was with me; I trod them in my anger and trampled them in my wrath; their lifeblood spattered on my garments, and stained all my apparel."
- Joel 3:13b: "Go in, tread, for the winepress is full. The vats overflow, for their evil is great."

211

II. The Introduction of the Bowls and the Believers' Worship of Almighty God (Rev. 15:1–4)

Revelation 15:1. Just as there was an interlude between the opening of the sixth and seventh seals and the blowing of the sixth and seventh trumpets, so here we see an interlude between the giving of the sixth and seventh signs of Revelation 12:1–15:4. The purpose of this interlude is to introduce the seven bowls of judgment in Revelation 15:5–16:21. "Then I saw another sign in heaven," like the almost exactly similar phrase used in Revelation12:1, conveys the idea that another new section of the book is beginning. That the plagues are the "last" does not mean that they are the last plagues within the book chronologically (as those who interpret chapters 4 and following to be referring to the future only believe), but that they are last in terms of how John saw his visions. Otherwise, the phrase "for with them the wrath of God is finished" would be a contradiction, since we have already seen the final judgment portrayed in the seven seals, trumpets, and signs. The first five bowls precede the timeframe of chapter 14 then, since they deal with judgments upon unbelievers throughout the church age. And the sixth and seventh bowls would be temporally parallel with the seventh seal, sixth and seventh trumpets, and fourth through seventh signs, which all describe the final judgment. "Last" for John is chronological in the sense that it refers to the entire last days between Christ's first and second comings, the timeframe that is covered by the seals, trumpets, and signs as well. However, the bowls do convey God's judgment more intensely than the seals, trumpets, and signs do, so in this light, they are "last" as in the grandest description of wrath.[3]

Revelation 15:2. This is the seventh of the seven signs portrayed in Revelation 12:1–15:4. With the final judgment portrayed in the sixth sign, the seventh sign portrays the final exodus of the people of God from this world. Thus, the "sea of glass mingled with fire" is an allusion to the Red Sea crossing of the Israelites during the exodus from Egypt. Just as the Lord allowed his people to cross on dry land with the waters as a wall on each side of them, and drowned the Egyptians

---

3. Beale, *The Book of Revelation*, 784–88.

behind them, so too the Lord allows his people at the end of the age to cross into the Promised Land while destroying the beast before them. That the believers were able to stand beside the sea, which in the Old Testament represented the abode of evil chaos, is further testimony that God has triumphed over evil. Not only has he triumphed over it, but he has also put it to rest forever and reclaimed it as his own abode, which was his right from the beginning.

The believers had conquered "the beast and its image and the number of its name" because the Lamb of God had already conquered him and they were in Christ, sharing in both his suffering and his victory. That they were "standing beside the sea of glass" conveys their active involvement in the war between God and Satan. Perhaps it also indicates their resurrected bodies. They had fought with the fire of witness and worship, which the waters of deception, persecution, and temptation could not quench. "Those who had conquered" are the same as the "144,000" of chapters 7 and 14:1–5, which represents the entirety of God's people. The "harps of God" that they hold are specifically and solely for God alone, to aid in their worship of him.[4]

This world is our Egypt. We are enslaved here, forced to labor under circumstances that are difficult, burdensome, and grueling. The pharaohs who rule us are hardened to the ways of God, trying to force our servitude to the gods of this world. But the people of God rise up and ask for deliverance. We ask to be delivered from persecution, from temptation, from deception. And God hears our prayers. There is coming a day when he will once more part the waters of this world and allow his people to cross to the Promised Land of heaven, leaving the chaos of evil behind forever. Because he stands, we stand too. Because he conquered, we conquer too. Because he reigns, we reign too, forever, with our Lord and Savior Jesus Christ. What should be our response? *Worship*. We worship him with our lives that are to be for God's glory alone. And as we do so, we bear *witness* to a watching world that our God reigns.

4. Ibid., 791.

Old Testament Background to Revelation 15:2.
- Exodus 14: The crossing of the Red Sea.
- Isaiah 51:10: "Was it not you who dried up the sea . . . for the redeemed to pass over?"
- Ezekiel 32:2: "You consider yourself [Pharaoh] a lion of the nations, but you are like a dragon in the seas."
- Daniel 7:10–11: "A stream of fire issued and came out from before [the Ancient of Days] . . . the beast was killed and its body destroyed and given over to be burned with fire."

Revelation 15:3a. Appropriately, the saints who have experienced the second exodus sing the "Song of Moses" that was sung after the first exodus. It was not really the "Song of Moses," though; it was the "Song of the Lamb," because, though Moses wrote it, it was not about him as the servant of God, it was about *the* Servant of God, Jesus Christ. We have seen this song before in Revelation (the "new song" of Rev. 5:9 and 14:3). While it celebrates the redemption of God's people, at the same time it pronounces judgment over God's enemies.

Too often the crossing of the Red Sea only remains a historical story that we teach in children's church or to our own children at home. We read with awe and amazement that it happened, but we leave it in the world of the Old Testament, rarely applying it to our lives today. We believe it really happened, but don't look for it to happen again. But John tells us differently. John tells us that we are going to sing and shout, praising God for delivering us from the chaos of this world. And isn't "chaotic" how we so often portray our days as women? But our God reigns. And, one day he is going to completely calm the chaos of our lives, and we are going to stand beside the sea, which has been sovereignly claimed by God, and peace in all of its fullness will be ours forever. There will be no more chaotic days with our careers, our husbands, our children, our health, our emotions, and our ministries. We are going to sing a new song because it will be a new day in a new land with a new body. Isn't that something to sing about *now*?

Old Testament Background to Revelation 15:3a. Exodus 15 and Deuteronomy 32: "The Song of Moses."

Revelation 15:3b. The actual contents of the "Song of Moses" are not used here in Revelation, but rather, several Old Testament texts are tied together (see the Old Testament backgrounds noted below).[5] "Great and amazing" points back to the interlude in Revelation 15:1, where the bowls are seen as "great and amazing." This is a further confirmation that the visions in the book are not in chronological order, for Revelation15:3b is at the time of the consummated kingdom of God, whereas the bowls begin again with the time of the church age. So, "great and amazing are your deeds" refers to the seals, trumpets, signs, and bowls, as their judgments attest to the fact that God is almighty, sovereign over all. They display his justice and truth, and his saints validate that his ways are indeed just and true. He was never a God confined to Israel alone, but always the King over the nations, which in these verses have now been made to recognize him as such (Phil. 2:9–11). And, as King over the nations, he alone had the ability to use the nations in his purposes and plans for his people. Thus, not only is God's character worshiped, but his conduct is worshiped as well.

Let us look at the deeds that our God has done in our lives. Let us count them, meditate upon them, tell our families about them, and praise God for them. Let us recognize his sovereignty over the events in our lives. There is no such thing as chance, no mistakes, and no luck with God. God has orchestrated the events of our lives for his purposes. His ways are just and true. We can trust him even when we cannot trust ourselves. We can trust his way when we cannot see our own way through the darkness. We can trust that he rules over all of the circumstances and relationships in our lives and is using them for our good.

Old Testament Background to Revelation 15:3b.

- Exodus 34:10: "Behold, I am making a covenant. Before all your people I will do marvels, such as have not been created in all the

---

5. Ibid., 794.

earth or in any nation. And all the people among whom you are shall see the work of the LORD, for it is an awesome thing that I will do with you."

- Deuteronomy 28:59–60: "And he will bring upon you again all the diseases of Egypt."
- Psalm 111:2–4: "Great are the works of the LORD."
- Haggai, Zechariah, Malachi: "The LORD, the Almighty God."

Revelation 15:4. There is no one who will not fear and glorify God's name, for at the end of the age, every knee will bow and every tongue confess that Jesus Christ is Lord to the glory of God the Father (Phil. 2:9–11). His righteous acts will have finally been revealed in all of their fullness and "the kingdom of the world will become the kingdom of our Lord and of his Christ, and he shall reign forever and ever" (Rev. 11:15). His holiness is not just moral purity, but a sum of all of his divine attributes, which distinguish him from his creation as Creator God. That "all nations" will come and worship God is not a reference to every person, but every nation will be represented among the elect of God who bring him the worship that he is due.

Old Testament Background to Revelation 15:4.
- Psalm 86:9–10: "All the nations you have made shall come and worship before you, O LORD, and shall glorify your name. For you are great and do wondrous things; you alone are God."
- Psalm 98:2: "The LORD has made known his salvation; he has revealed his righteousness in the sight of the nations."
- Jeremiah 10:7: "Who would not fear you, O King of the nations? For this is your due; for among all the wise ones of the nations and in all their kingdoms there is none like you."

CONCLUSION

As I left my friend that night I felt so useless. I had little on my heart to say. And words didn't seem to be what she needed. As she spoke, I identified with her pain, but knew the answer was to continue to pray for our loved ones and continue to be a witness to them through the worship of God in our lives. I don't know the day or the hour when our Lord and Savior Jesus Christ will come again. And I don't know what the condition of my loved ones will be on that day. But I know that God is just and true, and that I can trust him with the souls of those I love. And I know that you can too.

LESSON 15

Revelation 15:5–16:21

PLEASE USE THE QUESTION paradigm from pages 353–54 as you work through the following. See the introductory comments there that explain each part of the process below in more detail.

- **Pray**.
- **Ponder the Passage**. Read Revelation 15:5–16:21 once a day from different translations for the entire week, looking for its:
  - Point
  - Persons
  - Patterns
  - Persons of the Trinity
  - Puzzling Parts
- **Put It in Perspective**.
- Place in Scripture
- Passages from Other Parts of Scripture

1. Based on your observations of the text, what is the basic content of Revelation 15:5–16:21? Try to summarize it in your own words, using a sentence or two.
2. To what does "the sanctuary of the tent of witness in heaven" in 15:5 refer (see Ex. 40:34)? For "witness" see Exodus 25:21; 31:18; Revelation 12:16.

3. Of whose clothing does the saints' clothing in Revelation 15:6 remind you (see Rev. 1:13)?

4. Who gave the seven angels the bowls? From what you know of their location in the throne room, what does this signify? Who really gave the bowls (see Rev. 5:6)?

5. To what Egyptian plague does the first bowl allude in Revelation 16:2? Compare this bowl with the first trumpet. What similarities do you see? What differences?

6. To what Egyptian plague does the second bowl allude in Revelation 16:3? Compare this bowl with the second trumpet. What similarities do you see? What differences?

7. To what Egyptian plague does the third bowl allude in Revelation 16:4? Compare this bowl with the third trumpet. What similarities do you see? What differences?

8. What character and what conduct does the angel praise God for in Revelation 16:5–6?

9. Who did we see at the altar in Revelation 6:10? How does that inform the meaning behind 16:7? How are the bowls an answer to the saints' plea in 6:10?

10. To what Egyptian plague does the fourth bowl allude in Revelation 16:8–9? Compare this bowl with the fourth trumpet. What similarities do you see? What differences?

11. Compare the final phrases in Revelation 16:9, 11, and 21. What do you see? How does this remind you of Pharaoh during the time of the Egyptian plagues?

12. To what Egyptian plague does the fifth bowl allude in Revelation 16:10–11? Compare this bowl with the fifth trumpet. What similarities do you see? What differences?

13. To what Egyptian plague does the sixth bowl allude in Revelation 16:12–16? Compare this bowl with the sixth trumpet. What similarities do you see? What differences?

14. How does Revelation 16:12 allude to the Red Sea? Also read Isaiah 44:27–28 with Jeremiah 50:38 and Zechariah 10:11. How does Revelation 16:12 reflect Cyrus's defeat of Babylon?

15. How does Revelation 12:14 define the "three unclean spirits like frogs" in 12:13? How does this enforce the symbolic interpretation of the plagues in Revelation?

16. Where else have we seen that Christ is "coming like a thief" in Revelation? Where else have we seen a blessing in the book (remember there are seven of them)?

17. Armageddon is "mount of Megiddo" in Hebrew. Look up "mount of Megiddo" or "mountain of Megiddo" in a concordance. Does one exist? What does this tell you about names in the book of Revelation? Are they usually literal or symbolic?

18. To what Egyptian plague does the seventh bowl allude in Revelation 16:17–21? Compare this bowl with the seventh trumpet. What similarities do you see? What differences?

19. How does the seventh bowl allude to Israel at Mount Sinai (Ex. 19:16–19)?

20. What did Christ utter on the cross? What similarities do you see here in Revelation 16:17? How is Christ's victory on the cross consummated at the end of history?

21. What are the other three places in the book where you have seen the phrase used in Revelation 16:18?

22. How does Revelation 16:19 reflect 14:8?

• **Principles and Points of Application.**

1. God's wrath also brings his blessing. Revelation 15:8 tells us that God's wrath opens the entrance to the sanctuary. Read Hebrews 4:14–16 and 10:19–22. How did Christ's drinking of God's wrath on the cross open our way to the sanctuary? Thank God today that you can boldly approach the throne of grace with confidence.

2. Meditate on Revelation 16:5–6. Think about a situation you are in right now in which you would like to take vengeance on the other party. The Scriptures say that we are to leave vengeance with the Lord because he is the only one just and the only one able to repay what sin deserves. By God's grace, commit to leaving vengeance with the Lord today.

221

3. Read Revelation 16:7. Do you believe this? Do you embrace the Word of God as absolute truth and do you believe that God is just in all that he does? If not, ask him to reveal this to you this week in his Word.

4. In what area of your life are you "cursing God," being unrepentant, and not giving him glory? By the power of the Holy Spirit, repent and bless the name of God this week while giving him glory.

5. How are you "staying awake" for the great day of God the Almighty? What sins do you need to confess today? What relationships do you need to repair? What service do you need to fulfill? What person do you need to tell about Christ? Don't delay; do these things today.

6. Meditate on Revelation 16:17, "It is done." Christ uttered the words, "It is finished," on the cross, but the kingdom of God was only inaugurated at that time. It will not be consummated until Christ's second coming. Spend time today thanking God that Christ's work on the cross is finished and that one day our battle with sin, Satan, and this world will be finished as well.

NOTES FOR REVELATION 15:5–16:21

Aim: Ponder the aim of this lesson concerning our:

Mind: What do we need to know from this passage in Scripture?

That God judges unbelievers' idolatry, unrepentant hearts, and persecution of believers throughout the church age and ultimately, at the final judgment.

Heart: How does what we learn from this passage affect our internal relationship with the Lord?

It prepares us to be kingdom disciples who repent of our sin, give God all the glory, bless God for all that he does, and leave vengeance to the Lord.

Hands: How does what we learn from this passage translate into action for God's kingdom?

It enables us to:

1. Embrace God's Word as absolute truth, believing that he is just in all that he does, and share the truth of his justice with others to both warn and encourage them.
2. Repent of any "cursing of God" and turn to glorifying him instead, leading others to do the same.
3. "Stay awake" for the great day of God the Almighty, confessing any sin, repairing any relationships, fulfilling any service, and sharing the gospel with any who are lost by relying on the Spirit's power.
4. Spend time thanking God that Christ's work on the cross is finished and that one day our battle with sin, Satan, and this world will be finished as well.

INTRODUCTION

The cross has long been held as a symbol of Christianity, but I wonder how many Christians who wear it or have it in their homes, businesses, and churches know the depth of its meaning. So often it is heralded as a symbol of our own belief as we wear it around our necks, or of our own salvation from our personal sin. While this is certainly true, it does not plumb the depths of Christ's sacrifice on the altar of the cross in order to atone for the sins of believers. The cross continued a war, a battle between Satan and God, that began before the fall of mankind. It was the beginning of the final judgment of Satan by God. At the cross, Jesus Christ drank obediently the cup of wrath that all of mankind deserved in order to redeem God's people for God's glory. But he also defeated Satan.

While the war between Satan and Christ ended in spiritual victory at the cross, the prince of this world is still allowed to have authority on earth. Defeated, he is angry and looking for people who pledge allegiance to his enemy, Jesus Christ, to devour. He tries to deceive us with lies,

lies that God doesn't really love us, that we're not really good enough for God, that we're worthless and insignificant, that this world is what really matters, that materialism provides happiness, and that superficial relationships give worth and meaning.

He also tries to tempt us. He uses temptations to make us think that we can control our own lives and the lives of those around us, to make us take pride in thinking that no one can take care of our families like we can, to make us flirt with the man at work, to make us love the gods of this world more than the God who reigns over the world, to make us dishonor our parents and in-laws. He uses temptations to get us to discount the holiness and rest of Sunday, to kill our spouse and children with our words, and to steal time and money from others.

He also tries to persecute us. He uses the persecution of physical pain that distracts us and leads us to pity ourselves, of emotional pain that sucks all of our energy away from ministry and work for the kingdom, of mental pain that clouds our minds from clear thinking about God, and of despair that leads to the taking of our very lives and seems to end in the defeat of Christianity.

But, there is coming another battle, the final battle to end Satan's power completely, a battle which, though it will be fierce, was drastically reduced at the cross. This battle will end in physical, emotional, mental, and spiritual victory. God's people will be delivered for all time from the suffering of this world, from the temptations of this world, and from the lies of this world. There will be no more war of words. There will be no more war of wills. There will be no more war with the wiles of our enemy. There will be no more war with the world. Revelation 15:5–16:21 has much to say about this final battle.

We can divide this lesson into three sections:

  I. The Introduction of the Bowl Judgments (Rev. 15:5–8)
 II. The First Five Bowl Judgments (Rev. 16:1–11)
III. The Last Two Bowl Judgments (Rev. 16:12–21)

I. The Introduction of the Bowl Judgments (Rev. 15:5–8)

Revelation 15:5–6. The brief introduction to the trumpets found in the interlude between the sixth and seventh signs (Rev. 15:1) is now continued. Just as God was with Israel through the wilderness by way of the tabernacle, so too the heavenly counterpart is the "sanctuary of the tent of witness." The "witness" is the Ten Commandments of God that resided in the ark of the tabernacle during Moses' day (Ex. 16:34). Thus, the Law is God's witness that he is just in condemning unbelievers. The "witness" is not just the Law, but also the one who came to fulfill the Law.[1] In turn, believers become witnesses of the Witness by sharing in his suffering. The imagery here conveys that God's judgment on unbelievers is just according to the revelation of his Law and that he will enforce it.

Out of the sanctuary come the seven angels who have been assigned the job of pouring out the seven plagues/bowls of God's judgment (seven here, like the other sets of judgments, is figurative for complete judgment). Leviticus 26:21 is the only other place in Scripture where "seven plagues" is used. In the broader context of Leviticus 26, it is said four times that God will judge Israel seven times if the people are unfaithful (Lev. 26:18, 21, 24, 28). Each judgment gets more severe, as we see in the four sets of seven judgments (seals, trumpets, thunders, and bowls) in Revelation, the bowls being the most severe. Just as in Leviticus, the warnings of the bowl judgments are to serve the purpose of repentance among true believers and of further hardening in unbelievers.[2]

The clothing of the angels is almost the same as the clothing of Christ, the "Son of man," in Revelation 1:13. Thus, believers are identified with him as they aid in carrying out his justice on earth. We too are clothed in the garments of Christ as believers and are to be his representatives here on earth. We are to walk as he walked, talk as he talked, love as he loved, serve as he served, and fulfill the Law of God as he fulfilled the Law of God. So often we feel rejection by unbelievers, not because we have done anything wrong, but because we are a

---

1. G. K. Beale, *The Book of Revelation: A Commentary on the Greek Text*, New International Greek Testament Commentary (Grand Rapids: Eerdmans, 1999), 801–2.

2. Ibid., 802–3.

walking Law of God before them, which condemns their sin. This helps me when I feel attacked by family members for no reason; it is not that I have done anything wrong, but that I represent the light, the Light of the World. And darkness always hates the light.

Old Testament/New Testament Background to Revelation 15:5–6.

- Exodus 16:34: "[The manna] was placed before the testimony to be kept."
- Leviticus 26:21: "Then if you walk contrary to me and will not listen to me, I will continue striking you sevenfold for your sins."
- Psalm 79:12: "Return sevenfold into the lap of our neighbors the taunts with which they have taunted you, O LORD!"
- Daniel 10:5: "And behold, a man clothed in linen, with a belt of fine gold."
- Revelation 1:13: "One like a son of man, clothed with a long robe and with a golden sash around his chest."

Revelation 15:7–8. Just as bowls were used at the altar in the Old Testament sacrificial system to carry away the ashes and fat of the sacrifices, so here bowls are used at the heavenly altar to carry out the judgments of God that result in part from the saints' pleas at the altar for vindication (Rev. 5:8; 6:9–11; 8:3–5). Furthermore, the "bowl of the cup of [God's] wrath" is said to be poured out on Babylon in Isaiah 51:17, 22, which is fulfilled in the bowls of Revelation. The phrase "who lives forever and ever" further conveys that the judgment of believers is eternal.[3]

The "smoke from the glory of God and from his power" strongly portrays that it is God alone who is able to execute judgment and he does so in his own time. Once he has decreed it, no one is able to enter the sanctuary and interfere. He is answering his saints' pleas for vindication.

Old Testament Background to Revelation 15:7–8.

- Exodus 40:34–35: "Then the cloud covered the tent of meeting, and the glory of the LORD filled the tabernacle. And Moses was

3. Ibid., 806.

not able to enter the tent of meeting because the cloud settled on it and the glory of the LORD filled the tabernacle."

- Isaiah 6:1–4: "And the foundations of the thresholds shook at the voice of him who called, and the house was filled with smoke."
- Isaiah 51:17, 22: "Wake yourself Jerusalem, you who have drunk from the hand of the LORD the cup of his wrath . . . your God who pleads the cause of his people; behold, I have taken from your hand the cup of staggering; the bowl of my wrath you shall drink no more."
- Ezekiel 10:2–4: "Burning coals . . . scatter them over the city . . . and a cloud filled the inner court . . . and the court was filled with the brightness of the glory of the LORD."

II. The First Five Bowl Judgments (Rev. 16:1–11)

We noted at the beginning of chapter 12 that chapters 12–20 would display the rise of the dragon, the first beast, the second beast/false prophet, and Babylon in chapters 12–15, and their fall in the reverse order (Babylon, second beast/false prophet, first beast, dragon) in chapters 16–20. We make note of that again here as we now begin the account of their fall. This aspect gives further evidence of a literary rather than a chronological structure to the book.

We also observed earlier in Revelation 15:1 that the first five bowls are judgments that take place throughout the church age, like the first five seals and the first six trumpets, whereas the sixth and seventh bowls are part of the final judgment of God.

Revelation 16:1. As we have noted at other points in the book, when a command comes from the temple, it always signifies judgment (Rev. 6:1–5; 9:13; 14:15, 17; 16:7, 17). We know from Revelation 6:6 and 15:8 that it is God who issues the command to pour out the seven bowls of his wrath.

Old Testament Background to Revelation 16:1. Jeremiah 10:25: "Pour out your wrath on the nations that know you not, and on the people that call not on your name, for they have devoured Jacob."

Revelation 16:2. We have already seen an allusion to the Exodus and the wilderness journey, most recently a reference to the Red Sea in

Revelation 15:2 and to the tabernacle and ark in 15:5. So, it is not surprising that the bowls, like the trumpets, are modeled on the Egyptian plagues. In fact, the trumpets and the bowls describe the plagues in the same order, giving us reason to believe that though they are not identical, they are related to one another and should be seen as temporally parallel with one another. The first bowl alludes to the Egyptian plague of boils (Ex. 9:9–11). As punishment for bearing the mark of the beast, the unbelievers will now bear the mark of boils. The "evil" sores (so Deut. 28:27, 35) display the evil nature of the mark of the beast. Though they were literal boils on the Egyptians, here they are figurative for what is most likely spiritual and emotional distress.[4] Just as unbelievers inflicted pain and harm on believers during persecution, now God vindicates his people by inflicting pain and harm on their persecutors.

As hard as it is to turn the other cheek, to protest silently rather than fight, to respond kindly to anger, and the like, we must remember that God will have the final word on those who harm and afflict us physically, emotionally, and/or spiritually. We can endure the hardships of persecution, not only because Christ did, but also because God will vindicate us.

Revelation 16:3. The second bowl, like the second trumpet, is based on the Egyptian plague of the Nile being turned into blood (Ex. 7:17–21). When we studied the second trumpet, we concluded that economic downfall was in view, especially in light of Revelation 18, where the sailors mourned Babylon's demise because of what it meant for them, economic deprivation. Here, though, the effect is total. "Like the blood of a corpse" and "every living thing died that was in the sea" most likely refer to unbelievers dying who were strategic in upholding the economic system.[5] Thus, at times during the church age, economic hardship can be seen on a universal scale.

Revelation 16:4. Just as the third trumpet continued the second trumpet's allusion to the Egyptian plague of the Nile being turned into

---

4. Dennis E. Johnson, *The Triumph of the Lamb: A Commentary on Revelation* (Phillipsburg, NJ: P&R Publishing, 2001), 225.

5. Beale, *The Book of Revelation*, 815.

blood (Ex. 7:17–21), so too the third bowl continues the same allusion from the second bowl. The only difference between the third trumpet and the third bowl is in its extent. The third bowl has a complete effect, whereas the trumpet was only partial. Like the second bowl, this is most likely a reference to economic distress, either the same or a foreshadowing of the economic distress caused by Babylon's fall, especially as it relates to sea commerce.[6]

Revelation 16:5–7. The angel who was in charge of pouring out the third bowl credits the judgments to God and emphasizes that he is just, holy, and sovereign in bringing them upon unbelievers. The reason why is because of their persecution of believers. Verse 6 confirms our conclusion that the second and third bowls referred both to the unbelievers' literal physical deaths and to their emotional and spiritual suffering. Since they shed the innocent blood of the believers, their blood also would be shed. But God's judgment is just, whereas their persecution of believers was not. Like the events associated with the previous bowls, this too occurs throughout the church age, as is evident from the phrase "who is and who was." God is sovereign over all of history, vindicating his people throughout the ages, though only completely at the end of the age.

That the vindication of the saints is in mind is clear from verse 7, where the altar, the place under which the saints await vindication (Rev. 6:10), speaks. The saints praise God for his judgment, declaring them true and just, and ascribing to him sovereignty over the nations and over what happens to his people ("the Almighty"). Just as the Israelites in the "Song of Moses" praised God for his works and his just ways following the Egyptian plagues and the first exodus, so too God's people praise him for his just and true plagues prior to the second exodus.

Old Testament Background to Revelation 16:5–7.

- Deuteronomy 32:4: "The Rock, his work is perfect, for all his ways are justice. A God of faithfulness and without iniquity, just and upright is he."
- Psalm 79:3, 10, 12: "They have poured out their blood like water all around Jerusalem, and there was no one to bury

---

6. Ibid., 816.

them . . . why should the nations say, 'Where is their God?'
Let the avenging of the outpoured blood of your servants be
known among the nations before our eyes . . . return sevenfold
into the lap of our neighbors the taunts with which they have
taunted you, O LORD!"

- Isaiah 49:26: "I will make your oppressors eat their own flesh,
and they shall be drunk with their own blood as wine. Then
all flesh shall know that I am the LORD your Savior, and your
Redeemer, the Mighty One of Jacob."

Revelation 16:8–9. In the events related to the fourth bowl, we see
the imagery of the sun scorching people with fire to convey God's judgment. This alludes to the judgment by fire that is prophesied in the Old
Testament (Isa. 66:15; Joel 2:3; Mal. 4:1–2).[7] That this imagery refers to
destruction of economic security is apparent from the use of the same
imagery in Revelation 7:16 as applied to believers: "neither will the sun
strike them or any heat." This states negatively that believers will have
no lack of provision in the heavenly city.[8] The plague did not bring about
the repentance of unbelievers; instead, it furthered their blasphemy and
idolatry. They have become like the "god" that they serve (Rev. 13:1, 5,
6; 17:3). Though the fourth bowl correlates with the fourth trumpet, it
also has similarity to the sixth trumpet with regard to the unbelievers'
response of further hardening (Rev. 9:20–21), as well as the correlation
of the sixth trumpet's "fire and smoke and sulfur coming out of the
[horses] mouths" with the fierce heat of the fourth bowl.

We become like those we follow. If we follow pop culture, we will
begin to think and make decisions based on the values of pop culture.
If we follow our favorite talk show host, we will begin to act like him
or her. If we follow our favorite news channel, it will shape our political
and economic views. If we follow our friends, we will begin to talk and
think like them. If we follow our own hearts and minds, they will lead

7. Vern S. Poythress, *The Returning King: A Guide to the Book of Revelation* (Phillipsburg,
NJ: P&R Publishing, 2000), 156.
8. Beale, *The Book of Revelation*, 822.

us astray. If we follow the god of this world, he will deceive us. But if we follow Jesus Christ, he will show us the way because he *is* the way. We will become like him, we will know truth, we will know life, and we will be witnesses to others about him in our worship of him.

Revelation 16:10–11. Like the fifth trumpet, the fifth bowl also alludes to the Egyptian plague of darkness (Ex. 10:21ff.). The plague was poured out on the "throne of the beast," which is equivalent to "Satan's throne" in the letter to Pergamum (Rev. 2:13). Because of Rome's immorality, idolatry, and persecution of the people of God, the pagans were to suffer from spiritual darkness and anguish of their souls. All through the church age, unbelievers will, at certain times, come face to face with the fact that they are separated from God, and they will feel the horror and desperation of the situation, though it will not produce change in the majority of them. That the kingdom was plunged into darkness means that it lost much of its power to rule. Though the unbelievers had inflicted pain and sores on others, they wanted no part of it themselves and cursed the God of justice and holiness for repaying them according to their own deeds. Just as Pharaoh did not repent of his deeds and only grew more hardened toward the Lord, so the majority of the unbelievers only drew farther away from God.

III. The Last Two Bowl Judgments (Rev. 16:12–21)

Revelation 16:12. The first five bowls speak of God's judgment throughout the church age, but the sixth and seventh bowls speak of God's final judgment at the end of history. The sixth angel pours out his bowl on "the great river Euphrates." We have already seen this in the sixth trumpet and concluded that it referred to demons deceiving nonbelievers, which is also the case here. That "its water was dried up" refers to the nonbelievers who end their religious allegiance to "Babylon." "The kings from the east" describes the political sphere of the kingdom of this world, which will turn against and destroy the economic and religious sphere. Both Babylon and the Euphrates here are symbolic for the universal kingdom of this world. In the Old Testament, God is always the one who dries up the water for judgment or redemption, and here too God directs the final judgment of and victory over the evil kingdom. The Old Testament prophesied that God's judgment of Babylon would include the drying up of the Euphrates River (Jer. 50:35–38). Originally fulfilled by Cyrus's defeat of Babylon, the final end time defeat of "Babylon" will be fulfilled by God's final judgment at Armageddon.[9]

Revelation 16:13. Here we see the details behind the big picture presented in Revelation 16:12. The members of the counterfeit trinity are listed together, with the same unclean spirits coming out of their mouths, a further confirmation that they all have the same purpose and goal to persecute, deceive, and tempt humanity. The dragon symbolizes Satan, the beast symbolizes the evil political realm, and the false prophet symbolizes the religious support of the evil political system. God uses them to execute his final judgment. "Like frogs" is an allusion to the Egyptian plague of frogs (Ex. 8:1–15), but literal frogs are not in view here; rather, it is the deceptive spirits that try to lead one to idolatry.[10]

Revelation 16:14. Now the symbolic use of the literal frogs of the Egyptian plague is plainly spiritualized. They are demonic spirits. Just as the Egyptians tried to use their own magic to reproduce the plagues and thus disprove God, so too the counterfeit trinity performs signs to try and show that they are worthy of worship. They go abroad to the kings of the whole world to assemble them for battle on the great day of God the Almighty. These political rulers who worship the kingdom of darkness gather together, thinking they will defeat the people of God. But instead, God has used Satan to gather those he will defeat in this final war of history, in which God will destroy the kingdom of this world forever. We have already seen this war in Revelation 11:7, as part of the interlude between the sixth and seventh trumpets that spoke of the final judgment. Again, this confirms that the book's themes run through all seven cycles of judgment that lead to the second coming; this displays the

9. Ibid., 827–29.
10. Ibid., 831.

inward unity of the cycles and points to the fact that the same battle is described more than one time.[11]

Old Testament Background to Revelation 16:14.

- Zephaniah 3:8: "For my decision is to gather nations, to assemble kingdoms, to pour out upon them my indignation, all my burning anger; for in the fire of my jealousy all the earth shall be consumed."

- Zechariah 12:2; 13:1–2; 14:2, 13: "Behold, I am about to make Jerusalem a cup of staggering to all the surrounding peoples . . . there shall be a fountain opened for the house of David . . . to cleanse them from sin . . . I will cut off the names of the idols from the land . . . I will gather all the nations against Jerusalem to battle . . . a great panic from the LORD shall fall on them . . . and the hand of the one will be raised against the hand of the other."

Revelation 16:15. We now come to a parenthetical break in the description of the events of the sixth bowl in order to exhort believers to be alert for the second coming of Christ. The church at Sardis was told the same thing in Revelation 3:3: "If you will not wake up, I will come like a thief, and you will not know at what hour I will come against you." The imagery is seen in the Gospels as well (Matt. 24:43; Luke 12:39). Since in the eyes of nonbelievers the war is directed toward believers' demise, believers are exhorted to remain firm and steadfast so that they are not taken off guard or found on the wrong side when the true Warrior comes to war with his saints and win the battle. This is the third of seven blessings in the book (Rev. 1:3; 14:13; 16:15; 19:9; 20:6; 22:7; 22:14). The blessing recalls Genesis 3, where we see that Adam and Eve were found naked and ashamed. Having been properly "clothed" in their initial sinless state, they "disrobed" themselves by sinning and were found naked and exposed before the almighty God. Here the Lord warns his people to not be found sinning again. They are to be ready to be identified with the King of kings when he comes.

11. Poythress, *The Returning King*, 156.

Revelation 16:16. The counterfeit trinity deceptively assembles the political leaders of the worldwide system at the place of the great and final war. "Armageddon," like "Babylon" and "Euphrates," is not a literal reference to a geographical location, but is symbolic for the whole world. The translation from the Hebrew is "mount of Megiddo." But, while there was a city of Megiddo during Old Testament times, there was not a "mountain of Megiddo," another confirmation that this name is symbolic. However, the events that took place at Megiddo in the Old Testament are surely behind the text here in Revelation.

Old Testament Background to Revelation 16:16.

- Judges 5:19–21: "The kings came, they fought; then fought the kings of Canaan, at Taanach, by the waters of Megiddo; they got no spoils of silver. From heaven the stars fought, from their courses they fought against Sisera. The torrent Kishon swept them away."
- 1 Kings 18:40: "Seize the prophets of Baal; let not one of them escape. And they seized them. And Elijah brought them down to the brook Kishon and slaughtered them there."
- 2 Kings 23:29: "In his days Pharaoh Neco king of Egypt went up to the king of Assyria to the river Euphrates. King Josiah went to meet him, and Pharaoh Neco killed him at Megiddo."
- 2 Chronicles 35:20–25: "[Josiah] did not listen to the words of Neco from the mouth of God, but came to fight in the plain of Megiddo. And the archers shot King Josiah . . . and he died."
- Zechariah 12:9–12: "On that day I will seek to destroy all the nations that come against Jerusalem."

Revelation 16:17. That the seventh bowl is poured out into the "air" continues the allusion to the Egyptian plague of hail (Ex. 9:22–35). Like the fourth through sixth bowls, the seventh bowl is judgment upon the evil world system of earth. Just as Christ shouted, "It is finished!" when he defeated Satan spiritually on the cross, so too God shouts, "It is done!" when Satan is defeated both physically and spiritually at the final battle. But Christ's shout only inaugurated God's judgment, whereas here the shout by God consummates it. God's redemptive-historical plan to redeem a fallen people for his praise and glory is finally accomplished and final judgment will occur before the new heaven and earth are revealed.

Revelation 16:18. We have already seen the phrase in this verse in the book. It was first used in chapter 4 at the throne in heaven. From the throne came "flashes of lightning, and rumblings and peals of thunder" (Rev. 4:5). Then it occurs at the end of each series of seven judgments, the seals (Rev. 8:5), the trumpets (Rev. 11:19), and here, the bowls. As the judgments increase in severity, so too the phrase expands.

- Revelation 4:5: "Flashes of lighting, and rumblings and peals of thunder."
- Revelation 8:5: "Peals of thunder, rumblings, flashes of lightning, and an earthquake."
- Revelation 11:19: "Flashes of lightning, rumblings, peals of thunder, an earthquake, and heavy hail."
- Revelation 16:18–21: "Flashes of lightning, rumblings, peals of thunder, and a great earthquake such as there had never been . . . and great hailstones, about one hundred pounds each."

Each use of the phrase alludes to Israel meeting God at the foot of Mount Sinai and Moses being called up to the top of the mountain to receive the Law of the Lord (Ex. 19:16–20). It is appropriate then for John to recall the giving of the Law in the context of judgment for breaking the Law. Here we also see an allusion to Daniel 12:1, which alludes to Exodus 9:18, 24.

Old Testament Background to Revelation 16:18.
- Exodus 9:18, 24: "I will cause very heavy hail to fall, such as never has been in Egypt . . . there was hail and fire flashing continually in the midst of the hail."
- Daniel 12:1–2: "At that time shall arise Michael, the great prince who has charge of your people. And there shall be a time of trouble, such as never has been since there was a nation till that

time. But at that time your people shall be delivered, everyone whose name shall be found written in the book. And many of those who sleep in the dust of the earth shall awake, some to everlasting life, and some to shame and everlasting contempt."

Revelation 16:19. Keeping with the earthquake imagery, the "great city . . . Babylon the great" was split into three parts, but it was not just "Babylon" that fell, it was all of the world's social, economic, and religious centers that promoted the kingdom of darkness. This confirms that this is the final, worldwide judgment of God upon the evil world kingdom. This verse expands on what has already been said about Babylon in Revelation 14:8, 10, where Babylon is pronounced as fallen because "she made all nations drink the wine of the passion of her sexual immorality." It also foreshadows the detailed account of Babylon's fall in 17:1–19:10, while emphasizing the judgment upon all nations for following Babylon, and a more severe judgment upon Babylon itself as the instigator in leading others astray.

It is a serious thing to lead people astray. My son, as early as age four, would try to lead his younger sister to disobey me at times or would try to provoke her to anger or distress or whining. These were good opportunities for me to remind him that he was even more in the wrong than his sister would be if she listened to him because he was the one leading her into sin. Let us be careful where we lead people; let us be careful not to provoke our children or our spouses to anger or frustration or sin. God will call us into account. Though we will not face judgment as a believer, we will face God's discipline. We must always seek to lead others to be better witnesses and worshipers of Christ through the power of the Holy Spirit.

Old Testament/New Testament Background to Revelation 16:19.
- Haggai 2:6: "For thus says the Lord of hosts: Yet once more in a little while, I will shake the heavens and the earth and the sea and the dry land."
- Zechariah 14:4: "On that day his feet shall stand on the Mount of Olives that lies before Jerusalem on the east, and the Mount of Olives shall be split in two from east to west by a very wide valley."

- Hebrews 12:26–27: "This phrase, 'Yet once more,' indicates the removal of things that are shaken—that is, things that have been made—in order that the things that cannot be shaken may remain."

Revelation 16:20–21. These verses expand on the previous ones, showing the complete and worldwide destruction caused by the seventh bowl, which depicts the final judgment of God. We have seen the description "every mountain and island was removed from its place" in the sixth seal depicting the final judgment (Rev. 6:14), and we will see it again in Revelation 20:11, "Then I saw a great white throne and him who was seated on it. From his presence earth and sky fled away, and no place was found for them." And we have previously seen the allusion to the Egyptian plague of hail in previous trumpets/bowls. But the plague of hail here is universal and complete. It also results in hardened hearts. Just as Pharaoh continued to harden his heart in the midst of the Egyptian plagues despite their severity and testimony to God's reign, so too unbelievers continue in hardness of heart at the final judgment. There will be no universal salvation.

Old Testament Background to Revelation 16:20–21.

- Exodus 9:13: The Seventh Plague: Hail.
- Joshua 10:11: "And as they [the Amorites] fled before Israel . . . the LORD threw down large stones from heaven on them . . . and they died. There were more who died because of the hailstones than the sons of Israel killed with the sword."
- Ezekiel 38:19–23: "On that day there shall be a great earthquake . . . all shall quake at my presence . . . every man's sword will be against his brother . . . I will enter into judgment . . . will rain upon him . . . hailstones. . . . So I will show my greatness and my holiness and make myself known in the eyes of many nations. Then they will know that I am the LORD."

This is the purpose of the judgments of God throughout history, and especially at the final judgment: to display to a watching world that he is great, that he alone is holy, and that he alone is Lord.

CONCLUSION

The final battle between Satan and God will belong to the Lord. We will hear the shout, the walls will crumble, and we will walk through the gates of glory to dwell with God for eternity. So let us keep on marching. One day we will hear the trumpet blast and the shout of victory signifying that our Lord and Savior Jesus Christ has come to break down the physical barrier between heaven and earth forever. He will dwell with us in all of his fullness, all of his love, all of his power, and all of his sovereignty. Let us be his witnesses. Let us be his worshipers!

LESSON 16

Revelation 17

PLEASE USE THE QUESTION paradigm from pages 353–54 as you work through the following. See the introductory comments there that explain each part of the process below in more detail.

- **Pray**.
- **Ponder the Passage**. Read Revelation 17 once a day from different translations for the entire week, looking for its:
  - Point
  - Persons
  - Patterns
  - Persons of the Trinity
  - Puzzling Parts
- **Put It in Perspective**.
  - Place in Scripture
  - Passages from Other Parts of Scripture

1. Based on your observations of the text, what is the basic content of Revelation 17? Try to summarize it in your own words, using a sentence or two.
2. What angel shows John the judgment of the great prostitute (Rev. 17:1)? How does this relate to the previous section of Revelation 16:12–21?

3. Define the "great prostitute" by looking at Revelation 17:5 and 17:18.

4. Define the "many waters" by looking at Revelation 17:15.

5. Who do you think the "kings of the earth" and "the dwellers on earth" are in Revelation 17:2? What is the imagery conveying?

6. To what location is John carried to see the vision (Rev. 17:3)? What does he see? Where have we seen this beast before in the book? How do you know it's the same one?

7. Contrast the adornment of the woman in Revelation 17:4 with the bride of Christ in Revelation 21:2; 22:11, 18–19, 21.

8. Compare Revelation 17:5 with 7:3. What do you see? Do you remember from previous lessons what this represents?

9. What is John's reaction to the beast (Rev. 17:6)? How does the angel respond to John (Rev. 17:7)?

10. Compare and contrast Revelation 17:8 with 1:8; 3:11; 4:8; 16:15. What do you see?

11. Contrast the "dwellers on earth whose names have not been written in the book of life from the foundation of the world" with the "called and chosen and faithful" in Revelation 17:14.

12. List all the information you can about the seven heads/mountains/kings in Revelation 17:10.

13. How is the beast both identified with and distinguished from the seven heads (Rev. 17:11)?

14. How are the ten horns defined in Revelation 17:12 and 17:16a? With whom do they ally (Rev. 17:13)? With whom do they make war (Rev. 17:14)? Who wins? Why? Who allies themselves with the Lamb?

15. What does God use the ten horns to do (Rev. 17:17)? How does this illuminate the "mystery" in Revelation 17:7?

- **Principles and Points of Application.**
1. The Holy Spirit was active in John's life to reveal the prophetic vision to him so that he would record it for the Holy

Scriptures, which are completed. But this same Holy Spirit is active with the same power in our lives as believers. How have you experienced the Spirit of God working in your life in a particular area this week? It may be helpful for you to look up "Spirit" in a concordance to see the roles that he plays in believers' lives.

2. On whose side of the war are you, the Lamb's or the world's? What evidence do you see in your life that you are the "called and chosen and faithful"?

3. Meditate on Revelation 17:17. Now read Genesis 50:20; Isaiah 45:7; and Acts 2:23. The Scriptures plainly state that God is sovereign, even over evil, and uses it to accomplish his purposes. Have you accepted this truth? Spend time today thanking God for his sovereignty, even when it can't be completely grasped. Relinquish any areas of your life that you've deemed as a "mistake" or attributed to your own decisions, to a sovereign and holy God, who is orchestrating your life for his glory and your good.

NOTES FOR REVELATION 17

Aim: Ponder the aim of this lesson concerning our:

Mind: What do we need to know from this passage in Scripture?

That Babylon is destroyed because she is allied with the beast, who is also destroyed.

Heart: How does what we learn from this passage affect our internal relationship with the Lord?

It prepares us to be kingdom disciples who rely on God's wisdom to recognize Babylon and the beast, and who choose, by the power of the Spirit, to stand with the Lord's army as the chosen and faithful people of God.

241

Hands: How does what we learn from this passage translate into action for God's kingdom?

It enables us to:

1. Recognize the role and influence of the Holy Spirit in our lives, to rely on his power in a greater way, and help others to do the same.
2. Choose, by the power of the Holy Spirit, to stand on the Lamb's side of the war and to pray that the Lord would lead others there also by our witness and worship.
3. Spend time this week thanking God for his sovereignty in our lives, even in areas we see as "mistakes" or attribute to our own decisions.

INTRODUCTION

I have heard the kingdom of God referred to as the "upside down" kingdom, meaning that it is contrary to the kingdom of this world. From the world's perspective this is true, but from the believer's perspective God's kingdom is the "right side up" kingdom and the world's kingdom the "upside down" one. This is because the world has made that which will be first, last, and has taken that which will be lowly and exalted it. It has made kingdoms out of all that is not important and will not last. The world recognizes things that will not be recognized in God's kingdom, while disregarding things that will. It places importance on things that will have no significance in heaven. It makes unimportant matters important ones and spends time worrying about them. The world puts priorities in the reverse order of what they should be. It places idols at the top and the true God at the bottom. It puts falsehoods in place of truth. It is deceived and blinded into thinking that it is right and God is wrong. The world is living upside down.

As believers, we know this, but the pull to be part of the world is strong. There is something attractive about living upside down. It seems to lead to economic security, social security, religious security, and political security. So, we get sucked into it at different times in our lives and pledge allegiance to it. We have to go to the most prestigious college. We have to be married. We have to be thin and fit. We have to have children or more children than we already have. We have to have a bigger and better house. We have to have the most charismatic preacher who draws the largest crowd. We have to have exactly the people we want in political office. We have to have a good career. But this kind of security is false. And one day it will be exposed for what it really is. Ironically, the kingdom of this world will be divided against itself at the end of history and will crumble and fall. Ironically, the Lamb that was slain will defeat the world forces of this world. God himself is the one orchestrating the plan, and it is a plan that takes the world by surprise. If we are wise, we will be in the Word of God so that we are not taken by surprise, but instead are found fighting alongside the Lamb of God.

We can divide this lesson into three sections:

I. The Angel Introduces the Judgment of the Great Prostitute, Babylon (Rev. 17:1–7)
II. The Angel Explains the Destruction of the Beast (Rev. 17:8–14)
III. The Angel Explains the Beast Turning on Babylon (Rev. 17:15–18)

I. The Angel Introduces the Judgment of the Great Prostitute, Babylon (Rev. 17:1–7)

Revelation 17:1–2. While 17:1–19:21 begins a new section in the book, this is really an expansion of the account of the sixth and seventh bowls in the previous verses (Rev. 16:12–21). This is apparent from the fact that it is "one of the seven angels that had the seven bowls" that speaks to John in 17:1 and shows him the judgment of Babylon, and also from the fact that the sixth and seventh bowls spoke of Babylon's judgment, but not in the detail that Revelation 17:1–19:21 will give. The judgment of Babylon is partly in answer to the saints' plea in Revelation 6:10 that God would "judge and avenge their blood" on their persecutors. That the "great prostitute" is Babylon is defined for us in verse

243

17:5. She is seated on "many waters," which is defined as "peoples and multitudes and nations and languages" (Rev. 17:15). So, she is intricately tied to those who are the foundation of her economic-religious sphere.[1]

Just as prostitutes offer their bodies in sexual favors for payment, so too Babylon offers her "economic and religious security" (which is false) to the nations in exchange for payment, thus setting up a relationship between idol and idol worshiper. She pours out deception ("wine") upon the unbelievers in order to lure them into her world of idolatry, knowing that once she does so, her subjects will be too delirious and numb to have any sense of truth or any knowledge of the way out of darkness.[2]

This should warn us to be wise concerning what we "drink." If we choose to drink the concoctions of this world, we will be deluded by them and be led astray. If we choose to drink the pure Word of God, we will be wise and recognize Satan's deception and temptation.

Old Testament Background to Revelation 17:1–2.

- Isaiah 23:15–18: "It will happen to Tyre as in the song of the prostitute . . . will prostitute herself with all the kingdoms of the world on the face of the earth."
- Isaiah 29:9: "Astonish yourselves and be astonished; blind yourselves and be blind! Be drunk, but not with wine; stagger, but not with strong drink!"
- Jeremiah 51:13: "O you who dwell by many waters, rich in treasures, your end has come; the thread of your life is cut."
- Hosea 4:11–12: "For a spirit of whoredom has led them astray, and they have left their God to play the whore."

Revelation 17:3a. Like Ezekiel, John is carried away in the Spirit (Ezek. 2:2), and like Isaiah (Isa. 21:10), he is carried into a wilderness. This identification with two great Old Testament prophets further confirms and gives authority to John's vision. While the wilderness is sometimes seen as a place where good things happen, this chapter makes

---

1. G. K. Beale, *The Book of Revelation: A Commentary on the Greek Text*, New International Greek Testament Commentary (Grand Rapids: Eerdmans, 1999), 848.
2. Ibid., 848–50.

it clear that it is also a place where bad things happen. The desert is connected with the "many waters" in Revelation 17:1 since both refer to persecutors of believers.

That John was taken to the desert is significant. Only when we have been stripped bare of all of the worldly influences around us that so often tempt and deceive us can we truly see how destructive, tempting, and influential these things really are. John was removed from the world in order to see heaven's perspective on it and share that perspective with the church. Thank goodness! Let us take heed of this. Let us too "go to the desert" by getting away into God's Word so that we see God's perspective on this world in which we live and be better witnesses and worshipers of him.

Revelation 17:3b. John saw a woman, which we have already identified as "Babylon" (Rome in John's day), sitting on a scarlet beast (which denotes her close association with the state, the evil political realm). That the beast was full of blasphemous names and had seven heads and ten horns identifies this with the first beast in Revelation 13:1, the counterfeit to the Lamb of God. From the allusion to Daniel 7, we know that the heads and the horns represent the complete power of evil kingdoms that persecute the church. That the beast is "scarlet" conveys both its royalty and its persecution of the saints (since blood is scarlet red). The blasphemous names refer to the sovereignty that the beast claims, that is God's alone. So, Babylon, representative of the world's social, economic, and religious centers that promote the kingdom of darkness, is closely linked with the beast, representative of the state (the evil political realm).

Just as the hungry man is seduced by the prostitute's sexual favors and pays for them, so too hungry mankind is seduced by Babylon, the social-economic-political favors, and pays for them. He pays his own fare of judgment. Unbelievers pay their own fare for final and eternal destruction. We would too, except for the grace of our Lord and Savior Jesus Christ who has taken the judgment in our place.

Revelation 17:4. The objects that "Babylon" is arrayed with are listed again in Revelation 18:12–14, which depicts the cargo of the merchants of the earth. Thus, this is a way of saying that Babylon represents the economic center of the world, which in John's day would have been Rome. Babylon stands in contrast with the true church, described as "the holy city, New Jerusalem, coming down out of heaven from God, prepared as a bride adorned for her husband . . . its radiance like a most rare jewel, like a jasper, clear as crystal . . . the city was pure gold . . . the walls of the city were adorned with every kind of jewel . . . the twelve gates were twelve pearls" (Rev. 21:2, 9–21).

Just as in Revelation 14:8 and 17:2, she is again seen as having a golden cup of wine (representing abominations and the impurities of her sexual immorality, which in turn represent immorality and idolatry). Again, the wine blinds mankind's true senses and perceptions, leading them astray and trapping them in the kingdom of darkness. In John's day, as mentioned earlier in the letters to the churches, citizens of Rome were under pressure to associate in trade guilds that worshiped different gods in order not to be socially and economically ostracized. Thus, Christians faced persecution when they did not participate in such idolatry.

Though Christians give up the material and economic prosperity of this world in order to not compromise our faith, we are greatly rewarded with so much more by our heavenly Father through our Lord and Savior Jesus Christ. All of the jewels of this world cannot compare to the jewels of the kingdom of heaven. All of the materialism around us is as nothing in comparison with the grandness of what heaven has in store for those who claim Christ as King of kings and Lord of lords. That is why Jesus told his disciples not to build up treasure on earth where moth and rust destroy, but to build up treasure in heaven, because what treasure is in heaven will last forever (Matt. 6:19–20). In a society that is driven by materialism, by retirement savings, and by economic prosperity, we need to remember God's view. This world is not forever, while the next one is. If we are putting more energy into building the kingdom of our families, relationships, businesses, careers, and hobbies, than we are into building the kingdom of God, our priorities are out of line.

Old Testament Background to Revelation 17:4. Jeremiah 51:7–8: "Babylon was a golden cup in the LORD's hand, making all the earth drunken; the nations drank of her wine; therefore the nations went mad. Suddenly Babylon has fallen and been broken; wail for her!"

Revelation 17:5. In contrast to the people of God who have the name of God the Father and God the Son written on their foreheads (Rev. 7:3; 14:1; 22:4), which represents their identity and allegiance, is the name on the woman's forehead, representing her identity and allegiance to Satan (see also Rev. 13:16; 14:9; 20:4). Thus, in contrast to the church stands the false church, the satanic economic and religious organizations throughout the ages. That the woman's name is a "mystery" is not just a reference to eschatological events previously hidden but now being revealed, but also to the irony of how God is orchestrating events to accomplish his plan of judgment and redemption.[3] "Babylon the Great" is symbolic for the city's glory and power. That she is the "mother of prostitutes" stands in contrast to "the mother" (the church) who gave birth to "a male child" (Christ) in Revelation 12:1–6. This woman is the leader of all those who follow in her immoral and idolatrous footsteps.

Old Testament Background to Revelation 17:5. Daniel 4:27: "Therefore, O king, let my counsel be acceptable to you: break off your sins by practicing righteousness, and your iniquities by showing mercy to the oppressed, that there may perhaps be a lengthening of your prosperity."

Revelation 17:6–7. In John's vision, he sees Babylon drunk with the blood of persecuted Christians. They are persecuted because they are witnesses and worshipers of Jesus. That the imagery is one of drinking wine, which usually goes along with joyous occasions, displays the fact that Babylon (Rome) enjoyed persecuting the Christians. We know this persecution at least included exile (Rev. 1:9), imprisonment (Rev. 2:10), or capital punishment (Rev. 2:10, 13).[4] But all through the ages, the "Babylons" of this world have enjoyed the persecution of the people of God.

The word "marvel" may refer to shock, fear, and maybe even admiration, though not in the same sense that we will see in Revelation 19:10 and 22:8. In those contexts it is in relation to the marriage supper of the

3. Ibid., 858.
4. Ibid., 860.

Lamb and the totality of what God is doing to usher in his kingdom, while here it is in the context of Babylon's judgment. In relation to the angel's statement, "I will tell you the mystery of the woman, and of the beast," he said this most likely because John's marveling at her response implied confusion and he needed clarity; he does not yet understand what all of this means.[5] Thus, the angel will explain.

II. The Angel Explains the Destruction of the Beast (Rev. 17:8–14)

Revelation 17:8. In contrast to the Lord God Almighty "who is and who was and who is to come" (Rev. 1:8; 4:8; 16:5), Jesus' death and resurrection (Rev. 1:18a; 2:8), and Jesus' coming (Rev. 3:11; 16:15; 22:7, 12, 20), is the beast who "was and is not, and is about to rise from the bottomless pit and go to destruction." Ironically, John portrays the one who is so sure of his defeat of God and of his sovereignty as one who is doomed for destruction. The fact that the beast "is about to rise from the bottomless pit" identifies him with the demonic world. This same event will be described again in Revelation 20:1–10, but there it will concern Satan. Unbelievers will marvel because he was allowed greater power prior to his defeat by Christ on the cross, then when Christ defeated him on the cross, he seemed to overcome that defeat by the power he has since displayed in the world.[6] Satan will deceive unbelievers even more during the end of history when he will be allowed one last time to try and blot out the church more severely than ever before. The unbelievers will be deceived that he is winning because they have not been illuminated by the Holy Spirit of God to resist such deception (their names have not been written in the Lamb's book of life since the foundation of the world), but God will expose him for what he really is, the deceiver of the world who is doomed to destruction.

Old Testament Background to Revelation 17:8. Daniel 7:3, 11, 17–18, 23, 26: "And four great beasts came up out of the sea, different from one another. . . . I looked then because of the sound of the

5. Ibid., 862–63.
6. Ibid., 866.

great words that the horn was speaking. And as I looked, the beast was killed, and its body destroyed and given over to be burned with fire. These four great beasts are four kings who shall arise out of the earth. But the saints of the Most High shall receive the kingdom and possess the kingdom forever, forever and ever. . . . As for the fourth beast, there shall be a fourth kingdom on earth, which shall be different from all the kingdoms, and it shall devour the whole earth, and trample it down and break it to pieces . . . but the court shall sit in judgment, and his dominion shall be taken away, to be consumed and destroyed to the end."

Revelation 17:9. That believers who are sealed still need wisdom reminds us that God uses warnings and exhortations in his plan of redemption. He grants us the grace that we need to respond to them positively, but he uses them to accomplish his salvation in our lives. The wisdom is also that of knowing Scripture, and here knowing the prophecy in Daniel about believers' needing wisdom during the tribulation at the end of history. The end of history was already inaugurated by John's day because it began at the time of Jesus' death, resurrection, and ascension. Believers need wisdom in order to withstand the deceptive nature of the evil political realm.

Just as the dragon with the seven heads and ten horns, and the beast with ten horns, represented oppressive world kingdoms throughout history (Rev. 12:3; 13:1–2), so here the seven heads/seven mountains represent the complete oppressive power of world governments throughout history, which persecute God's people when they do not submit to their idolatrous notions. In John's day, the seven mountains represented Rome,[7] but every age has its own "Babylons" and "Romes."

Old Testament Background to Revelation 17:9.

- Daniel 7:4–7: "The first was like a lion and had eagles' wings. Then as I looked its wings were plucked off . . . another beast like a bear . . . another, like a leopard. . . . And the beast had four heads, and dominion was given to it. After this I saw . . .

---

7. Vern S. Poythress, *The Returning King: A Guide to the Book of Revelation* (Phillipsburg, NJ: P&R Publishing, 2000), 163.

a fourth beast . . . it was different from all the beasts that were before it, and it had ten horns."

- Daniel 11:33: "And the wise among the people shall make many understand, though for some days they shall stumble by sword and flame, by captivity and plunder."
- Daniel 12:10: "Many shall purify themselves and make themselves white and be refined, but the wicked shall act wickedly. And none of the wicked shall understand, but those who are wise shall understand."

Revelation 17:10. The seven heads/seven mountains are now also identified as seven kings. Rather than attempting to identify these seven kings as historical rulers, it seems best to continue to apply the symbolism from the previous verse here too and see it as referring to the complete oppressive power of world governments throughout history. Yet, the Roman emperor Nero is a good example of John's words here. Though Nero died, Domitian rose to replace him; this continued the mindset which saw the emperor as godlike, and also perpetuated the persecution of believers. There had already been five of these oppressive emperors and another was now in place (and John's readers would obviously have known his name); still another will come but only remain a little while. This encourages John's readers that the fall of the complete oppressiveness of Rome, which represents all worldly government, would soon come to an end. As elsewhere in the book, this must be understood in relation to how God sees hours and days. Only he knows the hour at which he will come, but believers are to be waiting expectantly for his coming "soon." The "little while" of the seventh king most likely refers to the end of history when the dragon will be "released for a little while" (Rev. 20:3). Thus, the previous six "kings" cover history up to the last stage, when the seventh kingdom will establish its evil for a little time. Then will come the culmination of history.[8]

Revelation 17:11. This verse does not contradict what we have just said about the seventh being the final stage of history, but rather makes

8. Beale, *The Book of Revelation*, 870–72.

the point that the beast will be manifest in its totality in every stage of history, as it "belongs to the seven." Though he belongs to the seven, he is also distinct in the sense that he embodies the totality of the dragon's and the beast's evil in *more intensity*. Thus, the time frame of the end of history would place it during the reign of the seventh/eighth king. Like the number seven, the number eight also has a symbolic meaning here. It has long been recognized in Christianity that God's seventh day of rest could have led to an "eighth day" when the normative operation of the new creation began. We could also say that Christ's death on the sixth day of the week and his time in the tomb on the seventh day led to his resurrection on the eighth day. So here, the beast, as was noted in Revelation 17:8, will mimic Christ's resurrection at the end of time as he is allowed to have one final time of onslaught against Christians that will be the most intense in history. The eighth belongs to the seven because it represents the same evil nature as that which the seven embodied.[9]

Revelation 17:12. Now the angel interprets the horns. Like the other numbers in the book, these ten kings are representative of the full power of these kings. They stand in contrast to the "called and chosen and faithful" who stand with the Lamb in Revelation 17:14. So these kings, like believers, span the ages of history, and are agents through which Satan and the beast work.[10] They will receive authority (by God) for "one hour" together with the beast. We will see this "one hour" again in Revelation 18:10, 17, 19 for the time that Babylon is judged. Thus, like the previous verses, this is speaking of the final time in history, when the kingdom of darkness will be given one more "hour" to rise up in severe persecution of the church.

Revelation 17:13–14. Like believers who have one purpose, to serve and glorify God and hand over their power and authority to the Lamb (hand over their allegiance), so too these "kings" reign with and submit to the beast in order to make war on the Lamb. But we are told here that the Lamb will conquer them, for he is Lord of lords and King of kings. And, his saints, the "called and chosen and faithful," fight alongside

9. Ibid., 875–77.
10. Ibid., 879.

him, thus displaying for all to see that they too overcome. The king in Babylon and the emperors of Rome who demanded that they be called King of kings and Lord of lords, will now be shown who the real King and Lord is. This too is part of the "mystery" in Revelation 17:7. It reminds us that God's ways are not our ways. Just as Jesus came as a baby instead of a king, just as he entered Jerusalem riding on a donkey instead of on a war horse, just as he died a death on a cross *appearing* to be defeated instead of victorious, so here God uses a Lamb to conquer the beast and his allies. This action further displays the power of our God in that he needs nothing that we deem powerful to defeat his foes.

And so it is for our time as well. All people and all things in our society that demand to be known as gods will be shown in the end to be powerless, deceived counterfeits as they bow their knee and confess that Jesus Christ is Lord to the glory of God the Father (Phil. 2:9–11). Let us be careful to whom or what we pledge our allegiance here on earth. Let us not make marriage, education, children, beauty, health and fitness, money and materialism, credentials, hobbies, or our ministries our gods. There must be one God on the throne of our hearts, and he is to be our Lord and Savior Jesus Christ, King of kings and Lord of lords.

Old Testament Background to Revelation 17:14.

- Daniel 4:37: "Now I, Nebuchadnezzar, praise and extol and honor the King of heaven, for all his works are right and his ways are just; and those who walk in pride he is able to humble."

- Daniel 7:21: "As I looked, this horn made war with the saints and prevailed over them."

III. The Angel Explains the Beast Turning on Babylon (Rev. 17:15–18)

Revelation 17:15. Now the angel defines the "waters" of Revelation 17:1, "where the prostitute was seated," as "people and multitudes and nations and languages." In Daniel 3–6 this same phrase is used of the Babylonian king's subjects and has already been used throughout Revelation to depict unbelievers under "Babylon's" influence. These are the foundation for Babylon's economic commerce and security.[11] That they are closely linked to the beast is clear from Revelation 17:3, in which the woman is also sitting on the beast along with the waters, as well as from the next verse.

Revelation 17:16–17. Ironically, the "ten horns" and the beast will turn on the prostitute and hate her before they try to destroy the Lamb of God. This is part of the "mystery" of Revelation 17:7. It reminds us that God's ways are the opposite of man's ways. The imagery of Jerusalem's judgment by God in Ezekiel 23:25–29, 47 is here applied to Babylon. The political sphere of the evil world system turns against the social-religious sphere by way of the multitudes over which Babylon rules. Awakened to their drunken state and tired of their addiction, they refuse to take part in her anymore. The phrase, "they will devour her flesh," alludes to the Old Testament Jezebel, who has already been alluded to in the letters to the churches. Those of the apostate church will be included in Babylon's destruction. Thus, John is warning the churches in his day of what will happen to them if they align themselves with the pagan trade guilds. They will be judged for it and prove themselves to be apostates. It is God himself who orchestrates this ironic turn of events. The kingdom of darkness destroys itself, but the almighty hand of God orchestrates its destruction. Just as God is behind the persecution of the saints throughout history, using it to bring about his ultimate purposes, so too he is behind the destruction of Babylon by her previous subjects at the end.

For those of us facing the power of addiction, let us take heed to the warning of Babylon. Though it looks good, tastes good, feels good, and seems good for the moment, it will make us sick in the end. Let us pray and ask God to reveal to us what obsessions and addictions are deceiving us. Let us turn on them, break free from them, and declare war on them by the power of the Holy Spirit so that we are free to witness to others of the power of our God and are free to worship him, as he alone deserves.

Revelation 17:18. Now the angel defines the woman as the "great city that has dominion over the kings of all the earth." This is not just

11. Ibid., 882.

Babylon (Rome in John's day), but all of the "Babylons" and "Romes" that exist throughout the ages and that, with the power of Satan, deceive, tempt, and persecute with economic and religious power, and even hold sway over the political powers, until the end, when, as we saw in the previous verses, the political powers will turn against them to destroy them.

Throughout the chapter, it is clear that the woman Babylon stands in stark contrast to the woman of chapter 12, the church. Let us ask ourselves whether we are women of the world or women of the Word, women of wisdom?

Table 16.1 The Woman of the World versus the Woman of the Word/Wisdom

WOMAN OF THE WORLD	WOMAN OF THE WORD/WISDOM
Is impure.	Is pure.
Hides her corruption.	Reveals her reflection of God's glory and her righteous deeds.
Will be persecuted at the end, leading to destruction.	Will be persecuted throughout her life, leading to eternal life.
Will ultimately be destroyed by sin.	Will ultimately be delivered from her sin.
Finds her security in the things of this world.	Finds her security in Christ.
Receives desolation and death through her desert experiences.	Receives liberation and life through her desert experiences.

CONCLUSION

The pull to be involved in the kingdom of this world will remain strong because Satan, the world, and the flesh will persecute, tempt, and deceive us on our journey until the very end. But as we read God's Word, the Holy Spirit gives us wisdom to identify these deceptions for what they are and to flee from them. Let us stand strong alongside the Lamb of God, our Lord and Savior Jesus Christ, pledging our allegiance to him, witnessing to others about him, and giving him all of our worship and praise, to the glory of God the Father.

LESSON 17

Revelation 18

PLEASE USE THE QUESTION paradigm from pages 353–54 as you work through the following. See the introductory comments there that explain each part of the process below in more detail.

- **Pray.**
- **Ponder the Passage.** Read Revelation 18 once a day from different translations for the entire week, looking for its:
  - Point
  - Persons
  - Patterns
  - Persons of the Trinity
  - Puzzling Parts
- **Put It in Perspective.**
  - Place in Scripture
  - Passages from Other Parts of Scripture

1. Based on your observations of the text, what is the basic content of Revelation 18? Try to summarize it in your own words, using a sentence or two.
2. From the description and what you know about the context of "glory" in the rest of the book, who do you think the angel is in Revelation 18:1?

3. Using a concordance, where have you seen "fallen, fallen" (Rev. 18:2) before in the book? Where have you seen "demons" and "unclean"? With whom does this mean Babylon is associated?

4. Where in the book have we already seen this description of Babylon (Rev. 18:3)? Use a concordance if needed.

5. Why are the people to come out of Babylon (Rev. 18:4)? Is this physical or spiritual withdrawal (see John 17:15)?

6. What sin is Babylon being judged for according to Revelation 18:7a? What about according to Revelation 18:7c, d?

7. How does Revelation 18:8 allude to the bowl judgments in chapter 16? How does it allude to Revelation 14:11?

8. What do you think is the cause of the kings', merchants', and mariners' fear in Revelation 18:9, 15, and 17b?

9. What seems to be so shocking about the judgment of Babylon to the three groups of people (Rev. 18:10, 17, 19)?

10. Read Revelation 18:11, 15, 19 carefully. Why are the three groups distressed over Babylon's judgment? How does this reflect their character?

11. Compare Revelation 18:20 with 12:12. What do you see? How are these contexts related?

12. Look up Revelation 5:2 and 10:1. These are the only other places in the book where we see a "strong angel." What is the context of each and how does it compare to the context of Revelation 18:21?

13. Look up "millstone" in a concordance. Where else is it used in Scripture? How does this illuminate your understanding of it in Revelation 18:21?

14. Compare Revelation 2:9 with 18:22–23. How does God repay Babylon for what she did to the Christians in Smyrna? How will he reward the saints in the new heavens with what is mentioned in Revelation 18:22–23?

15. What three sins is Babylon judged for in Revelation 18:23c, 23d, and 24?

- **Principles and Points of Application.**
1. Think about the culture in which you live. What kind of immorality and idolatry is depicted in it? Have you become desensitized in areas where you need to put up boundaries again? Ask God to reveal areas of immorality and idolatry in your own life, help you to repent of any of them, and begin taking steps to change old habits this week by the power of the Holy Spirit.
2. What worldly sphere of influence or relationship is God calling you out of right now, lest you take part in its sins? Come apart from it this week (spiritually and emotionally) in a gracious manner, by the power of the Spirit.
3. Read Revelation 18:17. Jesus tells us not to set up treasure here on earth, but to store up treasure in heaven (Matt. 6:19–20). Worldly wealth will come to ruin but spiritual wealth will reap great rewards. Living in a materialistic culture like America, it is not always easy to have that mindset. What is your view of wealth? In what way has materialism affected you? Pray and ask God today to teach you to use your wealth for his glory, and ask him to help you have a proper view of money as you seek his wisdom in His Word.
4. Read Revelation 18:24. For those of us living in a free country, it is easy to forget about the persecuted church in other areas of the world. Yet, our brothers and sisters need us to remember them in prayer. One day God will avenge the blood of the martyrs, but we need to be praying for them daily that they would be faithful to him in the midst of persecution. Spend time today praying for the persecuted Christians in northwest Africa, North Korea, China, Bangladesh, and other places in the world.

NOTES FOR REVELATION 18

Aim: Ponder the aim of this lesson concerning our:

Mind: What do we need to know from this passage in Scripture?

That God's people are to be separate from "Babylon," praising God for his judgment of her that displays his glory.

Heart: How does what we learn from this passage affect our internal relationship with the Lord?

It prepares us to be kingdom disciples who allow God to pass judgment upon our persecutors and, when he does so, to worship and praise him for it.

Hands: How does what we learn from this passage translate into action for God's kingdom?

It enables us to:

1. Ask God to reveal any areas of immorality in our lives, help us to repent of them, and begin taking steps to change old habits this week by the power of the Holy Spirit.
2. Come out in a gracious manner from the worldly sphere of influences that are doing harm to us, leaving judgment of them to God.
3. Evaluate our view of wealth and how materialism has affected us by praying that God would use our wealth for his glory, and gives us a proper view of money as we seek wisdom in his Word.
4. Spend time this week praying for the persecuted church in specific countries of the world.

INTRODUCTION

As I begin my sixth year of chronic physical pain, I find myself tired. Tired of the pain, tired of crying out for deliverance and healing. Tired of my own flesh wanting deliverance, when I know that God's grace is sufficient for me. Some days when the pain is really bad, tears of frustration slip down my cheeks, frustration not only that the pain is still around, but also that I am not fully embracing it as God's will for my life. There are days when I feel like I have earned deliverance; after all, five years is a long time, right? No, I still have vast lessons of perseverance and acceptance to learn. There are days when I want to demand deliverance, but I know that I cannot demand anything from my Father. He has every right to demand everything of me, but I have no right to demand anything of him.

How many times have we gone before the Lord with our "I want" lists, crying out to him, demanding him to fulfill them "or else we will die." We say things like, "I want a career. I want a husband. I want my husband to be different. I want a house. I want good health. I want financial security. I want wealth. I want a baby. I want a promotion. I want relief from caring for my parents. I want to be free from this burden. I want to be free from this problem." In and of themselves, these desires are not wrong, but when we demand them or compromise our faith to get them, they become idols in our lives. The times in my life when I have been the most distressed have been when circumstances, often outside my control, have not allowed me to have what I most wanted.

This is what happened to the kings, merchants, and mariners in Revelation 18. But we are not to follow their example. We are not to weep and mourn over the idols of our lives. We are to rejoice that God has exposed them and knocked them down so that we can be better witnesses for him and better worshipers of him.

We can divide this lesson into four sections:

I. The Angel Announces Babylon's Fall (Rev. 18:1–3)
II. The Angel Calls Believers Out from Babylon (Rev. 18:4–8)
III. The Unbelievers' Weeping Response to Babylon's Fall (Rev. 18:9–19)
IV. Believers Are Called to Rejoice over God's Display of Judgment and Glory in Babylon's Fall (Rev. 18:20–24)

Chapter 18, like chapter 17, continues to expand on the judgment of Babylon as initiated by the pouring out of the fifth and sixth bowls (Rev. 16:12–21). What the angel promised John in 17:1 ("I will show you the judgment of the great prostitute") was previously described in one verse (Rev. 17:16), but now in chapter 18 greater detail is given. It was important to understand the beast and its power in chapter 17 so that we better understand both the power and the significance of Babylon and her fall.

I. The Angel Announces Babylon's Fall (Rev. 18:1–3)

Revelation 18:1. Again, "after this" refers to the order of John's visions, not to the chronological order of events in history. Perhaps the angel who comes down from heaven is the same one as in Revelation 17:1. But since "the earth was made bright with his glory," the angel could very well be Christ, especially because every time "glory" is used with a heavenly being in the book it refers either to Christ or to God.[1] The allusion to Ezekiel 43:2 is appropriate here, as Ezekiel saw a vision of the restoration of Israel to its land and temple at the end of history. This allusion here also foreshadows the same allusion to the greater context in Ezekiel (Ezek. 40–48) of the glory of God illuminating the heavenly city in Revelation 21:10 and following. Regardless of whether the angel is taken to be an angel or Christ, this heavenly being has great authority, which gives certainty to the following description of judgment.

Revelation 18:2. The angel's authority and the certainty of judgment are further confirmed by the "mighty voice." We have seen this announcement before in Revelaion 14:8 and in the briefer description of Babylon's fall in Revelation 17:16. The imagery is taken from the prophets who declared historical Babylon's and Edom's fall and/or fallen state. That historical Babylon fell and was left desolate gives further certainty that "Babylon" as the worldwide economic-social-cultural-religious sphere will fall. She is closely identified with the dragon, the beast, and the false prophet who had "three unclean spirits

---

1. G. K. Beale, *The Book of Revelation: A Commentary on the Greek Text*, New International Greek Testament Commentary (Grand Rapids: Eerdmans, 1999), 892, takes this angel to be Christ, while Vern S. Poythress, *The Returning King: A Guide to the Book of Revelation* (Phillipsburg, NJ: P&R Publishing, 2000), 168, takes this to be an angel who reflects the splendor of God.

like frogs . . . demonic spirits" (Rev. 16:13–14), by having become "a dwelling place for demons, a haunt for every unclean spirit."

Old Testament Background to Revelation 18:2.

- Isaiah 13:21: "But wild animals will lie down there, and their houses will be full of howling creatures; there ostriches will dwell, and there wild goats will dance."
- Isaiah 21:9: "Fallen, fallen is Babylon; and all the carved images of her gods he has shattered to the ground."
- Isaiah 34:11, 14: "But the hawk and porcupine shall possess it, the owl and the raven shall dwell in it. He shall stretch the line of confusion over it and the plumb line of emptiness."

Revelation 18:3. The first part of this verse, "for all nations have drunk the wine of the passion of her sexual immorality," is almost identical to Revelation 14:8, "she who made all nations drink the wine of the passion of her sexual immorality." And, the second part of the verse picks up on Revelation 17:2. The cause of her judgment is the "wine" that she gives other nations to drink, which deceives them into thinking that economic security is greater than security in God. Those who give into drinking idolatry are deceived and numb to the truth. Their powers of discernment are clouded and they are led away to destruction. The "kings of the earth" are not only those in actual political power in Rome, but also those who hold political sway in any area of the empire.[2]

Old Testament Background to Revelation 18:3. Isaiah 23:17b: "The LORD will visit Tyre, and she will return to her wages and will prostitute herself with all the kingdoms of the world on the face of the earth."

II. The Angel Calls Believers Out from Babylon (Rev. 18:4–8)

Revelation 18:4–5. Another voice from heaven (God the Father, Christ, or an angel) calls believers out of Babylon, so that they will not drink of her idolatry and be judged alongside her. This is not a physical removal, but a spiritual removal, as is clear from the exhortation not to

---

2. Beale, *The Book of Revelation*, 896.

"take part in her sins." We are to remain in the world to witness, but are to stay out of the world of spiritual compromise (see John 17:5). It is important that believers do not pull out of secular spheres of influence. Though we will be persecuted for our witness, we are called to be witnesses as Christians. If we remove ourselves from government agencies, secular businesses, and other public venues, we are not fulfilling our commission. We must be in these spheres physically, but out of them spiritually. The Spirit will strengthen us as we gird ourselves with the armor of God (Eph. 6:10–20) before going into such realms, recognizing that this world is a battlefield.

The reason why God's plagues have come upon the people is that Babylon has heaped up her sin, and God must display his justice. He never turns a blind eye to sin. There is always judgment rendered. Thankfully, the judgment was rendered upon Christ for believers so that we do not have to endure God's wrath.

Old Testament Background to Revelation 18:4–5.

- Isaiah 52:11: "Depart, depart, go out from [Babylon]; touch no unclean thing; go out from the midst of her; purify yourselves, you who bear the vessels of the LORD."

- Jeremiah 51:45: "Go out of the midst of her, my people! Let every one save his life from the fierce anger of the LORD!"

Revelation 18:6. Who is being addressed here? Ultimately, God himself, as he is the only one who can answer this request. But it may also include all those involved in Babylon's judgment—believers, the ten kings, and the beast—who turn on Babylon in the end, and/or angelic beings that help carry out judgment. Rather than translating the Greek word "double," it would be better to translate it as "equivalent," which is in line with the Hebrew translation of the equivalent word.[3] Taken with the preceding phrase, "pay her back as she herself paid back others," and with the following phrase, "give her a like measure" in verse 7, this would be in keeping with God's justice as expressed by the principle of "eye for eye" in Leviticus 24:20.

3. Ibid., 901.

Old Testament Background to Revelation 18:6.

- Psalm 137:8: "O daughter of Babylon, doomed to be destroyed, blessed shall he be who repays you with what you have done to us!"
- Isaiah 40:2: "Speak tenderly to Jerusalem, and cry to her that her warfare is ended, that her iniquity is pardoned, that she has received from the Lord's hand double for all her sins."
- Jeremiah 16:18: "But first I will doubly repay their iniquity and their sin, because they have polluted my land with the carcasses of their detestable idols, and have filled my inheritance with their abominations."
- Jeremiah 50:29: "Repay [Babylon] according to her deeds; do to her according to all that she has done."
- Jeremiah 51:24: "I will repay Babylon . . . before your very eyes for all the evil that they have done in Zion, declares the Lord."

Revelation 18:7–8. Here we are reminded of Proverbs 16:18, "Pride goes before destruction, and a haughty spirit before a fall." Again, Babylon's due judgment is requested. The wording used is an allusion to the fall of the historical Babylon in Isaiah 47:7–8, which foreshadowed the fall of worldwide Babylon at the end of history. The pride is not just economic, but political as well. This would be especially pertinent to the church of Laodicea, which said, "I am rich and have become wealthy, and I have need of nothing" (Rev. 3:17). Let us be aware, those of us in American churches that are so wealthy, that we do not find our security in our bank accounts, our retirement plans, or our material assets, but rather in the Lord our God.

Because of Babylon's economic and political pride, God's judgment that results in his glory will come upon her quickly. "And she will be burned up with fire" is repeated from Revelation 17:16, which is an allusion to Isaiah 47:14. It was noted in Revelation 17 that the beast and the ten kings would be the very ones God uses to judge her. This only serves to confirm how "mighty" he is, as "the king's heart is a stream of water in the hand of the Lord; he turns it wherever he will" (Prov. 21:1).

Old Testament Background to Revelation 18:7–8.

- Isaiah 47:7–9: "You said, 'I shall be mistress forever,' so that you did not lay these things to heart or remember their end. Now therefore hear this, you lover of pleasures, who sit securely, who say in your heart, 'I am, and there is no one besides me.'"
- Isaiah 47:14: "Behold, they are like stubble; the fire consumes them; they cannot deliver themselves from the power of the flame."

III. The Unbelievers' Weeping Response to Babylon's Fall (Rev. 18:9–19)

This section alludes to the fall of Tyre in Ezekiel 26–27, which foreshadowed the fall of worldwide Babylon at the end of history. The same three groups of people, kings, merchants, and mariners, mourn over both Tyre and worldwide Babylon. The point of the entire section is the economic distress that comes with Babylon's fall, which exposes economic security for the idolatry that it is.

Revelation 18:9–10. If the "kings of the earth" here are the same ones as those in Revelation 17 (who unite with the beast to destroy Babylon), it seems contradictory; but they may not be the same group, or if they are, though they united to destroy her, they could still mourn over what that meant for their economic security.[4] Just as the anorexic finally wakes up to her starved state, grows tired of her addiction, and seeks help to recover from it (turning her back on anorexia), there is still part of her that mourns over the loss of the sense of control and security that her addiction gave her. So here, though the kings have awakened to their drunken stupor brought on by Babylon, they still mourn over their economic loss. "As they see the smoke of her burning," recalls the description of the same judgment in Revelation 14:9–11, which was an allusion to Sodom (Gen. 19:28) and Edom (Isa. 34:9–10). The response of the kings does not include only weeping and wailing, but also fear. It is fear of their own economic loss, but it is also fear of their own judgment that will follow Babylon's in the same manner.

4. Ibid., 906.

Old Testament Background to Revelation 18:9–10.

- Jeremiah 51:8: "Suddenly Babylon has fallen and been broken; wail for her! Take balm for her pain; perhaps she may be healed."
- Ezekiel 26:16: "Then all the princes of the sea will step down from their thrones and remove their robes and strip off their embroidered garments. They will clothe themselves with trembling; they will sit on the ground and tremble every moment and be appalled at [Tyre]."
- Ezekiel 27:27: "Your riches, your wares, your merchandise, your mariners and your pilots, your caulkers, your dealers in merchandise, and all your men of war who are in you, with all your crew that is in your midst, sink into the heart of the seas on the day of your fall."
- Daniel 4:33: "Immediately the word was fulfilled against Nebuchadnezzar. He was driven from among men and ate grass like an ox."

Revelation 18:11–14. Now we come to the second group that mourns, the merchants of the earth. Again, their weeping is not on behalf of Babylon, but on behalf of what Babylon's fall has cost them: loss of economic security. The twenty-nine items listed here must have been part of the Roman trade system of John's time. The churches in John's day were in danger of compromising their faith to gain these items and the supposed security that came with them. That these items, which were not bad in and of themselves, became cause for sin in order to achieve economic affluence is seen clearly in the reference to "slaves, that is human souls" at the end of verse 13. Whenever we sacrifice our relationships with others for the sake of economic gain, we are headed down a sinful path.

Old Testament Background to Revelation 18:11–14. Ezekiel 27:7–25: A lament for Tyre.

Revelation 18:15–17a. In verse 15 the judgment of Babylon is repeated again from verses 9–11, but with different words to highlight it and display its certainty. Their words of weeping and mourning begin

265

like the king's words in verse 10, thus highlighting the distress and certainty of the judgment. The kings called Babylon the "mighty city," whereas the merchants call her the "great city." The description of the clothing not only emphasizes the economic sphere of Babylon, but also the religious sphere, as the high priest's clothing and the sanctuary were adorned with such.[5] Thus, she stands in stark contrast to the pure bride of Christ, and shows that the apostate church is also in view here alongside the pagan world. That the economic destruction of Babylon came swiftly and shockingly is seen in verse 17. This stands behind the fear of the merchants; if Babylon is destroyed so quickly, they also will be.

Old Testament Background to Revelation 18:15–17a.

- Ezekiel 16:13: "Thus you [Jerusalem] were adorned with gold and silver, and your clothing was of fine linen and silk and embroidered cloth. You ate fine flour and honey and oil. You grew exceedingly beautiful and advanced to royalty."
- Ezekiel 27:12–25: A lament for Tyre.
- Ezekiel 28:13: "You were in Eden, the garden of God; every precious stone was your covering . . . and crafted in gold were your settings and your engravings. On the day that you were created they were prepared."

Revelation 18:17b-19. Now the third and final group who mourns is mentioned, the mariners. Their mourning too is not on behalf of Babylon, but on what Babylon's fall means for their own economic demise. The "smoke of her burning" is another allusion to Revelation 14:9–11, which alludes to Sodom (Gen. 19:28) and Edom (Isa. 34:9–10). Verse 19 repeats the same exclamation as verses 10 and 16, but here the emphasis is on the sea commerce. The same phrase, "for in a single hour she has been laid waste," of verses 10 and 17 is repeated as well, further highlighting the suddenness of judgment.

So often we weep and wail over that which we think will give us security, but which is really an idol that we have set up in our hearts. We must examine our hearts and see if the root of our depres-

---

5. Ibid., 912.

sion, the root of our bad mood, the root of our distress, is not some "idol" that has either come crashing down or not been fulfilled in our lives. Selfishly, we want what we want when we want it, and when we don't get it, we cry, "Woe is me, for I am undone." But we are undone in the wrong way. We are to be undone by the glory of God, but too often we are undone because God has not granted our selfish wishes and desires.

Old Testament Background to Revelation 18:17b–19. Ezekiel 27:28–33: A lament for Tyre.

IV. Believers Are Called to Rejoice over God's Display of Judgment and Glory in Babylon's Fall (Rev. 18:20–24)

Revelation 18:20. When Satan was thrown down to earth at his defeat by Christ's death on the cross, which was the inauguration of the kingdom of God, believers were told to "Rejoice, O heavens and you who dwell in them!" (Rev. 12:12). Now, at the final defeat of Satan's world system, which is the consummation of the kingdom of God, believers again are told to "Rejoice over her, O heaven." Though all believers are exhorted here, the ones under the altar in Revelation 6:9–11 are especially in view, since this is God's answer to their plea for vindication. Ironically, the same response that the unbelievers had to the death of the two witnesses (symbolic of the church), to "rejoice over them and make merry . . . because [they] had been a torment to them," is now the response of the believers over the death of Babylon, which had been a torment to them.[6]

Old Testament Background to Revelation 18:20. Jeremiah 51:48: "Then the heavens and the earth and all that is in them, shall sing for joy over Babylon, for the destroyers shall come against them out of the north, declares the LORD."

Revelation 18:21. This is the third time in the book that an angel is referred to as "strong/mighty." The first strong angel was seen in the context of the scroll that only the Lamb of God was worthy to open and which concerned God's plan of judgment and redemption (Rev. 5:2). The

6. Ibid., 916–17.

second strong angel was found in the context of the little scroll which concerned the church following the example of Christ's suffering as she took part in God's plan of judgment and redemption (Rev. 10:1). So it is appropriate that the third strong angel is found in the context when God's plan of judgment and redemption is completed.

The imagery of Babylon's fall is taken from the historical destruction of both Tyre and Babylon (see the Old Testament background mentioned below). That these cities fell provides certainty that worldwide Babylon will fall as well.

The words of Jesus in Matthew 18:6 (see the New Testament background mentioned below) are instructive here, as Babylon was she who caused people to stumble and is now being thrown down in violence. John is warning the church so that she does not become like those who lead people astray, which, as we saw in the letters to the seven churches, was a serious problem. We too need to heed the warning so that we are not part of those who deceive. This includes making sure that the Bible studies we use to teach women, or those that we participate in, do not contain any false teachings. This will require diligence and wisdom on our part as we sift through them, knowing that most false teachers are subtle in their deception and masquerade under a great deal of truth.

Old Testament/New Testament Background to Revelation 18:21.
- Exodus 15:4–5: "Pharaoh's chariots and his host he cast into the sea, and his chosen officers were sunk in the Red Sea. The floods covered them; they went down into the depths like a stone."
- Nehemiah 9:11: "And you divided the sea before them, so that they went through the midst of the sea on dry land, and you cast their pursuers into the depths, as a stone into mighty waters."
- Jeremiah 51:63–64: "When you finish reading this book, tie a stone to it and cast it into the midst of the Euphrates, and say, 'Thus shall Babylon sink, to rise no more, because of the disaster that I am bringing upon her.'"

- Ezekiel 26:12, 21: "They [Babylon] will plunder your [Tyre] riches . . . I will bring to you [Tyre] a dreadful end, and you shall be no more."
- Matthew 18:6: "But whoever causes one of these little ones who believe in me to sin, it would be better for him to have a great millstone fastened around his neck and to be drowned in the depth of the sea."

Revelation 18:22–24. Once a place of merry making, Babylon has no reason to rejoice anymore. She has lost all that she thought she had and tied her own hands to destruction. We know that the church in Smyrna (Rev. 2:9) struggled with economic poverty because of its choice to not take part in pagan trade guilds. By choosing to do so, the people were ostracized from the guilds, which often resulted in loss of jobs or, at the very least, economic hardship. In keeping with the "eye for eye" judgment, God now removes the craftsmen, the sound of the mill, the light of a lamp, and the joyous occasion of weddings from Babylon. The reasons for such removal are, first, because they gloried in themselves rather than giving glory to God ("merchants were the great ones of the earth"); second, because of the deception that she used to lead people to idolatry ("all nations were deceived by your sorcery"); and third, because she persecuted believers ("in her was found the blood of all who have been slain on earth"). This third reason also confirms that Babylon represents the worldwide system of evil, not just one nation ("all . . . on earth").

The imagery in these verses stands in stark contrast to the new heaven and earth, where there are harpists and musicians assisting in the worship of God, where the light will be God himself, and where the bridegroom (Christ) and the bride (the church) will sit down to a marriage supper together.

I have known some wonderful Christian people whom the Lord has blessed with great wealth. Rather than glorying in themselves and in their wealth, though, they gloried in God. Rather than keeping their money for themselves, they graciously gave it away in large amounts to further the kingdom of God. Instead of being deceived into thinking that wealth was their security, they continued to find their security in God. Wealth in itself is not wrong. It is what we choose to do with wealth and how we view wealth that gets us into trouble. Babylon is the prime example of this.

Old Testament/New Testament Background to Revelation 18:22–24.

- Isaiah 23:8–9: "Who has purposed this against Tyre, the bestower of crowns, whose merchants were princes, whose traders were the honored of the earth? The LORD of hosts has purposed it, to defile the pompous pride of all glory, to dishonor all the honored of the earth."

- Isaiah 24:8: "The mirth of the tambourines is stilled, the noise of the jubilant has ceased, the mirth of the lyre is stilled."

- Isaiah 47:9–10: "These two things shall come to you [Babylon] in a moment, in one day; the loss of children and widowhood shall come upon you in full measure, in spite of your many sorceries and the great power of your enchantments."

- Jeremiah 51:49: "Babylon must fall for the slain of Israel, just as for Babylon have fallen the slain of all the earth."

- Ezekiel 24:7: "For the blood she has shed is in her midst; she put it on the bare rock; she did not pour it out on the ground to cover it with dust."

- Ezekiel 28:5, 9: "By your [Tyre's] great wisdom in your trade you have increased your wealth, and your heart has become proud in your wealth . . . will you still say, 'I am a god,' in the presence of those who kill you, though you are but a man, and no god, in the hands of those who slay you?"

- Matthew 23:35, 37: "So that on you may come all the righteous blood shed on earth, from the blood of innocent Abel to the blood of Zechariah the son of Barachiah, whom you murdered between the sanctuary and the altar. . . . O Jerusalem, Jerusalem, the city that kills the prophets and stones those who are sent to it! How often would I have gathered your children together as a hen gathers her brood under her wings, and you would not!"

CONCLUSION

I have no idea how long I will struggle with chronic physical pain. But I know this. While I can pray that the Lord will deliver me from it, I have no right to demand that God remove it from my life. I am not to make good health an idol in my life. By God's grace, I am learning to accept his lessons and plans for me, thanking him for exposing my own idols through such pain. It is my prayer that it will make me a better witness for him and a better worshiper of him, as this brings glory to his name. That is my hope and prayer for your distress as well. May we allow him to knock down our idols so that his name might be glorified through the witness and worship of our lives.

LESSON 18

Revelation 19

PLEASE USE THE QUESTION paradigm from pages 353–54 as you work through the following. See the introductory comments there that explain each part of the process below in more detail.

- **Pray**.
- **Ponder the Passage**. Read Revelation 19 once a day from different translations for the entire week, looking for its:
  - Point
  - Persons
  - Patterns
  - Persons of the Trinity
  - Puzzling Parts
- **Put It in Perspective**.
  - Place in Scripture
  - Passages from Other Parts of Scripture

1. Based on your observations of the text, what is the basic content of Revelation 19? Try to summarize it in your own words, using a sentence or two.
2. Look up "hallelujah" (Rev. 19:1) in a concordance. Is this word used in any other book of the New Testament? If so, where?
3. Why do "salvation and glory and honor" belong to our God (Rev. 19:1–2)? Why is the great prostitute judged? What has God's

judgment accomplished? How does this relate to Revelation 6:9–11?

4. Look up "smoke" (Rev. 19:3) in a concordance. Where have we seen this before in Revelation? What was the context? What is the context here?

5. Who joins the great multitude in heaven in Revelation 19:4? What do they affirm?

6. Look up "hallelujah" in a Bible dictionary. What does it mean? Do you see its meaning spelled out in Revelation 19:5? Where? Who is to praise God? How are they described?

7. How are the "roar" and "mighty peals of thunder" in Revelation 19:6 an answer to 19:5? Compare Revelation 19:6 with 19:1. What do you see?

8. What word do you see used again in Revelation 19:6 that has already been used several times in this chapter? How many times is it used in chapter 19? Does this last time signify an end to the section? Compare Revelation 19:6 with 11:17. What similarities do you see?

9. What is the exhortation in Revelation 19:7? Why? How has the bride made herself ready (think about the context and the relationship of the believers to Babylon)?

10. Does "it was granted her to clothe herself" contradict "and his Bride has made herself ready" or does it display the mystery of man's perseverance and God's preservation?

11. What is the fine linen? Who provides these? What does this imply? To what do righteous deeds on earth lead (see Matt. 6:4; Mark 9:41; 1 Cor. 9:17; Heb. 11:26; Rev. 22:12)?

12. What is the "blessing" in Revelation 19:9? What and where are the other six blessings in the book?

13. What does John do in Revelation 19:10? Why is he rebuked for it? How does the angel describe himself? What does this tell you about angels? How does Revelation 19:10 define "the testimony of Jesus"? What is the "spirit of prophecy" (see Acts 2:17–18 and Rev. 11:3)?

14. Contrast Revelation 19:11 with 6:2. How are the contexts different (go back and look at your notes!)?

15. Why does Christ have the right to come and make war (Rev. 19:11)?

16. Where else have you seen "diadems" in the book? How does this contrast with Christ's "many diadems" in Revelation 19:12?

17. How does Revelation 19:13 help explain the "name by which no one knows" in 19:12? What do you think "by which no one knows" means (see Luke 10:22)?

18. Why are the armies (Rev. 19:14) arrayed in fine linens (see Rev. 19:8)?

19. Where else in the book and in Scripture do you find the same imagery as portrayed in Revelation 19:15?

20. How does Revelation 19:16 help to further explain the "name by which no one knows" in 19:12?

21. Compare Revelation 19:17 with 18:1. What similarities do you see?

22. Contrast Revelation 19:7, 9 with 19:17–18.

23. Who is gathered against whom in Revelation 19:19? Who is ultimately behind this gathering? Have Revelation 11:7 and 16:14 alluded to the same final battle?

24. Who is captured and thrown into the lake of fire first, second, and third in Revelation 19:20–21? Is this significant? Why?

• **Principles and Points of Application.**

1. What persecution from unbelievers are you facing right now in which you want to play the part of avenger? Give that role to God this week. Continue to be a faithful servant of God by the power of the Holy Spirit and rest in him, knowing that he will be the avenger.

2. What righteous deeds are you doing in the power of the Spirit to prepare for the marriage supper of the Lamb? What righteous deeds should you be doing in the power of the Spirit? Pray and ask God to reveal these to you this week and then begin doing them, relying on the Spirit of God to work through you.

3. Who or what are you worshiping in your life? Scripture is clear that God alone is worthy of our worship. Confess any idols you may have, repent, and worship God alone.

4. How does God's Word tell us to fight the spiritual battle between the kingdom of God and the kingdom of Satan? Read Ephesians 6:10–20 again this week, and ask God to gird you with his armor. Then engage in warfare at his side in the strength of his Spirit.

NOTES FOR REVELATION 19

Aim: Ponder the aim of this lesson concerning our:

Mind: What do we need to know from this passage in Scripture?

That Babylon's judgment leads to the saints' worship of God and their marriage to the Lamb. God will finally judge the beast, the false prophet, and the nations.

Heart: How does what we learn from this passage affect our internal relationship with the Lord?

It prepares us to be kingdom disciples who respond to God's justice and glory with worship, and who look forward to the marriage supper of the Lamb with joy and hope.

Hands: How does what we learn from this passage translate into action for God's kingdom?

It enables us to:

1. Be God's faithful servants in the face of persecution, leaving vengeance of our persecutors to him.

2. Prepare for the marriage supper of the Lamb by doing righteous deeds through the power of the Holy Spirit for the glory of God.

3. Confess any idols in our lives, repent, and give glory and worship to God alone this week.
4. Be engaged in the battle between God and Satan by girding ourselves with the spiritual armor of God (Eph. 6:10–20) daily.

INTRODUCTION

I have never been one who enjoys shopping malls. Besides the atmosphere that is so full of temptation and deception, I suppose I am too frugal and too tall; too frugal because nothing seems to fit my budget and too tall because nothing seems to fit my size. But I know that I am in the minority. Many women enjoy shopping and love buying designer fashions. I am always amazed at the price difference between the name brand versus the store brand. I'm yet to be convinced of why I should pay for a name.

The same tendency to desire "name brands" seems to have crept into our churches. Women seem to be satisfied only if they are getting the name brand teachers, the name brand Bible studies, and the name brand conference speakers and teachers. Women in leadership know this and often play to this. I was amazed at how many large manila envelopes came in my mailbox when I worked as the director of women's ministry at a large church. It was not unusual to open one to find an 8-by-11-inch glamour shot of a Christian speaker, along with a biography telling me all the reasons why I should have her come to our church, and if she did, pay her an astronomical fee. Many will pay these fees to hear the big name speakers thinking that they are better than others, that their words are more powerful, and that their conferences are more life changing. But we are sadly confused. It is not the words of the woman, but the Word of God that changes our lives. The most powerful message could just as easily come to us through the no-name woman of a tiny country church as by the big-name woman of the huge metropolitan church in a well-known city.

Revelation 19 has much to say about misplaced worship. It tells us not to do it! It tells us to worship God, for he alone is worthy of the glory and the honor and the praise.

We can divide this lesson into two sections:

I. Babylon's Judgment Results in the Saints' Worship of God and Marriage to the Lamb (Rev. 19:1–10)
II. The Final Judgment of the Beast, the False Prophet, and the Nations (Rev. 19:11–21)

I. Babylon's Judgment Results in the Saints' Worship of God and Marriage to the Lamb

Revelation 19:1–10. The first eight verses of this section stand closely connected to Revelation 18:9–24; those verses gave us a picture of the response of unbelievers to Babylon's fall and 19:1–8 gives us a picture of the response of believers. We have already learned that the main thrust of chapter 18 is for believers to respond in worship to the fall of Babylon because it displays God's justice and glory (Rev. 18:20). Now we see the saints do this. This section also continues Revelation 11:15–19, in which the seventh trumpet resulted in the "kingdom of the world [becoming] the kingdom of our Lord and of his Christ."

Revelation 19:1–3. Now John sees all the believers at the end of history praising God for his judgment of Babylon, which displayed his justice and power and completed his plan of redemption for his people. The term "hallelujah" is taken from the Hebrew phrase that means "praise Yahweh." This word is only found four times in the New Testament, all occurring in the first six verses of this chapter.[1] Yahweh is to be praised because of his salvation, glory, and power, which were all displayed through his judgment on Babylon. God has avenged on her the blood of his servants as his answer to the saints' plea in Revelation 6:9–11 for vindication. It is an allusion to 2 Kings 9:7, where God avenges the blood of his servants who were slain at the hand of Jezebel.[2] Jezebel

---

1. Robert H. Mounce, *The Book of Revelation*, New International Commentary on the New Testament, rev. ed. (Grand Rapids: Eerdmans, 1998), 341.
2. G. K. Beale, *The Book of Revelation: A Commentary on the Greek Text*, New International Greek Testament Commentary (Grand Rapids: Eerdmans, 1999), 928.

has already been alluded to in the letters to the churches concerning false teaching; God indeed will judge the apostate church.

Again, the believers cry out in praise for the eternal destruction of Babylon. We have already seen this phrase in Revelation 14:11 in the context of individual unbelievers being judged. The city and the city's supporters suffer the same destruction. The deceived followers were led to the same demise. Let us be careful whom we follow. For where they go, we will go also. Let us follow only our Lord and Savior Jesus Christ, for though he went to the cross, and thus we will also, he also went to glory and we know that we will too.

Old Testament Background to Revelation 19:1–3.

- 2 Kings 9:7: "And you shall strike down the house of Ahab your master, so that I may avenge on Jezebel the blood of my servants the prophets, and the blood of all the servants of the LORD."
- Psalm 79:10: "Why should the nations say, 'Where is their God?' Let the avenging of the outpoured blood of your servants be known among the nations before our eyes!"
- Psalm 104:35: "Let sinners be consumed from the earth, and let the wicked be no more! Bless the LORD, O my soul! Praise the LORD!"
- Isaiah 34:9–10: "And the streams of Edom shall be turned into pitch, and her soil into sulfur; her land shall become burning pitch."
- Jeremiah 51:25: "Behold, I am against you, O destroying mountain, declares the LORD, which destroys the whole earth; I will stretch out my hand against you, and roll you down from the crags, and make you a burnt mountain."

Revelation 19:4. Now the elders and living creatures fall down and worship God, agreeing with the praise of the saints ("amen") and repeating the "hallelujah" for God's destruction of Babylon, which reveals his justice and glory and consummates his plan of redemption and judgment.

279

Old Testament Background to Revelation 19:4. Psalm 106:48: "Blessed be the LORD, the God of Israel, from everlasting to everlasting! And let all the people say, 'Amen!' Praise the LORD!"

Revelation 19:5. Now a voice from the throne exhorts all of God's servants to worship God because of his judgment of Babylon. This voice is either Christ's, which conveys that he is our elder brother and leads us in worship of our Father (John 20:17), or this is the voice of a heavenly being around the throne that exhorts believers to worship God.[3] "Praise our God," means the same as "hallelujah."

Revelation 19:6. The great multitude in heaven responds to the previous exhortation with even greater magnitude (compare "loud voice" of verse 1 with "roar of many waters" and "sound of mighty peals of thunder" in verse 6). They again say, "Hallelujah," praise Yahweh! For the destruction of Babylon has displayed that he is almighty and that he reigns. This clearly expands on Revelation 11:17, "We give thanks to you, Lord God Almighty . . . for you have taken your great power and begun to reign."[4] With the final "hallelujah" being used here, it seems to be a conclusion to this section of verses.

Old Testament Background to Revelation 19:6.

- Psalm 47:8: "God reigns over the nations; God sits on his holy throne."
- Isaiah 52:7: "How beautiful upon the mountains are the feet of him who brings good news, who publishes peace, who brings good news of happiness, who publishes salvation, who says to Zion, 'Your God reigns.'"
- Ezekiel 1:24: "And when they went, I heard the sound of their wings like the sound of many waters, like the sound of the Almighty, a sound of tumult like the sound of an army. When they stood still, they let down their wings."

Revelation 19:7–8. The great multitude rejoices again and gives God the glory, for the destruction of Babylon has allowed the marriage

3. Ibid., 930.
4. Ibid., 931.

of the Lamb to come. The church made herself ready through the fires of persecution, deception, and temptation that she withstood among the world system of Babylon by the power of the Holy Spirit. She stood firm as a witness and as a worshiper, proving that she was worthy to marry the Lamb. Without the refining fires of persecution, she never would have been ready to marry the Bridegroom. The theological tension here of God's preservation and man's perseverance is seen. The church made herself ready, but it was granted her by God to clothe herself. That God granted her clothes of fine linen is the reward of her righteous deeds, both those done by the believers and those done by God for the believers (his judgment of their persecutors). That they are clothed this way gives indication that they stand alongside Christ as he avenges their blood on their persecutors. Their righteous acts stand in stark contrast to Babylon's "sins heaped high as heaven" (Rev. 18:5). It also indicates the intimacy that they now share with Christ, which was initiated by him, and the purity of Christ that has been transferred to them.[5]

Not only are we clothed with fine linen, bright and pure at the marriage of the Lamb at the end of history, but also we are even now clothed with pure linen by the Holy Spirit of God, so that we may stand alongside our Lord and have access to the throne of grace (Heb. 4:16). The relationship that we now have with Christ is an intimate one. Because of his righteousness, we are able to perform righteous deeds as well. Enabled by the Holy Spirit, we can do good works here on earth, which will serve as our reward in heaven. We can also rest assured that God has clothed us with garments of vindication. No matter how much we might be persecuted here on earth, these garments serve to remind us that we are righteous in the eyes of our heavenly Father, the only judge that matters. We can be bold witnesses and worshipers of him, knowing that we wear his armor, his robes of righteousness, and his robes of righteous deeds.

Old Testament/New Testament Background to Revelation 19:7–8.
- Isaiah 61:10: "I will greatly rejoice in the LORD; my soul shall exult in my God, for he has clothed me with the garments of

---

5. Ibid., 934–44.

salvation; he has covered me with the robe of righteousness, as a bridegroom decks himself like a priest with a beautiful headdress, and as a bride adorns herself with her jewels."

- Hosea 2:14–20: "Therefore, behold, I will allure her . . . you will call me 'My Husband' . . . and I will betroth you to me forever . . . in righteousness and in justice, in steadfast love and in mercy . . . in faithfulness. And you shall know the LORD."
- 2 Corinthiana 11:2: "For I feel a divine jealousy for you as a pure virgin to Christ."
- Ephesians 5:25: "Husbands, love your wives, as Christ loved the church and gave himself up for her."

Revelation 19:9. As in Revelation 14:3 and 21:5, John is commanded by the angel to write a confirmation that what has just been said in verses 7–8 are the true words of God and to write that those who take part in the marriage are "blessed." This is the fourth of seven blessings in the book (Rev. 1:3; 14:13; 16:15; 19:9; 20:6; 22:7; 22:14).

Whereas verses 7–8 portrayed the church as a whole as about to marry the Lamb, verse 9 portrays individual believers as invited to the marriage supper of the Lamb. What a beautiful picture! God is not just concerned about the entire community of believers as a whole, but he also invites each one of us individually to partake in an intimate relationship with him. He wants to clothe us with his righteousness. He wants to sing over us with his love. He wants to protect us and provide for us. He wants to lead us and guide us. In a confused world, he is the truth. Do we long to be married? Let us allow Christ to be our Bridegroom. Do we feel trapped inside a marriage? Let us look to Christ as our perfect Groom. Do we have needs that are going unmet from our spouse? Let us look for fulfillment from our heavenly Husband. He loves us, he wants us, he pays for us, he redeems us, he protects us, he nourishes us, he clothes us, and he gives us his name; blessed are we when we wed with him!

Old Testament/New Testament Background to Revelation 19:9.

- Isaiah 25:6–7: "On this mountain the LORD of hosts will make for all peoples a feast of rich food, a feast of well-aged wine, of rich food full of marrow, of aged wine well refined."
- Isaiah 65:13–17: "Behold my servants shall eat . . . drink . . . rejoice . . . sing for gladness of heart. . . . For behold, I create new heavens and a new earth."
- Matthew 22:1–14: Jesus teaches the "Parable of the Wedding Feast."
- Matthew 26:29: "I tell you I will not drink again of this fruit of the vine until that day when I drink it new with you in my Father's kingdom."
- Luke 13:29: "And people will come from east and west and from north and south and recline at table in the kingdom of God."
- Luke 14:15: "Blessed is everyone who will eat bread in the kingdom of God!"

Revelation 19:10. John confuses the angel with the angel's message, and because he does this, he bows in worship to the wrong being. The angel, who knows that all glory and honor belong to God, is quick to correct him ("You must not do that!"). The reason why he must not worship the angel is because the angel is simply a fellow servant along with all those who hold to the testimony of Jesus. Jesus came to bear witness of the Father, and now believers are to bear witness of Jesus. Thus, we have been given a prophetic role[6] ("spirit of prophecy") as we live our lives on this earth as witnesses of Christ.

How often we too confuse the message with the messenger. We worship the woman of the Word rather than the living Word. We worship the charisma rather than the Christ. We worship the personality rather than the Person of God. We are so prone to idolatry and fall into it more often than we realize or want to admit. But we must not do this! Our preachers, our Bible study teachers, our women's ministry directors,

6. Ibid., 948.

and our Christian heroes are all fellow servants and witnesses of Christ. We are to worship God and God alone.

II. The Final Judgment of the Beast, the False Prophet, and the Nations (Rev. 19:11–21)

The fall of Babylon was not complete until the forces behind Babylon were destroyed as well. God's avenging on Babylon the blood of his servants (Rev. 19:2) was not complete until he had destroyed the allies of Babylon. So this section describes the destruction of the beast, the false prophet, and the nations that supported Babylon. Though this is not the first time that we have seen a description of the final judgment at the end of history, this is the most detailed account of it in the book.

Revelation 19:11. From a literary point of view, the phrase, "Then I saw heaven opened," signifies the start of a new vision. John sees a white horse. As was noted in the notes on Revelation 6:2, this is not the same white horse that appeared in the section on the opening of the first seal. The horseman there represented an evil power masquerading as a heavenly one with the purpose being to deceive believers spiritually and persecute them physically. But here the horseman on the white horse is clearly Christ. He is called Faithful and True (Rev. 1:5). His war is completely righteous and just, as is proclaimed by the angels and the saints (Rev. 15:3–4; 16:5–7; 19:1). Again, as in Revelation 12:7ff, the war is not a literal battle on earth, but a spiritual battle that accomplishes judgment.

Old Testament Background to Revelation 19:11.
- Psalm 9:8: "And he judges the world with righteousness; he judges the peoples with uprightness."
- Psalm 71:2: "In your righteousness deliver me and rescue me; incline your ear to me and save me!"
- Psalm 96:13: "For [the LORD] comes to judge the earth. He will judge the world in righteousness, and the peoples in his faithfulness."
- Psalm 98:9: "For [the LORD] comes to judge the earth. He will judge the world with righteousness and the peoples with equity."

- Isaiah 11:4: "But with righteousness he shall judge the poor, and decide with equity for the meek of the earth; and he shall strike the earth with the rod of his mouth, and with the breath of his lips he shall kill the wicked."

Revelation 19:12. We have already seen in Revelation 1:14 and 2:18 that Christ's eyes are like a "flame of fire," which symbolizes his divine judgment. We learned in Revelation 5:6 that Christ has seven horns on his head, but there was no mention of diadems. In Revelation 12:3, Satan was described as having seven diadems and in 13:1 the beast was seen with ten, but here in contrast, Christ is said to have "many diadems," far exceeding theirs. That Satan and the beast were described as having "seven" and "ten" diadems (representing fullness) symbolized their false claim to the sovereignty that is God's alone.

In Revelation 2:17, the church in Pergamum was promised "a white stone, with a new name written on the stone that no one knows except the one who receives it," if the church conquered the persecution that it faced. Here Christ is seen coming to fulfill that promise. Christ's name is not literally kept a secret, for it has been revealed all throughout the book and especially here in Revelation 19:11, 13, and 16. The symbolic meaning is that though we know Christ now and identify with his name (his character), we will not know him fully until we have seen the climactic revelation of his character in bringing the end of history. It also symbolizes the fact that Christ is sovereign over when and where and to whom he reveals his name. Some know him in an intimate, saving way. Others know him only as Judge. Also, as in Revelation 3:12, where the "name of my God," symbolizing God's presence, was given to those who conquered, so too here the name of Christ represents God's presence. Only those who know him in the context of saving faith will experience this presence in its fullness in the new heaven and new earth.[7]

New Testament Background to Revelation 19:12.

- Luke 10:22: "All things have been handed over to me by my Father, and no one knows who the Son is except the Father, or

---

7. Ibid., 951–57.

who the Father is except the Son and anyone to whom the Son chooses to reveal him."

- 1 John 3:1: "See what kind of love the Father has given to us, that we should be called children of God; and so we are. The reason why the world does no know us is that it did not know him."

Revelation 19:13. That Christ is "clothed in a robe dipped in blood" is a fulfillment of Isaiah 63:1–4, where God is displayed as a warrior; here John defines the warrior as Christ. The warrior in Isaiah gains redemption and vindication of his people, just as here Christ gains judgment and salvation. He is called the "Word of God" (which defines the "unknown name") here because it is his standard for judgment. All throughout the Old and New Testaments, the final judgment has been spoken of, and here the Word of God, Jesus Christ, carries it out. As in Revelation 19:10, where we saw that "the testimony of Jesus" was the words and deeds of Jesus that revealed God, so here the "Word of God" is the same.

Old Testament Background to Revelation 19:13. Isaiah 63:1–4: "Who is this who comes from Edom, in crimsoned garments from Bozrah, he who is splendid in his apparel, marching in the greatness of his strength? 'It is I, speaking in righteousness, mighty to save.' Why is your apparel red, and your garments like his who treads in the winepress? 'I have trodden the winepress alone, and from the peoples no one was with me; I trod them in my anger and trampled them in my wrath; their lifeblood spattered on my garments, and stained all my apparel. For the day of vengeance was in my heart, and my year of redemption had come.'"

Revelation 19:14. Now the "armies of heaven," the saints, are seen arrayed in fine linen by Christ and like Christ. This represents that their vindication is just, because their message was right and they were following him. That they follow him gives witness to his judgment of their persecutors. Their white and pure clothing represents that they are innocent and their persecutors are guilty. Thus, Christ has every right to judge.

Revelation 19:15. The description of Christ with a sharp sword is also seen in Revelation 1:16 and in the letter to the church in Pergamum (Rev. 2:12), which also depicts his judgment. It is an allusion to Isaiah 49:2 and 11:4. Here John defines "servant Israel" as Christ, the one who accomplishes his mission of judgment and salvation. He judges in order to strike down the nations, so that they will no longer persecute the people of God, and the fullness of God's plan is ushered into history. That "he will rule them with a rod of iron" is an allusion to Psalm 2:9. Here Jesus is seen as the fulfillment of "my Son" who will "break [the nations] with a rod of iron and dash them in pieces like a potter's vessel." He will also "tread the winepress of the fury of the wrath of God Almighty," which alludes to Isaiah 63:2–6. We have already seen this imagery in Revelation 14:19–20. The judgment of the ungodly will be as complete as treading grapes in a winepress.

Old Testament Background to Revelation 19:15.

- Psalm 2:9: "You shall break them with a rod of iron and dash them in pieces like a potter's vessel."
- Isaiah 11:4: "But with righteousness he shall judge the poor, and decide with equity for the meek of the earth; and he shall strike the earth with the rod of his mouth, and with the breath of his lips he shall kill the wicked."
- Isaiah 49:2: "He made my mouth like a sharp sword; in the shadow of his hand he hid me; he made me a polished arrow; in his quiver he hid me away."
- Isaiah 63:2–6: "Why is your apparel red, and your garments like his who treads in the winepress? 'I have trodden the winepress alone, and from the peoples no one was with me; I trod them in my anger and trampled them in my wrath; their lifeblood spattered on my garments, and stained all my apparel. For the day of vengeance was in my heart, and my year of redemption had come. I looked, but there was no one to help; I was appalled, but there was no one to uphold; so my own arm brought me salvation, and my wrath upheld me. I trampled down the

287

peoples in my anger; I made them drunk in my wrath, and I poured out their lifeblood on earth.'"

Revelation 19:16. Now another name identifies the unknown name of Revelation 19:12, "King of kings and Lord of lords." That it was on his robe/thigh is appropriate, as when one rode a horse, the robe would have fallen over the thigh. The thigh is also significant because it was the place where the warrior would keep his sword, which Christ has already been described as having (Rev. 19:15), and it was also where one would place his hand when swearing oaths (Gen. 24:2).[8] Thus, Christ was swearing an oath that God's plan of judgment and salvation was sure and would be accomplished by him. Jesus Christ, as King of kings and Lord of lords, claims the divinity and power rightly due him alone, but which had been falsely claimed by all the earthly emperors, especially in Rome during John's day but also by the kings of Babylon, Tyre, and others all through history.

Old Testament Background to Revelation 19:16.
- Genesis 24:2–3: "Put your hand under my thigh, that I may make you swear by the Lord."
- Exodus 32:27: "Put your sword on your side each of you."
- Daniel 4:37: "Now I, Nebuchadnezzar, praise and extol and honor the King of heaven, for all his words are right and his ways are just; and those who walk in pride he is able to humble."

Revelation 19:17–18. Just as an angel appears in Revelation 18:1 to announce the fall of Babylon and the earth is made bright with glory, so too an angel appears here to announce the fall of the beast, the false prophet, and all those associated with Babylon, and the earth is made bright with the sun. In contrast to the marriage supper of the Lamb, we see here "the great supper of God." Thus, we have a complete picture between the two of them of God's plan of judgment and salvation. This verse is an allusion to Ezekiel 34:4, 17–20, where the defeat of Gog and Magog is described. That the angel calls for the birds to "eat the flesh"

8. Ibid., 963–64.

is significant because it conveys the certainty of death in that there will be flesh to eat. Like the eagle that flies overhead to announce judgment in Revelation 8:13, so here the birds flying overhead are symbolic for judgment. God will make known his holy name to both his people and his enemies on a worldwide scale at the final judgment. That "the flesh of" is repeated so many times adds further emphasis to this being the time of final judgment. Also, the "small and great" among unbelievers at the end of the verse stands in contrast to the "small and great" of believers who are exhorted to "praise God" in Revelation 19:4.

Old Testament Background to Revelation 19:17–18. Ezekiel 39:4, 17–20: "You shall fall on the mountains of Israel, you and all your hordes and the peoples who are with you. I will give you to birds of prey of every sort and to the beasts of the field to be devoured. . . . Speak to the birds of every sort and to all beasts of the field, 'Assemble and come, gather from all around to the sacrificial feast. . . . You shall eat the flesh of the mighty and drink the blood of the princes of the earth . . . till you are filled."

Revelation 19:19. Now John sees the vision of the actual judgment taking place. We have seen this language before in Revelation 16:14 and will see it again in 20:8 to describe the last battle of history (see also Rev. 11:7). We know from these passages that both demonic spirits and Satan are behind this war, along with the beast. They are the forces that "gather" the world powers together. But ultimately it is God himself who uses these as his agents to gather the world powers together (Ezek. 38:2–9; 39:2). We also know from Revelation 16:14 and 20:8–9 that the war is also against God, his saints, and "the beloved city" (the church).

Old Testament Background to Revelation 19:19.

- Psalm 2:2: "The kings of the earth set themselves, and the rulers take counsel together, against the Lord and against his Anointed."
- Ezekiel 38:2–9: "Son of man, set your face toward Gog, of the land of Magog, the chief prince of Meshech and Tubal, and prophesy against him and say, . . . 'I am against you, O Gog . . . I will bring you out . . . Be ready and keep ready . . . After many days you will be mustered . . . You will advance . . . like a cloud

covering the land, you and all your hordes, and many peoples with you.' "

- Ezekiel 39:2: "And I will turn you [Gog] about and drive you forward, and bring you up from the uttermost parts of the north, and lead you against the mountains of Israel."

Revelation 19:20. Now we see that the beast and the false prophet are captured because they pretended to be divine and because they deceived others to give allegiance to them. Their eternal destruction portrays the eternal destruction that awaits all those who function as the beast (evil political realms) and false prophet (that which gives religious support to the evil political realm).

Revelation 19:21. The beast and the false prophet (and Satan, as we will see in Revelation 20:7–10) were thrown first into the lake of fire because they were the ones claiming divinity and deceptively leading unbelievers into idolatry and immorality. But the unbelievers are still held accountable and are the next and final group to receive eternal judgment. The "great supper of God" commences with the birds being stuffed to the brim with the flesh of judged unbelievers, a symbolic way of portraying final and complete worldwide judgment.

CONCLUSION

We all find ourselves drawn to the woman of the Word who teaches with the most charisma. But we must resist this and pledge our allegiance to the Lamb of God alone. We must not skip Bible study because the substitute teacher is teaching. We must not skip Sunday night service because the regular preacher is out of town. We must not grumble about the unknown name of the speaker at the women's event. The Holy Spirit of God works through the most humble means. We just might be surprised at what we learn from the lesser known names after all. But more importantly, we must remember that we are witnesses of God to others, not witnesses of the well-known Christians of our world. And this God to whom we bear witness is the one who will judge the evil powers of this world at the final battle at the end of history.

LESSON 19

Revelation 20

PLEASE USE THE QUESTION paradigm from pages 353–54 as you work through the following. See the introductory comments there that explain each part of the process below in more detail.

- **Pray**.
- **Ponder the Passage**. Read Revelation 20 once a day from different translations for the entire week, looking for its:
  - Point
  - Persons
  - Patterns
  - Persons of the Trinity
  - Puzzling Parts
- **Put It in Perspective**.
  - Place in Scripture
  - Passages from Other Parts of Scripture

1. Based on your observations of the text, what is the basic content of Revelation 20? Try to summarize it in your own words, using a sentence or two.
2. Look up "key" in a concordance. Where else does it occur in Revelation? How do these other uses fit with the use in Revelation 20:1?

3. List all the names used for Satan in Revelation 20:2. Do they recall to mind any Old or New Testament passages? If so, which ones? Now use a concordance to help you. Where else do you see these names in Scripture? What do you learn about Satan?

4. From what you have learned about numbers in the book of Revelation, do you think "one thousand years" in Revelation 20:2–3 is symbolic or literal? Why do you think that? To what do you think this period of time refers? Look up John 12:31–33.

5. Look up Mark 3:27. What does "binds" refer to here? Is it complete or partial? How does this inform the meaning in Revelation 20:2? What is the purpose of Satan being bound (Rev. 20:3)? In light of this, what would be the purpose of releasing him for a little while at the end of history?

6. Compare Revelation 6:7–11 with 20:4. When did these believers "come to life" and reign with Christ (see 3:21)? Where are they reigning (remember that they are "on thrones")? Is the "first resurrection" a physical one or a spiritual one?

7. What blessing does Revelation 20:6 contain? Where are the other blessings found in the book of Revelation (remember there are seven of them!)?

8. What is the second death (Rev. 20:6; see also 20:14)? Why does it have "no power" over those that have participated in the first resurrection?

9. Skim Ezekiel 38–39. What is "Gog and Magog"?

10. Look up "camp" in a concordance. What do you find? How would this apply to the church in Revelation 20:9? What is the "beloved city" in light of Revelation 21:2?

11. What happened to the nations when they surrounded the people of God (Rev. 20:9)? Where else in Scripture has God displayed his glory in a similar way (see 2 Kings 1:10–14)?

12. Where was Satan thrown (Rev. 20:10)? Who else was thrown in there with him (Rev. 19:20; 20:14–15)? How long will they be tormented?

13. Where in the book have we seen the throne in Revelation 20:11 before? To what end time event does "earth and sky fled away" refer?

14. Are both believers and unbelievers standing before the throne (Rev. 20:12)? How do you know? What books are mentioned? What is the difference between them? What is the full name of the "book of life" from Revelation 21:27? Why is this significant?

15. Do "the sea, death and Hades" all refer to the same place? What do they represent? Why will they be judged (Rev. 20:13–14)?

16. How is the "lake of fire" described (Rev. 20:14)?

17. Who is not thrown into the lake of fire (Rev. 20:15)?

PRINICPLES AND POINTS OF APPLICATION

1. In what area of your life right now do you feel like Satan has a foothold? Ask God to bind him from that area and to help you use the power that he has given you by the Holy Spirit to overcome the weakness.

2. First Peter 2:9 tells us that we are a royal priesthood. How are you acting as a priest of God in your circles of influence? In other words, how are you interceding for your family, friends, brothers, and sisters in Christ? Intercede for your children, grandchildren, or those children in your church whom you know, asking that God's Holy Spirit would indwell them.

3. In what area of your life are you possibly being deceived? Ask God to reveal truth to you in this area and then act on it by the power of the Holy Spirit.

4. Is your name written in the "book of life"? How do you know? For whom do you need to pray today that they may receive the indwelling of the Holy Spirit in order that their names might be written in the "book of life"? With whom do you need to share the gospel, praying that the Lord would open up their eyes so that their names will be written in the book too? Make time to do this today.

NOTES FOR REVELATION 20

Aim: Ponder the aim of this lesson concerning our:

Mind: What do we need to know from this passage in Scripture?

> That the millennium began when Christ's victory on the cross limited Satan's deception, and that it will end when Satan is released one final time to deceive the nations and gather them for the last battle, culminating in his final destruction and the final judgment of all peoples.

Heart: How does what we learn from this passage affect our internal relationship with the Lord?

> It prepares us to be kingdom disciples who recognize Satan's deceptions and are prepared for God's final judgment between believers and unbelievers.

Hands: How does what we learn from this passage translate into action for God's kingdom?

> It enables us to:

1. Recognize any area of our lives where Satan has a foothold, ask God to bind him from that area, and rely on the Holy Spirit's power to overcome the stronghold.
2. Take our description as a "priesthood" seriously, interceding for our families, friends, and neighbors to come to a saving faith in Christ and/or to grow in the grace and knowledge of Christ.
3. Evaluate any areas of our lives where we think there might be deception, asking God to shine the light of his truth on it, and then flee from it by the Spirit's strength.
4. Acknowledge Christ as our Lord and Savior and pray that those in our circle of family, friends, and neighbors will as

well, recognizing that only the Spirit can open up our hearts and minds to the gospel.

INTRODUCTION

As I walked down the hallways the smell of death was prevalent. I had walked these hallways for more than two years, and every time the smell of death was the same. It's the smell that usually accompanies a retirement center or a nursing home. I had heard that Mrs. Nelson wasn't doing well and would probably not be with us much longer, so I had gone to visit her. I lived on another floor in the independent living side of the facility. I had interviewed for the position that was available to a seminary student and had gotten it. I received a free room in exchange for maintenance work, but I ended up doing a lot more than maintenance work. I played the piano during meals, I conducted a Bible study, and I made visitations. Residents in my half of the building were still able to care for themselves, but those in the other half, where I was that day, were not. I knocked and went in, knowing that this would be the last conversation I would have with Mrs. Nelson.

I can't honestly remember what I said. But I know that my heart weighed heavy for these residents who were near death. Many were lonely, dying, bitter at the world that had forgotten them, and trapped in their four walls. I often wondered if they were ready to meet their Maker. Did they care that they had only hours or days left to confess Jesus Christ as Lord and Savior of their lives? Did I care enough to tell them? So many have been deceived into thinking that death is natural, but it's the most unnatural thing that the body could go through. We were not created to die, but to live. Death entered this world because of God's curse on man for his rebellion. It was not supposed to be this way. But did these poor souls know that? Did they know that eternal suffering lay on the other side if they didn't have a relationship with the Lord as one of servant to Master, as one of subject to King? Did they know that they would stand before the Lord of glory condemned for their sin if they did not accept Christ as the perfect sacrifice and substitute on their behalf?

Revelation 20 has much to say about the day that we meet our Maker. Those of us who know Christ will be rewarded because we are in Christ, and he has done righteous deeds on our behalf. But those who do not believe will be cast away from God's presence forever and will suffer continual spiritual and mental anguish.

We can divide this lesson into four sections:

I. Satan's Deception Is Limited during the Millennium (Rev. 20:1–3)
II. Saints Are Avenged by the Heavenly Reign during the Millennium (Rev. 20:4–6)
III. Satan's Final Release to Deceive Nations for the Last Battle against the Church (Rev. 20:7–10)
IV. Saints and Unbelievers Are Judged before the Great White Throne (Rev. 20:11–15)

I. Satan's Deception Is Limited during the Millennium (Rev. 20:1–3)

Revelation 20:1. "Then I saw an angel coming down from heaven" has already occurred in similar form at Revelation 7:2; 10:1; and 18:1. In every case, it has either introduced a vision that serves as an interlude or introduces a vision that refers to a prior time period of the previous section. This is important because if the millennium begins with Christ's victory on the cross, then Revelation 20:1–6 would occur prior to the events written about in 17:1–19:21. And Revelation 20:7–15 would be temporally parallel with the judgment described in 19:11–21, which referred to the last battle and the great supper of God. Thus, chapter 20 spans the time from the beginning of the church age (Christ's resurrection) to the end (Christ's second coming).[1]

The angel is "holding in his hand the key to the bottomless pit and a great chain." These two objects should serve to remind us of the symbolic nature of this vision that stands alongside its literal nature.

---

1. G. K. Beale, *The Book of Revelation: A Commentary on the Greek Text*, New International Greek Testament Commentary (Grand Rapids: Eerdmans, 1999), 972.

Holding the symbolic, visionary, and literal together has been important all throughout the book, but it becomes especially important in this passage. Most likely, the "key to the abyss" is synonymous with the "key of Death and Hades" (Rev. 1:18), which conveyed Christ's sovereignty over Satan's sphere. And also with the "key of David" (Rev. 3:7), which conveyed that Christ alone has the power to raise some to life and others to everlasting destruction at the end of history, and is the one who gives spiritual life during the church age. We see in Revelation 6:8 another reference to the keys of "Death and Hades" during the opening of the third seal. We also see the "key" again in Revelation 9:1–2 where God gives the "star fallen from heaven to earth" the "key to the shaft of the bottomless pit" in order to release demons. All of these previous references occur during the church age, which gives support to the notion that Revelation 20:1–6 should be seen as occurring during the church age as well.[2]

Revelation 20:2–3. The angel seizes Satan. The four names that are used in this verse recall Satan's deceptive acts as portrayed all through history. They recall especially "that ancient serpent," which alludes to Genesis 3 and reminds us that just as there was war between God and Satan prior to the first creation—which led to Satan being allowed to tempt Adam and Eve in the garden—so too there is a war between Satan and God prior to the new creation, in which Satan will be allowed to persecute the church. When Christ came to earth the first time, he came with the purpose of saving the lost. Thus, Satan had to be bound in order for God's children to be saved. Satan is not bound from the believer in every way, though. He can still afflict believers physically, but not spiritually, since God seals them. This binding would last through the entire church age, until, just prior to Christ's second coming, he will be allowed one last time to deceive the nations and gather them together for the last battle with the Lamb and his army. When this release occurs, the entire number of God's elect will have been brought into the kingdom of God. Not one will have been lost to the kingdom of darkness. Even at Satan's release, he is still under Christ's authority,

2. Ibid., 984.

and used as an agent to deceive the nations and persecute the church, which results in the judgment of unbelievers, the vindication of believers, and the glory of God.

Isn't it encouraging to know that God has bound Satan from harming us spiritually? He may throw all kinds of attacks against us, but he cannot take away our salvation. We are bound to God for eternity, sealed and sanctified by his Holy Spirit. We can fight the battle here on earth because the Spirit of our Warrior indwells us and our Warrior has reserved a place in heaven for us.

The "pit" into which Satan is thrown is symbolic of the spiritual realm that exists within the earthly realm (see Eph. 6:10–17). As is clear from other New Testament passages (2 Cor. 10:3–5; Eph. 6:10–17), the fact that Satan is "shut" and "sealed" in this pit does not mean that he does not have any authority in the world, but rather that his authority has been limited by Christ's victory on the cross. This shutting and sealing was imperative in order that the church of God might fulfill its purpose. Satan began his deception with one man and one woman. After the fall, Satan continued his deception with all men and all women. Thus, many in Israel were deceived and unable to accomplish the purpose of God for them to be a light to the nations (Isa. 49:6). Israel's sin also pledged the people's allegiance to the kingdom of darkness. All of the deception and sin in the Old Testament came to a head at the cross. The true Israel came and battled with Satan, defeating him at the cross, but still allowing him to have limited authority in the world. The limit on his authority was that he was no longer to deceive the true Israel, the church of God. The church was given Christ's keys so that the gates of hell would not prevail against the church during the church age (Matt. 16:18–19). But just as Satan attacked Christ on the cross before his defeat, so too will he be allowed to attack Christians at the end of the church age. However, just as Christ won the victory at the cross, so too Christians will win the victory, which will culminate in the defeat of Satan forever and the climax of the revelation of the glory of God.[3]

3. Ibid., 984–89.

Old Testament/New Testament Background to Revelation 20:2–3.

- Isaiah 49:6: "I will make you as a light for the nations, that my salvation may reach to the end of the earth."

- Matthew 12:29 (Mark 3:27): "How can someone enter a strong man's house and plunder his goods, unless he first binds the strong man?"

- Matthew 24:14, 21–24: "And this gospel of the kingdom will be proclaimed throughout the whole world as a testimony to all nations, and then the end will come. . . . For then there will be great tribulation."

- Mark 13:9–22: Jesus' remarks on the signs at the close of the age and the Abomination of Desolation.

- Luke 10:17–19: " 'Lord, even the demons are subject to us in your name!' And he said to them, 'I saw Satan fall like lighting from heaven. Behold, I have given you authority to tread on serpents and scorpions, and over all the power of the enemy, and nothing shall hurt you.' "

- John 12:31–33: " 'Now is the judgment of this world; now will the ruler of this world be cast out. And I, when I am lifted up from the earth, will draw all people to myself.' He said this to show what kind of death he was going to die."

- 2 Corinthians 10:3–5: "For though we walk in the flesh, we are not waging war according to the flesh. For the weapons of our warfare are not of the flesh but have divine power to destroy strongholds. We destroy arguments and every lofty opinion raised against the knowledge of God, and take every thought captive to obey Christ."

- Ephesians 6:10–17: Paul's description of the whole armor of God.

- Colossians 2:15: "He disarmed the rulers and authorities and put them to open shame, by triumphing over them in him."

- Hebrews 2:14: "Since therefore the children share in flesh and blood, he himself likewise partook of the same things, that through death he might destroy the one who has the power of death, that is, the devil."

II. Saints Are Avenged by the Heavenly Reign during the Millennium (Rev. 20:4–6)

The millennium (and all of eternity) addresses the great paradox of Christianity. Those who die will live. Those who are crushed by rulers will rule. Those who are defeated are victors. If Christ's resurrection, which led to his ascension and enthronement, began the millennium, then believers were also given the right to reign with him at the beginning of the millennium.[4]

Revelation 20:4. John now sees thrones and those to whom the authority to judge was committed. This is a symbolic portrayal of deceased believers with angels who, along with Christ, were given the right to reign after Christ defeated Satan on the cross. They reign with Christ over his kingdom. When believers die and their souls go to heaven, they join Christ in his role as judge over the kingdom of darkness. This is not a new role, but a continuation and escalation of what was already their role on earth as "priests" and "kings" (see 1 Peter 2:9–10). We saw in Revelation 2:26–27 and 3:21 that Christ promised the overcomers the right to sit with him on his throne and to be judges over the nations, though the complete fulfillment of those promises will not take place until the final resurrection. Christ's judgment against the kingdom of darkness is in large part due to what Satan and his allies did to Christ's saints by way of persecution. That "they have been given authority to judge" is best understood, then, as "judgment was passed against Satan on their behalf," in partial fulfillment of God's vindication of them.[5]

"The souls of those who had been beheaded" is the same group that we saw in Revelation 6:9–11 positioned under the altar and crying out for complete vindication (this group is symbolic for all Christians who suffered for their faith, not just literal martyrs). Here God's answer in Revelation 6:11 is further expanded. They have been given white robes, rest, the role of priests, and are made a kingdom (Rev. 1:6; 5:10; 6:11; 14:13). Most likely, "those who had worshiped" are the same group

4. Ibid., 991.
5. Ibid., 996.

further defined. Again, we see the "thousand years," which is symbolic for the entire church age, in which the deceased saints come to life (their souls go to heaven) and reign with Christ.[6]

Old Testament Background to Revelation 20:4. Daniel 7:22: "This horn made war with the saints and prevailed over them, until the Ancient of Days came, and judgment was given for the saints of the Most High, and the time came when the saints possessed the kingdom."

Revelation 20:5–6. In contrast to believers who "came to life and reigned with Christ for a thousand years" stands "the rest of the dead who did not come to life until the thousand years were ended." These are unbelievers who are not given the privilege of reigning with Christ in heaven when they die. They are not given spiritual life when they "come to life," but rather they are physically resurrected only to be judged (see verse 12).

The phrase "first resurrection" does not occur anywhere else in Scripture. Commentators differ on its meaning depending on how they view the one thousand years. Hopefully, the following summary will prove to be helpful as we study: When believers first die physically, their souls take part in the *first spiritual resurrection* in heaven. When Christ comes again the saints' bodies take part in the *first physical resurrection* of both believers and unbelievers. Also, when Christ comes again, the ungodly, who have already undergone their *first death* (physically died), take part in the physical resurrection and the *second spiritual death*—eternal punishment (these are the ones emphasized in verse 5).[7]

Blessed are those who share in the spiritual (first) resurrection, for the second death (judgment to eternal wrath) has no power over them. They are sealed securely and will never lose their salvation. They will reign with Christ during the entire church age in heaven, while believers who are still alive will reign on earth. This is the fifth of seven blessings in the book (Rev. 1:3; 14:13; 16:15; 19:9; 20:6; 22:7; 22:14). We saw this same promise in Revelation 2:11 in the letter to the church in Smyrna: "the one who conquers will not be hurt by the second death." That they

6. Ibid., 997–1000.
7. Ibid., 1005.

will be "priests of God *and of Christ*" emphasizes Christ's divinity and equality with God.

Old Testament/New Testament Background to Revelation 20:5–6.

- Exodus 19:6: "And you shall be to me a kingdom of priests and a holy nation. These are the words that you shall speak to the people of Israel."
- Isaiah 61:6: "But you shall be called priests of the LORD; they shall speak of you as the ministers of our God; you shall eat the wealth of the nations, and in their glory you shall boast."
- Romans 6:4–13: Paul's description of beleivers being "dead to sin, alive to God."

III. Satan's Final Release to Deceive Nations for the Last Battle against the Church (Rev. 20:7–10)

Just as Satan attacked Christ on the cross before his defeat, so too he will be allowed to attack Christians at the end of the church age. But, just as Christ won the victory at the cross, so too Christians will win the victory at the last battle, which will culminate in the defeat of Satan forever and the climax of the revelation of the glory of God.

Revelation 20:7–8. At the very end of the church age, just prior to Christ's second coming, Satan will be allowed by God ("released from his prison," which in verse 1 was "the bottomless pit") to deceive the nations from all over the world ("at the four corners of the earth, Gog and Magog"). He will deceive them into gathering for battle against Christ and his church. "Gog and Magog" is an allusion to Ezekiel 37–38, which is here equivalent with "all the nations" (rather than distinguished from them as the mightiest prince, Gog, and land, Magog, as in Ezekiel). This battle is one that the nations will think they will win. After all, their "number is like the sand of the sea" in comparison to the smaller number of saints. But though the church is small in comparison, God is great and the Almighty is only leading the nations to their demise. He gathers them from all over the world in order to display his glory before mankind, to show that he alone is God Almighty and, to display before his people's persecutors that his children were always in the right while their persecutors were in the wrong. He is justified in his punishment of the persecutors. And this punishment is nothing less than the "second death" spoken of in verse 6, eternal suffering.

Old Testament/New Testament Background to Revelation 20:7–8.

- Isaiah 11:12: "He will raise a signal for the nations and will assemble the banished of Israel, and gather the dispersed of Judah from the four corners of the earth."
- Ezekiel 38:2–8: "Gog, of the land of Magog, the chief prince of Meshech . . . I am against you."
- Ezekiel 39:2: "And I will turn you about and drive you forward, and bring you up from the uttermost parts of the north, and lead you against the mountains of Israel."
- Zephaniah 3: The prophet speaks of judgment on Jerusalem and the nations.
- Zechariah 12–14: "The burden of the word of the Lord concerning Israel."
- Revelation 16:12–16; 19:19–21; 20:7: All the events depicted in these verses are temporally parallel.

Revelation 20:9–10. The imagery of the nations marching up over the broad plain of the earth, as referenced in Ezekiel 38–39, continues, but Habakkuk 1:6 is alluded to also. The nations are marching to make war on the church, which is spread out all over the world ("camp of the saints and the beloved city"). That the church is called "camp of the saints" here is an allusion to several Old Testament texts (especially Deut. 23:14), in which Israel camped in the wilderness around the tabernacle (symbolic of God's presence). Here it is applied to the church, in which God dwells. "The beloved city" is also another name for the church, which is equivalent to the "holy city, Jerusalem, descending from God" (Rev. 21:2, 10), which is also the bride of Christ.[8]

But before the nations can defeat the saints, God destroys them ("fire came down from heaven and destroyed them"). The imagery is taken from 2 Kings 1:10–14 (see Rev. 11:5 where the same allusion

8. Ibid., 1027.

is used for a time of judgment previous to the final one), where God delivers Elijah from evil King Ahaziah's armies. These verses also continue to use imagery from Ezekiel 38–39.

Not only does God destroy the nations, he also throws Satan into the "lake of fire and sulfur" in order to torment him eternally. This is done at the same time (or immediately after) Satan's allies, the beast and the false prophet, are thrown into the lake (Rev. 19:20), and unbelievers are thrown into it as well (Rev. 14:10–11; 20:15). The "lake of fire and sulfur" is symbolic for eternal spiritual and mental suffering.

Old Testament Background to Revelation 20:9–10.

- 2 Kings 1:10–14: "But Elijah answered the captain of fifty, 'If I am a man of God, let fire come down from heaven and consume you and your fifty.' Then fire came down from heaven and consumed him and his fifty."
- Ezekiel 38:11, 15–16, 22; 39:6: The prophet speaks of the prophecy against Gog and Magog.
- Habakkuk 1:6: "I am raising up the Chaldeans."

IV. Saints and Unbelievers Are Judged before the Great White Throne (Rev. 20:11–15)

Revelation 20:11. We have seen this "great white throne" before in Revelation 4:2 and 5:7 where God is "seated on the throne." These references all allude to Daniel 7:9 (and Ezek. 1:26–28). The difference is that in chapters 4–5 the context was the beginning (inauguration) of God's reign through his Son, Jesus Christ, but here, the emphasis is on the consummate judgment, which brings history to a close and brings in the new heaven and the new earth. Whether it is God the Father or God the Son on the throne here doesn't matter, as both carry out the final judgment. That the throne is white is appropriate since God is holy and the one who avenges the blood of his people as Judge. "From his presence earth and sky fled away, and no place was found for them" signifies the completeness of the final judgment and destruction of the evil world system. This same language is used in Revelation 6:14 and 16:20 (see the sections on those verses for relevant Old Testament background references). "And no place was found for them" is an allusion to Daniel 2:35.

Old Testament Background to Revelation 20:11.

- Ezekiel 1:26–28: "And above the expanse over their heads there was the likeness of a throne, in appearance like sapphire, and seated above the likeness of a throne was a likeness with a human appearance."
- Daniel 2:35: "And the wind carried [the iron, clay, bronze, silver, and gold] away, so that not a trace of them could be found."
- Daniel 7:9: "As I looked, thrones were placed and the Ancient of Days took his seat; his clothing was white as snow, and the hair of his head like pure wool; his throne was fiery flames; its wheels were burning fire."

Revelation 20:12. John sees all the dead, both believers and unbelievers who have been raised (in the first and only physical resurrection at the end of the millennium) standing before the throne for judgment. The first "books" that are opened are symbolic for God's perfect memory; in them are remembered all the sins that unbelievers have committed for which they are now held accountable. There is no substitute for them because they have rejected him. There is no payment on their behalf; they have paid their own fare to destruction. The book of life only contains the righteous deeds (not sins) of the saints that serve as the basis of their reward. All other sins that would have been recorded there have been erased, blotted out from God's memory, for he remembers our sins no more. Christ is our substitute; his blood covers our sin and blots them from the memory of the Almighty God. We stand before the throne, not in fear, but in worship and wonder, as we receive our reward for persevering in our faith in this world.

Old Testament Background to Revelation 20:12.

- Daniel 7:10: "A stream of fire issued and came out from before him; a thousand thousands served him, and ten thousand times ten thousand stood before him; the court sat in judgment and the books were opened."

- Daniel 12:1–2: "At that time shall arise Michael, the great prince who has charge of your people. And there shall be a time of trouble such as never has been since there was a nation till that time. But at that time your people shall be delivered, everyone whose name shall be found written in the book. And many of those who sleep in the dust of the earth shall awaken, some to everlasting life and some to shame and everlasting contempt."
- John 5:28–29: "Do not marvel at this, for an hour is coming when all who are in the tombs will hear his voice and come out, those who have done good to the resurrection of life, and those who have done evil to the resurrection of judgment."
- Acts 24:15: "Having a hope in God, which these men themselves accept, that there will be a resurrection of both the just and the unjust."

Revelation 20:13. The sea, the place where Satan stood (Rev. 12:17) and from which the beast arose (Rev. 13:1), now gives up the dead. It is obvious that this verse is not in chronological order since verse 11 has already portrayed the destruction of the created world and here the "sea" is mentioned.[9] That the sea here is pictured in a negative light foreshadows the phrase in Revelation 21:1, "and the sea was no more." In other words, evil and all those associated with it are no more. "Death and Hades" are synonymous with "the sea," added to emphasize the completeness of the judgment. The imagery is one of "death to death." Unbelievers are raised up only to be thrown down into the "lake of fire." Each one of them is held accountable for their sin. This stands in sharp contrast to believers, who are raised to eternal life and who stand forgiven, washed in the blood of the Lamb, Jesus Christ.

Revelation 20:14. Now John sees "Death and Hades thrown into the lake of fire." Different commentators interpret this differently. Some of the possibilities are: (1) this may indicate that death itself is destroyed

9. Ibid., 1033.

forever; (2) it may mean that in the eternal state, physical death no longer occurs;. (3) it may be a way of saying that unbelievers previously held in the temporary place of death and Hades are now cast into the eternal and permanent lake of fire; or (4) death and Hades could be symbolic for Satan's demonic forces. Though any of these possibilities would be in keeping with Revelation, it seems most likely that number 3 is the case.[10] "This is the second death, the lake of fire" clearly defines what the second death is, and thus, the "second death" in verse 6 is also now explained. This second death is not physical, for the punishment of unbelievers is eternal suffering, but is symbolic for spiritual and mental anguish that will be eternal.

Revelation 20:15. This verse emphasizes that only those who have been sealed by God, whose names are found in the book of life because of their identification with the Lamb of God, are saved from the lake of fire. It is because the Lamb of God has borne our iniquities, and because we are identified with his death, and thus, with his resurrection, that we will reign with him forever. The rest of mankind, those who never believed that Jesus was the Christ, the Son of the Living God, and did not put their faith in him, acknowledging him as both Lord and Savior, will enter into eternal suffering.

CONCLUSION

I was very much aware of my role as intercessor as I walked the halls of the retirement center in which I lived and worked. Who knew Jesus and who didn't? I prayed for those who did not that they would come to know him before they died, and I prayed for those who did know him to rest in him and find their hope in him. I was also aware of my role as witness. Who needed to see Jesus in my life? With whom did I need to share his comfort and love? And I was also aware of my role as worshiper. How could I better worship God as I walked those halls, and how could I lead others into true worship of him as they prepared to take their last breaths here on earth?

10. Ibid., 1034–35.

What about you? What hallways have you been walking lately? It may be the hallways of your own home, or perhaps of a school, maybe the hallways at a corporation or at a church. Are you aware of your role as intercessor, as witness, and as worshiper? Let us strive to seek the lost and intercede for both believers and unbelievers by the power of the Holy Spirit as we put our hands up in worship of our Lord and Savior Jesus Christ.

LESSON 20

Revelation 21:1–22:5

PLEASE USE THE QUESTION paradigm from pages 353–54 as you work through the following. See the introductory comments there that explain each part of the process below in more detail.

- **Pray**.
- **Ponder the Passage**. Read Revelation 21:1–22:5 once a day from different translations for the entire week, looking for its:
  - Point
  - Persons
  - Patterns
  - Persons of the Trinity
  - Puzzling Parts
- **Put It in Perspective**.
  - Place in Scripture
  - Passages from Other Parts of Scripture

1. Based on your observations of the text, what is the basic content of Revelation 21:1–22:5? Try to summarize it in your own words, using a sentence or two.
2. How does the "sea was no more" in Revelation 21:1 relate to 20:13? What does this mean in context?

3. How does Revelation 21:2 define the holy city and the New Jerusalem? To whom does this bride refer? Read Ephesians 5:23–24.

4. Look up the word "covenant" in a concordance and read several of the passages in which the word occurs. How does Revelation 21:3 sum up the covenants in Scripture?

5. How does Revelation 21:4 refer to 20:14?

6. Compare Revelation 21:6 with John 19:30. What do you see? What are the differences and the similarities of these two great events, the crucifixion and the new creation?

7. Compare Revelation 21:7 with the promises to the conquerors in the seven letters to the churches in chapters 2–3. What do you learn?

8. To what covenant in Scripture does Revelation 21:7 allude?

9. With what do the sins at the beginning and the end of the list in Revelation 21:8 have to do? How does this relate to the context of the seven letters to the churches in chapters 2–3?

10. Compare Revelation 21:9–11 with 17:1–6. What similarities and what differences do you see?

11. Look up the word "mountain" in a concordance. What do you find? How does this illuminate the significance behind John's location in Revelation 21:10?

12. What gave the holy city of Jerusalem its radiance (Rev. 21:10–11)?

13. What were walls of cities used for in the Old Testament? What does "a great high wall" signify in Revelation 21:12?

14. What is written on the gates and the foundations (Rev. 21:14)? How is this the reverse of what you would think from a historical perspective? Why is it significant?

15. Compare Revelation 21:15 with 11:1ff. What does the measuring signify?

16. Compare Revelation 21:19 with Exodus 28:17–20 and 39:8–14. What do you learn? Why is this significant? What role does this mean that believers now have in the new creation? What kind of access do they have to God?

17. Compare Revelation 11:8 with 21:21. How would this encourage John's readers?

18. Look up "temple" in a concordance. What was the significance of the temple in the Old Testament? What does it mean that the Lord God, the Almighty, and the Lamb will be the temple in the new creation (Rev. 21:22)?

19. Compare Revelation 21:11, 23, and 22:5. What will give the new creation its light?

20. Compare Revelation 21:24 with 5:9–10. What do you learn?

21. Why and when were gates in the Old Testament shut? Why is it significant that the gates of the new creation will not be shut (Rev. 21:25) and that there will be no night?

22. What is the "glory and honor" of the nations (see Rev. 19:8)?

23. Who will be allowed to enter the new creation? Why?

24. Read John 4:7–14. Now define "water of life" in Revelation 22:1. From where does this flow? Why is this important?

25. What do the "leaves of the tree" symbolize (Rev. 22:2)? Who has healed the nations (see Rev. 5:9)?

26. What are believers called in Revelation 22:3? What else are they doing? How does this define our heavenly role?

27. Compare Exodus 33:20–23 with Revelation 22:4. Why is this significant?

28. Compare Revelation 22:5 with 21:25 and 21:23. What do you see? Is there any additional information? How does this further define the believer's role in heaven (see also Rev. 22:3)?

- **Principles and Points of Application.**
  1. How is the Holy Spirit using you to adorn the church for Christ? Pray and ask God to reveal to you what areas of your church he wants you involved with, then commit to serving these through the power of the Holy Spirit.
  2. What mourning, pain, and/or crying are you experiencing right now? Thank God today that one day it will be no more and recognize that at the present time it is conforming you to Jesus Christ.
  3. Meditate on Revelation 21:6. Spend time today thanking God that we do not have to pay for our sin or for the "water of life."

311

4. Read Revelation 21:8. For whom in your life do you need to pray who is ensnared in one of these sins? Intercede for them today and be sensitive to the Holy Spirit's leading concerning confronting them with their sin in a loving way.

5. What is the Holy Spirit doing in your life right now to ensure that you will bring glory and honor to the new creation? Pray and ask God to reveal to you what he wants you to be in character and what he wants you to do in action in order to glorify and honor him.

NOTES FOR REVELATION 21:1-22:5

Aim: Ponder the aim of this lesson concerning our:

Mind: What do we need to know from this passage in Scripture?

That the imperfect, earthly church (chapters 1–3) will become the perfected church of God in the new creation.

Heart: How does what we learn from this passage affect our internal relationship with the Lord?

It prepares us to be kingdom disciples who conquer the persecution, deception, and temptation of Satan and the world in order to be part of the consummated church, radiating the glory of God.

Hands: How does what we learn from this passage translate into action for God's kingdom?

It enables us to:

1. Help the church be adorned for Christ by living a holy life in dependence upon the Holy Spirit and helping others to do the same.

2. Recognize in the midst of our present mourning, crying, and pain, that one day such suffering will be no more, and to take great comfort and hope in that fact.

3. Thank God that we do not have to pay for our sin or for the water of life.

4. Intercede for someone we know who is consumed with one or more of the sins listed in Revelation 21:8, and be sensitive to the leading of the Holy Spirit to confront them with their sin in a loving way.

5. Pray and ask for God to reveal to us through his Word what he wants us to be in character and what he wants us to do in action in order to glorify and honor him.

INTRODUCTION

My children and I will sing a children's song together if they are having a hard time with the darkness of the night. The song speaks of all kinds of scary creatures that children are usually afraid of when it is dark. But the song goes on to speak of Jesus as being much stronger than monsters and that God will hold us all through the night, so we don't have to be afraid.[1]

As I have sung this song, I am struck at how applicable it is to adults as well as to children. I don't know about you, but it's when the lights are off and it's dark outside that thoughts come into my mind of all the suffering in my life. The chronic physical pain, the struggles in marriage, the rebelliousness of the children, the lost family members, the stress of present circumstances, loneliness, my sins, and lots more. We all have our "spiders, snakes, and creatures of every scary kind." And most of them are real. But, we have learned through the book of Revelation that Jesus is much stronger than the fiercest monster, Satan, and all of his allies. So, we don't have to be afraid of the night. I often

1. The song is "Don't Be Afraid of the Night" and is from the CD *J is for Jesus* (published by Matthias Media USA). The songs are led by Karen Pang and the Emu kids band. The liner notes say that the "collection of songs grew out of [a] desire to integrate Jesus into the everyday world of little kids."

313

tell my children that they can sleep because God doesn't (Ps. 121:3). He is watching over us, so that we can slumber. God will hold us through the dark nights of our lives. But in chapter 21 John goes a step further. John tells us that there will no longer be any night at all.

We can divide this lesson into five sections:

I. The Contrast between the Inheritance of the Faithful and the Faithless (Rev. 21:1–8)

II. The Vision of the Church Radiating the Glory of God (Rev. 21:9–14)

III. The Church Is Secure in God's Presence (Rev. 21:15–21)

IV. Only the Faithful Will Enter God's Eternal Presence (Rev. 21:22–27)

V. Believers Will Be Kings and Priests Who Radiate God's Glory (Rev. 22:1–5)

I. The Contrast between the Inheritance of the Faithful and the Faithless (Rev. 21:1–8)

These verses both conclude the previous section of the book (Rev. 17:1–21:8) and introduce the seventh and final major section (Rev. 21:9–22:5). What is said in these verses will simply be expanded upon in verses 21:9–22:5.

Revelation 21:1. This verse should be seen as temporally parallel with the preceding section, in which we read, "From his presence earth and sky fled away, and no place was found for them" (Rev. 20:11). John now sees "a new heaven and a new earth, for the first heaven and the first earth had passed away" after the second coming of Christ. Just as Jesus' resurrection body was very different from his former one and yet identifiable with it, so too the new creation will be very different from the old one, yet identifiable with it. The new creation will be permanent in contrast with the old creation that will "pass away." We will see in this chapter that for John, the emphasis of the new creation will be the people of God. "And the sea was no more" picks up on Revelation 20:13 when "the sea gave up the dead who were in it" and implies that no longer is there any evil.

314

In the book of Revelation, we have seen that the sea was the place where Satan stood and from where the beast arose (Rev. 12:17; 13:1). So, implicit here is that in the new creation there will be no evil, no threat of Satan or his allies. We have also seen that the sea refers to the rebellious nations that were a constant threat to the church (Rev. 17:2). So the people of God will no longer have to worry about being overtaken or persecuted. The sea has also been symbolic for death (Rev. 20:13), so there will also be no more dying in the new creation. The sea is related with the idolatry of sea trade as well (Rev. 18:10–19), so there will be no more idolatry in the new creation. And finally, seas have also separated people physically from one another (Rev. 5:13; 7:1–3), but in the new creation, all of God's people will be together glorifying God and serving him.

Old Testament Background to Revelation 21:1.

- Isaiah 65:17: "For behold, I create new heavens and a new earth, and the former things shall not be remembered or come into mind."
- Isaiah 66:22: "For as the new heavens and the new earth that I make shall remain before me, says the LORD, so shall your offspring and your name remain."

Revelation 21:2. The "new heaven and new earth" of verse 1 is now called "the holy city, the New Jerusalem." The imagery is from Isaiah 62:1–2 where it is prophesied that God's people will not always suffer exile, but will one day be returned to God's presence forever. Here is the ultimate fulfillment of that promise. This "holy city" is none other than the bride of Christ, the church. She has been adorned for her husband and is finally united to him for all of eternity, always to be secure both physically and spiritually in his presence.

Old Testament/New Testament Background to Revelation 21:2.

- Isaiah 52:1b: "Put on your beautiful garments, O Jerusalem, the holy city; for there shall no more come into you the uncircumcised and the unclean."
- Isaiah 62:1–2: "For Zion's sake I will not keep silent, and for Jerusalem's sake I will not be quiet, until her righteousness goes forth

as brightness, and her salvation as a burning torch. The nations shall see your righteousness, and all the kings your glory, and you shall be called by a new name that the mouth of the LORD will give."

- Ephesians 5:25–27: "As Christ loved the church and gave himself up for her, that he might sanctify her, having cleansed her by the washing of water with the word, so that he might present the church to himself in splendor, without spot or wrinkle or any such thing, that she might be holy and without blemish."

Revelation 21:3. Now God himself declares that he has been faithful to his covenant promises. All the covenants in Scripture could be summed up with this one phrase, "I will be their God and they will be my people." Here the covenant promises are completely fulfilled and declared by the one who perfectly fulfilled them (2 Cor. 1:20). The city and the bride are now defined as the intimate relationship and presence that God and his people share. What tabernacles and temples once symbolized is now reality; God himself is with his people in all of his fullness and glory.

Old Testament Background to Revelation 21:3.

- Genesis 12:2–3: "And I will make of you a great nation, and I will bless you and make your name great, so that you will be a blessing. I will bless those who bless you, and him who dishonors you I will curse, and in you all the families of the earth shall be blessed."
- Leviticus 26:11–12: "I will make my dwelling among you, and my soul shall not abhor you. And I will walk among you and will be your God, and you shall be my people."
- Jeremiah 11:4–5: "So shall you be my people, and I will be your God, that I may confirm the oath that I swore to your fathers, to give them a land flowing with milk and honey."
- Ezekiel 37:27: "My dwelling place shall be with them, and I will be their God, and they shall be my people."
- Ezekiel 43:7: "This is the place of my throne and the place of the soles of my feet where I will dwell in the midst of the people of Israel forever."

- Galatians 3:16: "Now the promises were made to Abraham and his offspring. It does not say, 'And to offsprings,' referring to many, but referring to one, 'And to your offspring,' who is Christ."

Revelation 21:4. With the old creation gone and the fullness of God's presence in the new creation, there will be no more threat of persecution, deception, or temptation, which in the old creation were the sources of grief, suffering, and death. We will have fully redeemed and eternal bodies and will be in God's presence both physically and spiritually for all of eternity.

Old Testament Background to Revelation 21:4.

- Isaiah 25:8: "He will swallow up death forever; and the LORD God will wipe away tears from all faces, and the reproach of his people he will take away from all the earth, for the LORD has spoken."
- Isaiah 35:10: "And the ransomed of the LORD shall return and come to Zion with singing; everlasting joy shall be upon their heads; they shall obtain gladness and joy, and sorrow and sighing shall flee away."
- Isaiah 51:11: Same as Isaiah 35:10.
- Isaiah 65:19: "I will rejoice in Jerusalem and be glad in my people; no more shall be heard in it the sound of weeping and the cry of distress."

Revelation 21:5. God himself declares that he is making all things new. And to emphasize the truth and trustworthiness of his declaration, he has John write it down for the church.

Old Testament Background to Revelation 21:5.

- Isaiah 43:19: "Behold, I am doing a new thing; now it springs forth, do you not perceive it? I will make a way in the wilderness and rivers in the desert."
- Isaiah 65:16: "Shall bless himself by the God of truth . . . shall swear by the God of truth."

Revelation 21:6. God himself continues to speak from the throne. Just as Christ cried out from the cross, "It is finished" (John 19:30), when he had defeated Satan and accomplished the work that the Father planned for him to do, so too God, at the end of history, when he has made all things new, cries, "It is done!" The completion of judgment and redemption has occurred.

We have seen the title "Alpha and Omega" already at the beginning of the book (Rev. 1:8), which was also declared by God himself. Now we see it reiterated at the end of the book by God again (these are the only two times in the book that God himself speaks), with the consummation of the new creation. From the beginning of the creation of our present earth to the beginning of the new eternal creation, God has been sovereign. He has directed and orchestrated all events according to his perfect plan. Not one thing is outside of his control. Not one part of our lives goes unseen by him. He is intricately involved in our lives and the lives of those around us. He directs even evil for his plan of judgment and salvation. Not only the beginning and the end, but also all that happens in between is in his sovereign hand. With the addition of "beginning and end" his sovereignty is further emphasized.

In another allusion to Isaiah, God's people are promised God's provision and protection. They are fully redeemed by the blood of the Lamb and will drink the waters of eternal life forever. And it is "without payment." God's grace is always free. There is no payment for our sin, and no payment for eternal life. Salvation is the free gift of God alone.

Old Testament Background to Revelation 21:6.

- Isaiah 49:10: "They shall not hunger or thirst, neither scorching wind nor sun shall strike them, for he who has pity on them will lead them, and by springs of water will guide them."
- Isaiah 55:1: "Come, everyone who thirsts, come to the waters; and he who has no money, come, buy and eat! Come, buy wine and milk without money and without price."

Revelation 21:7. The promises that God made to the conquerors of the seven historical churches in chapters 2–3 are now reiterated.

Those who overcome the persecution, temptation, and deception of Satan and the world will inherit the presence of God for all of eternity in the new creation. Again, the fulfillment of the covenants is seen in the statement, "I will be his God and he will be my son." This time it specifically alludes to the Davidic covenant (2 Sam. 7:14). The "he" in 2 Samuel refers to Christ, but now it is applied to all of God's people as individuals who stand in Christ.

Old Testament Background to Revelation 21:7. 2 Samuel 7:14: "I will be to him a father, and he shall be to me a son."

Revelation 21:8. In contrast to the one who conquers stands the unbeliever whose life was characterized by idolatry and immorality. That the apostate church is John's focus is clear from the words "cowardly, faithless" at the beginning of the list and "liars" at the end. But all unbelievers are included here, as is clear from all the sins in the middle of the list. They will have no part in the kingdom of God, but instead will share in the second death, the eternal torment of Satan, his allies, and all unbelievers.

Let us take an honest look at this list. John's purpose is to encourage believers to persevere through the temptation they are facing to compromise with pagan trade guilds in Rome, to persevere through any persecution they are facing, and to not be deceived by Satan's schemes that stand behind the Roman system. But his purpose is also to warn those who are already dabbling in these things to stop or else they will be counted with the pagans. Are we cowardly when it comes to standing up for our faith in circles where it may not be convenient to mention that we are Christians? Are we faithful to God in all areas of our lives, both private and public? Are our lives characterized by immorality and idolatry? Have we ever lied about our faith in order to secure a job or a relationship? Let us repent and be those who are called courageous, faithful, and bold in our witness and our worship as we walk by the Spirit of God.

II. The Church Radiates the Glory of God (Rev. 21:9–14)

These verses begin the seventh and final section of the book. It expands on what has already been described in Revelation 21:1–8 with much greater detail. The entire section of Revelation 21:12–22:5 alludes to the vision of Ezekiel 40–48, but here the temple, city, and land of Ezekiel's description are all shown to be the glorious truth of God's presence with his people. In keeping with the symbolic nature of the book, this section is not describing a literal city, but rather describes the reality of God's people in the presence of their God.

Revelation 21:9–11. The "bride" in verse 2 is picked up again here, as John begins a more detailed description of Revelation 21:1–8. It is appropriate that the same angel who showed John the judgment of the great prostitute would now be the one to show John the bride, the wife of the Lamb. What a stark contrast there is between the two of them! The angel had carried John away to the wilderness to see the great prostitute, Babylon. But now the angel carries John to a great, high mountain to see the church coming down out of heaven from God. Unlike the prostitute, who was arrayed in colors of royalty and adorned with common jewels, the bride has "the glory of God, its radiance like a most rare jewel, like jasper, clear as crystal." We are nothing without Christ. All of our glory is simply a reflection of his. We have no jewels of our own; we radiate his. We have no royalty apart from him. We are the city and the temple in which he dwells and in which we radiate his glory, his presence, with us.

It is important for us to see clearly the contrast that John is making between the world system and the church. For like the seven churches of John's day that were giving way to social, political, and cultural pressure, many of our churches today are doing the same. We must remember who and whose we are (the body of Christ) and live like it. We must know what we will be at the end of history (the radiance of the glory of God) and live in constant anticipation of it. We must remain faithful so that we are able to take part in the new creation, of which the new covenant, new temple, new Israel, and New Jerusalem are but parts. And most importantly, we must give God the glory for the completion of his plan of judgment and salvation. But how do we do this? By recognizing that the Holy Spirit will accomplish these things through us as we walk in him.

320

Old Testament Background to Revelation 21:9–11.

- Isaiah 58:8: "Then shall your light break forth like the dawn, and your healing shall spring up speedily; your righteousness shall go before you; the glory of the LORD shall be your rear guard."
- Isaiah 60:1–2, 19: "Arise, shine, for your light has come, and the glory of the LORD has risen upon you. . . . The sun shall be no more your light by day, nor for brightness shall the moon give you light; but the LORD will be your everlasting light, and your God will be your glory."
- Ezekiel 40:1–2: "On that very day the hand of the LORD was upon me, and he brought me to the city. In visions of God he brought me to the land of Israel and set me down on a very high mountain, on which was a structure like a city to the south."
- Ezekiel 43:5: "The Spirit lifted me up and brought me into the inner court; and behold, the glory of the LORD filled the temple."

When we look up the word "mountain" in Scripture, the first place we see it used is in Genesis 22:14 where God told Abraham to sacrifice his only son, Isaac. But after seeing Abraham's obedient faith, God provided a ram for the sacrifice instead. This was a type of what was to come in Jesus Christ, the only Son of God who would be sacrificed on the cross. The next times we see the word are in the books of Exodus, Numbers, and Deuteronomy. Mount Sinai was the place where God spoke with his people from a cloud. Moses was the great prophet who went up on the mountain, but even he could not see the Lord's face. He received the Ten Commandments at the top of the mountain, and was able to see the Promised Land from the top of the mountain before he died (Deut. 32:50). The psalms speak of the mountain as the place where God chooses to reign (Ps. 68:16). In the prophets, the mountain is spoken of as the place where the Lord's temple will be established (Isa. 2:2; Mic. 4:1). In the New Testament, the mountain was the place where Peter, James, and John saw the Lord transfigured before them. Hebrews reminds us that Moses was instructed to make the tent according to the pattern shown him on the mountain (Rev. 8:5) and that even now believers have come to Mount Zion and the city of the living God (Rev. 12:22).

So it is appropriate that John would be taken to a "great, high mountain," symbolic of God's presence throughout Scripture, now revealing the vision that God's presence is with his people forever. We are reminded of Mount Moriah and know that because Jesus was slain, God is with us. We are reminded of Moses not being able to see the glory of God and having to turn his back, but in the new creation we will be able to see God face to face. We are reminded of the prophets who spoke of the mountain as God's temple and know that God establishes himself with us in the new creation. And we are reminded that the people of Israel came to worship at the foot of the mountain, and that we too will be characterized as worshipers in the new creation. Glory be to the Father and to the Son and to the Holy Spirit for bringing us through the wilderness to the Promised Land where God himself will tabernacle among us forever!

Revelation 21:12–14. Nothing will be able to penetrate or destroy the saints' fellowship with God because of the "great, high wall." He has ensured that there will be no evil in the new creation by removing its presence and casting it into the lake of fire, which, wherever it exists, is not where God's people exist.

Like the angels of the churches and the twenty-four elders who represent the people of God, the angels at the gates are representative for God's people as well. There is a close connection with Revelation 4:3–4 here. In both of these chapters the number twenty-four is symbolic for the entire people of God. That the gates have the names of the twelve tribes of Israel and the foundation of the walls had the names of the twelve apostles on them is a beautiful picture of the true Israel, Jews and Gentiles, the church of God unified. It might be expected that Israel, coming first in history, would be on the foundation, but it is Christ, the chief cornerstone, and the apostles who built upon his foundation, that are the new Israel, the church of God. Thus, the city is the new Israel, the people of God.[2]

2. G. K. Beale, *The Book of Revelation: A Commentary on the Greek Text*, New International Greek Testament Commentary (Grand Rapids: Eerdmans, 1999), 1070.

Old Testament Background to Revelation 21:12–14.

- Ezekiel 40:5–6: "There was a wall all around the outside of the temple area, and the length of the measuring reed in the man's hand was six long cubits. . . . So he measured the thickness of the wall."
- Ezekiel 48:31–34: "Three gates . . . the gate of Reuben, the gate of Judah, and the gate of Levi, the gates of the city being named after the tribes of Israel. On the east side . . . the gate of Joseph . . . Benjamin . . . Dan. On the south side . . . the gate of Simeon . . . Issachar . . . Zebulun. On the west side . . . the gate of Gad . . . Asher . . . Naphtali. . . . And the name of the city from that time on shall be, The LORD is there."

III. The Church Is Secure in God's Presence (Rev. 21:15–21)

Revelation 21:15–17. In Revelation 11:1 John was given a measuring rod and told to "rise and measure the temple of God and the altar and the ones who worship there." Now it is the angel who has a measuring rod to measure the city. In both places, the city is symbolic for the people of God. We saw that the measuring in chapter 11 was synonymous with the sealing in chapter seven, but there the temple represented God's people as the invisible city on earth. Only the inner court was sealed while believers were on earth because they were only spiritually protected from their enemies. But now we see that God has sealed his people for all of eternity in the new creation both physically and spiritually. They are secure from Satan, his allies, and immoral and idolatrous people forever. Never before in history had this been true. Jerusalem's walls had fallen to her enemies many times, but now enemies will no longer threaten them. God himself will be his people's wall and he is impenetrable. He will have cast the enemies far away from them.

The measurements of the city should be taken as symbolic. They are all multiples of twelve, symbolizing the complete number of Jews and Gentiles, like the twelve tribes and twelve apostles. That the wall is 144 cubits correlates with the 144,000 in Revelation 7:4–9 and 14:1–3, which represented the complete people of God. Here too God's people are complete. He has been sovereign over the elect since the beginning of history and has not lost one of them to Satan or his allies. He seals us and preserves us until he brings us home to glory where we are protected behind the mighty wall of God. That the city had only one wall is significant, as temples on earth had separated Jews and Gentiles and men and women from one another, but God's people in the new creation will be unified for all of eternity.

John clarifies that the vision in which he sees literal measurements (human measurement) is also to be understood symbolically (angel's measurement). We have seen this double layer of meaning throughout the entire book. John's literal and historical visions have a deeper, symbolic meaning. The city of God stands in stark contrast to the city of man. The incident of the Tower of Babel, where mankind set out to build a city and a tower that reached to the heavens in order to make a name for themselves, foreshadowed Babylon and all great empires that followed in her footsteps. The city of man has always sought to be independent from God, to make a name for itself, and to prove itself as powerful and in control. While man's city went up brick by brick to reach the heavens, God's city comes down from heaven and its height is of unimaginable proportion. With the foundation in the heavens, nothing can destroy it. Whereas God looked down from heaven in disfavor and dispersed those at the Tower of Babel, he now looks at his people in favor, unifying them in the new creation. Thus, this is a reversal of Babel. There is no longer any confusion, and the people are no longer dispersed. The people of God have been unified forever as the true Israel in the true temple of God, Jesus Christ.

Old Testament Background to Revelation 21:15–17.

- Genesis 11:4: "Come, let us build ourselves a city and a tower with its top in the heavens and let us make a name for ourselves, lest we be dispersed over the face of the whole earth."
- Ezekiel 40:3–5: "There was a man . . . with a linen cord and a measuring reed in his hand . . . for you were brought here in order that I might show it to you . . . there was a wall all around

the outside of the temple area. . . . So he measured the thickness of the wall."

- Ezekiel 45:2–3: "Of this a square plot of 500 by 500 cubits shall be for the sanctuary . . . and from this measured district you shall measure off a section 25,000 cubits long and 10,000 broad, in which shall be the sanctuary, the Most Holy Place."
- Zechariah 2:2: "And he said to me, 'To measure Jerusalem, to see what is its width and what is its length.'"

Revelation 21:18–21. That the wall is built of jasper picks up on verse 11, which described the jasper as radiating the glory of God. Again, along with the description of "gold" and "clear as glass," the radiance of God's glory is emphasized. The "foundations of the wall of the city" is parallel with the bride in Revelation 21:2, 9, who is adorned for her husband. The "twelve" jewels again are symbolic for the complete and perfect radiance of God's glory. But more than that, they allude to the twelve stones that were on the high priest's breastpiece of judgment.[3] One of the names of the twelve tribes of Israel was written on each stone. Thus, all of Israel was represented before God's presence in the temple. But now, these stones are not applied to Israel, but to the church (the foundations of the wall), representing that true Israel, all Jews and Gentiles who are in Christ, have been granted the right to stand in God's presence, which, in the Old Testament, was reserved for the high priest alone. The garments of the high priest were even seen as a replication of the earthly tabernacle, which was symbolic for the heavenly tabernacle. Thus, John picks up on Old Testament passages rich in symbolism to show how God's presence is now with his people.

The gates are symbolic of the twelve tribes of Israel; together with the previous reference to the foundations of the wall, symbolic of the twelve apostles, they convey the perfect unity of the people of God. Not only is the city pure gold (verse 18), but the street of the city was pure gold as well, again emphasizing that everything

---

3. Vern S. Poythress, *The Returning King: A Guide to the Book of Revelation* (Phillipsburg, NJ: P&R Publishing, 2000), 191.

radiates the glory of God. "Transparent as a glass" recalls the "clear as crystal" in verse 11.

The description of the city does not just portray the radiance of God's glory, though. It also contrasts sharply with the old earth and the idolatrous and immoral city of Babylon. It is also a great encouragement to the saints as they follow in the footprints of their suffering Savior, especially in light of Revelation 11:8 where the "dead bodies [of their persecutors] will lie in the street of the great city . . . where their Lord was crucified."

Old Testament Background to Revelation 21:18–21.

- Exodus 28:17–20: "You shall set in it four rows of stones. A row of sardius, topaz, and carbuncle shall be the first row; and the second row an emerald, a sapphire, and a diamond; and the third row a jacinth, an agate, and an amethyst; and the fourth row a beryl, an onyx, and a jasper. They shall be set in gold filigree."
- Exodus 39:8–14: "He made the breastpiece, in skilled work, in the style of the ephod, of gold, blue and purple and scarlet yarns, and fine twined linen. It was square. They made the breastpiece doubled, a span its length and a span its breadth when doubled. And they set in it four rows of stones. A row of sardius, topaz, and carbuncle was the first row. . . . There were twelve stones with their names according to the names of the sons of Israel. They were like signets, each engraved with its name, for the twelve tribes."
- Isaiah 54:11–12: "O afflicted one, storm-tossed and not comforted, behold, I will set your stones in antimony, and lay your foundations with sapphires. I will make your pinnacles of agate, your gates of carbuncles, and all your wall of precious stones."

IV. Only the Faithful Will Enter God's Eternal Presence (Rev. 21:22–27)

Revelation 21:22. The temple in Ezekiel's vision is now fulfilled in the Lord God the Almighty and the Lamb. That which had been a type from the beginning of Israel's theocratic establishment is now fulfilled in all of its glory in God himself. No longer would believers have to meet with God in a physical temple where he spoke from above the mercy seat. Now God would be in the midst of his people in all of his fullness. Jesus spoke of himself as the "temple" when he was here on earth, but here we see the consummation of that inaugurated truth. In John's day, this clearly separated the belief of Christians from Judaism, which strongly affirmed that there would be a literal, future, and final temple that would be grander than any that had been before. Christians place no hope in the material; they know that God himself will be greater than any physical structure as he dwells in the midst of his people in all of his fullness for eternity.

Old Testament Background to Revelation 21:22. Ezekiel 40–43: Ezekiel sees a vision of the new temple.

Revelation 21:23. Just as the people of God have no need for a physical temple because God is the temple, so too there is no need for the sun or moon because the glory of God the Father and the Son is the light. As in Revelation 21:1, where we saw that "the sea was no more," this could be symbolic in meaning. There could be seas, sun, and moon in heaven, but if so, they will serve to represent the goodness of God, for in comparison to the glory of God, they will be as nothing.[4]

Old Testament Background to Revelation 21:23.

- Isaiah 60:19: "The sun shall be no more your light by day, nor for brightness shall the moon give you light; but the LORD will be your everlasting light, and your God will be your glory."
- Ezekiel 43:2, 5: "The glory of the God of Israel was coming from the east. And the sound of his coming was like the sound of many waters, and the earth shone with his glory . . . the Spirit lifted me up and brought me into the inner court; and behold, the glory of the LORD filled the temple."

Revelation 21:24–26. The nations will walk by the glory of God illuminating their path. There will never be night, never a time when they cannot see God or be in his presence. Because there is no more

---

4. Beale, *The Book of Revelation*, 1093.

evil, there is no more darkness, for God is able to dwell in fullness where there is complete holiness. Added to God's glory will be the glory of the "kings of the earth" and "the nations." It is so encouraging that we find these words here, for we know from chapter 19 that these, like Saul (turned Paul), were persecutors of the church, but evidently repented and were included in God's plan of redemption. But the focus here is not primarily on former persecutors, because in Revelation 5:9–10 we read of those brought from "every tribe and language and people and nation, and you have made them a kingdom and priests to our God and they shall reign on the earth."[5] It is not anything material that believers will bring, for nothing material can add to the glory of God, and we don't carry material riches with us from this earth. But rather, it is "the deeds that follow" us (Rev. 14:13; 19:8), which we will continue to do by worshiping and serving God in the new creation.

That "the gates will never be shut" does not imply that the door to heaven stands open to any in the lake of fire who are willing to repent and come into God's presence. After the Day of Judgment, there will be no further opportunity for repentance. What this means is that there is no longer any need for the gates to serve as protection from enemies (as they did for Jerusalem when they were closed at night), for there will be no enemies in the new creation. Furthermore, unlike the garden of Eden being blocked by angels after the fall, now the gates to God's presence are flung wide open, giving believers access to God's presence at all times for all of eternity.[6]

Old Testament Background to Revelation 21:24–26.

- Genesis 3:24: "He drove out the man, and at the east of the garden of Eden he placed the cherubim and a flaming sword that turned every way to guard the way to the tree of life."
- Isaiah 60:3, 5: "And nations shall come to your light, and kings to the brightness of your rising. . . . Then you shall see and be radiant; your heart shall thrill and exult, because the abundance

5. Ibid., 1097.
6. Ibid., 1099.

of the sea shall be turned to you, the wealth of the nations shall come to you."

- Isaiah 60:11: "Your gates shall be open continually; day and night they shall not be shut, that people many bring to you the wealth of the nations, with their kings led in procession."

Revelation 21:27. This verse serves to further confirm that the gates that stand wide open are not an invitation for those in the lake of fire to come into the new creation. Rather, God's people are assured that nothing unclean or immoral nor any idolatrous person will be in the presence of the new creation. The threat of persecution, temptation, and deception is gone forever. Only those names that are written in the Lamb's book of life will be in God's presence, and the only reason they are there is because of the Lamb himself. It was the Lamb who covered our sin, so that we might stand in the presence of the Lord God Almighty and have full access to his presence for eternity. And it was the Lamb of God and the Holy Spirit that protected us from persecution, deception, and temptation so that we could stand before God forever. Let us praise him!

V. Believers Will Be Kings and Priests Who Radiate God's Glory (Rev. 22:1–5)

These verses belong with the preceding chapter, as they form a conclusion to its entirety.

Revelation 22:1–2. Now John sees the river of the water of life and the tree of life. Though the prophets are rich with this same imagery, we see it first in the first book of the Bible, in Genesis 2:10, where "a river was going forth from Eden." Thus, the new creation will be a restoration, a return to the beginning of the old creation, but in a much grander way. The "water of life" is symbolic for the eternal life of the believers that comes from God himself. Some see the "water" as symbolic of the Holy Spirit proceeding from both the Father and the Son on the throne. The main point, though, is eternal life in the presence of God the Father and the Son. "Bright as crystal" conveys

329

the cleansing aspect of the water that allows the people to be in the presence of God.[7]

"The tree of life" refers to the tree in the garden of Eden, but most likely in the new creation it refers to a number of trees on either side of the river, emphasizing the grander scale of the new creation. The water flowing from God himself will completely nourish the trees so that they will provide perfect and complete fruit for eternity. This would have been a great encouragement to Christians who were enduring famine during times of judgment on earth, that one day there would be perfect and complete provision of produce. It is also a great encouragement to us now as we endure famine of all sorts in our own lives, knowing that one day our needs will be completely met and satisfied. That the "leaves of the tree were for the healing of the nations" is symbolic for Revelation 5:9, "for you were slain and by your blood you ransomed people for God from every tribe and language and people and nation." Both water and leaves were thought in the ancient world to have medicinal effects, so the imagery here conveys that Christ alone is the ultimate source of healing.[8]

Old Testament Background to Revelation 22:1–2.
- Genesis 2:10: "A river flowed out of Eden to water the garden."
- Isaiah 35:6–9: "Then shall the lame man leap like a deer, and the tongue of the mute sing for joy. For waters break forth in the wilderness, and streams in the desert . . . and the thirsty ground springs of water . . . and a highway . . . called the Way of Holiness; the unclean shall not pass over it. It shall belong to those who walk on the way; even if they are fools, they shall not go astray."
- Ezekiel 47:1–9: Ezekiel's vision of water flowing from the temple.
- Ezekiel 47:12: "And on the banks, on both sides of the river, there will grow all kinds of trees for food. Their leaves will not wither, nor their fruit fail, but they will bear fresh fruit every

7. Ibid., 1104.
8. Ibid., 1106–7.

month, because the water for them flows from the sanctuary. Their fruit will be for food, and their leaves for healing."

- Joel 3:18: "And in that day the mountains shall drip sweet wine, and the hills shall flow with milk, and all the streambeds of Judah shall flow with water; and a fountain shall come forth from the house of the LORD and water the Valley of Shittim."
- Zechariah 14:8: "On that day living waters shall flow out from Jerusalem, half of them to the eastern sea and half of them to the western sea. It shall continue in summer as in winter."

Revelation 22:3. The "healing of the nations" is further described here as being in the presence of total holiness, with nothing accursed. Instead, the throne of God and of Christ, representing purity and holiness, will be in the midst of the people and they (servants) will serve and worship him (both God the Father and Christ) forever. The unity between God the Father and God the Son is emphasized here, as it is in the title "Alpha and Omega" being applied to both of them (Rev. 1:8; 21:6; 22:13).

Can you imagine what this will be like? For the first time we will be able to worship God perfectly in glorified bodies. We do that now in part, but we are still hindered by our own flesh, the distractions of this world, and the deception, persecution, and temptation of Satan. But in the new creation, we will finally be able to worship God, as he alone deserves. We will be unhindered, undistracted, and unlimited in time. It will be glorious to sing praises to the glory of God the Father and his Son, Jesus Christ, in glorified bodies.

Now and then I get a glimpse of what it might be like in the new creation. The choir of our church sang the "Hallelujah Chorus" at a recent Sunday night service. I was almost weeping as I listened to saints here cry out in worship for God. If such worship could be so moving on earth now, what will it be like in the new creation when throngs of believers are worshiping around the throne of the King? I cannot even begin to fathom the depth of the riches of what that worship will be like, but I know that I want to be a part of it!

Old Testament Background to Revelation 23:3. Zechariah 14:11: "And it shall be inhabited, for there shall never again be a decree of utter destruction. Jerusalem shall dwell in security."

Revelation 22:4. In Exodus 33:12 and following, Moses pleads with God to go with his people into the land of promise. During this exchange, the Lord tells Moses that he has known him by name and has found favor with him. He tells Moses that he will make all of his goodness pass before him and proclaim his name to him, but that Moses could not see his face, for man cannot see God and live. So God covered Moses' face with his own hand until he had passed by Moses. But in the new creation, God's hand will be removed from our faces, and we will see him face to face. We will be completely holy, and thus will be able to look in the face of the perfect holy One. Because he knows our names, his name will be written on our foreheads. This symbolizes our presence with him, our protection by him, and our reflection of him. It also represents our priesthood, for "holy to the LORD" was written on the high priest's turban, signifying that he was accepted in the presence of the Lord. Now the right that was given only to the high priest of Israel is granted to all who are part of true Israel.

Old Testament/New Testament Background to Revelation 22:4.

- Exodus 28:36–38: "You shall make a plate of pure gold and engrave on it, like the engraving of a signet, 'Holy to the LORD.' And you shall fasten it on the turban . . . it shall be on Aaron's forehead, and Aaron shall bear any guilt from the holy things that the people of Israel consecrate as their holy gifts. It shall regularly be on his forehead, that they may be accepted before the LORD."
- Isaiah 62:2: "And you shall be called by a new name that the LORD will give."
- Isaiah 65:15: "But his servants he will call by another name."
- 2 Corinthians 3:18: "And we all, with unveiled face, beholding the glory of the Lord, are being transformed into the same image from one degree of glory to another. For this comes from the Lord who is the Spirit."

- 1 John 3:2: "Beloved, we are God's children now, and what we will be has not yet appeared; but we know that when he appears we shall be like him, because we shall see him as he is."

Revelation 22:5. "And night will be no more." I love that phrase. How many times have you thought, "I just want this night to be over"? Suffering seems to intensify in the night. With no distractions we are brought face to face with persecution, temptation, or deception in our lives. Our deepest desires that have gone unmet seem much stronger in the darkness and quiet of the night. Our pleas before God seem much louder. Our suffering seems much stronger. But one day it will be no more. And we will reign with our King forever.

CONCLUSION

The reason why the song "Don't Be Afraid of the Night" still speaks so powerfully to me is because I am still so often afraid in the dark nights of my pain, struggles, deceptions, temptations, and persecutions. But God's Word tells us that there is coming a day when there will be no more night, no more nights of physical or emotional pain. The Lord God himself will have disposed of any darkness in our lives, and we will reign with him forever and ever. God himself will answer the prayer that saints have prayed through the ages, and he will answer it in complete fulfillment: "The LORD bless you and keep you; *the LORD make his face to shine upon you and be gracious to you*; the LORD lift up his countenance upon you and give you peace" (Num. 6:25–26). I don't know about you, but that's something to witness and worship about!

LESSON 21

Revelation 22:6–21

PLEASE USE THE QUESTION paradigm from pages 353–54 as you work through the following. See the introductory comments there that explain each part of the process below in more detail.

- **Pray.**
- **Ponder the Passage.** Read Revelation 22:6–21 once a day from different translations for the entire week, looking for its:
  - Point
  - Persons
  - Patterns
  - Persons of the Trinity
  - Puzzling Parts
- **Put It in Perspective.**
  - Place in Scripture
  - Passages from Other Parts of Scripture

1. Based on your observations of the text, what is the basic content of Revelation 22:6–21? Try to summarize it in your own words, using a sentence or two.
2. How many times are the phrases "coming/come/time is near" used in this chapter?

3. Using a concordance, where do we find "trustworthy and true" in the book? What about "has sent to his angel to show his servants what must soon take place" (Rev. 22:6)?

4. Of the seven blessings in the book, which one is this (Rev. 22:7)? Where have you seen the other ones? What are they? Do you see any similarities between this one and others?

5. Compare Revelation 19:10 with 22:8–9. What does this tell you about the deception of idolatry?

6. What does the angel tell John to do in Revelation 22:9? How does this relate to the book as a whole?

7. Compare Revelation 10:3–4 with 22:10. What differences do you see? Now look up Daniel 12:4. How does this illuminate our understanding of the "time is near" in John's day? What event inaugurated the end times?

8. Compare Daniel 12:10 with Revelation 22:11. Also see Exodus 9:12; Isaiah 6:9–10; and Matthew 13:9–17, 43. What is the purpose of God hardening people's hearts? What do you think Revelation 22:11 means?

9. Compare Revelation 19:8 and 20:11–15 with 22:12. What does Revelation 22:12 mean for the believer? For the unbeliever?

10. Where else have you seen each of the three titles for Christ in Revelation 22:13 and to whom did they apply?

11. Compare Revelation 7:13–17; 2:7; and 3:12 with 22:14. What do you find?

12. Compare the lists in Revelation 21:8 and 21:27 with 22:15. What similarities and differences do you see?

13. Where in the book have we already seen the words and the titles for Christ that are used in Revelation 22:16?

14. What five groups of people (there may be some overlap) are mentioned in Revelation 22:17? What four exhortations are given? Is the church, the apostate church, or the world primarily the focus here? Why?

15. Compare Deuteronomy 4:1–2; 12:32; 29:19–20 with Revelation 22:18–19. What do you find? Why is this significant?

16. To whom does the "he" in the phrase, "he who testifies to these things," in Revelation 22:20 refer? Why is this significant? What kind of language is "testify" associated with? How does this confirm our own role as witnesses?

- **Principles and Points of Application.**

1. Do you believe that God's Word is trustworthy and true? Do you display this in your life? Ask God to increase your trust in his Word and to deepen your faith that his Word is absolute.

2. Who or what are you tempted to worship other than God in your present circumstances? Spend time confessing this to God today and then spend time worshiping him alone.

3. Read Revelation 22:15 carefully. Ask God to reveal to your heart any of these sins that might be in your own life. Confess, repent, and begin to live a life of holiness, faithfulness, and obedience today.

4. Is Jesus saying, "Come," to you? Or is he asking you to say, "Come," to another person in your life who needs Jesus? If so, don't delay; say yes to Jesus today or invite someone else to do so, recognizing that the Holy Spirit is the one who opens up hearts and minds to a saving knowledge of Jesus Christ.

NOTES FOR REVELATION 22:6-21

Aim: Ponder the aim of this lesson concerning our:

Mind: What do we need to know from this passage in Scripture?

That the book of Revelation is written to exhort believers to remain faithful in holiness and obedience, and to give glory to God for completing his plan of judgment and salvation.

Heart: How does what we learn from this passage affect our internal relationship with the Lord?

It prepares us to be kingdom disciples who live our lives as faithful witnesses and worshipers of God, giving him the glory for faithfully completing his plan of judgment and salvation.

Hands: How does what we learn from this passage translate into action for God's kingdom?

It enables us to:

1. Display practically our belief that God's Word is trustworthy and true by living lives of holiness and obedience by the power of the Holy Spirit.
2. Turn away from any idolatry in our lives to worship God alone and to help others to do the same, relying on the power of the Holy Spirit to do so.
3. Examine our lives in light of the sins listed in Revelation 22:15, repenting of those of which we are guilty, and replacing those sins with holy and obedient living as we walk by the Spirit, so that we might be an example to others.
4. Come to Jesus with our whole lives and invite others to do the same, recognizing that it is the Spirit that draws God's children to him.

INTRODUCTION

Women wear a lot of "hats" in our world. As daughters, we honor our parents by spending time with them and taking care of them in their older years. As sisters, we encourage and serve our siblings. As employees, we fulfill our job descriptions. As wives, we love, submit to, and respect our husbands. As mothers, we are teachers, referees, coaches, nurses, taxi drivers, full-service salons, counselors, and a host of other roles. With all of these "hats" it is not difficult to see why we are usually tired by the end of the day, and a lot of times still tired the next morning.

The moment we awake we are faced with a long day of responsibilities before us. Others are depending on us to perform our roles, and we often jump out of bed to begin our long "to do" list. But perhaps we have allowed these roles to define our purpose in life more than they should. Perhaps we have exchanged the greater purposes for the lesser ones. This wouldn't be surprising. The world's ideologies seem to creep into our churches, our homes, and our own hearts and minds, distracting us from the most important roles that God has given us to perform.

Revelation 22:6–21 has much to say about what should define who we are and what we do. We are to worship God by living lives of faithfulness, holiness, obedience, and perseverance, to the glory of God. And we are to be witnesses of God by exhorting those who know him but are faltering to persevere, and by calling those who do not know him to come to him in faith.

We can divide this lesson into five sections:

I. Exhortation to Keep the True Prophetic Word (Rev. 22:6–7)
II. Exhortation to Worship God (Rev. 22:8–10)
III. Exhortation to Be Holy in Anticipation of Christ's Coming (Rev. 22:11–12)
IV. Exhortation to Wash One's Robes (Rev. 22:13–17)
V. Exhortation to Not Add to or Take Away from God's Word (Rev. 22:18–21)

Each section is a call to holy and obedient living in anticipation of Christ's coming. The five sections are defined by their references to Christ's coming, which hold together several exhortations.

I. Exhortation to Keep the True Prophetic Word (Rev. 22:6–7)

Revelation 22:6. We have just seen the phrase "these words are trustworthy and true" in Revelation 21:5. And the second part of the verse repeats what we saw way back in verse 1:1, "The revelation of Jesus Christ, which God gave him to show to his servants the things that must soon take place. He made it known by sending his angel to his servant John." Thus, not only does this serve as a conclusion to the previous section (Rev. 21:1–22:5), but also to the entire book. The fact that God will establish his kingdom on the new earth and will judge the evil world system of this present world is trustworthy and true. We will not be disappointed or deceived by putting our faith in his Word. God's plan of judgment and salvation will certainly come to pass. The God of "the spirits of the prophets" has orchestrated the words of Scripture from beginning to end, and God's people can be sure that every single promise will be fulfilled. God has used these prophets to show all of the church the truth of his coming kingdom to complete his plan of judgment and salvation.

Old Testament Background to Revelation 22:6.

- Isaiah 65:16: "So that he who blesses himself in the land shall bless himself by the God of truth, and he who takes an oath in the land shall swear by the God of truth; because the former troubles are forgotten and are hidden from my eyes."
- Daniel 2:45: "A great God has made known to the king what shall be after this. The dream is certain, and its interpretation sure."

Revelation 22:7. We have also seen in the letters to the seven churches that Christ "will come." Thus, believers should live in anticipation of the fact that all throughout history Christ comes either to bless or to judge. But only at the end of history will he come visibly and bodily to complete God's plan of judgment and salvation. We also see the sixth of seven blessings in the book (Rev. 1:3; 14:13; 16:15; 19:9; 20:6; 22:7; 22:14). Its wording is almost exactly like that of the first blessing in Revelation 1:3, "Blessed is the one who reads aloud the words of this prophecy, and blessed are those who hear, and who keep what is written in it, for the time is near." The word "blessed" refers to God's free gift of salvation and is seen at the beginning and end of the book to highlight the fact that one of John's purposes is to exhort his readers to lives of faithful, holy, and obedient living that culminates in their salvation, which is a gift of God.

II. Exhortation to Worship God (Rev. 22:8–10)

Revelation 22:8–9. Again, as in Revelation 1:1, 4, 9, John claims authorship of the book, but he also explains his response to the revelation.

John shares these words with the church as both an encouragement and a warning. Though an apostle and chosen by God to have the visions of Revelation shown to him, he still was prone to idolatry like we are. He still confused the message with the messenger. What is an even greater warning is that this isn't the first time he has done it. In Revelation 19:10 we learned that John also had fallen down to worship the angel who had revealed the marriage supper of the Lamb. And there too he was told not to do that. But John had not yet learned his lesson, because here we see him flirting with idolatry again. How prone we are to do the same! How willing we are to give worship to other things and other people instead of to God alone! But God's Word makes it clear that we must not do that. We must pledge our allegiance to God. No one and nothing else is worthy of our worship.

Revelation 22:10. In contrast to Revelation 10:4 where John was commanded to "seal up what the seven thunders have said, and do not write it down," John is now commanded not to seal up the words of the prophecy of Revelation. This verse gives us the reason why we are to worship God. We worship him because of God's revelation to John that the Old Testament prophecies of the end of history have begun to be fulfilled with Christ's death, resurrection, and ascension. This verse is an allusion to Daniel 2:28–29, 45 and 12:9, which records the Lord's words to Daniel: "Go your way, Daniel, for the words are shut up and sealed until the time of the end." But in John's day, the time of the end had come since Christ had been crucified, resurrected, and taken up to heaven. So, the words were no longer to be sealed. The church was then and is now to live in light of the fact that the Old Testament prophecies are being fulfilled for the end of history, and we are to live holy and obedient lives in anticipation of Christ's second coming. If the message were sealed we would not be able to do so.

Let us not seal the message either. Let us be bold witnesses who proclaim the Word of God to our families, neighbors, friends, communities, and to the nations of the world, with the hope that more and more will come to a saving knowledge of faith in Jesus Christ and live holy and obedient lives to the glory of God.

Old Testament Background to Revelation 22:10.

- Daniel 2:28–29, 45: "But there is a God in heaven who reveals mysteries, and he has made known . . . what will be in the latter days . . . he who reveals mysteries made known to you what is to be . . . A great God has made known . . . what shall be after this. The dream is certain, and its interpretation sure."
- Daniel 12:9: "He said, 'Go your way, Daniel, for the words are shut up and sealed until the time of the end.'"

III. Exhortation to Be Holy in Anticipation of Christ's Coming (Rev. 22:11–12)

Revelation 22:11. The allusion to Daniel continues in this verse. Daniel 12:10 says, "Many shall purify themselves and make themselves white and be refined, but the wicked shall act wickedly. And none of the wicked shall understand, but those who are wise shall understand." As was noted in the previous verse, Daniel's prophecies that were to be sealed in his day have been opened in John's day by the death, resurrection, and ascension of Jesus. Thus, the change to the use of exhortations in Revelation (rather than decreed prophecy as in Daniel) is appropriate.[1] John recognizes the apostate church and true church in his own day and recognizes that it is a fulfillment of Old Testament prophecy. Since the beginning God has purposed to save some and judge others. We saw it with Esau and Jacob, of whom it is said, "Jacob I loved, but Esau I hated" (Mal. 1:2–3; Rom. 9:13). We saw it with Pharaoh and Moses, of whom it is said, "the LORD hardened the heart of Pharaoh" (Ex. 9:12). For purposes beyond our understanding, God chooses to harden hearts and soften hearts according to his glorious grace. In the letters to the seven churches we see the phrase, "He who has an ear, let him hear what the Spirit says to the churches." This is an allusion to Isaiah 6:9–10, "And [the LORD] said, 'Go, and say to [Israel]: Keep on hearing, but do not understand; keep on seeing, but do not perceive. Make the heart of this people dull, and their ears heavy, and blind their

---

1. G. K. Beale, *The Book of Revelation: A Commentary on the Greek Text*, New International Greek Testament Commentary (Grand Rapids: Eerdmans, 1999), 1133.

eyes, lest they see with their eyes and hear with their ears and understand with their hearts and turn to be healed.'" John is warning the churches of his day that God will judge their apostasy by hardening their hearts even more, just as he did with rebellious Israel in Isaiah's day. So too, God warns the apostate church today through the book of Revelation that if we do not open our ears and hear the truth of his Word, he will judge us by hardening our hearts even more. Though the doctrine of election has always been difficult for believers to understand, the Word of God, including this verse, testifies to its truthfulness.

Old Testament/New Testament Background to Revelation 22:11.
- Isaiah 6:9–10: "Keep on hearing, but do not understand; keep on seeing, but do not perceive. Make the heart of this people dull, and their ears heavy, and blind their eyes; lest they see with their eyes, and hear with their ears, and understand with their hearts, and turn and be healed."
- Daniel 12:10: "Many shall purify themselves and make themselves white and be refined, but the wicked shall act wickedly. And none of the wicked shall understand, but those who are wise shall understand."
- Matthew 13:9–17, 43: Jesus explains the purpose of the parables.

Revelation 22:12. Whereas the phrase "I am coming" in chapters 2–3 referred to both Jesus' first coming and his final coming at the end of history, the "I am coming soon" of this verse only refers to Christ's final coming. This gives further support for John's exhortation in the previous verse. He urges the church to remain faithful to living a holy and obedient life for the glory of God in anticipation of being united with Christ at the marriage supper of the Lamb. Believers need to be clothed with righteous deeds, so that they are rewarded (not saved, which is based on grace alone, but rewarded, which is based on the believer's proof of his faith by doing good works). We saw this promise in the letter to the church in Thyatira, "And I will give to each of you according to your works" (Rev. 2:23). The ungodly will be repaid for their evil deeds with judgment. That John wrote, "I am coming soon," and the church is still waiting for Jesus' return should not be seen as problematic. John's use of "soon" should be read in terms of the sudden nature of Christ's appearing *whenever* it occurs. Thus, we live the same way John's readers lived, prepared for the fact that Christ's return will be sudden whenever it does occur, and we need to be ready for it on any given day.

Are we really living our lives this way? What if today was the last day that we had to witness to our husbands, our children, our neighbors, our friends, or our coworkers before Christ returned? How would that change our agenda for today? What if today was the last day that we had to worship God in these bodies on this earth? How would that change our schedule today? I imagine even the mundane tasks would become glorious as we turned them into opportunities to witness and to worship. The things that seem most important and most urgent to us would fade into the background as our perspectives and priorities aligned with God's Word. We would not engage in petty arguments with our spouses and children. We would not engage in mindless and worthless activities. Our entire purpose would be to worship and to witness. Why do we not live with that intensity every day? We get lazy, grumpy, tired, weary, consumed, distracted, tempted, deceived, persecuted, and a host of other things. But the Lord himself reminds us, "Behold, I am coming soon, bringing my recompense with me, to repay everyone for what he has done." Oh, may we still be found doing good deeds on that day by the power of the Holy Spirit! May we still be found witnessing and worshiping when he returns so that we hear our Master say, "Well done, good and faithful servant" (Matt. 25:21, 23)!

Old Testament/New Testament Background to Revelation 22:12.

- Isaiah 40:10: "Behold, the LORD God comes with might, and his arm rules for him; behold, his reward is with him, and his recompense before him."
- Isaiah 62:11: "Behold, the LORD has proclaimed to the end of the earth: Say to the daughter of Zion, Behold your salvation comes; behold, his reward is with him, and his recompense before him."

- Malachi 3:1–5: "Behold, I send my messenger, and he will prepare the way before me. And the LORD whom you seek will suddenly come to his temple; and the messenger of the covenant in whom you delight, behold, he is coming, says the LORD of hosts! But who can endure the day of his coming, and who can stand when he appears? For he is like a refiner's fire and like fuller's soap. . . . Then I will draw near to you for judgment. I will be a swift witness against the sorcerers, against the adulterers, against those who swear falsely, against those who oppress the hired worker in his wages, the widow and the fatherless, against those who thrust aside the sojourner, and do not fear me, says the LORD of hosts."
- Matthew 16:27: "For the Son of Man is going to come with his angels in the glory of his Father, and then he will repay each person according to what he has done."

IV. Exhortation to Wash One's Robes (Rev. 22:13–17)

Revelation 22:13. We have already seen the titles "the Alpha and the Omega" (Rev. 1:8; 21:6) and "the beginning and the end" (Rev. 21:6) for God in Revelation 1:8 and 21:6. And we have seen the title "the first and the last" for Christ in Revelation 1:7 and 2:8. But here all three titles are applied to Christ, highlighting his divinity and his capability to consummate all of history when he comes.

Revelation 22:14. This is the seventh and final blessing in the book (Rev. 1:3; 14:13; 16:15; 19:9; 20:6; 22:7; 22:14). We have seen the promise to eat of the tree of life in the letter to the church in Ephesus: "To the one who conquers I will grant to eat of the tree of life, which is in the paradise of God" (Rev. 2:7). And we have seen the promise to the church in Philadelphia that the one who conquers will be made a pillar in the temple of God and will have the name of the city of God written on him (Rev. 3:12). We have seen as well "the ones coming out of the great tribulation [who] have washed their robes and made them white in the blood of the Lamb" (Rev. 7:14). Thus, it is not the believer, but the Lamb who has made the believer worthy to stand before God. However, believers' perseverance through persecution, temptation, and deception is proof that Christ has washed them. Because Christ has saved them they are able to have eternal life and access to God's presence for all of eternity.

Old Testament Background to Revelation 22:14.

- Genesis 3:24: "He drove out the man, and at the east of the garden of Eden he placed the cherubim and a flaming sword that turned every way to guard the way to the tree of life."
- Psalm 118:20: "This is the gate of the LORD; the righteous shall enter through it."
- Isaiah 26:2: "Open the gates, that the righteous nation that keeps faith may enter in."
- Isaiah 62:10: "Go through, go through the gates; prepare the way for the people."

Revelation 22:15. This verse recalls the lists of those excluded from the city of God in Revelation 21:8 and 21:27. It is significant that all three lists finish with "liars" because it highlights the apostate church, which was so prevalent in John's day, according to the seven letters in chapters 2–3. This list adds some new descriptions. First, they have become lovers of falsehood because they have benefited from both the economic advantages of participating in pagan trade guilds and the spiritual advantages of participating in the church. Second, they are dogs, which in Scripture has a negative connotation, as dogs are concerned for their physical health, not their spiritual well-being. It is most likely that the term "dogs" is used as an overarching term to cover the terms "cowards, the faithless, the detestable" in Revelation 21:8.[2] All of these unbelievers are outside the city in the "lake of fire." They suffer eternal punishment, never having access to the city of God.

Let us examine our own lives. Are we consistent Christians? Would we recognize one another if we saw the other's actions in our homes, in our workplaces, or in our communities? Do the people we live with and work with see consistency between who we are Monday through

---

2. Ibid., 1141.

Saturday and who we are on Sunday? Do nice clothes on Sunday dress up what is really hypocrisy hidden underneath them? Do we grumble and complain and whine with the same mouths with which we worship God? Are we "convenience only" Christians? Do we only go to church when it is convenient for us or do we only mention our faith when it is to our advantage? Do we pray over our meals at work and in public or only in private? Would those on our street be surprised that we are Christians from what they know about us? Let us seek to be consistent in our witness and consistent in our worship by the power of the Holy Spirit. Our God is worthy of our witness and worship in every aspect of our lives.

Revelation 22:16. Again, information from Revelation 1:1 is repeated, but here Jesus himself is the speaker. He also claims the titles "the root and descendant of David, the bright morning star" (Rev. 2:28; 5:5). "You" and "the churches" are best seen as the same group of people here. Thus, "I, Jesus, have sent my angel to testify to you [believers] about these things in the churches" (see Rev. 1:4 where "to the churches" is also "you"). The titles that Jesus uses for himself here are extremely significant. They allude to two Old Testament prophecies in Numbers 24:17 and Isaiah 11:1, 10 that refer to the Messiah's victory over his enemies at the end of history. Thus, Jesus is saying that he has already begun to fulfill these prophecies (with his death, resurrection, and ascension) that will be completed at the end of history. That this is a reference to the Davidic covenant is clear since that covenant promised that one of David's descendants would be on the throne forever (2 Sam 7:12–16).

Old Testament/New Testament Background to Revelation 21:16.
- Numbers 24:17: "I see him, but not now; I behold him, but not near: a star shall come out of Jacob, and a scepter shall rise out of Israel; it shall crush the forehead of Moab and break down all the sons of Sheth."
- 2 Samuel 7:12–16: "I will raise up your offspring after you . . . and I will establish his kingdom . . . I will establish the throne of his kingdom forever. I will be to him a father, and he shall be to me a son. . . . And your house and your kingdom shall be

347

made sure forever before me. Your throne shall be established forever."

- Isaiah 11:1, 10: "There shall come forth a shoot from the stump of Jesse, and a branch from his roots shall bear fruit. . . . In that day the root of Jesse, who shall stand as a signal for the peoples—of him shall the nations inquire, and his resting place shall be glorious."
- 2 Peter 1:17–19: "For when he received honor and glory from God the Father, and the voice was borne to him by the Majestic Glory, 'This is my beloved Son, with whom I am well pleased,' we ourselves heard this very voice borne from heaven, for we were with him on the holy mountain. And we have something more sure, the prophetic word, to which you will do well to pay attention as to a lamp shining in a dark place until the day dawns and the morning star rises in your hearts."

Revelation 22:17. The Spirit of God who speaks powerfully through the prophets and the church calls people to "come." In this context, the four exhortations are not for the world at large, but for believers to persevere in their faith. Those in the church who do hear are to be faithful to call those still dull of hearing (Heb. 5:11) to persevere. We must remember, though, that it is also one of the church's primary purposes to call unbelievers to come to Christ (Matt. 28:18–20). Just as Revelation 22:14, which opened this section, spoke of a reward for those who persevere, so too this closing verse of the section speaks of the reward of the water of life for all who come. The water is free; there is no payment necessary. We must simply accept Jesus Christ as our Lord and Savior by faith, resulting in a life lived in thanksgiving, service, and praise by the power of the Holy Spirit.

Old Testament/New Testament Background to Revelation 22:17.

- Isaiah 55:1: "Come, everyone who thirsts, come to the waters; and he who has no money, come, buy and eat! Come, buy wine and milk without money and without price."
- John 7:37–38: "On the last day of the feast, the great day, Jesus stood up and cried out, 'If anyone thirsts, let him come to me

and drink. Whoever believes in me, as the Scripture has said, "Out of his heart will flow rivers of living water." ' "

V. Exhortation to Not Add to or Take Away from God's Word (Rev. 22:18–21)

Revelation 22:18–19. Now a warning is issued for the church, the new Israel. Alluding to Deuteronomy 4:1–2; 12:32; and 29:19–20, John issues a warning for those who hear the words of the prophecy of Revelation. If anyone adds to the prophecy, then the plagues recorded in the book will be added to him. If anyone takes away from the prophecy, their share in the eternal presence of God will be taken away. The warning then is against what was occurring in the churches in John's day and what is occurring in our day, false teaching that says that compromise with the gods of this world can coexist with one's faith. John's warning is directed toward the apostate church, but is also an exhortation to the faithful to remain strong, pure, and holy.

As in verse 14, we have seen the promise to eat of the tree of life in the letter to the church in Ephesus: "To the one who conquers I will grant to eat of the tree of life, which is in the paradise of God" (Rev. 2:7). And we have seen the promise to the church in Philadelphia that the one who conquers will be made a pillar in the temple of God and will have the name of the city of God written on him (Rev. 3:12). Here those promises are put in a warning statement instead of a blessing; they will be taken away. This is not describing a genuine believer who loses salvation, for that conclusion would be inconsistent with other passages of Scripture that clearly teach that God preserves his chosen ones (John 17:12). But rather, this refers to those of the apostate church who have confessed Christ outwardly, but deny him inwardly. They talk the talk, but don't walk the walk.

Old Testament Background to Revelation 22:18–19.

- Deuteronomy 4:1–2: "And now, O Israel, listen to the statues and the rules that I am teaching you, and do them, that you may live, and go in and take possession of the land that the LORD, the God of your fathers, is giving you. You shall not add to the word

349

that I command you, nor take from it, that you may keep the commandments of the LORD your God that I command you."

- Deuteronomy 12:32: "Everything that I command you, you shall be careful to do. You shall not add to it or take from it."
- Deuteronomy 29:19–20: "One who, when he hears the words of this sworn covenant, blesses himself in his heart, saying, 'I shall be safe, though I walk in the stubbornness of my heart.' This will lead to the weeping away of moist and dry alike. The LORD will not be willing to forgive him, but rather the anger of the LORD and his jealousy will smoke against that man, and the curses written in this book will settle upon him, and the LORD will blot out his name from under heaven."

Revelation 22:20. It is the Lord Jesus who testifies to the plan of God. He is the fourth witness listed in this chapter. The angel (Rev. 22:16), John (Rev. 22:8, 18), and the Holy Spirit (Rev. 2:7, 11, 17, 29; 3:6, 13, 22) are the other three. Thus, the legal nature of the book is highlighted.[3] From the beginning, especially chapters four and five, we have the sense that we are in the divine courtroom of the Almighty Judge. That Jesus says, "Surely," emphasizes the certainty that God's plan of judgment and salvation will be fulfilled through his second coming. Just as he was obedient to come to earth the first time to save, so now he is obedient to come the second time to judge and reward. "I am coming soon" applies to every generation since Jesus comes in judgment and blessing throughout the church age, although his final coming is primarily in mind here. This coming serves as the purpose for the warning in the previous two verses. If the apostate church does not heed God's warning given through John then it will be found guilty on judgment day. John's "Amen" is a confession of faith and affirmation that Jesus will come just as has been said all through the Scriptures.

Revelation 22:21. Similar to other New Testament letters, the book closes with a benediction for the grace of the Lord Jesus to be with all

3. Ibid., 1154.

believers in the seven churches of John's day and thus, to all churches everywhere throughout the church age. John knows that it will only be by God's grace that those flirting with the world will turn to God in repentance to a life of obedience and holiness, and that it will only be by God's grace that the faithful will withstand the pressure of persecution, deception, and temptation, to live holy and faithful lives until Christ comes. So it is with all of us. It will only be by God's grace that we persevere through this journey on earth where we meet so many deceptions, temptations, and persecutions. And thankfully, "God is able to make *all* grace abound to [us], so that having *all* sufficiency in *all* things at *all* times, [we] may abound in *every* good work" (2 Cor. 9:8, emphasis mine).

CONCLUSION

The "hats" I wear as a woman often leave me parched and dry, thirsting for living water. Thankfully, by God's grace, I know where to go for refreshment. The invitation, "Let the one who is thirsty come," rings all through Scripture, from Genesis to Revelation. The Lord calls us over and over again to quench our thirst in him. And once we drink, the Holy Spirit will lead us to perform our ultimate purpose in life. We are witnesses and worshipers of Christ. Every interaction we have with others during the day and every moment we have for praise is to be looked at through this purpose. God's Word, not the world, defines our life purpose. And it tells us very clearly who we are and what we are to do. We are witnesses and worshipers, and we are to be witnesses of God and worshipers of God every moment of every day of our lives.

So, let the one who is thirsty to be more than just a daughter, more than just a sister, more than just another employee, more than just a wife, more than just a mother, more than just a homemaker, more than just a _____ (you fill in the blank) come! We have been given a glorious purpose. Let us witness! Let us worship! "Hallelujah! For the Lord our God the Almighty reigns. Let us rejoice and exult and give him the glory" (Rev. 19:6–7) forever and ever. Amen.

Question Paradigm for Revelation

THIS QUESTION PARADIGM should be kept close at hand for every lesson. Each lesson's questions will follow this paradigm, but only this master page includes the explanations under each of the P's.

- **Pray**. Ask that God will open up your heart and mind as you study his Word. This is his story of redemption that he has revealed to us, and the Holy Spirit is our teacher.
- **Ponder the Passage**. Read Revelation several times a day at different times of the day from different translations for the entire week.
  - *Point*. What is the point of this passage? What is the point of the entire book? What is the point of the entire Bible?
  - *Persons*. Who are the main people involved in this passage? What characterizes them?
  - *Patterns*. What are the patterns of the text? Is there any chiastic structure, prose, or poetry?
  - *Persons of the Trinity*. Where do you see God the Father, God the Son, and God the Holy Spirit in this passage?
  - *Puzzling Parts*. Are there any parts of the passage that you don't quite understand or that seem interesting to you or confusing?

- **Put It in Perspective.**
  - *Place in Scripture.* Where does this passage fit contextually? What is the original context? What is the redemptive-historical context—what has happened or hasn't happened in redemptive history at this point in Scripture? Where do you see the covenant(s) of God with his people? How is the gospel presented in this passage? How do the life, death, and resurrection of Christ connect with this passage? See especially the following passages of Scripture: _____.
  - *Passages from Other Parts of Scripture.* Look up any cross-references listed. How do these help illuminate the text? How is the main truth of this passage seen in earlier parts of Scripture? How is it seen in later parts of Scripture? Based on your observations of the text, what is the basic content of this passage? Try to summarize it in your own words, using a sentence or two. Questions will continue here that are specific to each lesson's passage.

- **Principles and Points of Application.**
  - What do I learn about God in this passage? How does this reshape how I view present circumstances?
  - What do I learn about God's Son, Jesus Christ? How does this impact my relationship with God and my relationship with others?
  - What do I learn about God's covenant with his people? How am I to live in light of this?
  - How will I apply this information to my life today and in the future? How should we apply this in our churches?
  - Questions will continue here that are applicable to each lesson's passage.

APPENDIX A

Comparison between the Trinity and the Counterfeit Trinity[1]

THE TRINITY

- *God the Father*: originator of the divine plan of judgment and salvation.
- *God the Son*: executor/witness of the divine plan of judgment and salvation.
- *God the Holy Spirit*: enabler/witness of the divine plan of judgment and salvation.

THE COUNTERFEIT TRINITY

- *The Dragon*: originator of the satanic plan to thwart the divine plan; symbolizes Satan.
- *The Beast*: executor/witness of the satanic plan to thwart the divine plan; symbolizes evil ideologies/government (communism, Islamic ideology, etc.).
- *The False Prophet*: enabler/witness of the satanic plan to thwart the divine plan; symbolizes religious support of the state (through media and education).

1. Vern S. Poythress, *The Book of Revelation: A Guide for Understanding* (Glenside, PA: Westminster Theological Seminary Bookstore, 2002), 2.2.

It is important to recognize that there is truth within secular spheres that believers can and should use. However, we must always filter it through a biblical worldview, with Scripture as the ultimate authority. Everything is subject to the Word of God. We must be wise and discerning as to what we accept and/or reject as truth, but willing to use the truth wherever we find it, even from secular minds, for the glory of God.

COMPARISON BETWEEN THE BRIDE AND BABYLON

- *The Bride*: symbolizes the elect church of God.
- *Babylon*: symbolizes all of the world's social-political-economic-religious centers that promote the kingdom of darkness (corrupt entertainment, corrupt hobbies, corrupt business practices, corrupt sexuality).

Comparison between Three Views of the Millennium

NOT ALL BELIEVERS, nor all evangelicals, nor all those within certain traditions of evangelicalism, interpret the "thousand years" in chapter 20 of Revelation the same way. It is clear from the notes what my own position is, although I want to emphasize that I hold it humbly, knowing that many of my past professors, friends, and brothers and sisters in the worldwide body of Christ, people whom I respect greatly and love dearly, hold to different views. It is not my intent to try and teach one view as right and the others as wrong. Rather, I am bound by my own conscience to set forth what I believe to be the view that aligns most closely with Scripture as a whole, and to allow others to do the same. With that said, I lay forth below the following three main views held for the "thousand years."[1] I encourage you to pray, study, and come to your own conclusions, holding them humbly, while loving and respecting those who see the text differently.

1. See Darrell L. Bock, ed., *Three Views on the Millennium and Beyond* (Grand Rapids: Zondervan, 1999).

Table A.1 Three Views of the Millennium

	PREMILLENNIALISM	AMILLENNIALISM	POSTMILLENNIALISM
Old Testament Prophecy	Daniel 2:34–35, 44	Typological images in Old Testmant used for new covenant: true Israel, Canaan, holy city of Jerusalem, kingdom of David, temple of God	Genesis 12:2–3: "All peoples on earth will be blessed."
	Isaiah 2:2–4	Christians are the Israel of God, Abraham's seed, heirs of promise, the true Israel, the seed of Abraham who is blessed by God	Messianic Psalms
	Micah 4:1–8		Isaiah 2:2–4; Micah 4:1–3; "last days" begin with Christ's first coming
Christ's First Coming	Totally new universal and national world-order with literal restoration of Jews to geographic Israel. Promises and blessings extend to saved Gentiles as well.		
	Pretribulationists believe church is raptured prior to start of tribulation.	Millennium (symbolic for church age) begins	Millennium (symbolic for long time of glory established at first coming) begins
	Tribulation occurs throughout seven years prior to second coming of Christ	Deceased saints reign from heaven during church age	Deceased saints in heaven and saints on earth reign with Christ
		First of two stages of Christ's victory over Satan	
	Midtribulationists believe church is raptured halfway through tribulation	Satan bound from saints spiritually	Satan bound from saints spiritually

	Postribulationists believe church is raptured at the end of tribulation, at second coming		Christ brings his kingdom into world to battle with Satan during earthly ministry
			Christ is exalted as King at his resurrection/ ascension
			Christ promises that the church will grow until end of history
			Christ issues Great Commission, promising to bless it
			Christians overcome and are seated with Christ who already rules
Christ's Second Coming	Destruction of Babylon, Beast, and False Prophet	Second climactic point of Christ's victory over Satan	General resurrection of all mankind
	Satan bound for 1,000 years First stage of resurrection, Christ raises martyrs to reign with him in millenial kingdom on earth Millennium ends	Resurrection of believers and "change" of living believers; resurrection of unbelievers	
	Christ raises the rest of the dead for final judgment Separation of believers and unbelievers for eternity Destruction of Satan	Judgment for all, the end	Great Judgment of all
	New earth/heaven Everlasting reign of Christ Eternal reign of saints on earth	The new heaven and new earth, inauguration of final kingdom of God, blessed eternal state of believers	New heaven/new earth

Bibliography

Beale, G. K. *The Book of Revelation*. New International Greek Testament Commentary. Grand Rapids: Eerdmans, 1999.

Bock, Darrell L., ed. *Three Views on the Millennium and Beyond*. Grand Rapids: Zondervan, 1999.

Celenza, Anna Harwell. *The Heroic Symphony*. Illustrated by JoAnn E. Kitchel. Watertown, MA: Charlesbridge, 2004.

Johnson, Dennis E. *The Triumph of the Lamb: A Commentary on Revelation*. Phillipsburg, NJ: P&R Publishing, 2001.

Kline, Meredith G. *Kingdom Prologue: Genesis Foundations for a Covenantal Worldview*. Eugene, OR: Wipf & Stock Publishers, 2006.

McCartney, Dan, and Charles Clayton. *Let the Reader Understand: A Guide to Interpreting and Applying the Bible*. 2nd ed. Phillipsburg, NJ: P&R Publishing, 2002.

Morris, Leon. *The Book of Revelation: An Introduction and Commentary*. Tyndale New Testament Commentaries. Leisester: IVP; Grand Rapids: Eerdmans, 1987.

Mounce, Robert H. *The Book of Revelation*. New International Commentary on the New Testament. Rev. ed. Grand Rapids: Eerdmans, 1998.

Poythress, Vern S. *The Book of Revelation: A Guide for Understanding*. Glenside, PA: Westminster Theological Seminary Bookstore, 2002.

Poythress, Vern S. *The Returning King: A Guide to the Book of Revelation*. Phillipsburg, NJ: P&R Publishing, 2000.

Wilcock, Michael. *The Message of Revelation: I Saw Heaven Opened*. The Bible Speaks Today. Downers Grove, IL: InterVarsity Press, 1975.

Sarah Ivill (B.A., University of Georgia; Th.M. Dallas Theological Seminary) has been leading, teaching, or writing women's Bible studies since she was eighteen. She has served at the Howard G. Hendricks Center for Christian Leadership, in Bible Study Fellowship, and as a Director of Women's Ministry in the church. Presently a stay-at-home mom, she continues writing and teaching women's Bible studies. A member of Christ Covenant Church (PCA), Sarah lives with her husband and two children in a suburb of Charlotte, North Carolina.